The Sexual Adolescent

Duxbury Press
North Scituate, Massachusetts

Sol Gordon, Ph.D.
Professor of Child and Family Studies
and Director of The Institute for Family
Research and Education at
Syracuse University

Peter Scales, Ph.D.
Research Analyst
and Consultant on Youth
Affairs, Washington, D.C.

Kathleen Everly, Ph.D.
President, Ed-U Press, Inc.
Charlottesville, Virginia

Second Edition

The Sexual Adolescent
Communicating with Teenagers about Sex

The Sexual Adolescent: Communicating with Teenagers about Sex, 2nd edition, was edited and prepared for composition by **Bowden Anderson.** Interior design was provided by **Trisha Hanlon.** The cover was designed by **Trisha Hanlon.**

Duxbury Press
A Division of Wadsworth, Inc.

Library of Congress Cataloging in Publication Data

Gordon, Sol, 1923–
  The sexual adolescent.
  Bibliography: p.
  Includes index.
  1. Sex instruction for youth. 2. Adolescence.
I. Scales, Peter, 1949–   joint author.
II. Everly, Kathleen, 1946–   joint author.
III. Title.
HQ35.G653 1979   612.6'007   79–174
ISBN 0-87872-209-2

Printed in the United States of America
1 2 3 4 5 6 7 8 9 — 83 82 81 80 79

Our book is dedicated to American youth, who need models more than critics; and to Ann Landers, a splendid and influential model who is respected by millions of young people, including those "critical" of her "traditional" views, because—she freely speaks her mind without apologies, acknowledges her mistakes without loss of dignity or status, and advocates sex education and planned parenthood.

Contents

Contents

Contents

Contents

Contents

Preface

This is an action-oriented book. We have not tried to discuss adolescence within a particular developmental scheme or theory. Our intent has been to describe many of the steps necessary to promote sexual health, and to outline the contributions parents, educators, legislators, religious leaders, and the media can make. The book is designed as a supplementary text for college students, physicians, nurses, teachers, youth leaders, guidance counselors, social workers—everybody working for and with young people.

Our book is biased. We believe that it is best for teenagers not to impregnate, become pregnant, or have children. It is small comfort that some teen parents can handle the challenges posed by early childbearing. For most, the joys of the "experience" are far outweighed by the sorrows. It is adults' responsibility to provide young people with the knowledge and services they need to avoid ignorant, perhaps tragic behavior in their sexual lives. We have no argument with the idea that once children are born—no matter to whom or under what circumstances—everything must be done to ensure their, and their parents', well-being. We fully realize that for some young people, sexual intercourse is part of a joyful, nonexploitative relationship. This does not deter us from our main and most generalizable conclusion: Primary prevention programs must enhance self-acceptance, discourage sexual intercourse among teenagers, and promote contraception and prophylactic use for those young people not impressed or affected by our convictions.

Acknowledgment

We would like to acknowledge the valuable research and editorial assistance from Craig Snyder and Emily Nelson, freelance journalists whose works have appeared in *The Journal of Current Social Issues* and *Impact*, and Leslie Weiser and Jane Lanzendorf, staff members of the Institute for Family Research and Education, Syracuse University, New York. We would also like to thank the following individuals who reviewed the entire manuscript in its early stages and made many helpful suggestions: Paul Ephross, University of Maryland; Ramona Mercer, R.N., University of California, San Francisco; and Pedro A. Poma, M.D., Mt. Sinai Hospital Medical Center, Chicago, and Rush Medical College, Chicago.

Introduction

Young people will have sex whether we like it or not, whether they like it or not, whether there are restrictive laws or not, and whether there is sex education in the schools or not. Operating on the simple assumption that teenagers should not have sexual relations effectively bars them from the information and contraceptives they should have, and the laws that can protect their interests. The argument that the less teenagers know about sex, the less they will "act out," is not valid. Evidence shows that the majority will engage in non-marital sexual relations no matter what adults think they should do.

Admittedly, there are moral questions involved in whether teenagers should have sexual relations, and there is nothing wrong with society suggesting they should not. However, it is wrong for society to avoid facing the fact that *they do*. The known consequences of adolescent sexual behavior are crucial to our society and are the primary concerns of this book.

U.S. statistics demonstrate that since 1974 there have been more than 1 million pregnancies among teenage girls each year. Divorce rates run two to two and a half times higher in teenage marriages, compared to marriages between persons twenty-one and thirty-five years old (Carter & Glick, 1976). Each year about 600,000 babies are born to women under twenty. In 1975, nearly 40 percent of these births were to unmarried teenagers; one-third were conceived prior to marriage, and the marriage then "legitimized" the pregnancy after the fact (Menken, 1975). The Commission on Population Growth and the American Future (1972) estimated that one-fourth of American teenage women reaching their twentieth birthday had already borne a child. In addition, many sexually active young people are remaining single longer: in 1976, 43 percent of women twenty to twenty-four were single, an increase of more than one-half from 1960 (Glick & Norton, 1977).

E. James Lieberman (1970) has remarked:

> Those who are anxious about the problem of premarital sexuality as a moral issue should be aware that the technology which has led to freedom is not so much the contraceptive technology as it is the telephone, the automobile, and the mass media. If there are no reasons for abstinence other than fear of pregnancy or loss of virginity per se, then our moral platform is very flimsy. If there are no very good psy-

3

chological reasons for abstinence or virginity, then we can expect a sexual revolution far beyond anything already seen. There are arguments for chastity and fidelity which do not depend on tradition or intimidation. But we can hardly argue such nuances until we face up to the tragedy of unwanted pregnancy and tell the contraception story like it is.

The huge number of teenagers and their mostly unwanted babies whose lives are ruined is tragic. Most teenage pregnancies *are* unwanted. The psychological explanation that virtually all teenage girls have a conscious or subconscious desire to become pregnant is a speculative theory that seriously interferes with efforts to organize constructive birth control programs for adolescents. Whether or not the theory is correct (and there is ample reason to believe that it is not), it should not impede the effort to help teenagers prevent unwanted pregnancies.

Giving birth to unwanted children is not the only tragedy. In 1976 more than 3 million Americans were estimated to have newly contracted a serious venereal disease. The greatest risk was in the twenty-to-twenty-four-year age group, followed closely by the fifteen-to-nineteen-year-old age group (Center for Disease Control, 1977). Many teenagers contract VD and do not know where to go for diagnosis and treatment. Some do not know that they have it. Until 1976, adolescents in some states could not even seek information and treatment without parental consent—and how many adolescents want to tell their parents that they might have VD?

The concept of parental responsibility is a sound principle of family life, but when written into law, it effectively bars many adolescents from attaining the medical help they need. In *Planned Parenthood of Missouri* v. *Danforth*, the courts have explicitly rejected the argument that "parental consent" should be required in the interests of "strengthening the family" (Paul, 1977). Of course, the ideal development would be for adolescents to feel freer to go to their parents with their problems, but it is more immediately effective to change laws than to change established patterns of parent-child relationships. Instead of being used to "discourage" adolescent sexual activity, the law should be applied to the conditions where it can be most effective: increasing the availability of contraceptives, medical abortions, and venereal-disease care for minors. *All teenagers should be able to obtain contraceptives and confidential medical advice and treatment related to pregnancy or venereal disease without parental consent.* The law's first line of defense against teenage pregnancy and VD can be established only at this point.

In addition, if an adolescent is already pregnant and wishes to bear her child, she should be able to receive medical care without parental consent. Early prenatal care is essential for the health of a mother and the developing fetus. An adolescent denied access to health care by the restrictions of parental consent or notification, remains at risk medically, socially, educationally, and, consequently, emotionally. Thus, the requirement of parental consent often works against the best health interests of the adolescent.

Adolescents are having sexual relations earlier and more frequently today than in previous generations; ironically, it appears that the earlier a person has intercourse, the less likely he or she is to know the facts of reproduction and contraception. Adolescents will make use of information presented in a straightforward and orderly way that they can see is in their own interests. Overintellectualized or moralistic presentations are remarkably ineffective, which may account for the failure of most school programs.

Our social responsibilities force our hand. We must redirect our priorities toward increased resources and more thorough education. Only then can adolescents make intelligent choices in a society that offers few alternatives to youth, especially those from impoverished families. We should provide the knowledge and insight that permit access to the best information regarding the consequences of sexual behavior. We must eliminate legal restrictions that thwart access to the information, materials, and medical services needed by adolescents to make healthy decisions. We must develop programs that enable young people to become sexually responsible.

Basic sex education begins in the home, and it is here that we must direct and intensify our efforts. We must prepare parents to understand, accept, and facilitate the development of their children as sexual beings. At this point the schools, community agencies, and religious groups can become partners with parents as primary educational forces in the lives of today's youth.

To accomplish the above tasks, we need to make clear what *we mean* by sex education (sometimes referred to as "sexuality education"). We subscribe to the definition developed by the World Health Organization (1975) that sex education programs should be "far more broadly and imaginatively conceived" to deal, not only with reproductive physiology, but with "questions of ethics in interpersonal relationships and responsibility in reproductive behavior." As described and interpreted by one of the world's most distinguished pioneers in the field, Dr. Mary Calderone (president of the Sex Education and Information Council of the United States), the intent of sexuality education is the development of mature individuals capable of making wise and responsible decisions in the fulfillment of their sexual lives. The best sex education programs explore the moral values underlying all relationships.

In our view, the very essence of mature sexual behavior involves people who feel good about themselves and thus are not available to exploit or be exploited by others.

In order to maintain the separate integrity of several chapters, some statistics and material have been repeated. This will be appreciated by many people who find figures difficult to absorb on first reading.

References Carter, H., & Glick, P. C. *Marriage and divorce: A social and economic study.* Cambridge, Mass.: Harvard University Press, 1976.

Center for Disease Control, *VD fact sheet, 1976.* Atlanta, 1977.

Commission on Population Growth and the American Future. *Population and the American future.* New York: New American Library, 1972.

Glick, P. C., & Norton, A. J. Marrying, divorcing, and living together in the U.S. today. *Population Bulletin,* 1977, *32* (5).

Lieberman, E. J., David, H. P., Hilmar, N. A., & Williams, P. R. Behavioral research in population planning. *Professional Psychology,* Spring 1970, *1* (3).

Menken, J. *The health and demographic consequences of adolescent pregnancy and childbearing.* Paper presented at National Institute of Child Health and Human Development, Conference on the Consequences of Adolescent Pregnancy and Childbearing, Rockville, Maryland, October 1976.

Paul, E. W. Danforth and Bellotti: A breakthrough for adolescents. *Family Planning/Population Reporter,* 1977, *6,* 3–5.

World Health Organization. *Education and treatment in human sexuality: The training of health professionals* (Technical Report No. 572). Washington, D.C.: WHO Publications, 1975.

One

Facing Facts—
An Adult
Responsibility

The majority of a child's sex education takes place during the preschool years. Given the special nature of the parent-child relationship, most children want to learn about sexuality from their parents in preference to any other sources. Thus, information and attitudes communicated by parents have a special importance and meaning for children. Too often, however, the parents' own sexual misconceptions and inhibitions stand in the way of meaningful communication, thus fostering unhealthy attitudes that may cause a child to have sex-related problems during adolescence. A desirable way to reduce or eliminate irresponsible sexual conduct, unwanted pregnancy, and venereal disease is to create within the home a climate of acceptance and honesty about sex. Research reveals that teenagers who have talked to their parents about sex are likely to delay first intercourse, and then to use contraception when they do take that step. This is true especially if their parents have refrained from being evasive, sanctimonious, contemptuous, or threatening (chapter 9).

This chapter attempts to lay to rest some mistaken assumptions, especially the ideas that sexual information encourages sexual activity and that today's "sophisticated" adolescent is already well informed. The main concerns of this chapter are *how* parents and other adults can communicate with children about sex, and *what* specifically they should strive to communicate.

The Fear of Encouraging Sexual Activity

In the Gallup Poll released January 23, 1978, 77 percent of the public favored teaching sex education, a significant increase over the 65 percent figure recorded in 1970. In general, there were little differences between Catholics and Protestants, even regarding the teaching of birth control in the schools. Thus, less than one-fourth of the public objects to sex education.

Yet the most common objection to educating adolescents about sex is the fear that such information will encourage them to be sexually active. The issue of contraception is particularly sensitive. Many adults think that once the fear of pregnancy is removed, teenagers will feel free to become sexually involved. The threat of venereal disease is often similarly used to discourage sexual activity. The very words *sex education* are often misinterpreted as teaching young people how to have sex and, coincidentally, condoning immorality and perversion. The myth seems to be that the less teenagers know about sex, the less likely they are to experiment with it.

The fear of "putting ideas into their heads" is wholly unfounded. The ideas and the felt need for pertinent information in sex education courses are already there. *What adolescents want to know about sexuality corresponds very closely with what they need to know.* They want to know about the areas of greatest anxiety. Basic anatomy lessons masquerading as sex education have not been very effective. Nor will scare tactics suffice to prevent undesirable sexual behavior. Ignorance about sexuality, as in all things, can be dangerous. Recognizing this would help resolve much of the controversy over the content of sex education courses and dispel the fears of many parents.

The notion that in this pluralistic society children can or should be protected from ideas and information reflects a grossly inaccurate assessment of the extent to which parents can exert control over their children. Many parents have a conscious, and some an unconscious, desire for their children to act *only* in accordance with what the parents say or believe. But everybody, whether protected or not, will sooner or later be exposed to a multitude of ideas. The important question is how they will receive and respond to these ideas.

The most explicit information about sexuality does not corrupt even young children. The worst that can happen is that the child will not understand or will become bored. Trying to keep "provocative" material out of adolescent hands or heads is as impractical as it is unreasonable. No matter what they read or do not read, adolescents are in the process of becoming sexually aware and sensitive. Sensations, impulses, and desires spring naturally from the unconscious. The child will associate these forces with many random ideas and materials in his or her life and attach a sexual significance to them.

In many aspects of life, sexuality simply cannot be avoided. It is not confined to intimate contact. Even in small children, for example, almost all physical, sensory contact is related to sexuality. It is widely understood that the physical attention and care infants receive will have an important influence upon the sex life they choose to have as adults.

How Much Do Teenagers Already Know?

There are those who cite the high incidence of intercourse among the young and argue that adolescents do not have to be told anything more because they already know everything. Sex education, according to this argument, is a waste of time and money; if young people had any interest in preventing pregnancy or VD, they would act to protect themselves. Since they choose not to do so, they stand to gain nothing by a formal program of sex education.

While one group wants to protect children from information, another wants to spare the expense of a program that would only repeat what young people already know. Professional experience suggests that the second argument is as fallacious as the first. Having sex does not cure adolescents of ignorance, and ignorance does not deter adolescents from having sex. Despite all the talk about a sexual revolution, there is among adolescents a high level of ignorance. As mentioned earlier, this level of ignorance is often highest among those who are most sexually active.

The use of *fear* (of out-of-wedlock pregnancy, of venereal disease, or of social disapproval) to influence behavior has not reduced adolescent sexual activity. It is, however, very successful in increasing confusion, anxiety, and exploitative behavior. *Relevant* and *specific* information, without moralizing and without euphemisms, is needed to reduce confusion.

In one carefully conducted study (Libby, 1970) more than 70 percent of parents thought that a fear of pregnancy would effectively deter young people from having intercourse. What usually happens, however, is that birth control, not intercourse, is discouraged, because young people are not encouraged to accept themselves as sexual beings. In another study (Mosher, 1973), people who felt the most guilty about their sexual experiences were the *least* likely to use birth control themselves or to approve of its being made easily available. (Chapter 9 reviews several other studies that reached the same conclusion.)

Most teenagers need information *and* services to avoid the consequences of careless sexual activity. The Alan Guttmacher Institute (1976) estimated that *half* of the nearly 4 million sexually active teenage girls in the U.S. and most of the 7 million sexually active teenage boys have never made use of professional birth control services. Reducing the incidence of unwanted pregnancies and venereal disease cannot be accomplished by wishful thinking about abstinence or a return to "traditional morality." Current research strongly suggests that the lack of knowledge of effective birth control methods does not deter adolescents from engaging in sexual intercourse (Zelnik & Kantner, 1977; Sorensen, 1973). Instead, they continue to have sex while relying on such absurd measures as using laxatives, avoiding orgasm, and having intercourse standing up. Teaching adolescents not to use such sorry substitutes without simultaneously providing information about effective contraception is not likely to reduce the level of teenage pregnancy. New myths would be invented, sexual activity would continue, and more girls would become pregnant against their wishes.

This is not to say that teenagers do not need moral guidance, or that parents have no right to suggest that teenagers should not have sex. We are, nonetheless, failing to confront the problems of adolescent sexuality if we restrict sexual communication to a list of shoulds and should nots.

What Adolescents Themselves Say

Ironically, adolescents are often the least consulted group on matters of sex education. Adults seem to forget at times that adolescents have opinions and feelings. The views of youth, however, are well represented in the book

Adolescent Sexuality in Contemporary America (1973) by Robert C. Sorensen. (It is significant that no teenager in Sorensen's study voiced opposition to sex education.)

The data in Sorensen's report on 411 adolescents aged thirteen to nineteen are not conclusive but nonetheless are of considerable interest. Here are some of the findings:

1 Fifty-two percent of his sample have had sexual intercourse. Fifty-nine percent of the boys and 45 percent of the girls are nonvirgins.

2 Three major reasons given for not having sexual experiences, in the order agreed to by adolescent virgins, are: because I'm not ready for it; because I haven't met a girl/boy who I would want to have sex with; and because I haven't met a girl/boy who wants to have sex with me.

3 Sixty-nine percent of the boys and 55 percent of the girls affirm, "So far as sex is concerned, I do what I want to do, regardless of what society thinks."

4 Fifty-five percent of all nonvirgin adolescents report that neither sex partner used birth control in their first intercourse; another 13 percent are not sure. Seventy-four percent of the girls whose sex partners were thirteen to sixteen years old did not use birth control; however, the older the boy at the time of first intercourse, the more frequently his partner made an effort to avoid pregnancy.

5 In answer to the question, "This very last time that you had sex with a girl/boy, did either of you use any kind of contraceptive or birth control method?" 47 percent of the boys and 60 percent of the girls responded, "Yes."

6 Eighty-nine percent of the girls who did not always take precautions say they do not know where to get birth control pills or any other kind of reliable contraceptive.

7 Thirteen percent of all adolescents with sexual experience (17 percent of the boys and 7 percent of the girls) had their first intercourse at or before the age of twelve. By age fifteen, 71 percent of the nonvirgin boys and 56 percent of the nonvirgin girls had had sexual intercourse.

8 Seventy-two percent of the boys and 70 percent of the girls say that they and their parents do not talk freely about sex. In fact, most adolescents are at a loss to know what their parents want them to know about sex. They feel a great need to learn specific facts about techniques and problem situations rather than hear abstract discussions and morality lectures.

9 A majority of adolescents tell their parents only what they think their parents will accept in matters of sex. Fifty-seven percent of the boys and 58 percent of the girls agree with the statement "My parents think that I pretty much agree with

their ideas about sex, and I don't say anything that would make them think different."

In Their Own Words

The language of youth reflects their anxiety, which often focuses upon the inconsistencies they perceive between what adults say and what they do. Their anger is also directed at arbitrary and inconsistent laws, practices, and conditions. Lacking the sophistication of adults but striving for directness, adolescents have evolved a special language which is often more straightforward and emotive than adult speech and is, perhaps, more prone to oversimplification and irrational anger. Thus, the militant language of youth sometimes hinders communication with adults, who too often perceive only the irrationalities and conclude that youths have little constructive to say.

Here are some young people's thoughts on "What is sex," made available to us by Monmouth County (New Jersey) Planned Parenthood:

> At one point I thought, "Bleck, that's gross" but I've grown and I'm really not sure how I feel. I know what I'm talking about and a few guys have asked me if I want to get to it. Now I'm not above kissing or even a little more than that. But right now I'm only thirteen and I got a whole lifetime ahead of me. But maybe some guy I know and me get serious, then I don't know (seventh grade).

> Sex is a good thing you should share with your husband and/or boyfriend. It is not something you fool around with. And you should not put down how anybody does (it's none of your business) or why or when. You should always be honest with your children about sex (seventh grade).

> It's something that goes on between a man and a woman, or intercourse. Sex to me is something that you feel about a person to show that you love a person. But having sex before your married to me is alright. I feel that it can help you. Because people who are between the ages of 11 or 12 or 17 or 18 have not have sex gets all still when the opposite sex is near them. And many people between those ages get hard-up, you know what I mean. Because I know plenty about sex as you already know. But I think sex can do you some good before your married. I was reading a sex joke book and they had one in there about a couple who never had sex and after they got married they didn't know what to do. So I think sex before your married is alright (sixth grade).

> To me sex is a three letter word which most families care not to discuss with their children. But it is something everyone must learn. Most families think if you teach their children about sex they'll run out and try it, but what they don't under-

13

stand is their children must know what they're getting into if it happens more than once. For in my case the word sex does not raise my blood or anything, it's just a three letter word (eighth grade).

Sex is something you do when you're out of school completely and are ready to accept this responsibility. I don't think sex is something you do anytime or with just anyone (eighth grade).

I think there is nothing wrong with sex because it's natural and if a boy and girl want to do it well why not, but there are some limits, like their age should be at least over 12 at least. And if a girl got pregnant around 14 her mother or father should not say anything because when they were young they probably did it too, even though her mother didn't get pregnant at 14, she still did it. Sex to me is a way of life. Some people do it for enjoyment, some to have children, younger people just do it because if they don't they can't hang, or it's just not like being like the others. But it's all right if you don't abuse it too much because you can get diseases like V.D., syphillis, or something even more terrible (eighth grade).[1]

Their search for answers to sensitive questions, or just a desire to talk about sex and feelings, leads many young people to write to us. Here is a letter from a girl in Florida:

I am 13 years old and go to junior high school. Both of my parents work all day and I only see them maybe once a week if I'm lucky. My mom taught me a few things about sex when I was six but I do not think I know enough. Usually my friends are always making jokes about it and sometimes I don't understand some of the things they're joking about!!! How can I get your book entitled "YOU"? I would love to sit in my room sometime and read a book like that maybe it could teach me what my parents don't have time for! "Shoot" I sure don't want to get into any trouble with a boy! ("Really!")

A fourteen-year-old from Milwaukee writes for information she never got from her parents:

I watched you on Donahue and I've come from a family where I have learned Sex from my friends my mother don't mention it to me and I still don't no what most of Sex & Love is all about. So I would like to no if you could send me a copy

---

[1] Reprinted by permission of Planned Parenthood of Monmouth County, Inc., Shrewsbury, New Jersey.

> of your book because I'm only 14 years of age and I've seen my friends get pregnant, I like to know what its all about.

Most poignant of all are letters such as the following, from a fourteen-year-old in Pennsylvania:

> I don't mean to be a pest to you. But a friend of mine has a problem. I let her read your book "You" but for some reason her question wasn't answered. So she has asked me to write and ask you personally.
>
> My friend had oral sex (she let him finger her) with her boy friend in February. On that day she come on her period. Since she went off her period 6 days leter she has not been on. She scared to death that she may be pregnant she hasn't gone to a doctor or told any except me. I told her that its probably her nerves and tension that is causion her to miss. But she insisted I write you. Dr. Sol please answer this letter.
>
> So she may relax.
>
> Could she be pregnant?

The Silent Parents

Parents are a child's earliest models of sexuality and authority, but most adolescents report that they have never been given any advice about sex by either parent, even though the majority of teenagers prefer their parents as counselors and sources of information. Schofield (1965) reported in his random survey of 1,873 English youths that 67 percent of the boys and 29 percent of the girls said they had never, at any time, been given advice about sex by their parents; of those who were "advised," more than two-thirds of the boys and one-fourth of the girls felt that neither of their parents had helped them to deal effectively with the matter of sex. More recent data reviewed by Fox (1978) support Schofield's findings.

The problem doesn't lie in children's unwillingness to talk as much as in parents' embarrassment about talking. The result is that most teenagers learn more from each other than from parents. The national study by the U.S. Commission on Obscenity and Pornography (1970) found that friends were the principal sex information source for 53 percent of the adult males and 35 percent of the adult females. Sixty-seven percent of males and 59 percent of females under age eighteen said friends were their main source of sex information. Our own three-year survey of more than eight hundred college students found that parents were consistently reported as minimally contributing to their children's education about sex.

A survey by *Seventeen* (July 1970) reported that although fathers were considered very reliable by the majority of teenage girls, 61 percent of the girls reported that they had never received any sex education from their fathers. The U.S. Commission on Obscenity also reported that fathers provided sex information for a mere 10 percent of adults and teenagers. Yet, as the *Seventeen* report commented, "Girls want and need to know the male point of view about sex, the facts about the male sex drive, the meaning of impotence, how men feel about sex before marriage, what the male orgasm is like, and many other such things about which they feel their mothers are far from the best informants."

How Parents Can Communicate

Parents contribute to their child's misinformation and sexual ignorance by withholding the facts. In a 1971 study (Libby & Nass, 1971) only one in twenty parents said they would give contraceptive advice to a teenage daughter who was already having sexual relations. All children think about sex, whether they are told anything or not. *Not* talking about it only increases their anxiety and strengthens their misconceptions.

While everyone agrees that parents should be open and frank when they talk to their children about sex, it is still not clear who is going to tell parents *how* to be open and frank. After centuries of silence and secrecy, parents are suddenly being told to liberate themselves and speak freely. But before parents can sit down to talk about sexuality with their children, they must first be able to talk with each other. Before there can be sex education for children, there must first be sex education for parents. Here are some suggestions that may help parents to be more relaxed and straightforward when discussing sex with children. A more detailed treatment of these issues is found in *Sex Education: The Parents' Role* by Sol Gordon and Irving R. Dickman (1977) and *Let's Make Sex a Household Word* by Sol Gordon (1975).

> The conventional American image of parent-child sex discussion is likely to be a scene from a television situation comedy. There sit Dad and Son, engaged in a man-to-man talk about the "facts of life." The laughs come, because while the one is relaxed, the other is obviously embarrassed. Who is the one who is tongue tied, red faced, flustered? Why, Dad, of course.
>
> That comic routine happens to be true to life often enough for even so respected an expert as Wardell Pomeroy to conclude, "Parents who feel reluctant, uneasy, or embarrassed about sex education at home should not attempt it; all the more reason, in such cases, for the school to take over." (It's worth noting that many teachers, including some assigned to teach those courses, do not feel "comfortable" either.)
>
> When it comes to adolescents, it has been suggested that the uneasy parent find an outsider, such as a counselor, a family doctor, or a member of the clergy, who is acceptable to the child. A conversation with such a person can be very useful. But sex education does not consist of one talk, or even a series; nor can it always be scheduled.

Of course, parents who are comfortable with their own sexuality will handle questions well and without losing their "cool" and will more easily help their children become comfortable about the role of sex in their lives.

Some parents feel that before they begin talking they must feel completely comfortable, totally at ease; otherwise, as some say, "the idea of talking about sex, to say nothing of saying 'penis' to our children, is just too much."

The answer is that it is okay to feel uncomfortable. It is even okay to feel nervous, upset, or frightened. But it is not okay to let these feelings paralyze you. Just because you feel uncomfortable does not mean you should stop functioning.

If you're a parent, how do you deal with this discomfort? One thing is to begin "sex education" before your children are old enough to make you feel uncomfortable. Your child's age has a great deal to do with how comfortable or uncomfortable you are. If you start early enough, being comfortable will become a habit.

But suppose your children are no longer preschoolers when you decide to talk with them openly and frankly? There are some specific steps you can take to make it easier. First, husbands and wives should begin to talk more freely with each other, in private, about sex and about their feelings. Second, parents can practice saying aloud the words they find difficult to say, until the words come out naturally.

If nothing else helps, you might simply acknowledge to your child that you don't feel comfortable talking about sex, possibly because your own parents never talked with you about it. Your child may hug and reassure *you*. That kind of frank statement, and a conscious effort to answer whatever you can as best you can, may well score points for you.

The parent who is more comfortable can take the lead, with the other joining in wherever he or she can. There is no reason why a father shouldn't answer some of his daughter's questions. Similarly, a mother can talk with a son as well as she can with a daughter. (In a one-parent family, that's certainly the way it has to be handled.) If both parents are equally prepared, questions should be dealt with as they occur, and answered by whichever parent happens to be present.

It is surprising how *little* technical information a parent needs to learn in addition to what he or she already knows. Depending on when you start, you may also overestimate just how much your youngster wants and needs to be told. Even if you do not know exactly what the Fallopian tubes are, chances are you will not be asked. If you are asked, the *way* in which you reply will tell your child a great deal about your attitudes toward sexuality.

17

Let's say you don't know the answer to a question. If you have only a general idea, say you'll find out, and do just that. It is more important to convey to your children that you are an askable parent than that you know everything.

And since it is legitimate to say you don't have the answer, it is just as legitimate to use a book—not as a substitute for talk, but as a supplement to it. There are books geared to parents as well as books youngsters can read as they choose.[2]

Examine Your Own Attitudes

Husbands and wives should start out by asking themselves questions. Am I satisfied with our sexual relations? Are we able to express the affection we feel for each other? How has our sex life changed during our marriage?

Husbands and wives are very often out of touch with their own feelings. By discovering what pleases them (never mind what the books say!), couples will understand and eventually become more comfortable with their own sexuality. They should remember that orgasm and even frequent intercourse are not as important as a loving relationship between two people.

In advertisements, magazines, novels, and television, our culture reinforces old sex-role stereotypes while defining intercourse as the primary expression of love. Because of this lopsided emphasis, husbands and wives have become needlessly anxious about their performance in bed. It is no coincidence that the leading sex clinics forbid sexual intercourse in the first days of treatment for impotence, poor ejaculatory control, and orgasmic problems. Husbands and wives should rediscover all forms of physical expression, from hugging and kissing to simple touching. Sometimes, just holding each other is the most pleasing form of sexual expression; at other times, couples will prefer other intimate means of expression.

Be Sure You Know the Facts

How much do you know about sex? Knowledge about masturbation, intercourse, birth control, and VD is essential to the development of guidelines for children. To find out what teenagers worry about, try reading the popular comic book *Ten Heavy Facts About Sex* or the adolescent guide *Facts About Sex for Today's Youth* (see "Selected List of Resources"). Women, especially, should become more knowledgeable about sex; they have labored too long under the belief that they aren't supposed to know much and that sex is something that is done to them. Particularly helpful in this regard are *Our Bodies, Ourselves; The Mermaid and the Minotaur;* and *Woman's Body and Woman's Right* (see "Selected List of Resources").

---

[2] From *Sex Education: The Parents' Role*, by Sol Gordon and Irving R. Dickman, Public Affairs Pamphlet No. 549. Copyright © 1977 by the Public Affairs Committee, Inc. Used with permission.

Talk Openly About Sex

Lastly, can you *talk* about sex? Many adults become embarrassed and flustered by the language of sexuality. People who consistently confuse mature discussions of sexuality with boasting or telling jokes are only trying to hide their own insecurity. Children are very sensitive about the emotional value parents give to certain words; if you are severely inhibited when talking about sex, you more than likely cannot transmit healthy attitudes to your children.

The pertinent question is: "Are you an askable parent?"

Special Feature: Putting Sex Education Back in the Home[3]

Parents are expected to be the primary sex educators of their own children. Yet in survey after survey, it has been found that fewer than 20 percent of young people today feel that their parents gave them a satisfactory sex education. In fact, some parents who report that they did educate their children about sex might be surprised to learn that their adult sons and daughters scarcely agree.

"My parents?" some laugh. "You must be kidding!"

"I learned more from my friends," others explain, "only to discover in college that most of what I learned was not true."

Let me first try to put to rest the two most prevalent and noxious sex myths which I see as largely responsible for the ever increasing incidence of irresponsible sexual behavior, particularly among young people.

Myth One: Today's Youth Already Know Everything There Is To Know About Sex

Some do, of course, but research reveals shocking ignorance about critical issues. Young people are having sex earlier, beginning at twelve, thirteen, or fourteen years of age. And the earlier a child has sexual intercourse, the less—repeat, *less*—he or she usually knows about it. Worse, sexually experienced young people will often feel compelled to exaggerate their knowledge, to pretend they understand as much as their experience suggests. In an important 1976 Johns Hopkins study of adolescent girls, for example, only 41 percent knew when in the menstrual cycle the risk of conception was greatest.

Don't believe the stories that all young people knowingly take risks, or that girls from disadvantaged homes deliberately try to get pregnant. Remember that research on teenage pregnancy usually involves asking pregnant girls if they originally wanted to conceive. In one such study of three hundred teenagers (in a *single* high school), we asked why the girls hadn't practiced

---

[3] An abridged, revised version of this section appears in the October 1977 *Good Housekeeping* magazine. As this article appeared in the publication *Community Sex Education Programs for Parents*—a project supported in part by a grant from the National Institute of Mental Health—it may be freely duplicated for educational purposes only. (Gordon, 1977)

19

birth control. "Oh, but we did," was the general response, but their specific answers revealed that quite the opposite was true.

"I used one of my mother's pills."

"I didn't think I could get pregnant standing up."

"He said he'd pull out in time."

"I didn't think I could get pregnant the first time."

"I used foam." (Careful questioning subsequently confirmed that many had used contraceptive foam, but as a douche *after* intercourse.)

When we asked three hundred sexually active girls if they wanted to become pregnant, a resounding 95 percent said they did not.

"What?" one asked in disbelief, "Do you think I'm stupid? I'm only fourteen!"

At this point, some readers may already be thinking that surely their own children are not involved in sexual experimentation. It should be remembered that whether anyone likes it or not (including the teenagers themselves), more than half of all high school students will have had sexual intercourse before graduation.

In surveys of high school students, more than 90 percent did not know that the original symptoms of venereal disease disappear after a while. Most assumed that the disappearance of symptoms meant the disease had been cured. A majority of the same students did not know that females are generally asymptomatic with respect to gonorrhea.

Each year our institute receives hundreds of poignant letters from teenagers. A large number begin something like this: "I'm 15, pregnant and I can't tell my folks (they'll kill me). What should I do?"

Myth Two: Knowledge Is Harmful

Virtually all opposition to sex education is based on the assumption that knowledge is harmful, that children who know about sex will practice it. It's not uncommon for editors of metropolitan newspapers to blame sex education for the rise of illegitimacy and venereal disease. Critics of the Scandinavian countries have long held sex education in the schools partly responsible for moral and social deterioration, as reflected in high rates of sex crime, suicide, and out-of-wedlock pregnancies. The truth of the matter, however, is that compulsory sex education in the public schools of Denmark, Sweden, and Norway is a recent development, and the best available statistics reveal sharp reductions in teenage birth rates and in serious sex crimes since that advent.

As for the United States, I couldn't name a dozen public schools that have what I would consider an adequate sex education program. I'd be hard-pressed to identify even one program that could be called a model in this regard. In fewer than 50 percent of the schools with any sex education program at all, the course usually consists primarily of a few lectures about plumbing, often a relentless pursuit of the Fallopian tubes. For the vast majority of American students, sex education is simply absent from the curriculum.

If you jump up and down real fast after sex you'll confuse the sperm and you won't get pregnant Birth control is the woman's responsibility don't worry I can't get pregnant the first time guys need sex more often than girls if you really love me you'll have sex with me guys are always on the make but they don't make rubbers in my size I can't be a real man unless I have sex if you douche after sex you won't get pregnant when a woman says no she really means yes I can't get birth control because I'm a minor girls really don't have a sex drive they just need love using birth control takes away all the romance if you jump up and down real fast after sex you'll confuse the sperm and you won't get pregnant I can't be a real woman until I have a baby if you're really careful about rhythm it always works but I'm a virgin I can't be pregnant but everybody said that withdrawal always works if you urinate right after sex you won't get pregnant birth control is the woman's responsibility they don't make rubbers in my size guys need sex more often than girls if you really love me you'll have sex with me guys know everything there is to know about sex if you're careful about rhythm it always works if you really love me you'll have sex with me don't worry but everybody said

STOP

To the question whether our communications media contribute to the responsible sex education of young people, we must give an emphatic "No." Certainly, we do find out about rape, violence, sadomasochism, and various forms of sexual titillation from newspapers, magazines, and especially television, but what have these to do with sex education? These are antisex messages. In television, sex education has been largely deemed inappropriate for family viewing!

Our research tells us that ignorance, not knowledge, leads to irresponsible behavior. In fact, knowledgeable young people are more likely to begin having sexual experiences later than their less knowledgeable peers and then to use effective contraception. In the whole world, literate and well-informed women usually take measures to control their fertility and limit the number of children they have to two or three.

A dangerously convoluted logic has prompted some to claim that the pill is leading young women to promiscuity. The fact is that no more than 30 percent of sexually active teenagers regularly use any reliable contraception whatsoever. If only they would use birth control, society wouldn't be in so much trouble.

Roadblocks to Effective Sex Education in the Home

Most parents, after all, want to educate their children about sex. They realize that schools, churches, community organizations, and the mass media can only offer supplementary sex education at best and, in any case, cannot be expected to mirror their personal values. Unfortunately, however, many parents also fear that too much information too soon will have the negative consequence of overstimulating their children.

Contrary to a *few* experts in this field, I've never been able to discover a documented case of a child's having been overstimulated by facts alone. Indeed, when was the last time you tried to tell your child too much about *anything?* Should parents err in the direction of too much information, children simply get bored, turn them off, or cut it short with an irrelevant question. This is not to say that overstimulation is not a problem. It is, and it derives from fears, unresolved curiosity, and ignorance. Our campaign against ignorance has led opponents of sex education to tell jokes about us. A popular example is about the child who asks where she came from and whose mother responds with an elaborate explanation of the seed and the egg. At the end, the child explains that she only wanted to know if she came from Philadelphia. To this, my response is very simple. "So what? Now the child knows not only where she was born but also how she got there." The moral of this and similar stories is that most children would learn very little if education was restricted to what they themselves chose to learn.

Quite understandably, many parents who did not receive sex education in their own homes feel uncomfortable talking about sex with their children. There is no instant remedy for such feelings, but it may be helpful to point out that no one is really comfortable about anything these days. When is the last time someone told you not to worry and you stopped? Contrary to much modern theory, it simply is not necessary to feel totally comfortable about your own, or anybody else's, sexuality in order to be an effective sex educator for your children.

As the primary force in your child's life, you are providing sex education in one form or another no matter what you do. The question is not whether you will teach your children about sex, but how well. Silence teaches no less eloquently than speech. Interestingly enough, if you convey to a young child, or even a teenager, the impression that you feel a bit awkward discussing love and sex, the chances are good that *you'll score.* Your child might well respond to your honesty with genuine affection and appreciation, with a hug and a kiss and with verbal assurances that your discomfort is perfectly understood. Many a parent has been happily surprised to hear a child say, "Don't worry. It's all right."

Parents who worry that they don't know enough about the subject to be effective teachers ought to pause to consider the questions. How much is it really necessary to know? How much really is there to know? To a particularly technical or baffling question, a parent can always respond with the truth. "I don't know, but I'll look it up for you and I'll tell you tomorrow." Or, better still, "Let's look it up together."

If you think about it, what do you really have to know that you don't know already in order to answer a small child's questions? Older children are more likely to ask questions about values than anatomy. And with hundreds of good books no more distant than your local library, what excuse do you really have?

Some parents are concerned about the possibility of traumatizing their children by making honest mistakes, by giving wrong answers. Remember that the resilience of children is legendary, and for good reasons. Parents should realize that they can make mistakes without harming their children. A few examples may be illustrative.

A child wanders into the bedroom while his parents are having sexual intercourse. What to do? Tell the child to leave. In the morning you can apologize for not having said, "Please." And then you can explain what you were doing. If you child asks to watch the next time, tell him he cannot. Kindly and firmly explain that sex is private. A child may not understand the prohibition, but later in life he will grow to appreciate the concept of privacy, not only for his parents but for himself as well. Most important, learn to laugh at the outrageous proposition that a child who has witnessed the "primal scene" will need five years of analysis to get over it. A more likely candidate for analysis is the person who, as a child, never once saw his parents being naturally and openly affectionate.

Some parents worry about the neighbors. What if your child tells the truth about sex to some little friends whose parents hear about it and inform

23

you, in no uncertain terms, of their horror and indignation? Let's take this one from the opposite point of view. What about parents who tell their children that babies grow in cabbage patches? Do you suppose they care about your feelings when your children come home with such news? Your responsibility is to tell your own children the truth, and without instructions to keep it confidential. If your neighbors don't like it, that's their problem. It's about time that the well-educated children—your children—become an important neighborhood resource with respect to sex education. No matter what parents do, children will share whatever information they might have about sex. Isn't it better that they share truth and fact?

Some parents believe that sex education belongs exclusively in the home, but it is grossly unrealistic to try to protect children from all external influences and viewpoints. No parents can have exclusive control over the sex education of their children unless they are prepared to rear them in virtual isolation—no friends, no books, no magazines, no television, and no school.

Of course, even the best-intentioned parents have questions to which the best-qualified professionals cannot give satisfactory answers. Of the thousands of questions I get from parents, the following are the most common. To be sure, some of the responses reflect my personal values, but if any of them conflict with yours, stick to your own. It is important to stress and respect the fact of individual differences. Perhaps we might have some differences which do not threaten a more fundamental agreement. In any case, it is you who must decide where you stand on specific issues. I make a special point of this because the subject of sex education often attracts extremists who try, often under the guise of "morality," to impose their personal views on everybody else.

The key question for all of us should be, "Am I an askable parent?" or put somewhat differently, "When should I tell?" The answer is simple. It is time to tell whenever the child asks. And if you are an askable parent, your child may begin to ask about sex from the time he is two. With young children, the questions are sometimes nonverbal. For example, a child may constantly follow you into the bathroom. Some shy children might ask no questions at all, even of the most askable parents. If your child hasn't raised sexual questions by the age of five, then you should start the conversation. Read a book with her. Tell him about a neighbor or a relative who is going to have a baby. While it's fine, on occasion, to refer to animals, do not concentrate on them in your explanations. People and animals have very different habits.

Askable parents should feel generally responsive to the suggested answers given in the series of questions that follow. Parents who are not askable may find themselves feeling somewhat provoked and perhaps indignant.

1. *How much should I tell?* You should tell your child a *bit* more than you feel he can understand.

2. *How explicit should I be?* In the first place, always make it a point to use the correct terminology. Avoid such infantile euphemisms as *pee-pee* or *wee-wee*. Say directly that when a man and a woman love each other and want to have a baby, the man's penis is placed into the woman's vagina. If the sperm from the man's body joins with the egg inside the woman's body at the right time, a baby gets started. Depending on the child's age and other factors, you might say more. "Sometimes it takes a year or more before a baby is conceived." Or "Your father (or mother) and I enjoy loving each other in this way. Right now we are using birth control because our family isn't ready for a new baby just yet."

The main idea is that parents can be explicit without overstating the case or feeling compelled to describe sexual techniques to a child who hasn't yet grasped much more basic ideas. It is also wiser to say at the start that a baby has its beginning in the mother's uterus, not the stomach.

3. *What about nudity in the home?* Many parents are relaxed about undressing in front of young children or about bathing with them. These are good opportunities for children to ask important questions. "How come you have one and I don't?" "How come yours is bigger than mine?" "How come you have two and I don't have any?" Parents should respond directly to these and similar questions.

A question also arises when a child wants to touch a parent's genitals or breasts. There are several perfectly acceptable responses, one of which is simply that you don't want her or him to do this. Even if a child protests against that familiar double standard—"but you touch me"—you can explain that that is because you have to bathe and keep the child clean. For parents who do not object to their children's requests to touch, it is important to remain casual about it. Generally speaking, a child's own growing sense of modesty will tell you when to start undressing in private. When a child wants to go to the bathroom alone or to undress without an audience, you will have indications that he is developing a sense of privacy that you need to respect.

4. *What do I do if I find my child playing doctor?* Almost all children, at one time or another, experiment with playing doctor. If parents discover their children examining a playmate's genitals or engaging in mutual stimulation, the best response is not to punish. Punishment—spanking, sending a child to his room, ordering the playmate home—suggests that sex play is sinful. Parents would do better simply to explain that they find this sort of behavior unacceptable. They can say, "In our family we feel that children should not play such games." This puts an effective end to the behavior without any harmful implications that the children have done something terrible.

5. *Is too much masturbation harmful?* Masturbation is a normal expression of sexuality at any age. The only thing wrong with it is the guilt that people are made to feel, and it is this guilt that creates the energy for impulsive and involuntary masturbation. All children old enough to understand should be taught that masturbation should be done in private. As they get older, they

25

will sense that masturbation is a normal enjoyable substitute for sexual intercourse, and they will realize that as long as it gives them pleasure, there is no such thing as too much.

6. *What about the use of obscenities?* Children invariably use vulgar language to get a rise out of their parents, to test a new and powerful weapon. If a child uses an obscenity, the parent should quickly and calmly explain its meaning, perhaps using the word itself in the explanation. Even the most common four-letter word can be handled in this way, provided the parent explains its gross intent as well as the fact that it's a crude synonym for sexual intercourse.

7. *What about the child who likes to look at his father's "girlie" magazines?* There is no harm in this. In fact, it may provide a teachable moment. You might point out that ordinary people don't look like that, or that people sometimes like to look at unusual photographs of the nude, or that women sometimes enjoy looking at pictures of nude men. It's not a big deal. Frontal nudity is becoming more common in established magazines.

Pornography, however, is something else again. True, it has not been proven harmful, but it is clearly not educational, and many parents would understandably prefer to keep their children away from it. While it may not always be possible to shield a child from pornographic material, parents can take some comfort in the fact that people who have received responsible sex education show a marked tendency to grow bored quickly with pornography.

8. *What about embarrassing questions in public?* Children have a great knack for asking the most delicate questions in the supermarket or when special guests have come to dinner. The best approach, no matter how embarrassed you are, is to tell the child that he has asked a very good question and, if you still have your wits about you, proceed to answer it then and there. In most cases, your guests will silently applaud. If you feel you can't answer the question right away, it is very important to praise the child for asking and to tell him specifically when you will discuss it with him. Generally speaking, it is better to risk shocking a few grown-ups than to embarrass your own child.

9. *What should I do if my husband says it's my job to tell?* Sex education is properly the responsibility of both parents, as it is reflected in their behavior with each other and in communication with children. If your husband stubbornly refuses to have any part of it, you must take it upon yourself to explain love and sex to all the children in your family. Incidentally, it has never been established that girls are better educated by their mothers or boys by their fathers. Single parents, relax.

10. *What can I do to keep my child from becoming homosexual?* Some parents have rather strange notions of what would constitute protection against homosexuality. Some fathers are not affectionate with school-age sons for fear of encouraging homosexuality, despite the absence of any compelling evidence linking a father's love with a son's homosexuality. There are cases where fathers have rejected sons and the sons are homosexual, but even here it

is very difficult to establish a connection between the rejection and the homosexuality. With as much research as we have on this subject, we still do not know why any one person, male or female, becomes homosexual. There is certainly no evidence that girls who are tomboys and boys who prefer books to footballs are more likely to become homosexual adults. Nor can we say that a child with a strong mother and a weak father has a greater chance of becoming homosexual. What we suspect is that between 4 and 10 percent of the population will develop an exclusive homosexual orientation, no matter what parents try to do about it. While it is all right not to want your children to become homosexual, it is important to understand that good mental health is not necessarily a function of sexual orientation. Just as homosexuals can be happy and creative people, heterosexual adults can turn to drugs, crime, and generally lead unhappy lives.

In dealing with homosexuality, parents should convey an attitude of consideration for people who have different orientations. At the same time they should make it abundantly clear that their children are to reject any sexual overtures made by adults. Moreover, they must emphasize that such overtures do not in any way suggest that a child was somehow to blame. A child should be discouraged from thinking that he must be a homosexual simply because he was approached by someone who is. Books that might be helpful for parents who believe their child may be homosexual are *A Family Matter: A Parents' Guide to Homosexuality* by Charles Silverstein (1977), *Consenting Adult* by Laura Hobson (1976), and *Gay: What You Should Know About Homosexuality* (Hunt, 1977).

11. *What if my children think I'm old-fashioned?* They may be right! Most parents are old-fashioned. The best thing to do is acknowledge it and continue expressing your views without worrying which label your child might attach to them.

12. *How can I talk to my teenage daughter about birth control without giving her the message that it's all right for her to have sexual intercourse?* Some parents erroneously believe that teenagers equate information with consent. Your teenage children know very well what your values are. It's one thing to tell a daughter that you will disown her if she becomes pregnant. It's quite another to explain your feelings something like this: "We really think you're much too young to have sex, but if you're not going to listen to us we urge you to practice birth control. In any case, you *should* know something about birth control and, more important, we don't ever want you to feel that there's *anything* you can't talk to us about."

13. *I worry about my children being molested. How can I talk about this without frightening them?* A little-known fact is that as many as 70 percent of all child molestation cases involve someone the child knows, such as a stepparent or babysitter. As part of a family's general discussions about sexuality, children should be taught never to go off with strangers or allow anyone to touch their genitals. Some individuals force children to submit to sexual activi-

27

ties and make them promise never to tell anyone what happened. Should you suspect that your child has been abused in this way, it is essential to make him understand that such promises should never be kept. The fact that most people are decent and kind must be balanced with the reality that some people take advantage of children. The critical point is not to let a child who has been molested feel guilt or blame. (Some parents unthinkingly ask, "Why did you let him do this?") Such crimes are the responsibility of the adult.

14. *We've never talked about sex. Now I want to, but my teenage son absolutely refuses. What should I do?* This is a common situation, and it is appropriate for a parent to begin the conversation something like this: "I really made a mistake by waiting this long and I wish we had talked when you were younger. Now I can understand why you might feel embarrassed to talk with me." Plan ahead for such discussions; have a book ready. Tell your son that you think he might be interested in it. Explain that some of the material might embarrass him, but that you're going to leave the book around just the same. The main thing is for him to understand that you are available to talk any time he is ready. Another technique is to "hide" a consciousness-raising book like *YOU* (Gordon, 1978). Most teenagers are very adept at finding such "hidden" material.

15. *What do you mean by normal or responsible sexuality?* Normal sexuality is voluntary, generally pleasurable, and inclined to enhance the personalities of the people involved. Abnormal or immature sexuality tends to be involuntary. People engage in it not because they want to but because they can't help it. Immature sexuality is generally exploitative, rarely enjoyable, and often degrading. Responsible sexuality, by contrast, is characterized by respect for oneself and by genuine caring for another human being.

16. *What is your opinion on premarital sex?* I'm opposed to teenagers having sexual intercourse. Teenagers are too young, too vulnerable. They do not have ready access to contraception. They tend to be impulsive. The double standard is still, alas, very much with us. Boys still use such lines as, "If you really love me, you'll have sex with me." Girls rarely reply with, "If you really loved me, you wouldn't put this pressure on me." In addition, teenage pregnancy is unsound from the medical, moral, and psychological points of view.

While I am opposed to sex for teenagers, I also must say that in my twenty-five years as a clinical psychologist, no teenager has ever asked for my consent. It is unrealistic for parents to assume their teenagers will not have sexual relationships in the absence of parental permission or consent. Thus, parents must face the possibility that however clear they have made their own values, their teenagers may just as clearly reject them. Should this occur, however, parents can *still* exert a positive influence. Without anger and without recriminations, parents can simply say, "We do not want you to have sex, but if your mind is already made up, at least be sure to use birth control." Young adults who are working or in college should receive similar parental messages.

The decision must be theirs, but if teenagers do choose to have sexual relationships, it is their duty, to themselves and to their partners, to act responsibly.

One of the most encouraging signs on campuses across the nation today is that women (and men) influenced by the women's liberation movement have become extremely sensitive to exploitation. More and more, young people of both sexes are coming to insist upon what they call egalitarian relationships in which the partners do not take advantage of one another.

There is little substantive evidence to suggest that people who are virgins at marriage have better marriages than people who are not. Let those who counsel against premarital sex refrain from the absurd argument that if people have sex before marriage they'll have nothing to look forward to after the wedding. My own view is that if sex is the only thing one looks forward to in a marriage, it's better not to marry, for marital sex takes on preeminent importance only if the partners are hung up on it or dysfunctional in it.

If I were to develop a ten-point scale of the most important things in a marriage, number one would be mutual love and caring. Second would be the ability to have interesting conversations. Third would be a good sense of humor. Ninth would be a satisfying sexual relationship. Last would be sharing household tasks together.[4] (Often I'm asked, "How come sex is number nine?" My reply: Of the 3,231 important aspects of a relationship, sex is one of the top ten. Not bad?)

17. *What should be the role of the public schools in sex education?* Sex education should be part of the regular curriculum. It is currently excluded because of censorship and because of extremist pressures exerted against school boards and administrations.

18. *My fourteen-year-old daughter worries about having lustful thoughts. Are these harmful?* One of the key concepts in the whole area of sexuality is that *all thoughts, desires and dreams are normal.* Anyone with the slightest imagination or creativity has occasional thoughts of lust, sadomasochism, incest, and rape. Behavior can be abnormal, but never thoughts by themselves.

Guilt is the energy for the repetition of unacceptable thoughts. For example, if a girl has homosexual fantasies and feels guilty about them, she will have these thoughts over and over again until they become part of a self-fulfilling prophecy. If, however, she recognizes that all thoughts are normal, nothing will happen and most of her thoughts will be voluntary; the remainder will be involuntary but of brief duration.

19. *How can I bring up my children to respect the values of other people?* This depends largely on the kind of life you lead and the kinds of

---

[4] Numbers 4, 5, 6, 7, and 8 are deliberately omitted to leave room for curriculum development.

values you translate into your behavior with others. For it is as a model for your children (which, of course, does not imply perfection), that you have the best opportunity to foster a true respect and appreciation for individual differences.

A Final Comment

Sex education is a family affair. It is related to how you feel about yourself and your ability to communicate with your husband or wife. Askable parents talk to each other. They also have a sense of humor. Not everything is a trauma. Children with askable parents tend to talk to them. While their developing sense of privacy prevents them from telling parents everything as they grow older, most want very much for their parents to respect that privacy. Askable parents have a lot of common sense. If you feel you've made mistakes, you can smile and say, "I've made some mistakes. My child will understand when I explain that I don't know everything." And then you'll feel more askable than ever.

References   Alan Guttmacher Institute. *11 million teenagers.* New York: Planned Parenthood, 1976.

Fox, G. L. *The family's role in adolescent sexual behavior.* Working draft prepared for Family Impact Seminar on Teenage Pregnancy and Family Impact: New Perspectives on Policy, Washington, D.C., October 1978.

Gordon, S. *Let's make sex a household word.* Charlottesville, Va.: Ed-U Press, 1975

Gordon, S. Putting sex education back in the home. *Community Sex Education Programs for Parents: A Training Manual for Organizers.* Charlottesville, Va.: Ed-U Press, 1977, 44–58.

Gordon, S. You—A survival guide for youth. New York: Times Books, 1978.

Gordon, S., & Dickman, I. *Sex education: The parents' role.* New York: Public Affairs Committee, Inc., 1977.

Hobson, L. Z. *Consenting adult.* New York: Warner Books, 1976.

Hunt, M. *Gay: What you should know about homosexuality.* New York: Farrar, 1977.

Libby, R. W. Parental attitudes toward high school sex education programs. *Family Coordinator,* 1970, *19* (3), 234–247.

Libby, R. W., & Nass, G. Parental views on teenage sexual behavior. *Journal of Sex Research,* 1971, *7* (3), 226–237.

Mosher, D. L. Sex differences, sex experience, sex guilt, and explicitly sexual films. *Journal of Social Issues,* 1973, *29* (3), 95–122.

Schofield, M. *The sexual behavior of young people.* Boston: Little, Brown, 1965.

Silverstein, C. *A family matter: A parents' guide to homosexuality.* New York: McGraw-Hill, 1977.

Sorensen, R. C. *Adolescent sexuality in contemporary America.* New York: World Publishing, 1973.

U.S. Commission on Obscenity and Pornography. *Report of the Commission.* New York: Bantam, 1970.

Zelnik, M., & Kantner, J. F. Sexual and contraceptive experience of young unmarried women in the United States, 1976 and 1971. *Family Planning Perspectives,* 1977, *9* (2), 55–71.

Two

What Adolescents Need to Know

Teenagers are beginning to have sexual intercourse earlier, and the proportion of teenagers who have had intercourse is increasing (Juhasz, 1976; Hunt, 1974; Sorensen, 1973; Kantner & Zelnik, 1972). The Alan Guttmacher Institute (1976) estimated that by 1975, there were 4 million teenage girls and 7 million teenage boys who had had intercourse. Kantner and Zelnik's (1972) national probability study conducted in 1971 sampled more than four thousand girls between fifteen and nineteen. A similar study of about two thousand teenage girls was conducted in 1976 by Zelnik and Kantner (1977). In 1971, 27 percent of teenage girls had experienced intercourse; by 1976, that figure had risen to 35 percent. By the age of nineteen, 55 percent of all teenage girls (49 percent of whites and 84 percent of blacks) have had intercourse. The increase has been twice as great for whites as for blacks, particularly between the ages of fifteen and seventeen.

From 1971 to 1976, there was a dramatic increase in the percentage of sexually experienced teenagers who said they "always" use contraception. Yet even though the percentage of those who said they didn't use birth control in their most recent intercourse dropped from 55 percent in 1971, the 1976 figure of 37 percent indicates that there was still a high degree of risk taking. This finding is supported by the increase in the percentage who said they "never" used birth control: from 17 percent in 1971 to 25 percent in 1976.

There was relatively very little improvement over the past five years in the extent to which teenagers were knowledgeable about the period of greatest fertility during the menstrual cycle; 60 percent were ignorant of this, and although white teenagers tended to become more knowledgeable with age and sexual experience, black teenagers continued to be generally ill informed regardless of age or experience.

When asked in 1971 why they had not used contraception, teenagers of all races consistently said it was because they had thought that for one of a number of reasons they could not become pregnant. Reasons included the beliefs that they were not fertile, they were too young, they did not have sufficiently frequent intercourse, or they had timed intercourse to coincide with what they erroneously believed to be the safest days of the menstrual cycle (Shah, Zelnik, & Kantner, 1975).

33

Sexual Ignorance Among Teenagers

Sexually active young people can be *less* knowledgeable than their sexually inexperienced peers (Crist, 1970). Early sexual experience seems to promote an unwillingness to learn about sex, partly because the individual feels he or she is already knowledgeable, and partly because there is a fear of appearing naive if one seeks information. In our society, few adolescents will admit to sexual confusion or ignorance. The dilemma is obvious, but it is still possible, and indeed vital, to provide adolescents with accurate information. On the basis of research and our own experience as counselors and educators, we find that adolescents' anxieties and sexual difficulties are due primarily to lack of accurate basic information, information they must have before they successfully confront the sophisticated and complex matters related to sexuality.

Unintentional Pregnancy and VD

A shocking and little-known fact is that in 1970 more pregnancies were reported among adolescent girls in the United States than among adolescent girls in any other Western nation (Committee on Maternal Nutrition, 1970). Whether this still holds is not easily determined, for as Kantner (1975) noted, "Comparisons that do not involve large differences in social and economic conditions are not readily available." The fact remains, however, that the illegitimacy rate among girls between the ages of fifteen and nineteen has continued to rise; in each year since 1973, more than half of *all* illegitimate births have been to teenagers (Jones & Placek, 1978; Menken, 1975; National Center for Health Statistics, 1975; 1976). The illegitimate birth rate among teenagers has risen dramatically in the last two decades: 15 percent in 1960, 27 percent in 1968, 36 percent in 1974, and near 40 percent in 1975 (U.S. Commission on Population Growth and the American Future, 1972; Menken, 1975; National Center for Health Statistics, 1975; 1976). We are also beginning to document the unintended and unwanted character of the overwhelming majority of out-of-wedlock births. Thus, there is a strong correlation between sexual ignorance and taking the risk of pregnancy.

There is also a powerful relationship between sexual ignorance and the recent increase in reported cases of venereal disease among teenagers. Most teenagers do not know how to prevent venereal disease or, if they have it, how to recognize symptoms and find treatment (Hayes & Littlefield, 1976).

Socioeconomic Differences in Sexually Active Adolescents

The lack of knowledge about sex among teenagers has been well documented (Shah, Zelnik & Kantner, 1975; Finkel & Finkel, 1975; Reichelt & Werley, 1974; Miller, 1973; Sorensen, 1973). In this regard, there are important correlations between a teenager's knowledge about sexuality and the socioeconomic status of his or her family. Evidence from thousands of questions submitted anonymously to us, as well as from hundreds of interviews with low-income and middle-income high school youths, supports the following conclusion: *Youth from low-income homes tend to have earlier and more frequent sexual experiences than youth from middle-income homes.* (In a "typical" Upward Bound program for sixteen- and seventeen-year-olds, about 80 percent of the males and 55 percent of the females had had sexual intercourse more than a few times prior to their enrollment in the program.)[1] While youth from poorer families also tend to feel less guilty about their sexual experiences, they generally lack the knowledge that offers true freedom from guilt. The fact is that poor teenagers know very little about the process of conception. They avoid and oppose masturbation and birth control, and entertain many false ideas about them.

By comparison, middle-class youth have tended, until recently, to avoid or postpone intercourse. They are somewhat better informed about the process of conception. They generally favor the use of contraception. While they have many false notions about masturbation, they do not avoid it themselves or oppose it for others.

In a study of eight-to-ten-year-olds, Elias and Gebhard (1969), reported that in the lower socioeconomic level, although 96 percent of the boys knew about sexual intercourse, only 4 percent of them knew about fertilization. Girls from the same socioeconomic level followed a similar pattern: half of them knew about intercourse, but only a few were informed about conception. The opposite pattern, however, emerged from the higher socioeconomic classes. These children were found to be better informed about fertilization and conception than about intercourse.

Teenage Sex and Ignorance

There is a strong correlation between sexual ignorance and the risk of pregnancy or venereal disease. In a study of black junior high school students, Kleinerman, Grossman, Breslow, and Goldman (1971) found a large discrepancy between the teenagers' awareness of various forms of sexual behavior and their knowledge of biological processes. The students had heard about masturbation, oral-genital relations, homosexuality, menstruation, and contraception, but their factual knowledge about these subjects was very limited. They knew about intercourse, but they did not know the details of the relationship between intercourse and conception or exposure to venereal disease.

Of 103 Upward Bound youths responding to a questionnaire, forty-eight believed that a girl could become pregnant only if she had sexual relations during her menstrual period. Elsewhere it was found that many girls used con-

---

[1] Upward Bound is a U.S. Department of Health, Education and Welfare project designed to assist high school students from poverty families to enter college. In 1971 there were 292 Upward Bound centers involving about 24,000 students.

35

traceptive foam, but not *before* sexual intercourse as directed in the complicated instructions that they could not read (Gordon, 1971).

Zelnik and Kantner (1977) also concluded that the older a girl is at her first intercourse, the more likely she is to use contraception, whereas in the typical teenage pattern, first use of contraception follows first experience with intercourse.

Sexual Ignorance Among College Students

The lack of sexual knowledge exists not only at the junior and senior high school levels. Takey Crist (1970) of the University of North Carolina at Chapel Hill administered a questionnaire on sexual anatomy to six hundred coeds. While difficulties with the research technique prevent us from considering the results conclusive, the findings are nonetheless interesting, even provocative. Among the sexually active women, more than one-fourth could not answer any of the questions. While 59 percent answered at least half of the questions correctly, *none* were able to score 100 percent. Less sexually active women scored much higher. Eighty percent of them answered at least half of the questions correctly, and 9 percent made perfect scores.

In light of these figures, it is difficult to persist in the notion that greater sexual knowledge is a sign of greater sexual activity. Ignorance goes hand in hand with an inclination toward risk in terms of more frequent intercourse as well as a more consistent failure to take precautions against pregnancy and venereal disease. By contrast, a high level of knowledge is generally associated with a more cautious and responsible approach to sexual behavior (chapter 9, "The Effects of Sex Education").

Failure to Use Birth Control—Not Ignorance Alone

The unwillingness or inability of sexually active girls to use effective contraception is well documented. Furstenberg, Gordis, and Markowitz (1969) reported a study made of 169 unwed pregnant teenagers at the Mt. Sinai Hospital in Baltimore. Only 30 percent had used any method of birth control. Less than half were able to name three kinds of birth control. One-third of those who had not practiced birth control were still not aware that they could have used contraceptives at all. Not surprisingly, 91 percent felt that they lacked adequate knowledge about how to use birth control.

Zelnik and Kantner found in their national study of teenage girls (1977) that more than 70 percent did not consistently use *any* kind of contraception; in seven cases out of ten this reflected the teenagers' belief that they could not get pregnant.

Some astute clinical observers of the "scene" have suggested reasons why couples don't use contraception. The eminent gynecologist/obstetrician Dr. Eugene Sandberg (1975) lists

    1 denial
    2 love

    3 guilt
    4 shame (embarrassment)
    5 sexual identity conflicts
    6 hostility
    7 masochism
    8 nihilism
    9 entrapment
  10 eroticism
  11 coital gamesmanship
  12 affectional poverty
  13 fear and anxiety
  14 abortion availability
  15 iatrogenesis
  16 opportunism (or desperation)

Another list was prepared by Robertson, Torrance, and Moore (1977):

    1 denial
    2 martyrdom
    3 guilt
    4 shame
    5 coital gamesmanship
    6 sexual identity conflicts
    7 naturalness/spontaneity
    8 hostility
    9 nihilism
  10 abortion availability
  11 instant gratification
  12 insecurity
  13 desperation
  14 nonacceptance of one's sexuality
  15 attention
  16 desire to become an adult through pregnancy
  17 fatalism
  18 "sex fiend" and "pick-up" myths
  19 babies as pets

It is clear that no single explanation can suffice for the nonuse of contraception. The above lists offer us opportunities to consider both the research and the action programs necessary to meet the needs of a wide range of personalities found among young people. It reminds us that adolescence is neither a diagnosis, nor a disease, but a developmental stage that "strikes" people in many ways.

Obviously, failure to use contraceptives cannot be attributed to ignorance alone. For example, the Furstenberg et al. study (1969) revealed that 78 percent of the pregnant girls had heard of the pill. The writers point out, however, that "girls tend to be most aware of birth control to which they have least access (pills, IUD) and over which they have the least control (condoms)." Many other studies have found that awareness of a birth control method is no guarantee that the method will be used (Kantner & Zelnik, 1972; Brown, Lieberman, & Miller, 1975; Gilbert & Matthews, 1974; Cobliner, 1974).

A *Circus* survey (September 29, 1977) of nearly two thousand young adults found that almost 40 percent *never* used birth control, despite the fact that 88 percent "usually" or "always" had easy access to contraception. Luker (1977) studied five hundred women seeking abortions at a San Francisco clinic during 1971–1973. The typical client was white, unmarried, middle class, about twenty-two years old, and had some college education. Although only 14 percent had *never* used any method of contraception, only 6 percent were consistently using the pill, IUD, or diaphragm in the month before they became pregnant. Luker's data suggested that failure to use contraception is often the result of a process of personal cost-accounting in which the *immediate* risks and benefits of contraceptive use are weighed against the *long-range* risks and benefits of pregnancy. She suggests that because women frequently face conflicting sexual pressures (e.g., to be responsive, but only at the "right" times and with the "right" man), use of contraception gets "caught in the crossfire and becomes too socially 'costly.' " Further, Luker's data show that if a woman has taken one or two chances without becoming pregnant, it is likely to reinforce her risk taking, because "if it hasn't happened yet, it won't happen."

Questions Teenagers Ask
The interests and the ignorance of adolescents are revealed in the following questions, largely unedited, submitted anonymously to the authors by high school and college students.

Urban Youth Speak
City teenagers are thought to be sophisticated and "with it." Their questions about sex tell a different story:

Can you get pregnant from having sex for five minutes?

If a boy has syphilis and a girl and boy has oral sex, will the girl get syphilis?

Can a boy get a girl pregnant without having sexual intercourse?

Can you still get VD if you use a rubber?

Do you have to use a different rubber after each sexual relationship?

Can Norforms be a guarantee for protection against pregnancy?

38

If you don't reach a climax, are you abnormal?

How do you put it in? Front or back?

Is it true that you can use dry mustard and vinegar to get rid of [the fetus]?

How is it that a girl gets pregnant faster standing up than in the bed?

During what periods of time are girls capable of becoming pregnant?

Is it true that a girl may not become pregnant unless she and the boy come at the same time?

Why is it easy for a girl to have a baby when she is on her period?

Can you get pregnant from fingering?

How many times must a woman have a sex relation before she gets pregnant?

Is it true that when a man eats a woman after a period of time, will it hurt her insides at all?

What makes a boy hard when he gets up in the morning time?

What Rural Youth Ask

Rural teenagers are thought to know it all because they are familiar with animals. The following questions from a large group of high school students in upstate New York suggest otherwise:

How long after sexual intercourse can you become pregnant?

How can I tell if I'm a lesbian?

Why do boys get more excited than girls?

If the shancre is only on the mouth, *can* you get VD by fucking?

Is it possible to get pregnant if he pulls out before he reaches his orgasm?

How many abortions can you have before it will effect your body?

Do men have menstrual cycles?

39

Is it true that "smell" causes sexual arousal?

Why is a chick such a Bitch when she is on the rag?

Why did our parent fuck when they were my age but don't want me to?

Is it possible for a girl our age to not have a large enough vagina to have successful sex?

Can you get pregnant without intercourse?

How many times a day can you withstand sex?

If your an athlete and you have sex with a girl before a game, does it help improve your playing ability?

Is there such a thing during intercourse as getting locked in?

How do you beat your meat?

What does it mean when your balls turn blue?

Can you get pregnant just by sleeping with a person of the opposite sex?

Is it sanitary to play with yourself?

Is it normal to materbate?

Here are some verbatim questions from Arkansas teenagers collected by the Arkansas Family Planning Council in 1975:[2]

What do you say when you go to the health clinic? Are you sure they won't consent with your parents?

I've heard the pill can make you pregnant. Is that true?

Do girls prefer rubbers or raw?

Can you get VD from kissing if you haven't had oral sex?

Can you die from VD if you've had it for about a year?

What if a boy makes a girl pregnant, and the boy didn't want to have anything to do with the baby?

Is it true that you can only become pregant 2 days out of the month?

---

[2] Reprinted with permission from the Arkansas Family Planning Council.

How come you can't get a bone when you're Drunk?

Do girls masterbate?

What if you eat someone and have sex afterwards could you get pregnant?

What goes on at drive-in movies?

How do you get a guy off after you get him on?

In February 1977, sixth-, seventh-, and eighth-graders attending a Shrewsbury, New Jersey school were asked what topics they would like covered in health class. Although each group requested basic information, the older children consistently expressed a greater concern about the social situation, morality, relationships, feelings, and communication.

Sixth Grade What happens when you have sex?

When you first have sex, what month does your stomach get big?

What age do you have to be to have a baby?

What is V.D.? Can it be in someone's family?

Is it normal to masturbate?

Why do only women have periods?

Seventh Grade I know about a period . . . what is menstruation?

Should young people be able to buy birth control pills?

How do you ask the other person if they want to have sexual intercourse?

How much sex do you have to do to get pregnant?

What do homosexuals do to each other?

In an abortion are you really killing your baby's life?

Why do some people think it's a sin to have sex?

Eighth Grade Why do I get embarrassed when I talk about sex?

How do you make a man stop if you don't want to?

41

Do boys have the same reactions toward sex that girls have?

Does having an abortion ever have any effect on the man's feeling about you?

When a girl gets pregnant do you think the boy should assume full responsibility?

Why can't we have coed health?

Should a girl get married without having had a sexual relationship?

How do you lose a slight fear of sex?[3]

Even College Students Need Answers

It is popularly assumed that college students are both knowledgeable and sophisticated in sexual matters. College students themselves will rarely admit to sexual ignorance or confusion. Yet consider such questions as these:

What is the significance of a fantasy?

What is a normal sex life?

Is jealousy inherent in sexual love?

Why is virginity a dirty word?

Why won't some girls let oral sex be performed on them?

Do you think women have a preoccupation with the size of a man's genitals and why?

Why do most sex partners lose at least some interest in each other over time?

What is the best way to discuss sex with your boyfriend? How open should you be and at what time during your relationship should you talk openly about it?

Is homosexuality abnormal?

Do men go through a state of menopause?

How can you get an orgasm when you can't get one?

Why does society feel that (the majority) the male should be the aggressive one in the act of sex?

---

[3] These questions were made available to the authors and reprinted by permission of Planned Parenthood of Monmouth County, Inc., Shrewsbury, New Jersey.

Is there a simple way to encourage a more open, verbal exchange about what in particular would most please your "partner?"

What extent, is it normal for a girl who is a virgin to be afraid of sex?

Are there other women who find orgasm painful? Is that natural?

How often does the normal teenager masterbate?

What are the moral ramifications of having sex only for pure physical enjoyment (even if you don't like or know the other person?)

What is an abortion like?

Meaningful Communication

Adolescents will have sex despite society's warning and raging. It is also clear, however, that adolescents want some sensible adult guidance about moral decision making. Merely saying "don't" does not make sense to them. By contrast, a plea not to exploit or hurt people by bringing an unwanted child into this world does make sense. In addition to an understanding of adult opinions, adolescents must have the facts and a knowledge of their personal op-

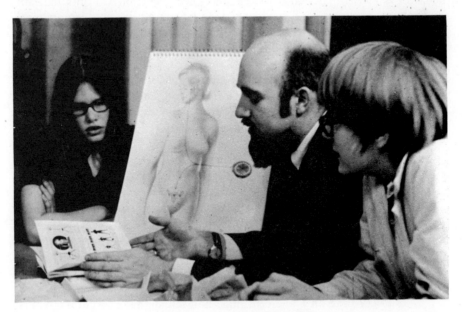

Sex education in a relaxed, informal setting.

By permission of the Unitarian Universalist Association.

tions before they can make up their own minds in a mature and sensitive way.

Few young people nowadays accept the notion that *all* sex outside of marriage is immoral, and that *all* sex within marriage is moral. They are sophisticated enough to notice that many married adults use sex for exploitation or corruption. They are also aware of older brothers and sisters and friends who are living with partners in what appear to be beautiful relationships. The Gallup Youth Survey of September 1978 found that 59 percent of the nation's teenagers believe premarital sex is acceptable, while only 30 percent disapprove. Only 23 percent feel it is "very important" to marry a virgin (*Behavior Today,* 1978).

Adolescents need to understand that they can—and must—make their own sexual decisions. Waiting for marriage is *one* of these options, despite the fact that a great number do not wait. They also need the security of parental support should they decide to use contraception before marriage. Whatever an individual's personal beliefs about morality, contraception must surely be preferable to forced marriages, unwanted children, and probable divorce.

Basis Facts Teenagers Should Know

At the very least, adolescents should be informed of certain facts. These can serve as a checklist for parents and professionals to refer to in raising sexually healthy children.

We must first advocate responsible sexual behavior; responsible behavior is loving, voluntary, and enhances self-acceptance of both partners. By contrast, irresponsible behavior tends to be compulsive and demoralizing. While teenagers are certainly sexual beings, they should be aware of the risks of sexual intercourse. Those in their early teens are generally too inexperienced, too vulnerable for sexual relationships. They rarely have access to birth control. They frequently are not able to deal with problems associated with early sexual experiences: pain, lack of orgasm, impotence, and premature ejaculation. The girls are not physically ready to handle the rigors of bearing children. Over the age of eighteen, young people can be free to make their own decisions; those who want to remain virgins until marriage should be encouraged to do so. The best we can strive for is loving behavior in the context of mutual understanding. We realize that eighteen is not a magic age and that some teenagers are more mature at seventeen than adults at twenty-five. Generally speaking, however, in our society high school graduation is a rite of passage for the child to either go to college or become employed. And even if it doesn't seem to make sense to some people, being eighteen or nineteen is different than being thirteen or fourteen.

Here are some concepts that should be considered in developing a sex education program for adolescents:

1. Every time an adolescent male and female have sexual intercourse without birth control, the female risks pregnancy. The risk is lessened

somewhat if coitus takes place during menstruation or a few days before or after. But since some women ovulate at that time as well, there is no *absolutely* safe time to have intercourse.

2. The major methods of birth control should be discussed: oral contraceptives, the IUD, the diaphragm, condoms, and contraceptive foam. The rhythm method has been proven ineffective, but is better than nothing. Both males and females should know how to use the condom, which also gives some protection against venereal disease.

3. Because teenage pregnancy is not a good idea, for both medical and psychological reasons, teenagers must know about abortion. Abortion is a legitimate way to end an unintended, unwanted, or dangerous pregnancy. If it is not contrary to a young person's religious beliefs, abortion is usually more defensible than bringing an unwanted child into the world. The main points to stress in a discussion about teenage pregnancy are that human beings, by their very nature, can make mistakes, and a girl who has made the very serious mistake of becoming pregnant retains the right to decide, with the help of family and counselors, which of the options (abortion, keeping the child, or surrendering it for adoption) would be best for her.

4. Masturbation is a normal expression of sexuality at any age, and for teenagers it is a healthy alternative to sexual intercourse. Like most forms of sexual behavior, it requires privacy. And again, like all other forms of sexual behavior, it can become a problem if one is compulsive or guilty about it.

5. Young people *don't* have to have sexual intercourse in order to be healthy. Our society has exaggerated the meaning and importance of sex in a person's life. It becomes desperately important only if one is hung up about it or having related problems. If one is generally happy with life, sex will almost naturally become a pleasant part of it. In marriage or other intimate relationships, sex is no more important than love, mutual interests, conversation, and humor.

6. Many young people needlessly worry because they feel, or once felt, attracted to someone of the same sex. Yet our definition of a homosexual is an adult who has and prefers sexual relationships with partners of the same sex. Little is known about why some people are exclusively homosexual. In any case, in a healthy society, nonexploitative sexual preferences are not a source of concern or anxiety.

7. Sexual preferences are undesirable only to the extent that they are exploitative. Being extremely uptight about, or hostile to, forms of behavior that other people may enjoy are signs of personal insecurities.

8. Both boys and girls need to know about wet dreams and menstruation. There is no excuse for any child to arrive unprepared at these points in life.

9. Venereal diseases have reach epidemic proportions. *Everyone* should understand that while the original symptoms (chancres, burning urina-

tion, etc.) may disappear, the disease can still be present. Women especially must know that with several forms of VD, they may have no symptoms at all.

10. Pornography is not educational but neither is it harmful. People with a good sex education may occasionally enjoy pornography, but they will usually find it boring.

11. Motherhood is not inevitable or desirable for every female; nor is fatherhood for every male. Some people can lead more fulfilling lives without children. Women and men should know that life offers many valid and satisfying choices, only one of which is parenthood.

12. Males needlessly worry about penis size. It is impossible to determine the size of a penis by observing its nonerect state. Small, flaccid (soft) penises may extend longer than those which appear larger. Sexual pleasure is unaffected by penis size. Similarly, females often needlessly worry that their breasts or vaginas are too small, or too large, or oddly shaped. Again, sexual pleasure depends on how one feels about one's body, not how it looks.

13. Parents need to inform their children about the problems of molestation and seduction. In the majority of such cases, the offender is someone the child already knows. In *all* cases, it is *never* the child's fault. Some parents mindlessly say, "Why did you let him do it?" Common sense and rationality are essential. Often the worst part of being molested as a child is the hysterical and traumatizing reaction of one's parents.

14. People who feel good about themselves and who have interests will find other people who are interested in them. People who feel inferior will find that few people care about them. People who feel they don't amount to anything *unless* someone marries them will not amount to much *after* someone marries them.

15. Knowledge Is *Not* Harmful. Research proves over and over again that educated people are more able to act responsibly. People who are ignorant of ovulation, reproduction, contraception, and the broader aspects of human sexuality find it difficult to choose what course to follow, what decisions to make.

16. We need above all to encourage an attitude of respect for the wide range of life-styles and sexual behavior patterns which fall within the bounds of normal experience.

Obviously, these are not the only things that people should know. But they are presented here to stimulate discussion and to start parents and teachers thinking about what it means to raise a sexually healthy human being.

Some Approaches to Teaching Adolescents: Sol Gordon Describes One Method

The following is an approach that I have used with high school youths for several years:

All the students, as many as a thousand, are called together for a two-hour meeting. The announced topic is "Sex." The students reveal little interest; many in fact, protest.

"Do we have to go?"

"Yes," they are told. "The assembly is compulsory."

All are assembled, but with a great deal of joking and horseplay. I request the attention of the group for a two-minute talk in which I explain that everyone has questions about sex. I then ask the students to write their questions, without signing their names, on index cards that have been provided. I suggest that if they do not have any questions, they are either not very smart, are limited in their imaginations, or aren't feeling well today. I tell them that if they do not have a question, they should pretend that they are writing one anyway so no one will know that there is anything wrong with them. *(Laughter.)* I explain that I will answer the questions on the spot, and I suggest that they not worry about spelling or using obscenities, because I will translate. The next two hours, during which everyone listens intently, are spent answering the questions. Not only are the students waiting for their own questions to be answered, but they are very curious about the questions that their friends have asked. Since most teenage conversation about sex involves lying, boasting, joking, and fooling around, this is for many the first opportunity to find out what their peers really want to know.

But it does not always go smoothly. Sometimes my taking a moral position about promiscuity arouses anger. The point that masturbation is normal occasionally elicits a noisy "You must be kidding!" (Sometimes in a black audience, to applause and shouts of approbation, a youth will get up and say, "Masturbation is what whites do because they are not man enough to get laid.")

One must also be prepared for the likelihood that from an audience of a thousand or more, one could receive 950 cards with questions and 50 with "Fuck you!"

How do we know that this approach is successful? We do not know for sure. Yet the following observations support its effectiveness:

1. I invariably manage, in response to some question, to remark, "Any girl who has sex with a boy who is too cheap to buy a rubber is just plain stupid." This soon becomes my most quoted statement. In the next several days, any number of boys will complain that I am inhibiting their sex lives.

"Girls are not making out hardly."

"Hey, Doc, rubbers are expensive."

"What are you trying to do, ruin me for life?"

2. At the end of the program, several observers from the Department of Health, Education, and Welfare reported that at the Upward Bound project where we held such a meeting, the pregnancy rate was among the lowest in the country.

3. Many youths who would not publicly acknowledge that they learned anything would later reveal privately how much they appreciated the lecture.

This was usually the starting point for more questions.

4. That almost all students asked questions and were attentive indicates that we were addressing major unfulfilled needs.

This is one effective approach. It can be easily duplicated, except that people administering such programs must be certain that the speaker is a well-trained sex educator who knows not only the facts, but the facts of life "like it is." Sometimes, merely inviting a physician because it is politically expedient (and not because he or she knows how to make a presentation) can do more harm than good. In addition, a single meeting is more effective when the speaker can return for follow-through talks.

Written Material for the Adolescent

Another important method of communication is written and illustrated material designed for unsophisticated or marginally literate teenagers. The Institute

© 1973, 1975 by Ed-U Press.

48

for Family Research and Education at Syracuse University, New York, has published several comic books about sexual relations, venereal disease, and birth control (Institute for Family Research and Education, 1975). Teenagers are comfortable with these comic books; they don't find them boring, and the humor reduces the anxiety that sometimes turns them away from reading what they really need to know. Consequently, the comic books have been very successful. Since 1971, more than 3 million have been distributed to social action groups, health departments, government agencies, and Planned Parenthood chapters in the United States and Canada.

Other Media

The Public Broadcasting Service presentation of "VD Blues," produced by WNET in New York City, combined humorous skits, contemporary popular music, and a straight delivery of facts about venereal disease in blunt vernacular language. The program has been aired several times, and each time thousands of viewers called the station to express their approval.

A multimedia curriculum, "About Your Sexuality," prepared by the Unitarian Universalist Association, includes films, records, and written material. This program has been used by schools and other nonsecular groups, as well as by Unitarian education classes.

Chic Thompson, a cartoonist and media specialist (founder of Creative Media Group in Charlottesville, Virginia) has produced a series of especially effective sex education films and film strips on subjects such as herpes genitalis and homosexuality.

Education directed to the common sense and sensibility of teenagers is, we believe, the best hope of reducing the current levels of VD, unwanted pregnancy, and sexual problems.

Who Should Teach About Sex?

Those who advocate increasing public knowledge about sex have consistently emphasized the role of the schools. Sex education classes, which have been organized in many schools, are usually conducted as separate courses or as sequences in the health education curriculum. The theory has been that such courses offer the best hope of reducing unwanted pregnancy and venereal disease while simultaneously helping to promote more satisfactory sexual adjustment among youth.

Sex education is appropriate in schools where morale is high, where students are enthusiastic and involved. In such an emotionally reinforcing environment, schools may be able to help adolescents develop a better awareness of their own sexuality as well as a greater sensitivity to others. But in schools where morale is low and students are generally apathetic, it is doubtful that a course in sex education can have a positive influence. In schools with high rates of pregnancy and venereal disease, it might be marginally helpful to provide information about contraception and prevention of VD. But among stu-

49

dents who are generally apathetic and clearly "turned off," traditional sex education designed to influence attitudes and sexual behavior are not likely to produce significant results.

Ideally, a child's models for healthy sexual behavior should be his or her parents. Unfortunately, many parents do not serve as effective models because of their behavior and their lack of information. (For a detailed discussion of the role of parents, see chapter 1, "Facing Facts—An Adult Responsibility.")

Community Services

A greater emphasis must be placed on the role of community services. Churches and synagogues can be very influential in developing counseling and information centers for parents as well as teenagers. Ideally, Planned Parenthood or similar centers should be available to adults and adolescents in every community. Community members should be trained to counsel individuals in their own peer, ethnic, or language groups.

Colleges, church groups, social action agencies, and PTAs should offer courses to teach parents how best to provide effective sex education for their children. There should be an expanded sex education curriculum in all institutions of higher learning that prepare students for careers in teaching, medicine, social work, and other areas of community service. Incredible as it may seem, most physicians, clinical psychologists, and social workers have not been educated at length and in depth about human sexuality and family planning. Professionals and paraprofessionals with some expertise in human sexuality not only would be better parents themselves, but also would be able to give sound advice to other concerned parents.

The Role of the Government

It is crucial to consider birth control programs, population education, and sex information in general apart from traditional establishment politics. In a democratic country, political authority is not likely to have a significant influence on an individual's sexual behavior. As in other intensely personal aspects of life, people will do what they think is in their own interests. Even the communist government of the Soviet Union has been unsuccessful in persuading couples to have more children, simply because the Russian people generally do not wish to have larger families. This remains true despite the ready availability of day-care centers, tax relief, and other incentives. It is also interesting to note that the pill is not generally available and that birth control does not insure that people will use it. Communist China, however, has been remarkably successful in its birth control program. One wonders if it could manipulate its people to have large families, especially if Chinese women were being educated equally as well as men.

In this country, government warnings about the dangers of drugs are more likely to be met with youthful derision than acceptance. The young are particularly given to rejecting anything pushed by the establishment and bearing its stamp. One way around this difficulty is to staff birth control clinics with community members ready to engage in candid and straightforward communication with young people. Adolescents will accept information they can use to their own advantage, but they will resist moralizing platitudes. Their needs are best met by straight talk in a sympathetic environment.

Conclusion

To reduce the rates of unwanted births and venereal disease, we should, of course, devote the major part of our endeavors to education and economic well-being. The lowest birth rates are consistently found among better-educated, middle-class individuals. College-educated women, Jewish women, and middle-class black women all produce children at a rate well below the national average. The problem of unwanted births is often a problem of poverty. As such, it is likely to continue until all Americans can expect a fair income and a decent education. However, immediate short-term efforts must still be made to reach adolescents with the information they need in order to reduce the number of unwanted children and incidence of venereal disease.

References   Alan Guttmacher Institute. *11 million teenagers.* New York: Planned Parenthood, 1976.

Behavior Today, October 23, 1978, 7.

Brown, S., Lieberman, E. J., & Miller, W. B. *Young adults as partners and planners.* Paper presented at annual meeting of the American Public Health Association. Chicago, Illinois, November 16–20, 1975.

Cobliner, W. G. Pregnancy in the single adolescent girl: The role of cognitive functions. *Journal of Youth and Adolescence,* 1974, *3,* 17–29.

Committee on Maternal Nutrition. *Report of the food and nutrition board.* Washington, D.C.: National Research Council, 1970.

Crist, T. *The coed as a gynecological patient in today's sexual revolution.* Chapel Hill: University of North Carolina, Department of Obstetrics and Gynecology, 1970.

Elias, J., & Gebhard, P. Sexuality and sexual learning in childhood. *Phi Delta Kappan,* 1969, *50* (7), 401–406.

Finkel, M. L., & Finkel, D. J. Sexual and contraceptive knowledge, attitudes, and behavior of male adolescents. *Family Planning Perspectives,* 1975, *7* (6), 256–260.

Furstenberg, F., Gordis, L., & Markowitz, M. Birth control knowledge and attitude among pregnant adolescents: A preliminary report. *Journal of Marriage and the Family,* 1969, *31,* 34–42.

Gilbert, R., & Matthews, V. G. Young males' attitudes toward condom use. In M. A. Redford, G. W. Duncan, & D. J. Prager (Eds.). *The condom: Increasing utilization in the United States.* San Francisco: San Francisco Press, Inc., 1974, 164–172.

Gordon, S. What should we stress in community programs for teenage sex education? Syracuse, N.Y.: Institute for Family Research and Education, 1971.

Hayes, J., & Littlefield, J. H. Venereal disease knowledge in high school seniors. *Journal of School Health,* 1976, *46* (9), 546–548.

Hunt, M. *Sexual behavior in the 1970's.* Chicago: Playboy Press, 1974.

Institute for Family Research and Education. *Ten heavy facts about sex; Protect yourself from becoming an unwanted parent; VD claptrap.* Charlottesville, Va.: Ed-U Press, 1975.

Jones, A. E., & Placek, P. J. *Teenage women in the U.S.A.: Sex, contraception, pregnancy, fertility, and maternal and child health.* Paper presented at Family Impact Seminar Conference on Teenage Pregnancy and Family Impact: New Perspectives on Policy, Washington, D.C., October 1978.

Juhasz, A. M. Changing patterns of premarital sexual behavior. *Intellect,* April 1976, 511–514.

Kantner, J. F. *Coming of age in America.* Baltimore: Johns Hopkins University, School of Population Dynamics, 1975 (unpublished paper).

Kantner, J. F., and Zelnik, M. Sexual experience of young, unmarried women in the United States. *Family Planning Perspectives,* 1972, *4* (1), 9–17.

Kleinerman, G., Grossman, M., Breslow, J., & Goldman, R. Sex education in a ghetto school. *Journal of School Health,* 1971, *41* (1), 29–34.

Luker, K. Contraceptive risk taking and abortion: Results and implications of a San Francisco Bay area study. *Studies in Family Planning,* 1977, *8* (8), 190–196.

Menken, J. *The health and demographic consequences of adolescent pregnancy and childbearing.* Paper presented at National Institute of Child Health and Human Development, Conference on the Consequences of Adolescent Pregnancy and Childbearing, Rockville, Md., October 1975.

Miller, W. B. Sexuality, contraception, and pregnancy in a high school population. *California Medicine,* 1973, *119,* 14–21.

National Center for Health Statistics. Advance report, final natality statistics, 1975. *Monthly Vital Statistics Report,* 1976, *25* (10), December 30, 1976.

National Center for Health Statistics. Final natality statistics, 1974. *Monthly Vital Statistics Report,* 1975, *24* (11), (supp. 2, HRA 76–1120).

Reichelt, P. A., & Werley, H. H. Contraception, abortion, and venereal disease: Teenagers' knowledge and the effect of education. *Family Planning Perspectives,* 1975, *7* (2), 83–88.

Robertson, P., Torrance, G., & Moore, M. *Sex education—a teacher's guide.* Ottawa, Ontario, Canada: Department of National Health and Welfare, 1977, Pamphlet #5, 3–4.

Sandberg, E. *An exploration of the limitations of contraception.* Proceedings of the Ontario Science Centre, November 1975. Don Mills, Ontario, Canada: Ortho Pharmaceutical Ltd.

Sex and today's teenager. *Circus,* 29 September, 1977, 20–21.

Shah, F., Zelnik, M., & Kantner, J. F. Unprotected intercourse among unwed teenagers. *Family Planning Perspectives,* 1975, *7* (1), 39–44.

Sorensen, R. C. *Adolescent sexuality in contemporary America.* New York: World Publishing, 1973.

United States Commission on Population Growth and the American Future. *Population growth and the American future.* New York: New American Library, 1972.

Zelnik, M., & Kantner, J. F. Sexual and contraceptive experience of young unmarried women in the United States, 1976 and 1971. *Family Planning Perspectives,* 1977, *9* (2), 55–73.

Zelnik, M., & Kantner, J. F. *Sexuality, contraception and pregnancy among unwed females in the United States.* Paper prepared for U.S. Commission on Population Growth and the American Future, 1971.

Three

Sexual Communication and the Persisting Double Standard

If you were a teenage girl in the 1950s, you probably read several books that gave you advice about social etiquette. "Talk about the things *he* is interested in. Let him be your teacher. Let him win at sports or games. Don't be pushy. Don't let him know how smart you are." Teenage girls in the 1950s learned not to be pushy. Meanwhile, the boys learned to be strong, to savor competition, to suppress emotions in order to get ahead, and to distinguish "nice" girls from "bad" girls. A boy might try to seduce girls, but he had no intention of marrying one who did have sex with him. Yet for both sexes, marriage was a common goal. The social etiquette of the 1950s dictated the pattern: the strong men and nonassertive women got married, grew dissatisfied, and ultimately got divorced in record numbers.

There are today the beginnings of new approaches to relationships and marriage. As the double standard has waned, more young men and women have begun to explore how to live and love without confining their own and other people's behavior only to standards deemed acceptable long ago. In the 1960s and 1970s, people began having children because they wanted them, not because they believed that parenthood is destiny or that life is meaningless without children. Of course, these emerging beliefs created problems for generations of parents who *were* taught that parenthood was necessary and normal, and who came to regard grandchildren as their birthright. But despite a trend toward new life-styles, the old double standard is still very much with us and is at least partly related to the tragedies of unwanted pregnancy and venereal disease among young people.

Many young people today still don't appreciate that unless you feel good about yourself and see life as worthwhile and an opportunity, you are a candidate for exploitation. People whose sense of worth depends on having someone else in love with them or who feel useless in the absence of romantic love find it difficult to look beyond expressions and declarations of undying passion to see whether they are being used.

Communication and Decision Making

Communication about sex is still too often rooted in the notion of unequal roles. Young people clearly begin relationships with different expectations, concerns, and preferred ways of resolving problems. But what the partners

57

usually and tragically share is an inability to talk about sex and birth control. This inability leaves open the door to sexual exploitation, one of the most blatant and insidious forms of the double standard.

Most young people do not talk about contraception. In their study of college males, Kirkendall and McDermott (1970) found that possible pregnancy as a discussion topic raised jointly by both partners increased in frequency *after* intercourse, but was much less commonly discussed prior to intercourse, regardless of the affection between the partners. In a study of inner-city males (average age, eighteen) who obtained condoms from neighborhood stores, Arnold (1972) found that only 17 percent had ever discussed birth control with their partners. Only 15 percent of their partners had apparently expressed an interest in the condom as a means of birth control. Goldsmith et al. (1972) found that nearly 20 percent of their sample of females said they either would be "embarrassed" to ask their partner to use contraception, or that they felt the male "wouldn't want to pull out or use a rubber." Sorensen (1973) reported that only a "small minority" of teenage males always know what method of birth control is being used, and about one-fifth *always* trusted luck to prevent pregnancy. His data revealed glaring inconsistencies in male and female estimates of contraceptives used and made clear that nonmarital sexual and contraceptive behavior occurs in a context of confusion, ignorance, and myth.

Gilbert and Matthews (1974) asked a group of San Francisco area male teenagers to respond to a vignette in which a male has condoms available, but doesn't use them because they are "too much hassle." These teenagers strongly appreciated the "role norms," with only 6 percent of the eighty-six teenagers saying the male character, "did the right thing." The overwhelming majority, however, said there should have been some communication between the partners prior to intercourse, either to "talk it over" (48 percent) or to urge the female "to get some birth control for her to use" (27 percent). This prior communication, however, is precisely what is too often lacking.

In one survey of over four hundred college students (Gordon & Scales, 1977), more than a third said that the first time or two they have sex with someone, it "just seems to happen without talking." It should be clear by now that young people badly need to learn how to handle a situation that otherwise seems inevitably to "flow" by its own momentum.

Moral Motivation and the Double Standard

There is evidence of a persisting double standard in regard to decision making about contraceptives. In Schofield's early study (1965), 46 percent of the sexually experienced males responded that their first intercourse occurred because of sexual "appetite" or desire, while only 16 percent of females responded in that way. Only 10 percent of the males said their first experience occurred because they were in love, while 42 percent of the females gave that response. The presence of a normative double standard was further underscored by Schofield's finding that more than half of the males wanted to have sexual intercourse, but that two-thirds of them still wanted to marry a virgin.

The males in Schofield's study actually had direct responsibility for use or nonuse of contraceptives, for condoms and withdrawal were the two most frequently cited methods. The number of males assuming this responsibility was low, however, with 57 percent not always using contraception while 29 percent of the males responded that they "didn't care." To make matters worse, nearly two-thirds of the females did not always insist that contraception be used. Yet, astonishingly, 51 percent of the same males and 70 percent of the females said they worried about the possibility of pregnancy.

Simon, Berger, and Gagnon (1972, data collected in 1967) supported this view of the conventional affectional context for sexual decision making. They found that nearly 60 percent of the females were planning to marry their first coital partner (including 52 percent of the women who reported *never* having been "in love"), whereas only 14 percent of the males were planning to marry their first partner. Although Simon et al. found that males and females in about equal proportions "planned" their first intercourse, they also pointed out that a substantial portion of males had their first coitus with a casual partner. This led them to the tentative conclusion that males planned for sexual success, while female planning was linked more to a long-term relationship with a single partner.

Thirty percent of the males in Sorensen's (1973) study agreed that they wouldn't want to marry a girl who "isn't a virgin at marriage." This figure is much lower than Schofield's finding eight years earlier in Great Britain, but closer inspection reveals a relationship between the preference for virgin brides and the sexual inexperience of the respondent. Although "virgins" and "nonvirgins" differed markedly in their responses (42 percent and 21 percent respectively agreeing with the statement), the difference can be traced to variations in the degree of "any sexual contact with another person, other than kissing, that either aimed at or resulted in pleasurable physical reaction." In other words, some virgins are more experienced in sexual relationships than others who have not yet begun to experience interpersonal sex. Using this standard to distinguish "inexperienced" and "beginner" virgins, Sorensen found that 54 percent of the inexperienced virgins, compared with 22 percent of the beginners, agreed with the statement about virginity at marriage. Agreement of this type of standard is thus most evident among those who have not yet experienced any sexual touching.

Other items in Sorensen's research, however, indicate that a sexual double standard still operates within many teenage relationships. When asked to describe the type of relationship they had with their first intercourse partner, 44 percent of the males, compared with 15 percent of the females, said they had known the partner only slightly. These 1973 figures, similar to those reported by Schofield (1965), and the data collected in 1967 by Simon et al.

(1972) indicate a consistent difference across time between male and female first-intercourse relationships. In addition, substantially more females than males agreed that "it would be wrong" to have sex with a partner who "I'd just met and hadn't gotten to know" (79 percent and 51 percent respectively). Only 44 percent of the males, compared with 75 percent of the females, agreed that they wouldn't want to have sex with a partner who didn't love them. In both of these last two findings, males demonstrated a difference depending on age, with the younger males (ages thirteen to fifteen) more likely to agree with both statements, as they had also been more likely to agree with the desirability of virginity at marriage. Nearly half of males apparently begin their sexual experience agreeing with the same moral absolutes to which the majority of females assent. With time, however, they seem to undergo a dramatic attitudinal shift. Sexual experience, not age, appears to be the crucial variable responsible for this change. Although the correlation between age and experience is obviously high, nevertheless, it seems that patterns of interpersonal sexual behavior account for this difference.

The double standard is also expressed in other ways. In Sorensen's study, fear about the consequences of unprotected intercourse was uncommon among males but common among females. Nearly 40 percent of the males said that they *never* worried about the possibility of the female becoming pregnant. When asked about a time frame limited to the "last month," only 51 percent of the males with recent intercourse experience, compared with 82 percent of the females, indicated that they had thought about whether or not the female might conceive. When Schofield (1965) asked his male British respondents about possible actions in case of pregnancy, 40 percent indicated that the "possibility had not been entertained."

Most men do not participate in decision making about birth control. Even at Yale, which offered one of the first university-sponsored programs in comprehensive sexual health care, less than half of the clinic's clients (mostly women) bring their partners with them. However, there has been improvement during the clinic's seven years of operation. In 1971 only one in ten clients brought her partner (Sarrel, 1976). Ironically, Cahn (1975) found that male partners are more frequently involved in crisis situations than in planning and prevention. Fewer than six out of ten of his New York City teenage girls discussed their need for contraception with their male partner before receiving counseling and services, but three out of four teenagers obtaining abortions had discussed the abortion with their partner.

There is evidence that family planning agencies and institutions systematically devalue the male role and exclude male participation in their services. If social-service professionals are to encourage male participation, awareness of this problem is essential.

Few would deny that sexism is perpetuated if women as a class are excluded from occupational opportunities. The exclusion of males from contraception planning is itself another, no less insidious, form of sexism because it perpetuates and/or reinforces conventional sex-role behavior by estranging the sexes.

Strategies for changing clinic receptivity toward men should be directed toward improving the various ways in which men can become involved in making birth control decisions, such as participating in the choice of method or helping the woman to use her contraceptives effectively (inserting the diaphragm or helping keep track of her menstrual cycle). Efforts should also be made to encourage family planning personnel to view clients as equal partners. Specific, immediate changes might include: lengthening the initial interview to explore individual concerns; requesting women who make initial appointments to have their partners accompany them; and stocking waiting rooms with literature that focuses on the male's potential role (not simply with pamphlets about vasectomy, which is more a concern of the older male). Birth control counselors should understand that male involvement is an issue worthy of their time and energy. (See *The Family Planner*, [Syntex Laboratories, 1977], for a review of some recent positive trends in male programs.)

Transition To Nonvirginity

One of our studies has focused on the first sexual experience (Buder, Scales, & Sherman, 1977), an event generally characterized by vague and inadequate communication, not to mention risk taking in regard to possible pregnancy. Typically, the experience is described as "losing" one's virginity. Implicit in the usual sex-role socialization differences between men and women, however, is the notion for males of "gaining" one's masculinity through the "loss" of the partner's virginity. For most males, that point of transition is welcomed, as evidenced by the proportional differences between males and females who say they are virgins only for want of partners. Brown, Lieberman, and Miller (1973) studied a group of 325 teenage males and 372 teenage females, over 90 percent of whom had completed the eleventh grade. Among the virgins, only 3 percent of the girls but 23 percent of the boys, said their virginity was due to "lack of opportunity." Seventeen percent of the 97 males and 12 percent of the 83 female teenagers attending a middle-class school in Miller's (1973) study of two San Francisco high schools reported that lack of opportunity had "been a factor on some occasion" in their sexual abstinence.

Sorensen (1973) found no difference in the proportion of males and females who hadn't had intercourse because they had not met an attractive partner. Yet twice as many males as females (36 vs. 18 percent) said they hadn't had sex because they had not met anyone who wanted to have sex with them. When asked to describe their feelings after the first intercourse, boys twice as frequently reported feelings of maturity, joy, and thrill; girls were nearly four times as likely to say they were afraid or worried, and twelve times more likely to say they felt guilty. The most glaring discrepancy was that only 1 percent of the males as compared to 25 percent of the females said they were sorry afterward.

The type of relationship felt to be necessary for intercourse has been a primary concern of much of the research on transition to nonvirginity. Reiss (1960; 1967) defined four attitudinal standards of sexual permissiveness depending on the affection for partner:

1 Abstinence for both sexes, regardless of affection;
2 Orthodox double standard: intercourse permitted for males, not females, regardless of affection;
3 Transitional double standard: intercourse permitted for males with or without affection, and for females with affection;
4 Single standard, high permissiveness: intercourse permitted for both sexes, regardless of affection (1960, pp. 82–85).

Jurich and Jurich (1974) added a fifth, based on Kohlberg's (1969) stages of moral development, called "non-exploitative permissiveness without affection."

The increase in the proportion of females who have had premarital intercourse has been cited as evidence of a declining double standard. But research on the *feelings* one has toward the first partner indicates that little has changed over the past decade; males are still far more likely to feel a casual relationship with their first partner, while females are much more likely to be "in love" and/or to have marriage plans (Scales, 1977). Farrell, Talone, and Walsh (1977) indicated in their study of two overlapping panels of college students (1967–71 and 1970–74) that males subscribe to the double standard more frequently, although males and females in both panels became more single standard, highly permissive between freshman and senior years.

More than 1,500 readers responded to a survey on dating, marriage, and sexual behavior conducted by *Circus* in 1977. Sixty percent of both sexes disapproved of the "traditional" dating situation; more than 40 percent of both said that emotional relationships did not have to coexist with sexual ones. About one-third of the males and only one-quarter of the females said that they have had sex with a "casual acquaintance" or a "stranger," providing further indications of greater male casualness with partners.

Lewis and Burr (1975) suggested, "Males and females in more equal numbers are limiting coitus to those with whom they have defined a relationship as one of some affection and commitment" (p. 78). However, their study of 2,453 college students may have seriously underestimated the extent of intercourse. They found that 60 percent of the males and 29 percent of the females had had intercourse. In contrast, Juhasz's (1976) review of most of the pertinent literature indicates that well over 80 percent of both sexes have had intercourse before graduation. Our three-semester study of 1,200 undergraduates enrolled in a human sexuality course also found that about 80 percent had had intercourse (Gordon & Scales, 1977). Zelnik and Kantner's (1977) national study of girls between fifteen and nineteen found that by age fifteen, nearly one-fifth had had intercourse. By age nineteen, that proportion had increased to 55 percent.

Even if Lewis and Burr are correct, an unlikely possibility, their suggestion of increasing emotional commitment in sexual relationships may overlook the difference between first and subsequent intercourse. Previous research discussed above indicates that the first intercourse is often perceived by males more as an *event* than as a personal interchange. Males tend to have powerful anticipatory feelings about reaching a milestone of maturity; they are generally without strong feelings toward their first sexual partner. Concern and emotional commitment become important for both sexes in later stages of dating. Most Americans do marry, though at later ages these days, and with increasing age and experience, both sexes usually begin to limit intimacy to those for whom they care deeply, and with whom they can envision more long-term, stable relationships.

Since males and females appear to approach the first sexual relationship with significantly different anticipations and emotions, it follows that their style of communication in that first sexual experience will differ markedly. One indication of this is found in Sorensen's (1973) data: girls can describe their partners' reactions after the first intercourse much more accurately than boys. It may be that the male's preoccupation with the significance of the moment seriously interferes with his ability to discern his partner's cues of fear, worry, or embarrassment. Possibly he is aware of these signals, but chooses to pursue his own sexual satisfaction in preference to dealing with his partner's concerns and anxieties.

Thirty percent of nonvirgin males in Sorensen's (1973) research agreed, "There's nothing wrong with telling a girl you love her—even if you don't, if that's what it takes so she will have sex with you" (p. 395, table 108). In Chicago Planned Parenthood's more recent study of more than a thousand urban, mostly black teenage males, 70 percent said it was "o.k. to tell a girl you love her so that you can have sex with her" (Syntex Laboratories, 1977). Depending upon other characteristics in these samples, it is apparent that at least 30 percent of young males feel that it is acceptable to lie about their feelings in order to have sex.

Such deceitfulness probably is also perceived as necessary by many young males. Sorensen (1973) found that 76 percent of teenage females "wouldn't want to have sex with a boy unless he loved me" (tables 174 and 168). After reviewing related data, Teevan (1972) found in his sample of 1,117 college students that a young person "conforms to what he perceives to be the norm among his peers" (p. 288). The young male who considers lying to get sex will find substantial support from his peers. Sorensen (1973) found that 26 percent of both males and females in his teenage sample agreed, "If a girl has led a boy on, it's all right for the boy to force her to have sex" (table 251).

It is vital that parents and young people understand the potentially destructive impact of this double standard. In one of our studies (Scales & Everly, 1977), mothers who had participated in a sex education program, as compared to mothers who had not, showed an increase in several aspects of

63

communication with their children. These included more frequent initiation of conversations about sex and a greater tendency to give children something to read on the subject. Fathers showed no such change. However, this was a predictable finding, for mothers in our society have traditionally had the primary child-care role. The difference between mothers' and fathers' involvement in sex education is another indication of a persisting double standard.

Further, parents continue to raise their children differently on the basis of sex. In a national sample of parents with children under thirteen (General Mills, 1977), 52 percent agreed that "boys and girls should be raised differently." Apparently, this belief *has* an effect on their children. The National Assessment of Educational Progress has found that almost 40 percent of the nation's seventeen-year-olds believe a woman's place is in the home, and an additional 20 percent believe women should be allowed to work only under certain conditions ("39 percent of youths," 1977). In our own research on the process of becoming a nonvirgin, we asked 165 university students how their parents had influenced their views on virginity. Males were much more likely to report either that parents hadn't influenced them or that the message had been to have sex when it was "right." Females were more likely to have been told not to have sex except within marriage (Buder, Scales, & Sherman, 1977).

Such patterns of childrearing help perpetuate the use by males (and some females) of sexual "lines." Publicizing these lines—and effective responses to them—is one of the best ways to help young people back away from sexual relationships for which they are pathetically unprepared. (See Gordon, 1978a, for these lines and responses.) The media should be used more frequently and creatively to raise such public awareness. Young people sometimes know a great many lines and understand them for what they are. The problem is that the young are not given sufficient opportunity to analyze these lines away from "the heat of passion."

Exposing the dangerously negative value of sexual lines is one way to help young people. Lines work best with people who feel inadequate and deprived, whose fleeting moments of self-respect and confidence depend exclusively on the approval and acceptance of others. The women's liberation movement is a great ally in the effort to prevent the tragedies of unwanted pregnancy, teenage abortion, and hasty marriage. All over the world, high and uncontrolled fertility rates plague societies in which women are poor, badly educated, and confined to the lowest rungs of the working ladder. We need to support movements that encourage women to demand equality, feel good about themselves, and that strive to increase the involvement of men in sexual and contraceptive decisions. Our primary message for helping youth destroy the double standard and its disastrous implications, the main theme of *You— A Survival Guide for Youth* (Gordon, 1978b), is simply this: *Nobody can make you feel inferior without your consent.*

References   Arnold, C. B. The sexual behavior of inner city adolescent condom users. *Journal of Sex Research,* 1972, *8,* 298–309.

Brown, S. S., Lieberman, E. J., & Miller, W. B. *Young adults as partners and planners.* Paper presented at annual meeting of the American Public Health Association, Chicago, Ill., November 16–20, 1975.

Buder, J., Scales, P., & Sherman, L. Virgins may be vanishing, but the double standard persists. Syracuse, New York.: Institute for Family Research and Education, 1977.

Cahn, J. *Adolescents' needs regarding family planning services.* Presented at World Population Society Conference, Washington, D.C., November 19–21, 1975.

Farrell, M. Z., Talone, W. L., & Walsh, R. Maturational and societal changes in the sexual double-standard: A panel analysis (1967–1971; 1970–1974). *Journal of Marriage and the Family,* 1977, *39* (2), 255–273.

General Mills Incorporated. *Raising children in a changing society.* Minneapolis: General Mills, Inc., 1977.

Gilbert, R., & Matthews, V. G. Young males' attitudes toward condom use. In M. A. Redford, G. W. Duncan, & D. J. Prager (Eds.), *The condom: Increasing utilization in the United States.* San Francisco: San Francisco Press, 1974.

Goldsmith, S., Gabrielson, M. O., Mathews, V., & Potts, L. Teenagers, sex and contraception. *Family Planning Perspectives,* 1972, *4,* 32–38.

Gordon, S. *You would if you loved me.* New York: Bantam, 1978a.

Gordon, S. You—A survival guide for youth. New York: Times Books, 1978b.

Gordon, S., & Scales, P. Sexual communication, attitudes, and socialization among undergraduates. Syracuse, N.Y.: Institute for Family Research and Education, 1977 (in progress).

Juhasz, A. M. Changing patterns of premarital sexual behavior. *Intellect,* 1976, *104,* 511–514.

Jurich, A. D., & Jurich, L. A. The effect of cognitive moral development upon selection of premarital sexual standards. *Journal of Marriage and the Family,* 1974, *36,* 736–741.

Kirkendall, L. A., & McDermott, R. J. Premarital intercourse. In J. P. Semmens & K. E. Krantz (Eds.), *The adolescent experience.* London: Macmillan, 1970.

Kohlberg, L. Stage and sequence: The cognitive—developmental approach to socialization. In Goslin (Ed.), *Handbook of socialization theory and research.* Chicago: Rand McNally, 1969, 347–480.

Lewis, R. A., & Burr, W. R. Premarital coitus and commitment among college students. *Archives of Sexual Behavior,* 1975, *4,* 73–81.

Miller, W. B. Sexuality, contraception, and pregnancy in a high school population. *California Medicine,* 1973, *119,* 14–21.

Reiss, I. L. *The social context of premarital sexual permissiveness.* New York: Holt, Rinehart, & Winston, 1967.

Reiss, I. L. *Premarital sexual standards in America.* New York: Free Press, 1960.

Sarrel, L. Sex counseling at Yale. *Personnel and Guidance Journal,* 1976, *54,* 382–384.

Scales, P. Males and morals: Teenage contraceptive behavior amid the double standard. *Family Coordinator,* 1977, *26* (3), 210–222.

Scales, P., & Everly, K. A community sex education program for parents. *Family Coordinator,* 1977, *26,* 37–45.

Schofield, M. *The sexual behavior of young people.* Boston: Little, Brown, 1965.

Sex and today's teenager. *Circus,* 29 September, 1977, 20–21.

Simon, W., Berger, A. S., & Gagnon, J. H. Beyond anxiety and fantasy: The coital experience of college youth. *Journal of Youth and Adolescence,* 1972, *1,* 203–222.

Sorensen, R. C. *Adolescent sexuality in contemporary America.* New York: World Publishing, 1973.

Syntex Laboratories. *The Family Planner,* 1977, *8* (2/3), 2–4.

Teevan, J. J. Reference groups and premarital sexual behavior. *Journal of Marriage and the Family,* 1972, *34,* 283–291.

39 percent of youths say women belong home. *New York Times,* 14 June 1977.

Zelnik, M., and Kantner, J. F. Sexual and contraceptive experience of young, unmarried women in the United States, 1976 and 1971. *Family Planning Perspectives,* 1977, *9,* 55–71.

Four

The Problems of Adolescent Pregnancy

A widespread and dangerously false theory holds that because many unwed girls become pregnant because of an unconscious psychological wish, it is virtually useless to try to reach them with birth control information and services. Whatever social or psychological causes contribute to the increasing rate of pregnancies among unmarried teenagers, the problem remains sufficiently serious to demand immediate and concerted attention. Research has made it unequivocally clear that a rigorous educational campaign is not only in order, but urgent.

In 1976, total births to teenagers were 570,672, of which 235,300 (41.2 percent) were to unmarried teens. Teens accounted for more than half the total number of births to unmarried mothers in the U.S. in 1976. In addition, there were an estimated 400,000 abortions to teenagers in that same year (1976), according to Forrest, Tietze, and Sullivan (1978). Illegitimacy rates among women over the age of twenty decreased by almost 25 percent between 1961 and 1974; teenage illegitimacy during the same period increased by 33 percent among eighteen- and nineteen-year-olds, and by 75 percent among fourteen-to-seventeen-year-olds (Alan Guttmacher Institute, 1976, table 4.1). And the numbers do not tell the whole story. Adolescent pregnancy almost invariably ends up a bleak and desperate tangle of serious psychological and social damage to both mother and child.

What Happens to the Unwed Adolescent Mother

Pregnancy is the major reason why teenage girls drop out of school in this country (Alan Guttmacher Institute, 1976). Presser (1975) also found that among fifteen- and sixteen-year-old new mothers, fully 74 percent gave pregnancy as the reason for leaving school.

If a single girl becomes pregnant and drops out of school, her chances of enjoying a rewarding, satisfying life are drastically diminished. How does the pregnancy get resolved? Nearly three in ten girls marry before the outcome of pregnancy, down from 35 percent in 1971 (Zelnik & Kantner, 1978). Of course, marriage undertaken because of a teenage pregnancy is a risky affair: six in ten of those couples will be divorced within five years (Alan Guttmacher Institute, 1976). Whites are nearly five times more likely to marry under these circumstances than blacks (Zelnik & Kantner, 1978). For the remainder who

	Age 15–44	15–19	20–24	25–29	30–34	35–39	40–44
1961	22.6[a]	16.0	41.2	44.8	28.9	15.1	3.8
1965	23.4	16.7	38.8	50.4	37.1	17.0	4.4
1968	24.1	19.8	36.1	39.4	27.6	14.6	3.7
1969	25.0	20.6	37.4	38.1	27.4	13.6	3.6
1970	26.4	22.4	38.4	37.1	27.0	13.6	3.5
1971	25.6	22.4	35.6	34.7	25.3	13.5	3.5
1972	24.9	22.9	33.4	31.1	22.8	12.0	3.1
1973	24.5	22.9	31.8	30.0	20.5	10.8	3.0
1974	21.4	23.2	30.9	28.4	18.6	10.0	2.6
1975	24.8	24.2	31.6	28.0	18.1	9.1	2.6
1976[a]	24.7	24.0	32.2	27.5	17.8	8.9	2.5

Table 4.1 Estimated Illegitimacy Rates by Age of Mother: United States, 1961, 1965, 1968–1976—Number of Illegitimate Births per 1,000 Women.

[a] Latest available statistics.

Sources: U.S. National Center for Health Statistics
Vital Statistics of the U.S.
1968, Vol. I, Natality, Table 1–25
1969, Vol. I, Natality, Table 1–30
1970, Vol. I, Natality, Table 1–30

Monthly Vital Statistics Report: Summary Report, Final Natality Statistics
1971, Vol. 23, No. 3, Table 4
1972, Vol. 23, No. 8, Table 3
1973, Vol. 23, No. 11, Table 3
1974, Vol. 24, No. 11, Table 11
1975, Vol. 25, No. 10, Table 12
1976, Vol. 26, No. 12, Table 12

do not marry, good data is available only for whites. Among this group, there has been a substantial reduction in the percentage of pregnancies ending in a live birth, down to 28 percent from 44 percent in 1971. This drop parallels a dramatic rise in the percent ending in induced or spontaneous abortion from 40 percent in 1971 to 60 percent in 1976. Among unmarried girls giving birth, the percentage giving their babies up for adoption has dropped markedly from nearly 8 percent in 1971 to only 3 percent in 1976. As Zelnik and Kantner (1978) observe, "The strategy of encouraging adoption in place of abortion that is being advocated by anti-abortion groups appears to be bucking a clear trend that is going in the opposite direction" (p. 18).

The U.S. has one of the highest infant mortality rates among the world's industrialized nations (Jones & Placek, 1978) which, according to Prescott

(1975), is primarily the result of inadequate prenatal and postnatal care (figure 4.2). Infants surviving this poor early care will have a higher risk of lower educational achievement, low income potential, poor health, and asocial behavior than those with adequate care.

Regardless of the decision, pregnant teenagers, particularly the poor, will have trouble finding services. Eight day-care centers out of ten will not accept infants under the age of two (Alan Guttmacher Institute, 1976). Legal abortions are also often difficult to arrange. It is estimated that *at least* 125,000 teenagers who want abortions don't have access to them. Recent congressional legislation granting state discretion in the use of federal funds for abortion only exacerbates this situation. Congress regularly sees the introduction of bills embodying the intent of the Hyde Amendment, that is, prohibiting federal support for abortion. Without federal aid, and without other recourse, poor teenagers will be largely restricted to three grim choices: illegal abortion, self-induced abortion, or the birth of an unwanted child. And Prescott (1975) has convincingly demonstrated that the last is likely to lead to an increase in child abuse.

If hasty marriage is not a good solution for the pregnant teenager, the alternative of remaining single is no more attractive. An analysis of national data (Bonham & Placek, 1975) confirms that earlier motherhood is associated with closer spacing of additional children, thus compounding the already serious problem of adolescent pregnancy and parenthood; women who begin childbearing before eighteen will have families 1.3 times larger than women who begin childbearing between the ages of twenty and twenty-four.

Physical and Mental Health Risks for Mother and Child

Adolescent pregnancy poses serious health risks for both mother and child. Studies have consistently found a significant relationship between the age of the mother and complications during pregnancy. Infant mortality is much higher when the mother is younger than fifteen or older than thirty (figure 4.2). The rate is more than twice as high for white teenagers fourteen or younger than it is among white women in their early twenties (Menken, 1975). Maternal mortality follows a similar pattern. Teenagers run by far the greatest risk of dying in childbirth; the second highest risk of maternal mortality is found among women between forty and forty-nine (Baldwin, 1976). After an extensive review of pregnancy and child development studies, Nortman (1974) concluded that childhood mortality between ages one and four was a compelling 41 percent greater among children born to adolescent mothers than among children of older mothers. This is a result of generally poor prenatal care and of incomplete biological maturation. The major complications are anemia, toxemia, premature birth, and infant mortality. A seven-year study found that children born to teenagers under fifteen (and in 1976 there were 13,000 such children!) are more than twice as likely to have neurological defects and mental retardation as the children of women in their early twenties (National Institutes of Health, 1972).

71

Figure 4.1

World Infant Mortality Rates, 1975[a] — Infant Deaths Under One Year of Age per 1,000 Live Births.

[a] Latest available chart, based on 1977 World Population Data Sheet (Population Reference Bureau, Inc.). Rates for China, North Korea, and Mongolia—designated as unknown when the chart was originally published—have been updated in this presentation.

Reproduced by permission of Population Reference Bureau, Inc.

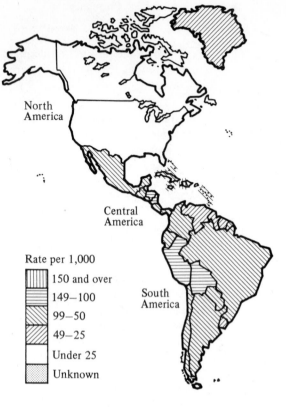

North America

Central America

South America

Rate per 1,000

150 and over
149–100
99–50
49–25
Under 25
Unknown

The risks to children of teenage mothers are not exclusively medical. Adolescent mothers generally lack the maturity needed for successful child-rearing. Oppel and Royston (1971) have reported that mothers under eighteen are less likely than older mothers to remain with their children. If they keep their children, they are less able to provide the necessary financial and emotional security. While they commonly believe that children should be independent, their own children tend to become psychologically dependent on others. Compared to the children of older mothers, children born to teenagers are underweight and shorter. They are also more likely to lag behind in grade level, to have lower IQs, and to develop behavioral problems.

One indicator of the disastrous psychological effects of adolescent pregnancy is the frequency of suicide attempts among teenage mothers. Gabrielson et al. (1970), in a study of 105 teenage mothers under eighteen, found that suicide attempts or threats were made by 22 percent of those who were single at the beginning of the study, and by 7 percent of those who were married. Based on comparisons with other studies, they calculated that teenage mothers in 1970 attempted suicide at a rate higher than that of the general population and of other adolescent groups.

A teenage girl who becomes pregnant is unlikely to find a decent job or to have the social skills needed for employment. As a result, she and her children often become dependent on public welfare.

Europe

Asia

Middle
East

Africa

Australia

In short, pregnancy is a major crisis for most unwed teenagers. Sarrel (1970) provided an excellent summary of the drastic costs involved:

> Pregnant teenagers are high risks medically, socially, and educationally. Without care, they have high rates of toxemia, prematurity, and perinatal infant mortality. They fail to complete their education or obtain vocational training. When they marry, they more often than not get divorced, and when they do not marry, they often become trapped in a self-destructive cycle consisting of failure to continue education, dependence on others for support, failure to establish a stable family life, and repeated pregnancies. Not infrequently, depressed, defeated, and dependent, the teenage mother is poorly prepared to cope with the demands of family life and in particular, the responsibilities of parenthood (pp. 15-16).

There is little reason to believe that the situation is any different today. On a more promising note, some young women, primarily those with better education, more financial support, and easier access to services, can overcome the setbacks of teenage pregnancy. Furstenberg's (1976) longitudinal study of young black mothers concluded:

> The principal reason that so many young mothers encounter

73

problems is that they lack the resources to repair the
damage done by a poorly timed birth. We have suggested
that those women who managed to overcome the problems
associated with early pregnancy had unusual personal
qualities, good fortune, and/or the ability to avail themselves
of the limited opportunities that existed.

He further described the kind of coordinated social services effort
needed by young women who decide to see their pregnancies through to term:

What would happen if service programs made it easy, not
difficult, for women to restore order in their lives following an
unplanned pregnancy? Let us imagine that instead of the
short-term, fragmented, and partial assistance that currently
exists, there were comprehensive and extended services for
young parents and their children. Suppose, for example, that
family planning programs to prevent unplanned pregnancies
and to counsel women who did have unwanted conceptions
were established in the schools. Suppose that a woman who
elected to bring her pregnancy to term would be granted a
child care allowance to purchase day-care services or to pay
a relative or friend to care for her child while she completed
her education or entered the labor force. And regardless of
whether or not she remained in school, took a job, or
assumed full-time child care responsibilities, the young
mother would receive an income sufficient to meet the needs
of her family. Furthermore, suppose the father were invited
to join special educational or job training programs or were
provided with a steady job. How many parental couples
would elect to marry under these circumstances is a matter
of speculation. This question aside, our results indicated that
under conditions of economic security most fathers would
contribute to the support of the family and willingly maintain
a relationship with their children (p. 226).[1]

Why Teenagers Become Pregnant

It is extremely doubtful that the majority of adolescent mothers originally
wished to become pregnant. Many researchers have attempted to determine
whether pregnant girls generally have promiscuous histories or share particular psychological traits. The evidence, however, shows that sexual experience
aside, pregnant teenagers have nothing in common save a lack of knowledge
about the reproductive process and birth control.

Did She Want To Get Pregnant?

A number of explanations have been proposed for why a teenage girl might
want to become pregnant. Khlentzos and Pagliano (1965) suggested that unmarried teenagers may become pregnant to satisfy oral dependency needs that
have not been met by members of her family, particularly her mother.
Kasanin and Handschin (1941) attributed the desire for an out-of-wedlock

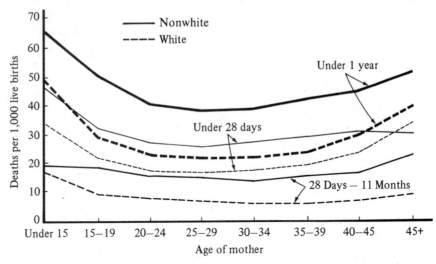

Figure 4.2   Infant Mortality Rates by Age of Mother and Race: United States, 1960 Birth Cohort.

Source: Committee on Maternal Nutrition, Food and Nutrition Board, National Research Council, *Maternal Nutrition and the Course of Pregnancy* (Washington, D.C.: National Academy of Sciences, 1970) p. 144.

child to an acting out of Oedipal incest fantasies in which the sexual partner serves as a substitute for the girl's father. Loesch and Greenberg (1962) viewed premarital pregnancy as a reaction to major loss—of a parent, boyfriend, or valued job. Typically, unmarried pregnant girls display signs of neurosis, depressive anxiety, schizophrenia, severe emotional deprivation, and ambivalence toward their mothers (Khlentzos & Pagliano, 1965), disorders presumed to be less common among the general population.

The problem with all these carefully documented conclusions is that they were all based on studies of girls who are already pregnant. In some cases, the girls were actually undergoing treatment for psychological problems. Thus, the data cannot apply to all adolescent girls. Often they cannot even be applied to all pregnant adolescents, but only to those whose disorders are so severe as to require psychiatric help.

Adolescence is a period of searching for identity, a process generally accompanied by uncertainty and emotional stress. The discovery by a teenager that she is pregnant can frequently intensify her feelings of uncertainty and anxiety, often to the point of psychological crisis. Forced to leave school, confronted by recriminations from parents and society at large, and faced with the decision of what to do with her unborn child, she is quite likely to develop symptoms of depression, anxiety, and withdrawal. She may have cause to feel

[1]   F. F. Furstenberg, *Unplanned parenthood: The social consequences of teenage childbearing.* © 1976 by The Free Press, a division of Macmillan Publishing Co., Inc. Reproduced by permission.

deprived of her family's emotional support and betrayed by her boyfriend. She may become heavily dependent on her mother while simultaneously resenting her for somehow allowing this thing to happen, for failing to advise her how to avoid pregnancy. In short, she is apt to develop most or all of the negative characteristics identified by researchers. While the research findings may accurately identify the psychological consequences of premarital pregnancy, the fact remains they shed no reliable light on what combination of factors leads a teenager to become pregnant in the first place.

In an attempt to reduce her acute psychological stress to manageable proportions, a pregnant teenager is likely to indulge in post facto rationalizations of her pregnancy, ill-fated efforts to convince herself and everyone else that she actually wanted a child.

One study of pregnant teenagers found nothing to suggest that girls find anything attractive about the role of unwed mother. "Notably absent was evidence of the conscious pre-pregnancy wish for a child. It is almost as if the pregnancy was a 'by-product' of sexual relations" (Barglow, 1968).

Diamond and his associates (1973) studied Hawaiian women who had conceived during a two-month period in 1971. While 90 percent of the women had planned or anticipated intercourse, fewer than 10 percent of those who were single had wanted to become pregnant. Again, these women were all pregnant at the time of the study, so it is quite probable that this 10 percent figure is higher than would be reported for a sample of never-pregnant, sexually active women. In her study involving New York City mothers, Presser (1974) found that 81 percent had not planned to conceive. Since this was also a retrospective study, the percentage would probably be higher among sexually active women who had never been pregnant. Wilson et al. (1973) surveyed more than 16,000 new teenage patients at Illinois family planning clinics in 1972 and found that only 1 percent were pregnant by choice.

Bogue (1975) reported on a probability sample of 315 Chicago women receiving federal aid to families with dependent children. He asked sixty-four single mothers how they had felt upon learning that they were pregnant. Nearly 88 percent were a "little unhappy" or "very unhappy."

Thus, the evidence suggesting that teenage girls become pregnant by choice is unimpressive. Even if it were possible to generalize about the relationship of certain personality factors to premarital pregnancy, such data would more likely than not confuse a predisposition toward sexual activity with a predisposition toward pregnancy itself. For some girls, sexual relations might represent a temporary escape from an otherwise unsatisfactory lifestyle, but even for them, sex is perceived as an end in itself, not as a means of becoming pregnant.

Pregnancy and Psychological Traits

If pregnant teenagers do not have a "pregnancy wish," are there other psychological differences between them and their nonpregnant peers? Vincent

(1961) compared the results of psychological tests for matched samples of pregnant and never-pregnant girls who were initially divided into two equal groups according to whether or not they came from broken homes. The observed psychological differences between pregnant and never-pregnant girls were much less significant than Vincent had anticipated. The group profiles were very similar along fourteen of the eighteen scales designed to measure psychological traits. Although the profiles of the unwed mothers from broken homes were significantly different from those of the never-pregnant girls from unbroken homes, the profiles of the pregnant and the never-pregnant girls from broken homes (1965) were very similar. This corresponds to Michael Schofield's findings in England that teenagers from broken homes were no more likely to be sexually active than teenagers from unbroken homes. On the basis of his findings, Vincent concluded, "Unwed motherhood is not the result of any one personality type, intra-familial relationships, or social situation."

In 1969, Jerome Pauker (1969) compared pregnant and nonpregnant high school girls of similar age and socioeconomic background. He wanted to determine whether there were any significant differences between the two groups in the areas of general intelligence, language facility, personality, and home-life situation. While he found some minor statistical differences, he does not attach much importance to them.

> The differences lie mainly in the area of statistical significance rather than of practical significance. *These two groups of girls are much more similar than they are different.* Even where the differences are statistically significant, the two groups overlap tremendously; and *one would be hard put to take individual matched pairs of girls and choose which one would become pregnant out of wedlock.* The weight of the evidence favors the point of view that girls who become pregnant out of wedlock do not fit one personality mold, nor do they show striking personality differences from other girls. (Italics added.)

Of course, certain factors, such as race and economic status, make it more likely that one girl will become pregnant instead of another. Even so, the effect of these factors is a predisposition toward sex, not pregnancy. Without belaboring the point, suffice it to say there remains grave doubt as to whether girls who become pregnant are psychologically motivated to do so.

Sexual Experience and Pregnancy

If, as we have suggested, unwanted pregnancy among teenagers in the vast majority of cases is only a "by-product (rather than an end goal) of sexual relations," the most immediately obvious approach to the problem is to educate teenagers about birth control and to make it available to them under supervised and controlled conditions.

According to one extensive study by Butman and Kamm (1965), the major difference between sexually active girls who become pregnant and those who do not is their knowledge about contraception. Butman and Kamm cited the following characteristics as typical of *all* sexually active girls:

1 A self-image stressing personal incompetence vis-à-vis adult authority both in school and out.
2 The expectation of marriage soon after graduation from high school.
3 The absence of specific career or educational goals.
4 A disinclination to discuss dating and/or social relationships with parents.
5 The belief that boys have greater sexual expectations than do girls.
6 Relatively lenient standards for personal conduct.
7 A deep psychological involvement in dating relationships; the feeling that going steady means a boy seriously cares about them.

To avoid the drawbacks of interviewing already pregnant teenagers, Butman and Kamm first gathered information and personality profiles on a cross section of high school girls. In follow-up studies, the girls were classified according to whether they had dropped out of school and whether they were pregnant.

Even so, the factors isolated by Butman and Kamm seem at best indirectly related to premarital pregnancy; they reflect a predisposition toward pregnancy only to the extent that they reflect a predisposition toward the necessary prerequisite of sex. Schofield (1965) also concluded that alienation from parents, "lenient" standards of personal behavior, and intense involvement in a dating relationship suggest that a girl will probably have sex, but these factors still do not verify a conscious or unconscious wish to conceive.

Pregnancy and Promiscuity

Girls who become pregnant are commonly thought to be more "promiscuous" than other girls. If promiscuity is defined as having indiscriminate intercourse with a large number of partners, this allegation is not supported by the evidence. Teenage pregnancies usually result from lengthy relationships with a single partner, not from casual sexual encounters. Schofield (1965) found that stable sexual relationships were typical of English adolescents. In his sample, 75 percent of the experienced girls had had intercourse with only one partner during the previous year; 65 percent of these girls had never had intercourse with anyone else. Kantner and Zelnik (1972) reported that about one-third of their national probability sample of teenage females fifteen to nineteen had intercourse with two or more partners. Vener and Stewart (1974) studied over four thousand fourteen-to-seventeen-year-olds in Michigan and reported that over 70 percent of the males and over 85 percent of the females had intercourse with three or fewer partners. There has been a shift in the typical number of partners, however, between 1971 and 1976: Zelnik and Kantner (1977) reported that in 1971, over 60 percent of sexually experienced whites and blacks had had only one partner, but by 1976, 53 percent of experienced white teenagers and 40 percent of experienced blacks had only one partner. Over 80 percent of all teenagers, however, still have had less than four partners.

Similar patterns also hold true of pregnant girls. Furstenberg, Gordis, and Markowitz reported (1969) that in a study of pregnant unwed adolescents at the Mount Sinai Hospital in Baltimore, only 17 percent of the girls reported having sex with more than one partner in the year preceding pregnancy.

Education to Prevent Pregnancy

The Need for Birth Control Knowledge

The general absence of a compelling wish to conceive suggests that efforts to prevent premarital teenage pregnancy can be successful. Traditional approaches to this problem have stressed only the risks involved in sexual activity and, not surprisingly, have been dismal failures. What can succeed is a program directed toward the key factor that differentiates sexually active girls who become pregnant from those who do not: the level of knowledge about birth control.

A large-scale educational program, combined with the availability of contraceptives for teenagers, could significantly reduce the rate of unwanted pregnancy. Such a program promises to be far more effective than attempts to deal with psychological patterns which may or may not bear some relationship to teenage pregnancy.

Difficulties in Educating the Disadvantaged

Contraceptive education is needed most acutely in poor areas that have a high rate of adolescent pregnancy. Yet it is in these very areas that the obstacles loom largest.

William R. Reevy (1961) has reported how social factors greatly effect the rate of coitus among adolescents, and Kinsey et al. (1964) could not find in low-income white communities "a solitary male who had not had sexual relations by the time he was 16 or 17." Kantner and Zelnik (1972) found that more than twice as many black as white females fifteen-to-nineteen-years-old had had intercourse. While they observed this pattern again in 1976, they also reported that the increase in the proportion of sexually experienced teenagers was twice as great for whites as for blacks. Since higher rates of sexual activity produce higher pregnancy rates, it is not surprising that low-income families have more adolescent pregnancies.

A pregnancy prevention program based on straightforward contraceptive advice can succeed with low-income families. Attempts to dictate responsible sexual behavior or to impose different moral values will be doomed.

Premarital pregnancy often has vastly different implications for inner-city adolescents than it does for their middle-class counterparts. The current "established" folklore suggests that in black families, sex apart from marriage, and its consequences, are not necessarily seen as deviations from an accepted life-style. It may not be viewed as an obstacle to career goals among poor black teenage girls who may have virtually no such expectations, whose prospects for happiness may be largely unaffected by pregnancy or motherhood. Once poverty has effectively closed off most of the avenues to a bright future, one baby more or less seems to make very little difference.

Yet when birth control services are made available in poverty areas, teenagers do use them. In the past several years, illegitimacy among black teenagers has leveled off, but has steadily increased among whites. From its major study of welfare and family planning services, the Urban Institute concluded that states that fail to provide birth control services to persons under eighteen have higher illegitimacy rates among blacks; moreover, states with restrictive abortion policies have higher rates of illegitimacy among whites (Moore & Caldwell, 1976). Furstenberg's (1976) longitudinal study found that at the five-year follow-up, 42 percent of single mothers receiving welfare two years earlier had become pregnant, as compared to 38 percent of those not previously on welfare, an insignificant difference. Janowitz (1976) also concluded that welfare status affects the legitimacy of births rather than the absolute number of births because it penalizes women who would otherwise marry a man capable of working. Most recently, the U.S. Department of Health, Education, and Welfare released a study showing that between 1973 and 1975 (the latest figures available), families with only one or two children had come to make up almost two-thirds of all recipients of Aid to Families with Dependent Children, and that for the first time since 1967, more than half of all AFDC families were white (Oberhau, 1977).

Resources for Educating the Disadvantaged

Middle-class expectations of propriety clash with inner-city realities. Most sex education literature and films, for example, are designed for white middle-class youth, not for adolescents from low-income areas where the rate of unwanted pregnancy is highest.

Leading sex education groups such as SIECUS, Planned Parenthood, the American Association of Sex Educators, Counselors, and Therapists, the E. C. Brown Foundation, and the Child Study Association (mentioned specifically because they are the pioneers and are doing a superb job in their areas of concern) prepare virtually all their material with the middle class in mind. This is not to suggest that the middle class does not need to learn. But the fact remains that almost no such material is designed specifically for disadvantaged youth, who usually do not like to read.

Some Planned Parenthood affiliates are now developing special materials for these audiences. Especially notable are the publications of the

Planned Parenthoods of Southeastern Pennsylvania, Philadelphia, Pennsylvania; Dayton, Ohio; Rocky Mountain, Denver, Colorado; Baltimore, Maryland; Columbus, Ohio; Chicago, Illinois; Rochester, New York; San Diego, California; San Antonio, Texas; and Syracuse, New York. The bulk of professional literature in the past, however, has not been so directed. For example, of the more than 250 books on adolescent sexuality published between 1960 and 1975, almost all were geared to college-bound youth and included diagrams incomprehensible to less able students. Professional educators tend to forget that the average American reads at about the sixth-grade level. No wonder so few people read the literature of sex education.

Although films and other visual materials are effective means of reaching the nonreader, these generally consist of "plumbing" and preaching, which alienates many adolescents. Exceptions to this are recent films distributed by Perennial (see "Selected List of Resources").

Furthermore, although there is a great demand for sex information in languages other than English, very little is available. Some urban agencies have translated material dealing with VD and birth control into Spanish, but the information too often is inadequate. *They do not teach adolescents what they want, and need, to know about sexuality.*

From their study of some 17,000 school systems, Wurtz and Fergen (1970) concluded, "Scarcely one school district in three makes any educational provision at all for its unmarried, pregnant school-age girls," and this despite the fact that in many cases state funds were available for such programs.

In school systems that do make provisions for pregnant girls, there is little or no consistency in the type of programs. Pregnant students may be permitted to continue in their regular courses or channeled into night school, adult education courses, or home-study arrangements. Sometimes they are assigned to special classes within their regular schools or sent away to special schools altogether.

In the spring of 1970, the NEA Research Division asked a nationwide sample of public school teachers, "What provision, if any, should school systems make for the continuing education of pregnant girls (whether or not married) who are pupils in their schools?" Although the results indicated a great variety in the type of curriculum teachers preferred, 80 percent of them believed that schools should make some provision for this education (Pregnant Teenagers, 1970).

These data emphasize the nationwide need to establish community approaches to meet the educational, medical, and social needs of pregnant teenagers. A growing awareness of this need is illustrated by the dramatic rise in comprehensive programs serving school-age pregnant girls, from thirty-five in 1968 (U.S. Department of Health, Education, and Welfare, 1968), to more than 175 serving close to 40,000 teenagers in 1971 (Sharing, 1971), to about 350 programs in 1976 (Furstenberg, 1976).

Many of these programs, however, are hampered by the effects of a

81

tightening economy and increasing competition for what has typically been one of the least supported efforts of government. As federal funds were made available for family planning services in the early 1970s, teen clinic enrollment rose; since 1973, however, the rate of increase has dropped by more than half, resulting in a squeeze that has raised awareness and increased demand but without expanding services and general counseling. The number of those who need services currently outstrips available resources by two to one (Alan Guttmacher Institute, 1976, p. 45). New York State, for example, nearly suffered a $200,000 cutback in funds to establish local clinics: This money was later tacked on to a Supplemental Budget, merely restoring the cut and leaving the budget at the same level for the seventh year in a row (Albany Memo, July–August 1977).

We believe that all comprehensive programs should have the following goals:

> 1 To improve the chances for normal pregnancy and childbirth and to protect the health of both mother and infant.
> 2 To help teenagers deal with the personal problems that may have led to their pregnancy or resulted from it, and to direct them toward a satisfying future.
> 3 To enable pregnant girls to keep up their studies and to increase the proportion of those who continue in school following childbirth (Howard, 1968/69).

To help solve the problems involved in establishing and maintaining comprehensive programs, the National Alliance Concerned with School-Age Parents (NACSAP), an independent organization serving as the advocate for school-age parents (and now concerned with *prevention* of pregnancy as well) was created in 1970. Its objectives are:

> 1 To improve existing programs and aid in the development of additional comprehensive programs for school-age parents.
> 2 To increase the knowledge and concern of all citizens about the specific and unique problems associated with pregnancy in adolescence.
> 3 To develop standards and guidelines for the establishment of services to school-age parents.
> 4 To provide consultant services to communities in the planning or early stages of program development.
> 5 To encourage the exchange of information between programs, thereby improving the quality of services offered.
> 6 To encourage or conduct research needed to establish the knowledge necessary for quality programming.

A promising development was the Consortium on Early Childbearing and Childrearing, begun in July 1972 through the Inter-Agency Task Force on Comprehensive Services to school-age parents. Its objectives were to increase the quality and quantity of comprehensive services to school-age parents and their children. Unfortunately, in 1975 the consortium was forced to disband because of lack of funds. Its tasks now come under the auspices of the U.S. Office of Education.

Finally, there has also been the recognition that teenage fathers need help too. Wirth (1970) has pointed out that the father is often seen only as a "shadow figure," whose educational needs will somehow take care of themselves. It cannot be overlooked that fatherhood may cause teenage boys to leave school, a problem that generally receives only scant attention in youth clinics.

Family planning programs that involve both teenage mothers and fathers can go a long way in preventing second pregnancies. Furstenberg's (1976) study and others reviewed in chapter 9 provide increasingly reliable evidence that when clinics insist upon more frequent and intense contact with patients, the rate of second pregnancies begins to decline. Avoiding subsequent unwanted pregnancies is obviously crucial, yet a study of 128 "comprehensive" programs across the nation (Baizerman, Ko, & Ellison, 1972) showed that three out of four offered no contraceptive services or abortion counseling. In 1979 our society still has not heeded the early warning signals.

Conclusions

In view of the facts presented here, it is our responsibility to establish sex education programs to increase the level of knowledge among teenagers. Research has failed to prove that pregnant girls are psychological misfits or self-destructive neurotics. Attempts to label them abnormal or deviant serve only to avoid the real problem. They are not pregnant because they are different; they are different because they are pregnant. Some admirable attempts have been made to provide for their education, but we need even more to educate teenage girls *before* they become pregnant, to ensure that they retain the option to prevent pregnancy, and thus to remain in control of their lives. In short, we need less moralizing and psychologizing and more commitment toward meeting the demonstrated needs of sexually active adolescents.

References   Alan Guttmacher Institute. *11 million teenagers.* New York: Planned Parenthood, 1976.

Albany Memo. (Family Planning Advocates of New York State), July–August 1977, *2* (5).

Baizerman, M., Ko, H., & Ellison, D. B. *National study of comprehensive programs for pregnant adolescents.* Paper presented at annual meeting of American Public Health Association, Atlantic City, New Jersey, November 13, 1972.

Baldwin, W. H. Adolescent pregnancy and childbearing—Growing concerns for Americans. *Population Bulletin,* 1976, *31* (2), (entire issue).

Barglow, P., Bornstein, M., Exum, D., Wright, M., & Visotsky, H. Some psychiatric aspects of illegitimate pregnancy in early adolescence. *American Journal of Orthopsychiatry,* 1968, *34* (4), 672–688.

Beasley, J. *Comprehensive services and the need for total community involvement: A report on the National Invitational Conference on Parenthood in Adolescence* (Sponsored by Yale University and the University of Pittsburgh in cooperation with the Maternal and Child Health Service, Health Services and Mental Health Administration and Children's Bureau, Office of Child Development, Washington, D.C., January 22–24, 1970).

Bogue, D. J. A long-term solution to the AFDC problem: Prevention of unwanted pregnancy. *Social Service Review,* 1975, *49* (4), 539–552.

Bonham, S., & Placek, P. J. *The impact of social and demographic, maternal health, and infant health factors on expected family size: Preliminary findings from the 1973 National Survey of Family Growth and the 1972 National Natality Survey.* Paper presented at annual meeting of the Population Association of America, Seattle, Washington, April 17–19, 1975.

Butman, J., & Kamm, J. The social, psychological and behavioral world of the teen-age girl. Ann Arbor: The University of Michigan Center for Research on Utilization of Scientific Knowledge, June 1965.

Center for Disease Control. *Abortion Surveillance,* 1974. Atlanta, 1976.

Diamond, M., Steinhoff, P. G., Palmore, J. A., & Smith, R. G. Sexuality, birth control, and abortion: A decision making sequence. *Journal of Biosocial Science,* 1973, *5,* 347.

Forrest, J. D., Tietze, C., & Sullivan, E. Abortion in the United States, 1976–77. *Family Planning Perspectives,* 1978, *10* (5), 271–279.

Furstenberg, F. F. *Unplanned parenthood: The social consequences of teenage childbearing.* New York: Free Press, 1976.

Furstenberg, F. F. The social consequences of teenage childbearing. *Family Planning* Perspectives, 1976, *8* (4), 159.

Furstenberg, F. F., Gordis, L., & Markowitz, M. Birth control knowledge and attitude among pregnant adolescents: A preliminary report. *Journal of Marriage and the Family,* 1969, *31,* 34–42.

Gabrielson, I. W., Klerman, L. V., Currie, J. B., Tyler, N. C., & Jekel, J. F. Suicide attempts in a population pregnant as teenagers. *American Journal of Public Health,* 1970, *60* (12), 2289–2301.

Howard, M. School continues for pregnant teenagers. *American Education,* December 1968/January 1969, *5* (1), 5–7.

Janowitz, B. S. The impact of AFDC on illegitimate birth rates. *Journal of Marriage and the Family,* 1976, *38,* 485–494.

Jones, A. E., & Placek, P. J. *Teenage women in the U.S.A.: Sex, contraception, pregnancy, fertility, and maternal and child health.* Paper presented at Family Impact Seminar Conference on Teenage Pregnancy and Family Impact: New Perspectives on Policy, Washington, D.C., October 1978.

Kantner, J. F., & Zelnik, M. Sexual experience of young, unmarried women in the United States. *Family Planning Perspectives,* 1972, *4* (1), 9–18.

Kasanin, J., & Handschin, S. Psychodynamic factors in illegitimacy. *American Journal of Orthopsychiatry,* 1941, *11* (1), 66–84.

Khlentzos, M. T., & Pagliano, M. A. Observations from psychotherapy with unwed mothers. *American Journal of Orthopsychiatry,* 1965, *35* (4), 779–786.

Kinsey, A. C., Pomeroy, W. B., Martin, C. E. Social level and sexual outlets. In R. Bendix and S. M. Lipset (Eds.), *Class, status, and power.* New York: The Free Press, 1964.

Loesch, J. G., & Greenberg, N. J. Some specific areas of conflict observed during pregnancy: A comparative study of married and unmarried pregnant women. *American Journal of Orthopsychiatry,* 1962, *32* (4), 624–636.

Menken, J. *The health and demographic consequences of adolescent pregnancy and childbearing.* Paper presented at National Institute of Child Health and Human Development Conference on the Consequences of Adolescent Pregnancy and Childbearing, Rockville, Md., October 1975.

Moore, K., & Caldwell, S. *Out of wedlock pregnancy and childbearing.* Washington, D.C.: The Urban Institute, 1976.

National Institutes of Health. *The women and their pregnancies: The collaborative perinatal study of the National Institute of Neurological Diseases and Stroke.* Washington, D.C.: GPO, 1972.

85

Nortman, D. Parental age as a factor in pregnancy outcome and child development. *Reports on Population/Family Planning,* 1972, *16.*

Oberhau, H. Characteristics of the AFDC population. *Social Security Bulletin,* 1977, *40* (9), 17–18.

Oppel, W., & Royston, A. Teenage births: Some social, psychological, and physical sequelae. *American Journal of Public Health,* 1971, *61* (4), 751–756.

Pauker, J. D. Girls pregnant out-of-wedlock. In National Council on Illegitimacy, *The double jeopardy, the triple crisis: Illegitimacy today.* New York: NCI, 1969.

Pregnant teen-agers. *Today's Education,* 1970, *59* (7), 26–29.

Prescott, J. W. Abortion or the unwanted child: A choice for a humanistic society. *The Humanist,* March/April 1975, 11–15.

Presser, H. B. *Social consequences of teenage childbearing.* Paper presented at National Institute of Child Health and Human Development Conference on the Consequences of Adolescent Pregnancy and Childbearing, Rockville, Md., October 1975.

Reevy, W. R. Adolescent sexuality. In A. Ellis & A. Abarbanel (Eds.), *The encyclopedia of sexual behavior.* New York: Hawthorn Books, 1961.

Sarrel, P. Caring for the pregnant teenager. *The Family Planner,* 1970, *3* (4), 15–16.

Schofield, M. *The sexual behavior of young people.* Boston: Little, Brown and Co., 1965.

Sharing. Washington, D.C.: Cyesis Programs Consortium, George Washington University, February 1971.

U.S. Department of Health, Education and Welfare, Children's Bureau. *Multiservice programs for pregnant school girls* (1968).

Vener, A., & Stewart, C. Adolescent sexual behavior in middle America revisited: 1970–1973. *Journal of Marriage and the Family,* 1974, *36,* 728–735.

Vincent, C. E. *Unmarried mothers.* New York: The Free Press, 1961.

Wilson, S. J., Keith, L., Wells, J., & Stepto, R. O. *A preliminary survey of 16,000 teenagers entering a contraceptive program.* Unpublished paper, Cook County Hospital, Chicago, Illinois, n.d. (c. 1973).

Wirth. T. Education for all youth. In *A report on the National Invitational Conference on Parenthood in Adolescence* (Sponsored by Yale University and the University of Pittsburgh in cooperation with the Maternal and Child Health Service, Health Services and Mental Health Administration and Children's Bureau, Office of Child Development, Washington, D.C., January 22–24, 1970).

Wurtz, F., & Fergen, G. Not much help for pregnant school girls. *American School Board Journal,* 1970, *157* (10), 22–24.

Zelnik, M., & Kantner, J. F. First pregnancies to women aged 15–19: 1976 and 1971. *Family Planning Perspectives,* 1978, *10* (1) 11–20.

Zelnik, M., & Kantner, J. F. Sexual and contraceptive experience of young, unmarried women in the United States, 1976 and 1971. *Family Planning Perspectives,* 1977, *9* (2), 55–71.

Five

The Abortion Controversy

January 23, 1978 marked the fifth anniversary of the Supreme Court decision establishing abortion as a constitutional right for all women. The law declared that the state could not interfere with the right of choice except to ensure the medical safety of the woman. Yet the abortion debate continues despite the 1973 ruling that affected the abortion laws of every state.

Why do some factions believe the law has gone too far, and why do others believe it has not gone far enough? What are the facts about abortion— its safety and its psychological effects? What has actually happened in New York, where a liberal abortion law was in effect for several years *before* the Court's ruling? These are some of the questions discussed in this chapter.

In 1977, an estimated 1,270,000 legal abortions were performed in the United States (Abortion Under Attack, 1978), which is an increase of 7 percent from 1976. Almost one-third of 1976 abortions were obtained by teenagers (Alan Guttmacher Institute, 1977). While Zelnik and Kantner (1974) and Furstenberg (1976) both discussed the greater use of abortion by whites than blacks, the latest data show a dramatic change: about one-third of those obtaining abortions in 1976 were nonwhite (Abortion Under Attack, 1978) as compared with 23 percent in 1972 (Center for Disease Control, 1977). In view of religious pronouncements on abortion, it also might be expected that Catholic women would elect abortion less frequently. Yet Catholic women, who constitute 25 percent of the population, obtain 30 to 33 percent of all abortions (Steinem, 1977), with other sources citing statistics ranging up to 55 percent (Abortion Under Attack, 1978).

Antiabortion forces have sometimes labeled abortion dangerous to the health of the mother, yet the bulk of evidence demonstrates the safety of abortion performed by a competent physician under sanitary conditions. Nine out of ten abortions are performed during the first trimester of pregnancy. The very young and poor, however, constitute a disproportionate number of second trimester patients (Alan Guttmacher Institute, 1977). This delay appears to be related to service accessibility (Zero Population Growth, 1976). Most abortion services are concentrated in a few metropolitan areas primarily on the East and West coasts, and only 18 percent of public hospitals in 1975 reported performing any abortions, despite their being the primary source of

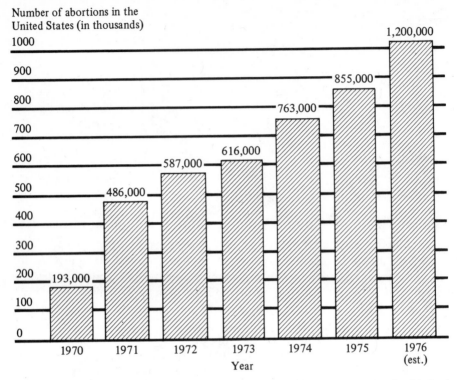

Number of abortions in the
United States (in thousands)

Figure 5.1 Trend in Abortions: Number of Abortions in the United
States, as Counted by the Federal Center for Disease
Control.

Note: Latest available statistics.

Source: U.S. Dept. of Health, Education, and Welfare.

medical care for many people with low incomes (Alan Guttmacher Institute,
1977).

The Gallup Poll released on January 22, 1978, reported that 77 percent
of adults support abortion under some circumstances. This contrasts with 22
percent favoring abortion being legal under all circumstances and 19 percent
suggesting that it should be illegal under all circumstances. In general, there
was very little difference in point of view between Catholics and Protestants.

The Supreme Court Decision

The Supreme Court decision in the cases of *Roe* v. *Wade* and *Doe* v. *Bolton*
gave every woman in the United States the right to abortion on request during
the first three months of pregnancy. Pregnant women can now control their
own bodies and decide their own futures, rights that women's liberation groups
have sought for a long time. However, these rights are greatly modified by the
Hyde Amendment that prohibits payment of abortion through Medicaid.

The Guidelines

The Supreme Court decision on abortion (January 1973) is as follows:

> We recognize the right of the individual, married or single, to be free from unwarranted governmental intrusion into matters so fundamentally affecting a person as the decision whether to bear or beget a child. That right necessarily includes the right of a woman to decide whether or not to terminate her pregnancy.

The Court's ruling was based on the following guidelines:

During the first trimester, "the abortion decision and its effectuation must be left to the medical judgment of the pregnant woman's attending physician."

In the second trimester, the abortion procedures may be regulated by the state in ways "related to maternal health." However, requiring approval by a panel of doctors is not constitutional.

During the third trimester, the state may regulate or forbid abortion, except in cases where it is necessary to save the pregnant woman's life or her health.

The Basis for the Decision

The protection of the individual's right to privacy contained in the due process clause of the Fourteenth Amendment provided the basis for the decision.

Medical factors were responsible for the three-part guidelines. The opinion stated that in the first three months, abortion has become safer than childbirth. After that, the dangers increase and the state has authority to protect the woman's health.

A fetus, the ruling states, has no legal right to life. It is not a person under the Constitution.

How Safe Is Abortion?

In a study of British and U.S. mortality rates, Tietze and Lewit (1977) flatly state, "The death rate is far lower for legal abortions done during the first 12 weeks of pregnancy than it is for the complications of childbirth" (p. 26). The comparison shows such abortion-related deaths at about 4 per 100,000 abortions, while about 48 deaths per 100,000 births are associated with childbirth. In another study, Tietze (1971) comments:

> If the use of contraception were maintained at or near its present level after the legalization of abortion, the increase in the number of abortions would be moderate and the number of deaths from abortion, and of nonfatal complications, as well, would be substantially reduced. The birth rate would also be lower. One would hope that this might be the outcome, but hope is no substitute for experience.

91

The Effects of Liberalized Abortion Laws

Although the *New York Times* reported (Schultz, 1977) that over 350 new abortion clinics have been opened in states where they were illegal before the Supreme Court ruling, it is too soon to have information available on their experiences and effects. However, studies in New York since 1970 can be examined as an example of what occurs under a liberal abortion law. Many of the pessimistic predictions regarding the law's results proved untrue.

The prediction that women seeking abortion would monopolize hospital beds needed for other urgent health problems was not supported. According to Pakter and Nelson (1971), "Almost 70% of all abortions were performed on an ambulatory basis with no overnight hospital stay." In 1971, hospitals were the providers of over 80 percent of all New York City residents' abortions; by 1974, they accounted for less than 60 percent. The shift was explained by the great increase in abortions provided by nonhospital clinics; these provided 16 percent of 1971 resident abortions and over 40 percent of 1974 abortions. Nationally, clinics now provide 55 percent of abortions, private hospitals 37 percent, public hospitals 10 percent, and doctors' offices 3 percent (Alan Guttmacher Institute, 1976). This shift was made possible by increasing proportions of residents obtaining the safest form of abortion, the first-trimester vacuum aspiration. In 1971, 79 percent of all resident abortions were first trimester; by 1974, 86 percent were first trimester. Among residents, four abortion-related deaths were recorded in 1971, but only one in 1974, despite a steady increase in that period in the number of resident abortions performed (51,000 in 1971 to 82,000 in 1974). During 1973, the first year of nationwide legal abortion, abortion-related deaths dropped 40 percent nationally (Pakter et al., 1975). Christopher Tietze of the Population Council estimated (1975) that legal abortion has a mortality rate of 4 cases per 100,000 population. Legal abortion is thus far safer than pregnancy and childbirth. Legal abortion is now the most commonly performed surgical procedure after tonsillectomy (Kramer, 1975), and Tietze demonstrated that it accounted for 20 percent of the reduction in expected births nationwide in 1974 (Tietze, 1975).

Among New York residents, this effect on the birth rate was especially dramatic and important. Because of New York's less restrictive application of the law, legal abortions accounted for 50 percent of New York's reduction in expected 1974 births (Tietze, 1975). This is particularly critical, because the increase in abortions provided to teenagers represented almost one-third of the total abortion increase from 1971–74; this was the largest increase of any age group, with the greatest change occurring among fifteen-to-seventeen-year-olds. Although teenagers, like other age groups, are having their abortions earlier, young people as a group are still more likely to have an abortion after the twelfth week of pregnancy, especially nonwhites and females under fifteen (Pakter et al., 1975). Despite their more difficult access to these services, teenagers accounted for 20 percent of all 1974 legal abortions in New York, with two-thirds being to unmarried women.

Legal abortion, which one observer has called "one of the great social equalizers of our times" (Kramer, 1975), has made possible a reduction in unwanted, "illegitimate" births. Contrary to the commonly held belief that blacks are less inclined to use abortion, New York statistics for the first year showed that black abortion rates *increase* with increasing economic status, education, and female labor force participation (Kramer, 1975). The prediction that the poor, and especially the black poor, would either oppose, or not seek, abortion was wrong. According to Pakter and Nelson (1971), of New York State *resident* women who sought abortion from July 1970 to March 1971, 31.9 percent were black, 58 percent white, and 10.1 percent Puerto Rican. By 1974, these figures had changed somewhat: Nonwhite use of abortion represented 49 percent of the total use of abortion (Pakter et al., 1975).

The abortion law also had a tremendous effect on adolescent pregnancy in New York, with teenagers accounting in 1971 for more than 16 percent of abortions and 13.8 percent of live births. One-third of abortions to teenagers were to girls seventeen or younger (Pakter and Nelson, 1971). In addition, all of the shelters in New York City caring for unmarried pregnant girls reported sharp declines in the number of applicants for admission, suggesting that legal abortions not only replaced illegal abortions but also terminated pregnancies that otherwise resulted in unwanted births (Pakter and Nelson, 1971).

Prescott (1975) has also pointed out that a reduction in unwanted births may well result in a reduction in child abuse and, eventually, in homicide. The articles by Prescott and Wallace (see appendix) provide supportive evidence for some of the inferences presented in this chapter on antiabortion views and behavior.

The New York experience indicates that when women are given the opportunity to go through legal rather than illegal channels, they choose the former wholeheartedly; moreover, when aware of the procedural safety, women will seek abortions earlier in pregnancy. Clearly, the myth that women are not capable of making decisions about their futures is not substantiated. In fact, Zero Population Growth noted (1976):

> Since the 1973 Supreme Court decision on abortion, lower court rulings have set the following precedents: that parental and spousal consent to abortion cannot legally be required, that public hospitals have a responsibility to provide abortion services, and that state Medicaid programs must reimburse for abortion if they do so for other pregnancy-related services (p. 2).

These kinds of rulings (as opposed to the more recent restrictions) have the effect of allowing women to have control over their futures, thus enhancing their status. The raising of women's status is a key element in reducing unwanted fertility, for as a regional Asian conference noted in 1973, there has been a "close relationship between the low status of women, early and universal marriage of girls, and a high fertility" (Soewondo, 1975).

The Religious Viewpoint

The Supreme Court's views on the safety of abortion and the status of the fetus are strongly opposed by antiabortion groups. Their principal argument has been that abortion is murder.

Probably the most consistent, vocal, and powerful opponent of abortion reform has been the Catholic Church, and its opposition is based on the belief that the fetus *is* a person. The position was stated at length in Pius VI's encyclical *Casti Connubii,* issued in 1930, and restated in Paul VI's encyclical *Humanae Vitae,* issued on July 29, 1968 (Westoff, 1970; von Geusau, 1970). The Catholic Church officially holds that the soul "enters" at the moment of conception; therefore, the death of the fetus is the death of an "unborn human."

Other major religious groups in this country hold different views on the humanity and sacredness of the fetus. The general position of Conservative and Reformed Jews is that the fetus is not human until after birth, although Orthodox Jews share the Catholic viewpoint, with the important exception that Orthodox Jewish law *always* gives the life of the mother priority over the fetus. The report on *Sexuality and the Human Community* (1970), ratified in 1970 by the General Assembly of the United Presbyterian Church in the U.S., states: "Exodus 21:22 and other instances of Old Testament laws concerning homicide suggest that the fetus is not to be regarded as a person, but as a part of (or property of) the mother, and that feticide is not homicide." (See chapter 7 for a compilation of current statements on abortion by major religious groups.)

Abortion and Public Opinion

The National Abortion Rights Action League has collected the results of polls on abortion since the Supreme Court decision (NARAL, 1976). While variations in response can often be attributed to wording differences, it appears that the majority of Americans agree that it is a woman's right to decide, with her doctor, whether or not to have an abortion, and that about the same percentage oppose a constitutional amendment to alter the current laws.

In 1976, a *New York Times*/CBS News Poll revealed that 67 percent of a national population sample agreed that "the right of a woman to have an abortion should be left entirely up to the woman and her doctor." A Knight-Ridder Newspapers 1976 survey in twenty-one cities revealed that 76 percent of Roman Catholics, 82 percent of Protestants, and 98 percent of Jews agreed that if a woman wants to have an abortion, it is a matter for her and her doctor to decide and the government should have nothing to do with it. According to a 1976 *Washington Post*/Harvard University Poll, 70 percent of Americans in national leadership groups "strongly agreed" that "it is the right of a woman to decide whether to have an abortion." And in 1978, 44 percent of respondents to a Gallup Poll conducted by the Catholic Press Association agreed that the church should "relax its standards forbidding all abortions under any circumstances," with "those with college degrees . . . increasingly likely to reject church teachings on such issues as abortion" (Educated Catholics, 1978). In the Devries Poll, conducted in December 1974 for the National Committee for a Human Life Amendment, 72 percent of four thousand adults nationwide mildly or strongly disagreed that "abortion should not be allowed under any circumstances," with virtually no difference between Catholics and Protestants; Jewish respondents in nearly all the surveys taken since the Court's decision are overwhelmingly in favor of abortion as a woman's choice and opposed by the same overwhelming percentage to any amendment to the Constitution that would limit the availability of abortion.

All this public approval hasn't been mobilized, however, with the result that twelve states have already passed resolutions calling on Congress to convene a constitutional convention in order to pass an antiabortion amendment, with thirteen more states having introduced such resolutions (Zero Population Growth, 1977). It is also apparent that in some communities, doctors are succumbing to the same antiabortion pressure directed against hospitals (Gratz, 1977). The complacency of prochoice advocates has accelerated a backslide on abortion to the point where, for hundreds of thousands of women, the Supreme Court's 1973 decision might as well have never been made. In fact, Forrest, Tietze, and Sullivan (1978) estimate that in 1977, nearly 560,000 women across the country who wanted an abortion were unable to obtain one. The passage of the Hyde Amendments has dealt a particular blow to women too poor to afford an abortion; about 279,000 such women obtained Medicaid-subsidized abortions in 1976 (Forrest, Tietze, & Sullivan, 1978).

The Current Abortion Controversy

The Supreme Court decision has not silenced the antiabortion forces; they are more vociferous in their opposition than ever. In addition, some Catholic groups have "forced" hospitals and medical groups under Catholic auspices to refuse to perform abortion on request. A health bill was passed in the U.S. Senate in 1976 with a rider stating that no federal funds shall be denied a hospital or medical facility because it refuses to perform abortions on ethical or religious grounds. Such legislative action can only encourage hospitals' continued failure to offer abortion: Abortion services are excluded from 70 percent of non-Catholic general hospitals and 80 percent of public hospitals in the U.S. (25% of Pregnancies, 1977).

The Hyde Amendment passed in fall of 1976 banned the use of Medicaid funds for elective abortions. In June 1977, the Supreme Court ruled that it was "not unreasonable for a state to pursue its 'valid and important interest in encouraging childbirth' by refusing to pay for abortions" (Wicker, 1977). On December 7, 1977 a "compromise" Hyde Amendment was passed:

> None of the funds contained in this Act shall be used to perform abortions except where the life of the mother would be endangered if the fetus were carried to term; or except for

> such medical procedures necessary for the victims of rape or incest, when such rape or incest has been promptly reported to a law enforcement agency or public health service; or except in those instances where severe and long lasting physical health damage to the mother would result if the pregnancy were carried to term when so determined by two physicians.

Final regulations issued by the Department of Health, Education, and Welfare went into effect February 1978, with stringent rules for obtaining a Medicaid-covered abortion following rape or incest.

Of course, all these legislative events have accomplished is a return to "kitchen-table justice" in which the poor, subsidized clinic user (60 percent of all abortions) is forced to an illegal and dangerous abortionist, while the affluent woman, as always, remains able to buy her needed care (Wicker, 1977). President Carter's contribution to the debate ("life is unfair") further weakens the force of the Supreme Court decision; citing moral concerns, neither he nor HEW Secretary Califano favor public financing of abortions. But as *Time* noted in its August 1, 1977 issue: "To say that abortion, while legal, is immoral but that only the poor shall be saved from this immorality by a fastidious government is not only unfair but absurd" (p. 49).

Aryeh Neier (ACLU Acts, 1978) executive director of the American Civil Liberties Union, has argued that the Hyde Amendment

> is no compromise. It is brutal treatment of women with medical needs for abortions. It is intended to intimidate doctors into refusing to perform all abortions for patients requiring Medicaid reimbursement, even where the woman's life would be threatened. The demand for rigorous enforcement threatens doctors with prosecution if their professional judgments do not conform to those of Uncle Sam. This law denies women the right to control their destiny; it denies doctors the right to practice medicine; it imposes the religious views of some groups on others; it interferes with the right to privacy; and it penalizes the poor.

As a reaction to such legislation many religious groups have voiced support of a woman's right to choose abortion as an alternative to unwanted children. For example, in 1977, more than two hundred American ethicists and theologians signed the "Call for Concern" sponsored by the Religious Coalition for Abortion Rights (1978a), which states:

> 1 The most compelling argument against the inflexibility of the absolutist position is its cost in human misery;
> 2 "Pro-life" must not be limited to concern for the unborn; it must also include a concern for the quality of life as a whole;
> 3 We believe it is wrong to deny Medicaid assistance to poor women seeking abortions;

4 We are saddened by the heavy institutional involvement of the bishops of the Roman Catholic Church in a campaign to enact religiously-based anti-abortion commitments into law, and we view this as a serious threat to religious liberty and freedom of conscience;

5 We call upon the leaders of religious groups supporting abortion rights to speak out more clearly and publicly in response to the dangerously increasing influence of the absolutist position.

A recent class action suit *(McRae* v. *Califano)* has challenged both the 1976 and 1978 Hyde Amendments, chiefly arguing that such legislation violates the First Amendment prohibition against "establishment of religion" because it favors the Roman Catholic religious viewpoint, while inhibiting or disfavoring other religious views. The effect of a ruling against McRae (Magar, 1978) would

signal a retreat of First Amendment rights in this country and give fuel to the anti-choice forces to redouble their efforts to eliminate abortion rights for all women. . . . Once you've gotten into motion a single issue, extremely fervent constituency, you have the force in place to move in a similar fashion on other issues such as restrictions on contraception, sex education or even aid to parochial schools. . . . Conversely, if the Court decides in our favor, it will serve as a strong defense of the First Amendment and act as a deterrent to those who would see their religious beliefs lawfully imposed on all other Americans.

Antiabortion Group Tactics

Antiabortionists have used such legislative tactics as attaching riders to federal legislation cutting off funds for abortion and pushing for enactment of prohibitive state laws and restrictive practices by physicians and hospitals. Pressure, however, has not stopped at the state and federal legislative levels. Antiabortionists have also harassed abortion clinics, implemented high-pressure "education" campaigns, such as public demonstrations, marches, debates, letters-to-editors, and pictures of fetuses enlarged to distort actual size as ways of influencing the general public. Another technique has been to exploit such issues as "parental rights" and the Holocaust. In the April 13, 1978 issue of the *Wanderer,* a conservative, right-wing Catholic newspaper, John J. Malloy wrote:

One wonders if our American advocates of abortion, so anxious to make certain that the unborn child is killed in the womb of its mother, did not take a page out of Hitler's book. . . . The issue of abortion is of such central importance for a discussion in understanding the holocaust, for it

97

shows clearly that Americans have their own holocaust, which is now being carried on in this country.

Is there not a far greater degree of guilt involved in the permissive attitude of many Americans toward abortion than there was in the German people for having failed to mount organized opposition to the Nazi killing of the Jews?

In response, a special release was issued April 14, 1978 by the Population Institute in which Rabbi Balfour Brickner, director of Interreligious Activities of the Union of American Hebrew Congregations, stated:

The effort to equate the Holocaust with the anti-abortion campaign in this country is an unbelievable outrage. It insults the memory of 6 million dead; it represents a crude, obvious, crass, even obscene exploitation of what should remain a tragically unique and hallowed memory.

The 'Holocaust' stands alone. It defies analogy and allegory. The Holocaust was the genocide of six million already born, living people. There was neither theological nor medical question as to the fact that those who were slaughtered were indeed alive. To suggest, even by implication, that a pro-choice stand by Americans, the majority of whom have at least serious reservations, if not differing ideals both religious and medical about when life begins, is tantamount to the atrocity of the genocide of six million Jews—an analogy no clear-thinking, decent-minded person can or should make or accept.

Dr. George H. Outen, General Secretary of the Board of Church and Society of the United Methodist Church also noted:

I deeply deplore the attempt to compare the systematic pogrom carried out in Nazi Germany to exterminate the Jewish people of Europe with the rights and the freedom granted to women of this nation by the courts, to choose to have a legal abortion. Such self-serving, but erroneous, comparisons serve to lessen the impact of the Holocaust and do a disservice to the memories of the millions of Jews who died in an atmosphere of fascism.

In 1975 the National Conference of Catholic Bishops adopted a plan to involve the Catholic Church and its members in a campaign against abortion rights. The three-fold public education, legislative, and political plan was to be carried out, in part, by the National Committee for a Human Life Amendment (Religious Coalition for Abortion Rights, 1978b). Although the intrusion of the Roman Catholic Church in America in politics to impose its morality on American citizens raises serious questions about violation of the First Amendment, the recent relaxation in its opposition to legalization of contraceptives by the Roman Catholic Church in Ireland represents the reverse position. A statement issued by Irish bishops, while reaffirming their opposition to contraceptives, also notes:

> It does not necessarily follow from this that the State is bound to prohibit the distribution and sale of contraceptives. There are many things which the Catholic church holds to be morally wrong, but which it has never suggested should be prohibited by the State. Those who insist on seeing the issue purely in terms of the State enforcing, or not enforcing, Catholic moral teaching are therefore missing the point.[1]

To date, nine major invasions have occurred in the Washington, D.C. area (Violence, 1978) including picketing by members of groups calling themselves "Concerned Citizens," "Peace" (People Expressing a Concern for Everyone) as well as members of the better-known National Right to Life Committee. Although Dr. Mildred Jefferson, president of the National Right to Life Committee, has dismissed the picketing as "so much side-show activity," claiming "we are not violent people," such demonstrations have caused injury at clinics (Surge of Vandalism, 1978). For example, demonstrators harassed patients, snapped photographs of clinic patients, and took over the telephone to tell callers the Northern Virginia Women's Medical Center in Fairfax County was closed. In an attempt to prevent this kind of pressure tactic, the Reproductive Freedom Project of the ACLU and the ACLU of Virginia has filed suit against the Fairfax County commonwealth attorney and two district court judges for denying pregnant women their constitutional right to choose abortion. The ACLU charges that trespassing and interference by trespassers at the Northern Virginia Women's Medical Center on four separate occasions were "not only permitted but encouraged by the refusal of the commonwealth attorney . . . and district court judges to uphold the law" (Sue to Stop, 1978). In some cases demonstrators have been acquitted of charges by utilizing the common law principle of "defense of necessity." Although this law does reside in "good faith belief that their actions were necessary to save lives," the legal theory on which this argument is based is that "a person may come to the aid of another who is under *unlawful* attack" (Violence, 1978, emphasis added).

From February 1977 to March 1979, sixteen abortion clinics were burned, and to date there has been one unsuccessful bombing attempt. Many of these acts have occurred during operating hours, thus endangering building occupants. Clinic personnel and their children have received death threats.

Although there have been no fatalities to date, it would appear that there is a hypocritical relationship between the view of antiabortionists that abortion is murder and the violent actions taken by some to promulgate this belief.

Adolescents and Abortion

It is now possible for an adolescent to obtain a legal abortion, but in many cases only with parental consent. Twenty-six states have "endorsed the principle" that unmarried minors should be able to get an abortion only with parental consent (Paul, Pilpel, & Wechsler, 1976). Abortion is surgery, and parental consent is required for surgery performed on minors except in emergencies. However, there is a fair amount of confusion as to who is a minor, since different states have different statutory ages, and even within a particular state ages may vary. An eighteen-year-old may be an adult in the alcoholic-beverage and voting statutes and a minor according to other laws. In New York any woman eighteen or older may obtain an abortion without parental consent. In New York, Governor Hugh Carey vetoed a 1976 bill that would have required parental consent for abortions performed on minors. In vetoing the bill, the governor called it "illusory" and stated that it was "an attempt to substitute symbolism for a substantial and legally sound treatment of a serious issue." In Massachusetts, an "emancipated" minor (an eighteen-to-twenty-one-year-old supporting herself and maintaining her own residence) does not need the consent of a parent, but a financially dependent woman of the same age must have consent. And in *Planned Parenthood of Missouri* v. *Danforth,* the Court ruled that a minor "mature enough" to understand the nature and consequences of treatment may give her own consent for abortion (Paul, 1977). On October 29, 1978, the United States Supreme Court again agreed to review whether a state may require unmarried females under eighteen to obtain the consent of their parents.

Illegal Abortion

Unmarried pregnant teenagers who are afraid to, or do not know how to, seek help may obtain a dangerous illegal abortion or attempt an even more dangerous self-induced abortion. Self-induced abortion can cause extreme pain and can lead to permanent disability or death. Teenage girls have inserted such things as knitting needles, coat hangers, curtain rods, lye, and alcohol into their uteri, and even have swallowed quinine and ergot compounds in their attempts to rid themselves of a fetus. Many are not aware that they are also risking their lives in the process. In their fear of being "found out" by those who probably mean the most to them, they go through tremendous agony, lacking the support they should have in this critical situation.

Giving Birth

If a girl gives birth to her child, she faces, in a majority of cases, a series of possibilities—forced departure from school, confinement to a life of poverty, repeated out-of-wedlock pregnancies, or a hasty, unstable marriage—all of which are highly injurious to her well-being as well as to society's. Or she may choose giving up her baby for adoption, even sometimes with severe emotional consequences.

These results of teenage pregnancies are the traditional "deterrents" to premarital sex. At present, most laws relating to teenage sexuality continue to be based, at least in part, on this "deterrent" theory, a theory that has very little validity. As Furstenberg et al. (1969) noted: "If the incidence of premarital pregnancy is to be reduced significantly, it will be by decreasing the rate of conception, not sexual intercourse."

Although more federal monies have been allocated in the current budget for unwanted pregnancy and venereal disease prevention among teenagers than ever before in history, the federal and state backlash against Medicaid-funded abortions will undoubtedly take its toll on teenage women. About 300,000 abortions on teenagers are performed each year (*U.S. News and World Report,* 1977), with about one-third paid through Medicaid funds (Steinem, 1977). Zelnik and Kantner's national probability sample survey of ever-married and never-married women fifteen to nineteen years of age has provided some of the richest data to date on teenage women. We concur with their observation that:

> While the greatly increased availability and accessibility of legal and medically safe abortion may lessen the impact of first pregnancy on the lives of young women, especially young unmarried women, (because of the dangers of births and illegal abortions averted), we believe this event still influences considerably their future decisions and options. Any reduction in the availability of legal abortion (as the result of recent congressional action and Supreme Court decisions) could again increase the impact of first pregnancy on the lives of young women involved.[2]

The adolescent abortion dilemma arises from fear of communicating with parents and from the unavailability of contraceptives and birth control information. Increasing the availability of contraceptives requires changing laws that restrict the places where nonprescriptive contraceptives can be sold. Increasing parent-adolescent communication requires parents to reevaluate many of their own attitudes and efforts to discuss sexuality and sex-related problems, such as unwanted pregnancy and venereal disease, with their children in a relaxed, nonjudgmental way.

An Opportunity for Research

Little is known about the psychological and social implications of abortion, and many of the medical effects and implications are still unknown. Until now, there has been little opportunity to pursue meaningful studies of abortion because of the secretiveness surrounding illegal abortions. The legality of

---

[2] Reprinted with permission from *Family Planning Perspectives,* Volume 10, Number 1, 1978, p. 11.

abortion creates an opportunity to perform some greatly needed research in the field.

Some of the assumptions regarding abortion have been carefully researched. Published data can be thoroughly investigated to ascertain whether the sample is biased in any way; whether the research, in fact, reliably measures what it states it measures; and whether the data are meaningful. Studies of psychological outcomes of abortion contradict each other and contain erroneous information. Care must be taken to define specifically what is meant by guilt, by sadness, by suffering. These terms are generally interpreted individualistically and are not easily adapted to group data. Moreover, the rationale for discrimination for terms such as "moderate" and "high" must be reported.

Some women experience guilt feelings following abortion, and little consideration has been given to the fact that cultural tolerance toward abortion may reduce these feelings. As more abortions are performed, cultural tolerance will increase, as will the number of women who can be studied (Pohlman, 1971).

Often, data do not take into consideration the mental state of the adolescent prior to the pregnancy. This, in fact, would be an arduous task—time consuming and costly. Nevertheless, studies continue to be published that report postabortion attitudes and feelings while not reporting the prepregnancy history of the adolescent or adults, leading to faulty conclusions. For instance, if an adolescent is emotionally disturbed after abortion and never was before pregnancy, abortion could be considered a cause, but if an adolescent has a history of emotional disturbance and is disturbed after abortion, the conclusions would be different.

Some data now available are more convincing because they avoid some of the above research limitations. In a carefully conducted nine-year study of 220 children born to Czechoslovakian mothers twice denied legal abortion and a matched control group of 220 boys and girls (Dytrych et al., 1975), it was found that, especially for boys, "the unwanted children (had) poorer health and poorer grades in school and (tended) to be less accepted by their peers than other children of similar socio-economic status, intellectual ability, birth order, and family size" (Zero Population Growth, 1976).

Conclusion

The Catholic position should be respected, as should the Protestant, the Jewish, and any other religious position on abortion, but, by law, no religion has the right to impose its teachings on others. According to Christopher Tietze, seven out of ten legal abortions done in 1974 would have been performed illegally if abortion were outlawed (Zero Population Growth, 1976), the only difference being the eight times greater rate of death from illegal abortion (Tietze, 1975) and the emotional damage done to the woman and perhaps her child, as shown in the Czechoslovakian study.

The American Academy of Pediatrics (1971) Committee Statement on Youth describes a caring and accepting attitude toward adolescent abortion which should be universal:

> Clearly, the decision by the patient to terminate her pregnancy by abortion does not end her need for further care. Continuing support and guidance are the essentials of a rehabilitative program, with the pediatrician acting as the coordinator. Regular health supervision, including contraception advice and other aspects of preventive care, is primary. In addtion, encouragement of continued education, job training, and assistance with employment must follow.
>
> The issue is not whether the Academy supports the concept of abortion in teenage girls; abortions are occurring and will continue to occur among teenagers with or without Academy approval. However, the Academy is resolved that the procedure must never become a routine technical event in the lives of young people. Every effort must be made to insure that a concerned, dignified, and enlightened care situation is developed for these young patients.[3]

We know that unwanted pregnancy and/or birth is a source of a great amount of pain and misery for the mother, the unwanted child, and society. To allow women to decide for themselves whether to have an abortion seems the most just and humane attitude that society can take. The Supreme Court decision is a giant step forward.

The Report of the Commission on Population Growth and the American Future (1972), recommended that federal, state, and local governments make funds available to support abortion services and that abortion be specifically included in comprehensive health insurance benefits, both public and private. This is now the focal point of the struggle of prochoice advocates.

The pioneer Alan F. Guttmacher (1971) stated our position precisely: "I can think of nothing more immoral than forcing an unwilling mother to bear an unwanted, unloved child. A great deal of emotional and unscientific literature has been written about the mental anguish of women who undergo abortion. I suggest that the suffering endured by both mother and child as a result of compulsory childbirth is far better documented."

The late John D. Rockefeller 3rd, chairman of the Population Council, wrote in *Newsweek* (1976):

---

[3] Reprinted by permission from "Teen-age pregnancy and the problem of abortion," American Academy of Pediatrics *Newsletter* (Supplement), Vol. 22, No. 18, December 1, 1971. Copyright American Academy of Pediatrics, 1971.

Those who support legalized abortion—and opinion polls demonstrate them to be in a majority—have been comparatively quiet. After all, they won their case in the Supreme Court decision. Legalized abortion is the law of the land. It is also in the mainstream of world opinion. The number of countries where abortion has been broadly legalized has increased steadily, today covering 60 percent of the world population.

In this situation, there is a natural tendency to relax, to assume that the matter is settled and that the anti-abortion clamor will eventually die down. But it is conceivable that the United States could become the first democratic nation to turn the clock back by yielding to the pressure and reversing the Supreme Court decision. In my judgment, that would be a tragic mistake. . . .

We must uphold freedom of choice. Moreover, we must work to make free choice a reality by extending safe abortion services throughout the United States. Only one-fourth of the non-Catholic general hospitals and one-fifth of the public hospitals in the country now provide such services. It is extremely difficult to have a legal and safe abortion if you are young or poor or live in a smaller city or rural area.

On a broader front, we must continue the effort to make contraceptive methods better, safer, and more readily available to everyone. Freedom of choice is crucial, but the decision to have an abortion is always a serious matter. It is a choice one would wish to avoid. The best way to do that is to avoid unwanted pregnancy in the first place.[4]

---

[4] "No retreat on abortion." *Newsweek,* June 21, 1976, p. 11. Copyright 1976 by Newsweek, Inc. All rights reserved. Reprinted by permission.

References Abortion under attack. *Newsweek,* 5 June 1978, 36–37; 39–42; 47.

ACLU acts to stop abortion foes. *Civil Liberties,* January 1978, 321, 8.

Alan Guttmacher Institute. *Planned births, the future of the family, and the quality of American life.* New York: Planned Parenthood, June 1977.

Alan Guttmacher Institute. *11 million teenagers.* New York: Planned Parenthood, 1976.

Alan F. Guttmacher. *Testimony presented to the Commission on Population Growth and the American Future,* April 14, 1971. Washington, D.C.: Superintendent of Documents, 1972.

American Academy of Pediatrics, Committee on Youth. Teen-age pregnancy and the problem of abortion. 1 December 1971.

Catholics are reported matching non-Catholics on birth control. *New York Times,* 26 September 1977, 18.

Center for Disease Control. *Abortion surveillance, 1975.* Atlanta: April 1977.

Dytrych, Z., Matejcek, Z., Schuller, V., David, H. D., & Friedman, H. L. Children born to women denied abortion. *Family Planning Perspectives,* 1975, *7* (4), 165–171.

Educated Catholics remaining in church. *Syracuse Post-Standard,* 3 March 1978, 5.

Forrest, J. D., Tietze, C., & Sullivan, E. Abortion in the United States 1976–1977. *Family Planning Perspectives,* 1978, *10* (5), 271–279.

Furstenberg, F. F. *Unplanned parenthood.* New York: Free Press/Macmillan, 1976.

Furstenberg, F. F., Gordis, L., & Markowitz, M. Birth control knowledge and attitudes among pregnant adolescents: A preliminary report. *Journal of Marriage and the Family,* 1969, *31,* 34–42.

Gratz, R. B. Never again! never again! *Ms.,* July 1977, 54–55.

Irish bishops clear way for sale of contraception. *New York Times,* 3 May 1978, 12.

Kramer, M. J. Legal abortion among New York City residents: An analysis according to socioeconomic and demographic characteristics. *Family Planning Perspectives,* 1975, *7* (3), 128–137.

Magar, M. Hyde Amendment challenged. *NARAL Newsletter,* 1978, *10* (2), 1–2.

National Abortion Rights Action League. Public opinion polls since the Supreme Court decisions of 1973. Washington, D.C.: NARAL, n.d., (ca. 1976).

Pakter, J., & Nelson, F. Abortion in New York City: The first nine months. *Family Planning Perspectives,* 1971, *3* (3), 5–12.

Pakter, J., Nelson, F., & Suigir, M. Legal abortion: A half-decade of experience. *Family Planning Perspectives,* 1975, *7* (6), 248–255.

Paul, E. W. Danforth and Bellotti: A breakthrough for adolescents. *Family Planning/Population Reporter,* 1977, *6,* 3–5.

Paul, E. W., Pilpel, H. F., & Wechsler, N. Pregnancy, teenagers, and the law, 1976. *Family Planning Perspectives,* 1976, *8* (1), 16–21.

Pohlman, E. Abortion dogmas needing research scrutiny. In R. Bruce Sloane (Ed.), *Abortion: Changing Views and Practices.* New York: Grune and Stratton, Inc., 1971.

Prescott, J. W. Abortion or the unwanted child: A choice for a humanistic society. *The Humanist,* March/April 1975, 11–15.

Religious Coalition for Abortion Rights. *Call for concern.* Washington, D.C.: 1978(a).

Religious Coalition for Abortion Rights. The abortion rights crisis. *Options,* February 1978(b), 2.

Report of the Commission on Population Growth and the American Future. *Population and the American future.* New York: New American Library, 1972.

Rockefeller, J. D., 3rd. No retreat on abortion. *Newsweek,* 21 June 1976, 11.

Schultz, T. Though legal, abortions are not always available. *New York Times,* 2 January 1977, E8.

Sexuality and the human community. The General Assembly of the United Presbyterian Church in America, 1970.

Soewondo, N. Marriage law reform in Indonesia. In P. Piotraw (Ed.), *Draper World Population Fund Report,* 1975, 1, 18–19.

Steinem, Gloria. Abortion alert. *Ms.,* 1977, *6* (5), 118.

Sue to stop abortion clinic raids. *Civil Liberties,* May 1978, 323, 4.

Surge of vandalism hits abortion clinics. *New York Times,* 2 March 1978, A16.

Tietze, C. The effect of legalization of abortion on population growth and public health. *Family Planning Perspectives,* 1975, *7* (3), 123–127.

Tietze, C. Abortion on request: Its consequences for population trends and public health. In R. Bruce Sloane (Ed.), *Abortion: Changing Views and Practices.* New York: Grune and Stratton, Inc., 1971.

Tietze, C., & Lewit, S. Legal abortion. *Scientific American,* 1977, 236, 21–27.

25% of pregnancies ended by abortion. *Syracuse Post-Standard,* 31 May 1977, 5.

Violence against the right to choose. *NARAL Newsletter,* 1978, *10* (1), 2.

von Geusau, L. A. International reaction to the encyclical Humanae Vitae. *Studies in Family Planning,* February 1970, 50, 8–12.

Westoff, C. F., & Ryder, N. B. United States: The papal encyclical and Catholic practice and attitudes. *Studies in Family Planning,* February 1970, 50, 1–7.

Zelnik, M., & Kantner, J. F. First pregnancies to women aged 15–19: 1976 and 1971. *Family Planning Perspectives,* 1978, *10* (1), 11–20.

Zelnik, M., & Kantner, J. F. The resolution of teenage first pregnancies. *Family Planning Perspectives,* 1974, *6* (2), 74–90.

Zero Population Growth of New York. *Abortion update,* August 1977.

Zero Population Growth. 15 facts you should know about abortion, Washington, D.C.: Zero Population Growth, n.d. (c. 1976).

Six

Sexually
Transmitted
Diseases

The dramatic increase in the incidence of gonorrhea in the last decade and of syphilis in the last five years is considered an epidemic that is "clearly out of control" (White House Conference, 1970). Since 1956, gonorrhea infection has increased by two and one half times among teenage males, and nearly fourfold among teenage females, 80 percent of whom show no easily recognized symptoms (figures 6.1, 6.2, 6.3, and 6.4). Samuel Knox, program director of the American Social Health Association, estimates that more than 2.5 million teenagers annually contact venereal disease (VD Alarm, 1978). It is also estimated that over 400,000 people in the United States now have unde-

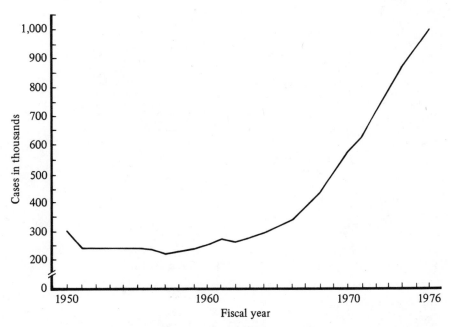

Figure 6.1 Gonorrhea. Reported Cases—United States: Fiscal Years 1950–1976[a].

[a] In figures 6.1–6.4, latest available statistics are for 1976.

Source: VD Fact Sheet, 1976. Center for Disease Control (Atlanta, Georgia).

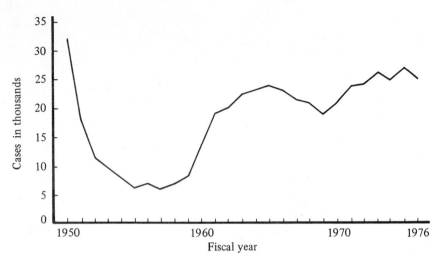

Figure 6.2   Primary and Secondary Syphilis. Reported Cases—United States: Fiscal Years 1950–1976.

Source: VD Fact Sheet, 1976. Center for Disease Control (Atlanta, Georgia).

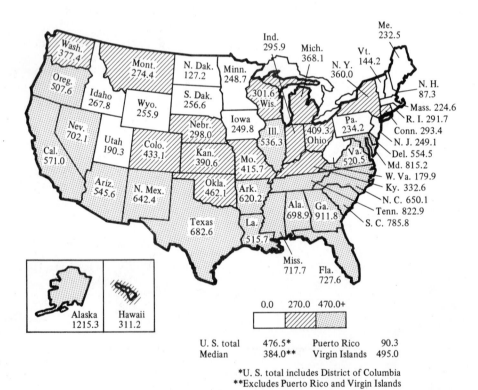

U. S. total   476.5*   Puerto Rico   90.3
Median   384.0**   Virgin Islands   495.0

*U. S. total includes District of Columbia
**Excludes Puerto Rico and Virgin Islands

Figure 6.3   Gonorrhea. Case Rates per 100,000 Population—Fiscal Year 1976.

Source: VD Fact Sheet, 1976. Center for Disease Control (Atlanta, Georgia).

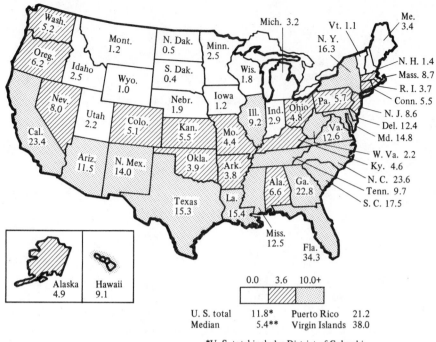

Figure 6.4   Primary and Secondary Syphilis. Case Rates per 100,000
Population—Fiscal Year 1976.

Source: VD Fact Sheet, 1976. Center for Disease Control (Atlanta, Georgia).

tected and untreated syphilis (Spence, 1978). In 1977, there was a reduction in the number of reported VD cases over 1976; syphilis cases dropped to 20,447 from 23,724, and there were 996,883 reported cases of gonorrhea as compared to 1,002,098 in 1976 (VD Cases, 1978). This first downward trend since 1969 has occurred during a period of greatly improved reporting techniques, and therefore is very encouraging.

Why Teenagers Need the Facts

In 1976 more than 500,000 VD victims were not yet twenty-one years old, and a significant number were in the eleven-to-fourteen age group (figures 6.3 and 6.4). The high incidence of teenage VD substantiates the need for VD education for teenagers, as do the following questions asked during a venereal disease prevention program developed by the Syracuse Board of Education:

"If a boy has a chancre on his finger can he give syphilis to a girl by masturbating her?"

"Does it help to prevent VD if a man uses a prophylactic kit (issued by the U.S. military) *after* intercourse?"

"Why is the VD rate higher now in teenagers?"

111

> "Should you ask a girl that you are planning to go with to be examined for G.C. and Syphilis?"

The unedited questions below are representative of those posed by high school students:

> "Can you still get VD if you use a rubber?"
>
> "Can a girl get syphlus from sucking a boy's penis?"
>
> "If a boy has syphillis and a boy and girl has oral sex will the girl get syphillis?"
>
> "What is sores on the dick?"
>
> "How many different kinds of VDs are there?"

The following myths are well established in some inner cities: "I may be poor and fuck a lot but I'm clean;" "You can only get VD from a whore;" "It (VD) proves you are a man."

In addition to providing teenagers with venereal disease information, professionals and parents need to encourage youth to create their own responses to sexual lines which are not in their best interests. For instance, if a male says that he won't use a condom because he gets no feelings out of it, a female could respond, "What's the matter with you? All the other guys I know get plenty of feelings out of it" (Gordon, 1978).

The Facts About VD

Venereal diseases are spread by sexual contact. They can be transmitted by an infected person any time he or she has sexual intercourse—homosexual or heterosexual—or mouth-genital contact. It is not necessary to have an orgasm or even to enjoy the sex act to contract VD. VD germs live only in warm moist areas like the genitals, the mouth, or the rectum. Air and dryness will kill them; therefore, they cannot be picked up from toilet seats or doorknobs, although they can be spread, in rare instances, by kissing.

The two most dangerous types of sexually transmitted diseases are gonorrhea and syphilis. People can have both diseases at the same time and can become reinfected after they have been cured.

Syphilis

Syphilis shows up in three stages. The first sign is a sore called a chancre (pronounced "shanker"), which shows up between ten and ninety days after sexual contact with an infected person. The sore usually appears on a man's penis and inside a woman's vagina, although sometimes a sore may show up on other parts of the body, such as the mouth or rectum. The sore first resembles a pimple or wart, but it soon becomes larger. Because it does not hurt or itch, it is often unnoticed.

112

The disappearance of the sore after a few weeks does not mean the disease is cured. Two to six months after the sore goes away, other signs may appear, such as rashes and sores on other parts of the body, sore throat, hair falling out in patches, fevers, and headaches. Some people think they have a heat rash or allergy because the rashes do not itch or sting. Again, the symptoms will disappear by themselves, but the disease is still inside the body doing serious damage.

Although the diseased person can still infect his sexual partners for another two to five years, he or she may feel healthy for a time after the second stage. However, from five to twenty years later the disease may reach the brain, heart, or other vital organs and result in death. If these people are not found and treated, one in thirteen will develop heart disease; one in twenty-five will become crippled or insane; one in two hundred will go blind; and one in four will die of the disease.

A pregnant woman should have a blood test early in her pregnancy, for she can give syphilis to the fetus, even after the contagious stage of the disease has passed. Brain damage, deformities, and other problems show up in the eventual baby—if it lives at all.

Gonorrhea

Gonorrhea is also very contagious. It usually shows up in men two to six days after sexual contact with a carrier, but sometimes symptoms do not appear for a month. Usually pus drips from the penis, and there is a burning sensation while urinating. However, between 10 and 20 percent of the male victims show no signs, even though they are spreading the disease and it is damaging their bodies.

Most women (about 80 percent) have no symptoms at all, except possibly a slight vaginal discharge with a burning sensation. A woman may not know she has gonorrhea for weeks, months, or even years after she is infected, and there are no reliable medical tests for it. Most doctors treat all female sexual partners of an infected man, since symptoms may not appear until late in the development of the disease when the germs have already done serious damage.

Untreated gonorrhea is the most prevalent cause of sterility in the United States. It can also cause arthritis and heart trouble. It can go from the vagina to the eyes of a newborn baby, causing blindness. Fortunately, silver nitrate can be put into the eyes of babies at birth to prevent this affliction.

Herpes Genitalis[1]

Herpes genitalis is now the second most common sexually transmitted disease, surpassed in frequency only by gonorrhea. There are an estimated 200,000 to 300,000 cases, with herpes 14 percent as common as gonorrhea in males and 9

[1] This section adapted from C. V. Horos. Herpes Genitalis. In K. Paulsen and R. A. Kuhn (Eds.), *Woman's almanac.* New York: J. B. Lippincott Co. 1975, 21–22.

113

percent as common in females (St. John and Jones, 1977). Herpes is usually spread by vaginal, oral-genital, or anal intercourse with an infected partner, but can also be passed through slight cuts or breaks of the skin. After the virus enters the body, an undetermined period of time (usually six to twenty days) passes before the first symptoms appear. One or several sores resembling fever blisters appear on or around the sexual organs. These blisters become red and very tender, and are painful when touched. Several days after the blisters form, they rupture. This leaves a very painful open sore covered by a yellowish-gray pus. During this stage, the disease is highly contagious and can be passed to other people as well as to other areas of the body. In about a week, a scab forms, often being mistaken for the chancre of syphilis. Some people also have flu-like symptoms (fever, aches) that accompany the sores.

Herpes has been linked to cervical cancer, and can kill newborns. A major problem with herpes is that, like gonorrhea, the symptoms are not easily noticed in women: the blisters usually form in the vagina or cervix. After the original blisters disappear, it is possible to have recurrences for years. Women with an active sex life involving more than one partner are advised to have an internal examination every six months to guard against cervical cancer. Treatment for herpes is still being developed and at the present time there is no cure. Other than antibiotic creams and ointments prescribed by a physician to prevent secondary infections and help reduce pain, most attempts at treatment of herpes are suspected of producing cancer. Aside from noticing whether you or your partner have blisters or pus-covered sores, women are advised to carry condoms and not simply to depend on the male having them. In fact, a recent survey of druggists nationwide (Kushner, 1976) showed that where condoms are openly displayed, 15 percent of the purchasers are women, in contrast to the usual 12 percent.

Curing VD
Gonorrhea and syphilis can be cured quickly—usually with penicillin therapy or antibiotics—if treated in the early stages. A teenager does not need parental consent for diagnosis and treatment even if he or she is a minor (Paul, Pilpel, & Wechsler, 1976). Therefore, he or she should go immediately to a VD clinic, health center, or private doctor if VD is suspected. VD centers test for VD without charge. Usually they will provide free treatment and contact the sexual partners of the infected person.

Self-treatment is almost always useless. Treating sores with a penicillin ointment often kills only the top layers and leaves the germs underneath alive and spreading.

Protection of Others
A VD center will contact the partners of an infected person. By law, government health centers cannot reveal the name of the person who has divulged the names of his sexual partners. Private doctors treat most VD cases, how-

ever, and it is commonly acknowledged that they report only about 20 percent to public authorities. Consequently, most cases are not traced for other possible victims. A person treated by a private doctor should tell his sexual partners that he has the disease so they can get treatment before serious damage occurs.

Prevention and Treatment of Adolescent VD

Dr. Richard Sherer, a leader of a statewide committee for the eradication of venereal disease in California, states: "All the moralizing in the world won't heal this epidemic; we have got to stop pussyfooting and encourage our young people to practice prevention. Talk about abstinence and moral laxity is no longer realistic. . . . Above all we must educate people to the plain fact that the use of prophylactics is now, literally, our only hope" (Holles, 1971).

Encouraging Use of Condoms

The best way to prevent sexually transmitted diseases is not to have sexual relations with someone who might be infected. However, for those teenagers who are sexually active, it makes sense to use a condom to prevent VD. Urinating and washing with soap and water or douching immediately after intercourse may sometimes help, but when used correctly and consistently, the condom is still the only proven preventative method that also has the additional value of being a contraceptive.

Unfortunately, use of the condom is decreasing among young people as the pill becomes more the method of choice. Between 1971 and 1976, pill use among teenage women more than doubled, so that 47 percent of those who had ever used a contraceptive had most recently used the pill in 1976. In the same period, use of the condom decreased by 27 percent among whites and by 55 percent among blacks (Zelnik & Kantner, 1977). Young people are also ignorant about how effective the condom is. In a study of over one thousand Detroit females under eighteen, only 18 percent knew that "rubbers do not break easily." After a program to improve their knowledge, there was marked improvement, but the 31 percent level of correct responses indicated that sizable degrees of ignorance remained (Reichelt and Werley, 1974). In a recent study of 740 high school teenagers, only 36 percent knew that a condom can protect against gonorrhea (Hayes and Littlefield, 1976).

In Darrow's (1974) research of 2,300 clinic attendees in Sacramento ("average" age, twenty-two), it was found that the most common reason for not using condoms was that they "interfere with sex" (26 percent). Attempts to improve the "image" of the condom by direct appeal may be misguided: there is still a need for providing basic facts about the condom and for dealing with more sensitive aspects of condom use. For instance, there are virtually no literature or courses which tell the young person how to use it in the sexual situation without "interfering with sex" or without making the partner feel "diseased." This kind of question must be creatively answered if the condom is to remain an important weapon in the fight against VD.

Articles, books, and pamphlets published for mass distribution need to mention the condom. Of the dozens of pamphlets on venereal disease published prior to 1972, only a few specifically mentioned the use of a condom in reducing the chances of venereal disease. *Venereal Disease—A Self-Instructional Booklet* (UCOM Education, Inc., 1971) talks about VD being spread through sexual contact; yet no mention is made of how to prevent or decrease the chances of catching a venereal disease. Nor does *Modern Sex Education* make any mention of the condom, although there is a slight (less than one-page) section devoted to contraception, as well as a full chapter on venereal disease (Jolian & Jackson, 1967).

Most newspapers and magazines, while printing ads for blatantly pornographic films, refuse to print advertisements on the use of the condom in reducing venereal disease, although these advertisements are discreet. The following letter came from a leading newspaper in response to a request for advertising from a company producing the condom:

> Thank you very much for your letter of March 22 enclosing proposed ads for Youngs Drug Products Corporation.
>
> I regret that the [newspaper] is unable to accept this advertising as a matter of policy.
>
> May we at the same time compliment you on your copy in the interest of education on this serious problem.

Making the Facts Comprehensible

If young people do not understand what they are reading, they are not likely to gain much from the information offered. The publications that have been produced are generally directed to the intellectual teenager and those fluent in English, although there seems to be a general shift in some organizations toward the nonintellectual adolescent. There is a pressing need for written material in Spanish as well as other languages for youths who find it difficult to read English. Material must also be written at a level that the majority of American youth can understand. Adolescents are turned off by highly intellectualized publications. Words such as *prophylactic, coitus, intercourse,* and *ejaculation* are but a few that have no association for some teenagers.

VD Claptrap and *Ten Heavy Facts About Sex,* pamphlets in comic book form designed for the nonintellectual adolescent, are produced by the Institute for Family Research and Education at Syracuse University. These books are an example of nonthreatening literature in language comprehensible to adolescents who don't enjoy reading, or who read poorly. They use the word *rubber* as well as *condom,* and explain the importance of the condom in preventing VD. *VD Claptrap* also includes a section on how to use the condom.

However, the comic books, like the condom advertisements, have met with some strong opposition. The Institute for Family Research and Education at the 1971 New York State Fair was forced to stop distributing *Ten Heavy Facts About Sex* because a state senator sent a protest letter stating the comic book "put thoughts in a teenager's mind that were never there." This "reasonable approach to contemporary sex education for teenagers promptly outstripped, in controversy, the Fair's strip shows (featuring the 'World's Oldest Stripper!') and the John Birch Society's exhibit" (Clinch, 1976).

Increasing numbers of well-researched articles on VD have been appearing in magazines such as *Teen* and *Circus*. A particularly important fact sheet was developed by the Boston Women's Health Book Collective in Somerville, Massachusetts. Called "Preventing Venereal Disease," it takes a no-nonsense approach by recognizing that many young people have more than one partner and that social embarrassment still keeps many people from taking precautions. The following is an excerpt from their pamphlet:[2]

> "No" isn't the only way. If you and your sex partner are anything but 100 percent monogamous this information will be important to you!
>
> There *are* ways to keep from getting VD. It seems that because sex has been considered sinful and VD a kind of punishment for it, the U.S. Public Health system has never adequately researched or publicized methods of VD prevention other than "no sex outside marriage." We are glad to be able to share with you some effective prevention methods. At first, these methods may seem messy or too much of a hassle. But talk over with your sex partner how you could bring one of them into your lovemaking, and probably both of you will end up feeling more at ease.
>
> VD organisms generally enter the body through the warm, moist surfaces (mucous membranes) of the vagina, urethra, anus, or mouth. There are four ways you can prevent them from entering:
>
> 1 Certain birth control products used during vaginal intercourse (for anal intercourse see note).
>
> Available in local drugstores or beauty-aid stores:
> Delfen Foam
> Emko Foam
> Cooper Cream
> Ortho Cream
> Certane Vaginal Jelly
> Preception Gel
> Milex Crescent Jelly
> Ortho-Gynol Jelly
> Koromex A-II Vaginal Jelly
> 2 Other products good for VD prevention but not for birth control:

[2] Excerpted from "Preventing venereal disease." Reprinted with permission from the Boston Women's Health Book Collective, Inc. © 1976.

Lorphyn Vaginal Suppositories
Progonysyl (by prescription only)

3 Condoms (rubbers, safes) used during vaginal and anal intercourse.

4 Washing genitals before and especially after sex.
Men: use soap and water
Women: effectiveness questionable. Use douche (1 TBL vinegar to one quart of water with bag held no higher than waist) *unless* your birth control method involves contraceptive foam, cream or jelly used alone or with a diaphragm. Douching is *not* a method of birth control.

Note: The products listed in 1 and 2 may be good for VD prevention in ANAL SEX also. But the absorption rates in the anus are different from those of the vagina, and no tests as far as we know have been done using these products in the anus. Women: if you are having anal sex as well as vaginal sex, be sure to put the cream, foam or jelly in both places.

None of the above methods is 100% foolproof, so have VD tests every 3–6 months if you are sexually active with more than one partner or have *any* reason to think you might have been exposed to VD.

Making Condoms Available

Condoms, as mentioned earlier, offer effective prevention of venereal disease and should be made easily available to teenagers. Of great interest is the work of Population Services, Inc., which distributes contraceptives by mail, mainly condoms and foam. It also has been refused advertising space in several leading publications.

Free condom distribution programs, such as the OEO-sponsored project in Raleigh, North Carolina, make condoms available in grocery stores, pool halls, drugstores, barber shops, and various places where teenagers hang out. These are of great benefit, not only in the reduction of venereal disease, but also in the prevention of unwanted pregnancy.

Reaching Teenagers with Information

Pamphlets

Information regarding detection, prevention, the importance of early treatment, and where to go for treatment should be easily available. Pamphlets and posters displayed in areas teenagers frequent should provide the telephone number and address of clinics where adolescents can go for help.

Hot Lines

The hot-line service is an excellent way to reach youth without forcing face-to-face contact. "Operation Venus," a Pennsylvania-based hot line in operation for eight years, is staffed by teenagers. Questions may be phoned in toll free by dialing 800–523–1885 or 215–567–6973 for Pennsylvania residents.

The Media

The media, especially TV and radio stations, can play an important role in "spreading the word" to audiences composed largely of youth. "VD Blues" presented nationally on October 9, 1972 on public television, and repeated on April 9, 1973, is an example in the public interest that commercial prime time TV could well emulate. The showing was followed by an invitation to phone questions to a hot line. The original broadcast was believed responsible for more than 200,000 inquiries to local public TV stations from people seeking help and a 50 percent increase in medical treatment for VD cases.

Organized Community Efforts

The New York Alliance for the Eradication of Venereal Disease, the state pharmaceutical society, and the city health department joined in a summer program to alert New York City residents to the VD problem, the means of prevention available, and the location of treatment centers. Teenagers were enlisted to conduct a house-to-house education campaign in selected neighborhoods. Local pharmacists put up displays advertising the neighborhood clinic, distributed free VD booklets in English and Spanish, and matchbooks with the cover "Fight Love Pollution (Venereal Disease)." The media announced a hot-line venereal disease message in both English and Spanish and described the VD program and where help could be obtained. The immediate result was an appreciable increase in the use of the city's VD clinics.

A public information campaign launched in May 1971 by the Onondaga County Board of Health in Syracuse, New York included a telephone hot line for a recorded message on venereal disease, in addition to distributing more than 200,000 pieces of literature about VD. A second VD information program, implemented in May 1971 by the city school system, featured films and a discussion of the VD problem. Both programs emphasized the need for community aid and approval. A series of five local newspaper reports on VD stressed: "As long as hush-hush embarrassment is the typical attitude toward syphilis and gonorrhea, these venereal diseases will continue to flourish among the nation's young. Facts, research, and money are necessary to break the conspiracy of silence that surrounds the disease" (Lawless, 1971). Two months later, reported gonorrhea cases reached a high for the year. A week's total of ninety-two cases was reported, thirty-eight more than in the previous week. The Health Department arranged for two extra clinics, in addition to the regular VD clinics, to be open primarily for the treatment of teenage infectees. Although this increase in reported cases may seem alarming, it can be interpreted as a measure of the program's success; that is, more people sought treatment.

119

Who Can Help?

Parents

Parents can help by learning about sexually transmitted diseases and then teaching their children. Adolescents must know how to recognize the symptoms of VD and where they can go for free medical care (without their parents' consent); out of fear that their parents will find out, adolescents will often delay seeking medical attention. Parents must respect and understand this fear, which in most instances is based on love for the parents.

Doctors

Doctors must continue to report cases of sexually transmitted diseases to health departments. Their understanding and sympathetic attitude can convince youth that the information they give to the medical profession via the health department will remain confidential, that parents will not find out, and that their names will remain anonymous.

Pharmacists

Pharmacists can help by freely distributing accurate and easy-to-read information provided from sources interested in preventing the spread of venereal disease. Many organizations provide such information as a public service. Pharmacists Planning Service, Inc., of Sausalito, California, is such an organization, reaching over 40,000 druggists nationally. In 1978, they sponsored the first National Condom Week, beginning, appropriately enough, on Valentine's Day. Each year, they sponsor a National Family Planning and Venereal Disease Awareness month to promote consciousness-raising projects all over the country. They also develop materials and sponsor health conferences around the world.

Organizations

Schools, churches, and parent groups can conduct coordinated programs to reach youth through educational efforts, while supporting the creation of treatment centers in hospital and community-based clinics.

Teenagers Themselves

Teenagers themselves are often willing participants, acting as outreach workers. Involvement with youth is necessary to achieve long-range goals, as are the continued efforts of community clinics, hospitals, and other groups involved with preventing venereal disease.

The Treatment of Sexually Transmitted Diseases and the Law

Because of the highly communicable nature of sexually transmitted diseases, immediate treatment is imperative, both for the safety of the individual and for the protection of society. If parental consent is required for treatment, a teenager may ignore symptoms rather than tell parents. In 1970, New York State enacted a law that serves as a model in the area of medical care for adolescents exposed to venereal disease. This law provides for mandatory examination and treatment by a public health officer of any person suspected of having VD. A subsequent amendment to the law permits private physicians to treat persons under twenty-one without the consent of parent or guardian. Anyone discovered to have VD by a public health officer is required to submit to treatment. The law prohibits the disclosure of medical records to the parent or guardian of the minor (Hofmann & Shenker, 1970).

Adolescents fear being labeled promiscuous by their own peer group if they are having multiple sex relations. New York State, recognizing this fact, secures the names of people with whom the individual has had sexual relations while keeping the name of the "informant" confidential. The adolescent is thus not only assured of proper treatment, but also confidentiality, both of which are essential if the problem of teenage venereal disease is to be dealt with effectively. Although no states still require parental consent for diagnosis and treatment of sexually transmitted diseases, the laws of some states still do not explicitly recognize the need for confidentiality.

Conclusion

How can we expect adolescents to make responsible decisions if the facts about VD are inaccessible to them? How can we expect sexually active adolescents to prevent exposing themselves to VD if we make it difficult for them to consider, to obtain, and to properly use what is at present their main source of protection—the condom?

Chapter Six

References Center for Disease Control. *VD fact sheet.* Atlanta, 1976.

Darrow, W. W. Attitudes toward condom use and the acceptance of venereal disease prophylactics. In M. A. Redford, G. W. Duncan, & D. J. Prager (Eds.), *The condom: Increasing utilization in the United States.* San Francisco: San Francisco Press, 1974.

Gordon, S. *You would if you loved me.* New York: Bantam Books, 1978.

Hayes, J., & Littlefield, J. H. Venereal disease knowledge in high school seniors. *The Journal of School Health,* 1976, *46* (9), 546–548.

Hofmann, A., & Shenker, I. R. Medical care of adolescents and the law. *New York State Journal of Medicine,* 1970, *70* (20), 2603–2611.

Holles, E. R. New strain of gonorrhea aggravates venereal disease epidemic on West Coast. *New York Times,* 11 April 1971, 53.

Kushner, D. The condom comes out of hiding. *American Druggist,* 1976, *173,* 26.

Lawless, D. Sex educators urged in all school grades. *Syracuse Post-Standard,* 23 July 1971, 5.

Lawless, D. VD cure simple . . . if victims seek treatment. *Syracuse Post-Standard,* 13 May 1971, 4.

Paul, E. W., Pilpel, A. F., & Wechsler, N. Pregnancy, teenagers, and the law. *Family Planning Perspectives,* 1976, *8* (1), 16–21.

Reichelt, P. A., & Werley, H. H. Contraception, abortion, and venereal disease. Teenagers' knowledge and the effect of education. *Family Planning Perspectives,* 1975, *7* (2), 83–88.

St. John, R. K., & Jones, O. G. *Nonreported sexually transmitted diseases.* Paper presented at American Public Health Association Annual meeting, November 1977.

Spence, M. R. Testimony presented to the Sexually Transmitted Diseases Work Group, Health, Education and Welfare, Washington, D.C., January 10, 1978.

VD alarm. *Parade,* 12 November 1978, 19.

White House Conference on Children. *Children and health,* December 1970, 1 (1).

Zelnik, M., & Kantner, J. F. Sexual and contraceptive experience of young unmarried women in the United States, 1976 and 1971. *Family Planning Perspectives,* 1977, *9* (2), 55–71.

Seven

The Religious Perspective

It is no longer sufficient for the churches to state that "sex is good" and is "God's gift to us," both of which statements I firmly believe, if they then proceed to hem sex in with attitudes and restrictions that prevent its full flowering.

Mary S. Calderone, 1974

Most contemporary American values regarding human sexuality derive from religious traditions. The Judeo-Christian ethic, Protestantism, Catholicism, Puritanism, Victorianism, and other social-religious movements provide the historic foundation for contemporary moral standards. One could endlessly debate the new liberalism versus conservatism, sin versus responsible sexual expression, and other points of difference in values. But since these are personal judgments, this chapter will not attempt to establish an "ideal" or preferable theology. Rather, we will provide an overview of recent statements on sexuality by various denominations. We acknowledge our obvious bias favoring separation of church and state.

Organized religion in the United States appears to be in a state of flux. While most religious organizations in the 1960s were quick to emphasize the positive force of human sexuality, the 1970s have seen rigid and sometimes bitter forces within each denomination battling over the specific interpretations of such issues as gay rights, contraception, abortion, and the role of women as clergy.

Most religious leaders acknowledge that they have a long way to go before agreement can be reached on how to cope with critical aspects of the "sexual revolution." Although religious leaders were in a sense caught unprepared by some of the questions posed to them, their responses, in many instances, can be characterized as courageous and visionary.

Human Sexuality—A Positive Force

An evolution in attitudes concerning human sexuality is taking place within the churches, write Minor, Myskens, and Alexander (1971). They point out that the sources of negativism toward sex developed from the Greek philosophy of mind-body dualism that considered sex evil and were thus cultural, rather than biblical. The Bible itself, in the Song of Solomon and many other

125

passages with sexual allusions, indicates a healthy acceptance of the sexual aspect of life. This view of biblical teaching is also shared by Billy Graham (1970): "Far from being prudish, the Bible celebrates sex and its proper use, presenting it as God-created, God-ordained, God-blessed. . . . The Bible makes plain that evil, when related to sex, means not the use of something inherently corrupt but the *mis*use of something pure and good."

The General Assembly of the United Presbyterian Church, in a report titled "Sexuality and the Human Community" (1970), notes, "The church has always attested [Christ's] full humanity. Therefore, one cannot imagine that he was unaware of his own sexuality, and there is no evidence that he denied this aspect of his humanity in the manner of some of his later followers." The report goes on to say that the moral significance of sex depends on whether it is alienating or reconciling, and that Jesus condemned most strongly those who misused each other, not the "sexually miscreant." Similarly, David R. Mace (1970) of the Society of Friends points out that Jesus was understanding and compassionate about sexual misdemeanors. By stating that the harlots would precede the publicans into the Kingdom of Heaven, Jesus was "clearly trying to correct a distorted religious judgment of his time (and of later times) which singled out sexual transgression for disproportionately violent attack."

A passage from the United Church of Christ's text *Approaching Christian Marriage* to some degree reconciles one of Freud's fundamental theories about sex with Christian teaching. W. Clark Ellzey (1964) wrote that sex is not something to be ashamed of. God gave us two basic drives: sex and hunger. Hunger makes us eat for self-preservation. "Sex drives us to seek self-realization through intimate companionship with another in love, and then through the relationships of the family, the community, and society in general."

Rabbi Robert Gordis (1978) gives a Jewish perspective of human sexuality:

> Since God created man with his entire complement of impulses, sex is a manifestation of the Divine. It is not to be glorified as an end in itself, as is paganism, or in the exaggerations of romantic love. Hence, the Bible and the Talmud are frank and outspoken in dealing with the sexual component of human experience. The pages of our classic literature are free from both obscenity and false modesty, from pornography and prudishness, which are essentially two sides of the same coin.

More and more religious thinkers are perceiving sexuality as natural and desirable. Gordis and others believe that sexuality is not antireligious but can have religious significance itself—a viewpoint far removed from the old ideas of sin and shame.

Sex Education

From our point of view one of the most significant documents of this decade has been *Human Sexuality—New Directions in American Catholic Thought* (1977).[1] The study, commissioned by the Catholic Theological Society of America, details its position on sex education:

> Sex education, acknowledged as necessary in a survey of the Sacred Congregations for the Clergy, the Religious, and for Catholic Education (April 1973) must extend beyond that called for in the home and permeate all areas of educational development. We acknowledge that there are powerful forces at work in the United States and Canada today that would curtail such programs, pleading that they are out of harmony with Christian principles and practice and insisting that such education belongs in the home only. We would point out that such education in the home does not generally take place (as attested to by numerous studies), and that it is sorely needed to stem the tide of hedonism and to instill wholesome attitudes and values regarding human sexuality.
>
> Programs of education consonant with the understanding of sexuality presented in this report call for guidelines that respect the Christian concept of human dignity and the goal of human destiny to which all persons are called in Jesus Christ. Because sexuality must not be divorced from a holistic view of life, sex education must grow out of life experiences. It must be adapted to the age and readiness of the individual and be appropriate to the life situation of the child or the adult. It must be realistic, challenging, and inspiring.
>
> Where programs of education are given to supplement and/or correct the information provided in the home, an effort must be made to awaken respect for life and reverence for love. Such programs should be of a nature to prepare every human being for an experience of sexuality that fosters "creative growth toward integration" within the framework of a chosen life-style.[2]

The Presbyterian Church in the United States, the Associate Reformed

---

[1] We are well aware that the hierarchy of the Roman Catholic Church has generally not accepted the principles in this volume. However, it does appear to be closer to Catholic practice inasmuch as Catholic use of birth control is not significantly different from that of other religious groups (Westoff & Jones, 1977). And, not only do the majority of Catholics favor the Supreme Court decision on abortion, but Catholic women also avail themselves of abortion to a *greater* extent than they are represented in the population (National Abortion Rights Action League; Steinem, 1977).

[2] Reprinted with permission from The Paulist Press.

127

Presbyterian Church, the Cumberland Presbyterian Church, the Moravian Church in America, and the Evangelical Covenant Church of America (Sexuality and the Human Community, 1970) have issued a sex education curriculum based on the following principle: "Since a Christian ethic of sex requires a knowledge of both the theology and the biology of sex, opportunity should be provided within the church for persons of all ages to be given appropriate information and to know Christian attitudes toward sex." The Presbyterian report expresses concern about the effect on children in our culture of "commercial corruptions of sex" and "erotic stimuli." The report states that it is a "matter of the highest importance in the Christian formation of children that they be equipped with a realistic understanding and appreciation of their own and others' sexuality."

The Unitarian Universalist Association has published a very frank and objective multimedia sex curriculum, which includes films, records, and books, and discusses such topics as homosexuality, masturbation, and changing male-female roles. (See a "Selected List of Resources" in the appendix for texts published by other denominations.)

Nonmarital Sex

Sexual expression within the context of marriage has traditionally been the only accepted mode of behavior in Western societies. In the last several decades, pre- and extramarital sex have been widely discussed. A major study by the United Church of Christ (1977) titled *Human Sexuality: A Preliminary Study* went beyond the debate of exactly which behaviors are acceptable and which are not by seeking to establish one morality consistent with all forms of human sexual expression:

> *First, love's justice requires a single standard* rather than a double standard. This should mean that there is not one ethic for males and another for females, one for the unmarried and another for the married, one for the young and another for the old, nor one for those who are heterosexually oriented and another for those oriented toward their same sex. The same basic considerations of love ought to apply to all.
>
> *Second, the physical expression* of one's sexuality in relation to another ought to be *appropriate to the level of loving commitment* in the relationship. Human relationships exist on a continuum—from the fleeting and casual to the lasting and intense, from the relatively impersonal to the deeply personal. So also, physical expressions exist on a continuum—from varied types of eye contact and casual touches, to varied forms of embraces and kisses, to bodily caresses and genital petting, to foreplay and genital intercourse. In some way or another, we inevitably express our sexuality in every relationship. The morality of that expression, particularly its more physical expression, will depend

128

upon its appropriateness to the shared level of commitment and the nature of the relationship.

Third, genital sexual expression ought to be evaluated in terms of the basic elements of a moral decision, informed by love:

Motive (why should I do, or not do, this?). Each genital act should be motivated by love. This means love for one's partner. It also, however, means a healthy love of oneself. Infusing both of those loves is love for God, whose good gift of sexuality is an invitation to communion.

Intention (at what am I aiming in this act?). Each genital act should aim at human fulfillment and wholeness, which are God's loving intentions for all persons. In marriage the procreation of children may also be the intent of certain times of intercourse, but statistically those times will be in a small minority, and even then the desire for children is part of our quest for wholeness, for wholeness is known in relationships. Fulfillment also requires sexual pleasure. Good genital sex is highly erotic, warm, intimate, playful, and immensely pleasurable. At times it can also be almost mystical in its possibilities of communication and communion. In each of these ways it can contribute to wholeness, a deep sense of being at one with oneself, with the other, and with God.

The Act (are certain sexual acts inherently right and good, and are certain others inherently wrong and bad?). It is notoriously difficult to label whole classes of acts as inherently right or wrong, since the moral quality of any act hinges so heavily upon what is being communicated by it in the particular context. What are our intentions and what are their effects? We can surely say that sexual acts which are characterized by loving motives and intentions will exclude all acts which are coercive, debasing, harmful, or cruel to another.

Consequences (what will most likely result from this act, and in what ways will I be willingly accountable?). Responsibility for the results of a sexual act is also a mark of love. This involves responsibility to the ongoing relationship, its commitments, and its promises. It means responsibility to the partner's emotional health insofar as that is linked with a given sexual act. If a child is conceived and born, it means responsibility for nurture. Responsibility also means that this particular act must be weighed in terms of its effect on the well-being of the wider human community. Will it endanger the love and justice by which communities must exist?[3]

[3] From *Human sexuality: A preliminary study* by The United Church of Christ. Copyright © 1977 United Church Board for Homeland Ministries and the United Church Press.

129

Commenting on "the relationship of the unmarried," the Presbyterian Church in Canada (1972) noted:

> Like anyone else the unmarried are offered a freedom and love of Christ. Their relationships with others ought to be free from shame, pretense, and anxiety, and to be characterized by acceptance and joy. They also live under the obligations which derive from the realities of their situation: they are not their own, but God's; they are to understand that sexual intercourse is part of a whole picture which involves lifelong commitment and a one-flesh relationship, and these only can be realized within lawful marriage.

Masturbation

In his book for teenagers, Rabbi Gittelsohn (1965) writes: "The greatest possible harm from masturbation springs from feelings of guilt about it, and such feelings are unwarranted."

Eugene Kennedy (1971), a Roman Catholic educator, notes:

> There is no doubt that masturbation has been considered a sin throughout the history of the Catholic Church . . . while this concern is laudable, it has been based on an undeveloped appreciation of man's sexuality and the overall pattern of human growth. I think we understand man better now and we also have some new opinions about sin. . . . I do not think the categories of moral right and wrong are the proper ones to use in trying to understand the meaning of masturbation.

Kennedy says that knowing whether or not masturbation is sinful does not help us understand its significance. He does not advocate masturbation as an "outlet to sexual tension" or any simplistic moral relativity.

In *Sexuality and the Human Community* (1970), the Presbyterians make a cautious, but significant statement on the church's view of masturbation:

> Since masturbation is often one of the earliest pleasurable sexual experiences which is identifiably genital, we consider it essential that the church, through its teachings and through the attitudes it encourages in Christian homes, contribute to a healthy understanding of this experience which will be free of guilt and shame. The ethical significance of masturbation depends entirely on the context in which it takes place. Therefore, we can see no objection to it when it occurs as a normal developmental experience or as a deliberately chosen alternative to inappropriate heterosexual activity. We can see valid ethical questions raised about masturbatory practices which become or which inhibit normal heterosexual development. In most instances, however,

130

we believe that masturbation is morally neutral and psychologically benign.

Birth Control

In *Human Sexuality—New Directions in American Catholic Thought* (1977),
the Catholic Theological Society presents its position about artificial methods
of contraception:

> As a general principle to guide parents in the moral evalua-
> tion of the various available methods, Vatican II suggests the
> following norm:
>
> Therefore when there is a question of harmonizing
> conjugal love with the responsible transmission of life, the
> moral aspect of any procedure does not depend solely on
> sincere intentions or on an evaluation of motives. It must
> be determined by objective standards. These, *based on
> the nature of the human person and his acts,* preserve the
> full sense of mutual self-giving and human procreation in
> the context of true love. Such a goal cannot be achieved
> unless the virtue of conjugal chastity is sincerely practiced.
>
> The insistence that the total nature of the human per-
> son and his actions constitute the norm for evaluating the
> morality of the method to be employed marks a significant
> development from earlier teaching of the Church which
> focused this judgment solely on the nature of the act. If one
> is to be true to this teaching of Vatican II, approved by the
> Holy Father and by bishops throughout the world, one can-
> not judge methods of contraception as immoral or unaccept-
> able solely for physical or biological reasons that flow from
> the nature of the act itself. Moral judgment must always
> reflect a concern for the total well-being of the person. It
> must be made in terms of the value conflicts and realistic
> possibilities that confront people in their concrete life situa-
> tion. Conscience must play a crucial role in honestly assess-
> ing the objective considerations on which the decision is to
> be based. The decision should not be purely subjective, rely-
> ing on a false sincerity that refuses to face the objective
> evidence. Parents need to consider honestly and carefully
> the medical, psychological, economic, and religious implica-
> tions of each method in regard to their total well-being
> before reaching a decision.
>
> Such an interpretation of the teaching of Vatican II on
> marriage recognizes that there are times when the decision
> to use artificial methods of contraception is both morally
> responsible and justified. In such instances, special consid-
> eration should be given to the particular effects a given
> method may have on the overall nature and well-being of the
> persons involved (p. 115).

The report goes on to list vital medical, psychological, personal, and religious considerations involved in the decision of what method of birth control, if any, should be used. These findings are decidedly more liberal than the official proclamations of Pope Paul VI (1968), who wrote in his encyclical *Humanae Vitae:*

> That teaching, often set forth by the magisterium, is founded upon the inseparable connection, willed by God and unable to be broken by man on his own initiative, between the two meanings of the conjugal act: the unitive meaning and the procreative meaning. Indeed, by its intimate structure, the conjugal act, while most closely uniting husband and wife, capacitates them for the generation of new lives, according to laws inscribed in the very being of man and woman. By safeguarding both these essential aspects, the unitive and the procreative, the conjugal act preserves in its fullness the sense of true mutual love and its ordination toward man's most high calling to parenthood.
>
> To use this divine gift destroying, even if only partially its meaning and its purpose, is to contradict the nature both of man and woman and of their most intimate relationship, and therefore it is to contradict also the plan of God and his will.

As with most sensitive issues confronting church leaders today, different denominations can hold strikingly different views. The Christian Life Commission of the Southern Baptist Convention (1970) uses the "population explosion" as its premise, stating, "The Christian faith stresses the responsibility of believers to help reduce suffering and pain. They are to love and to minister to all people. Since overpopulation causes widespread suffering, Christians should help reduce the world's birth rate." The statement recommends to individuals and families: "Limit your family to two children unless you adopt the others. Practice consistent birth control (and) support family planning clinics. Make sure such services are available to all." The Baptist commission also suggests that its members "be open to new insight on controversial subjects related to population limitation: sex and family life education in public schools, abortion, voluntary sterilization, contraceptives to the unmarried, revisions of tax policies at various levels." It recommends that churches "sponsor family planning clinics or make church facilities available for such meetings and conduct counseling sessions for engaged couples with an emphasis on the responsibility of family limitation."

The United Presbyterian Church Report contains a similar view and adds that without implying approval of nonmarital sex, the church recommends making contraceptives available to unmarried persons (A Synoptic, n.d.).

Abortion

Of all the issues involving human sexuality, none has aroused such intense emotions as abortion. The controversy hinges on the definition of when life actually begins. Proabortion or prochoice forces contend that life per se does not begin until viability, when the fetus is no longer dependent on the mother. Antiabortion forces, on the other hand, believe that life begins at the moment of conception.

Prior to the landmark 1973 Supreme Court decision making abortion a legal decision between a woman and her physician, many religious organizations had issued statements on abortion. For instance, the Washington State Council of Churches stated that since illegal abortions were widely tolerated and law-breakers involved were "rarely prosecuted" and since this "breeds cynicism about the law" the council resolved to "support a reform of the current state abortion laws and that a special committee be appointed by the council's president to study the Citizen's Committee for reform of the Abortion Law Bill" (A Compendium, n.d.). The United Church of Christ's Council for Christian Social Action (September 20, 1970) took a similar position. On May 31, 1968 the American Baptist Convention issued a statement calling for legalization of abortion by request before the twelfth week, specified reasons for legalization after this period, and encouraged their churches "to provide sympathetic and realistic counseling on family planning and abortion" (A Compendium, n.d.). The Southern Baptist Commission (1970) wrote, "There may be physical, social or emotional factors in a particular case indicating that the continuation of pregnancy would destroy more than it would preserve," and the United Methodist Church urged that abortion prohibition be removed from the criminal code and made simply a medical question (Responsible Parenthood, 1972). The Presbyterians also noted that historically abortion was not officially forbidden by the Roman Catholic Church until 1869, except for a three-year period in the sixteenth century. The postbiblical rabbinical view is that abortion "is not specifically forbidden in the Bible or the Talmud" (Sexuality and the Human Community, 1970).

Prior to and following the 1973 Supreme Court decision, many national religious organizations issued the following statements on abortion:[4]

The Abortion Debate

American Baptist Churches—Convention—June 2, 1968

> "Because Christ calls us to affirm the freedom of persons and sanctity of life, we recognize that abortion should be a matter of responsible personal decision."

---

[4] Reprinted with permission from *The Journal of Current Social Issues*, 1978, *15* (1), 74–75.

American Friends Service Committee, Inc.—Board of Directors—October 31, 1969

"Mindful that it does not speak for all Friends, . . . [the Board of Directors] arrived at the view that it is far better to end an unwanted pregnancy than to encourage the evils resulting from forced pregnancy and childbirth. . . . We believe that no woman should be forced to bear an unwanted child."

American Jewish Congress—Biennial Convention—April, 1976

". . . expresses its total support for the decisions of the United States Supreme Court of January 1973. . . . We respect the religious and conscientious scruples of those who reject the practice of abortion. However, to the extent that they would embody those scruples in law binding on all, we oppose them."

The American Lutheran Church—Seventh General Convention—October 14, 1974

". . . The American Lutheran Church accepts the possibility that an induced abortion may be a necessary option in individual human situations. Each person needs to be free to make this choice in light of each individual situation."

Central Conference of American Rabbis—June, 1975

"We affirm the legal right of a family or a woman to determine on the basis of their or her own religious or moral values whether or not to terminate a particular pregnancy. We reject all constitutional amendments which would abridge or circumscribe this right."

Christian Church (Disciples of Christ)—General Assembly—August, 1975

". . . affirm the principle of individual liberty, freedom of individual conscience, and sacredness of life for all persons . . . Respect differences in religious beliefs concerning abortion and oppose, in accord with the principle of religious liberty, any attempt to legislate a specific religious opinion or belief concerning abortion upon all Americans . . ."

The Church of Jesus Christ of Latter-Day Saints

"The Church opposes abortion and counsels its members not to submit to, perform, nor abet an abortion except in the rare cases where, in the opinion of competent medical counsel, the life or good health of the mother is seriously in danger or where the pregnancy was caused by rape and produces serious emotional trauma in the mother. Even then it should be done only after consulting with the local presiding priesthood authority and after receiving divine confirmation through prayer."

Church of the Brethren—Annual Conference—1972

". . . The Brethren ideal upholds the sacredness of human life and . . . abortion should be accepted as an option only where all other possible alternatives will lead to greater destruction of human life and spirit. . . . Laws regarding abortion should embody protection of human life, protection of freedom of moral choice, and availability of good medical care. . . ."

Episcopal Church—65th General Convention—1976

". . . the position of this Church, stated . . . in 1967 which declared support for the 'termination of pregnancy' particularly in those cases where 'physical or mental health of the mother is threatened seriously, or where there is substantial reason to believe that the child would be born badly deformed in mind or body, or where the pregnancy has resulted from rape or incest,' is reaffirmed. . . . expresses its unequivocal opposition to any legislation on the part of the national or state governments which would abridge or deny the right of individuals to reach informed decisions in this matter and to act upon them."

Lutheran Church in America—Fifth Biennial Convention—June 25–July 2, 1970

"Since the fetus is the organic beginning of human life, the termination of its development is always a serious matter. Nevertheless, a qualitative distinction must be made between its claims and the rights of a responsible person made in God's image who is in living relationships with God and other human beings. . . . On the basis of the evangelical ethic, a woman or couple may decide responsibly to seek an abortion."

National Association of Laity—The Assembly Annual Convention—June 24, 1973

". . . affirms the sanctity of life," asks church "to support woman . . . in a decision not to abort"—"affirms the right of individuals to hold opposing views"—"rejects . . . attempt to force a moral judgment on others."

National Conference of Catholic Bishops—1970

"The child in the womb is human. Abortion is an unjust destruction of human life and morally that is murder. Society has no right to destroy this life. Even the expectant mother has no such right. The law must establish every possible protection for the child before and after birth."

Administrative Conference—1973 ". . . a constitutional amendment is now the only viable means to correct the disastrous legal situation created by the Supreme Court's rulings on abortion."

National Council of Jewish Women—1969, Reaffirmed 1975

"It is resolved . . . To promote public understanding that abortion is an individual right and to work to eliminate any obstacles that limit this right."

National Federation of Temple Sisterhoods—Biennial Assembly—November, 1975

". . . affirms . . . strong support for the right of a woman to obtain legal abortion, under conditions now outlined in the 1973 decision of the United States Supreme Court. . . .Only by vigorously supporting this individual right to choose can we also ensure that every woman may act according to the religious and ethical tenets to which she adheres."

Presbyterian Church in the U.S.—General Assembly—1970

"Induced abortion is the willful destruction of the fetus. Therefore, the decision to terminate a pregnancy should never be made lightly or in haste. . . . Medical intervention should be made available to all who desire and qualify for it, not just to those who can afford preferential treatment. . ."

The Reformed Church in America—General Synod—June, 1975

". . . To use, or not to use, legal abortion should be a carefully considered decision of all the persons involved, made prayerfully in the love of Jesus Christ. . . . Christians and the Christian community should play a supportive role for persons making a decision about or utilizing abortion."

Reorganized Church of Jesus Christ of Latter Day Saints—Published by the First Presidency—February, 1974

"We affirm the right of the woman to make her own decision regarding the continuation or termination of problem pregnancies. Preferably this decision should be made in cooperation with her companion and in consultation with a physician, qualified minister, or professional counselor."

Southern Baptist Convention—June, 1977

". . . we call on Southern Baptists and all citizens of the nation to work to change those attitudes and conditions which encourage many people to turn to abortion as a means of birth control . . . we also affirm our conviction about the limited role of government in dealing with matters relating to abortion, and support the right of expectant mothers to the full range of medical services and personal counseling for the preservation of life and health."

Union of American Hebrew Congregations—General Assembly—November, 1975

"The UAHC reaffirms its strong support for the right of a woman to obtain a legal abortion on the constitutional grounds enunciated by the Supreme Court in its 1973 decision . . . we express our confidence in the ability of the woman to exercise her ethical and religious judgment in making her decision."

Unitarian Universalist Association and Unitarian Universalist Women's Federation—General Assembly—June, 1977

"We affirm the right of each woman to make the decisions concerning her own body and future and we stress the responsibilities and long-term commitment involved in the choice of parenthood. . . ."

United Church of Christ—Eleventh General Synod—July, 1977

"RESOLVED: that the Eleventh General Synod affirms the right of women to freedom of choice with regard to pregnancy expressed by the Eighth General Synod and interpreted as a constitutional right in the

136

January 22, 1973 decisions of the Supreme Court which remove the legal restrictions on medical termination of pregnancy through the second trimester."

United Methodist Church—General Conference—1976
"Our belief in the sanctity of unborn human life makes us reluctant to approve abortion. But we are equally bound to respect the sacredness of the life and well-being of the mother, for whom devastating damage may result from an unacceptable pregnancy. . . . We support the legal option of abortion under proper medical procedures . . . a decision concerning abortion should be made after thorough and thoughtful consideration by the parties involved, with medical and pastoral counsel."

United Methodist Church, Women's Division—April, 1975
"We believe deeply that all should be free to express and practice their own moral judgment on the matter of abortion. . . . We affirm our belief in freedom of conscience on this matter . . . where there is no religious or moral consensus in our society, the attempt to embody one particular moral viewpoint in the U.S. Constitution does serious injury to our cherished freedom of religious belief and conscience."

United Presbyterian Church, USA—184th General Assembly—May, 1972
". . . the General Assembly . . . declares that women should have full freedom of personal choice concerning the completion or termination of their pregnancies and that the artificial or induced termination of pregnancy, therefore, should not be restricted by law, except that it be performed under the direction and control of a properly licensed physician."

United Synagogues of America—Biennial Convention—1975
". . . affirms once again its position that 'abortions involve very serious psychological, religious, and moral problems, but the welfare of the mother must always be our primary concern' and urges its congregations to oppose any legislative attempts to weaken the force of the Supreme Court's decisions through constitutional amendments. . ."

Women of the Episcopal Church—Triennial Meeting—1973
"Whereas the Church stands for the exercise of freedom of conscience by all and is required to fight for the right of everyone to exercise the conscience, therefore, be it resolved that the decision of the U.S. Supreme Court allowing women to exercise their own conscience in the matter of abortion be endorsed by the Church, and . . . that the Church provide all possible support and counseling to persons faced with this decision."

Women's League for Conservative Judaism—1972—Reaffirmed at Convention, 1974
"National Women's League believes that freedom of choice as to birth control and abortion is inherent in the civil rights of women."

There are, however, still many opponents of abortion who are actively campaigning to make it illegal. As a result of judicial actions and congressional mandates, Medicaid funding was cut off in 1978 for all abortion except those where the life of the mother would be endangered if the fetus were carried to term, or those involving rape or incest. Even prior to this decision, however, such organizations as the Committee for a Human Life Amendment began to lobby for a constitutional convention at which Congress would adopt an amendment to the U.S. Constitution prohibiting elective abortion. On October 23, 1977, *The New York Times* reported, "The Committee for a Human Life Amendment receives direct support from the National Conference of Catholic Bishops, as well as local Roman Catholic dioceses and archdioceses. But the anti-abortion movement in general, including the committee, cuts across spiritual lines, attracting support from Orthodox Jews, Mormons, Black Muslims, Jehovah's Witnesses, many Baptists and other conservative Protestant sects."[5]

Homosexuality

Our position on homosexuality is included in chapter 11. For those who wish to pursue the religious perspective, an important review of the church and homosexuality appears in the *Journal of Current Social Issues* (Sex Is Aweful, 1978). In our view the most significant book on this subject is *The Church and the Homosexual* by the Roman Catholic priest Father John McNeill (1976).

Women in Religion

Neither the Catholic nor Mormon Churches allow women to become priests. However, the Episcopal Church has begun ordaining women priests amidst a storm of controversy that is causing some congregations to secede. The role of women in the church increasingly has become a legitimate theological issue.

Religions are encountering the same questioning of traditional sex roles with which other institutions have come face to face. The patriarchal societies where men were the providers, and also attended to intellectual and political concerns, are passing. In a society in which making a living no longer depends mainly on physical strength and where women are learning the lessons of equality and opportunity, however, even the essence of canon law and spiritual enlightenment have come under the influence of women's liberation.

The Role of Religious Organizations in the Community

By and large, the religious organizations that represent the majority of this country's population favor an open acceptance of healthy sexuality and a more understanding attitude toward controversial issues related to human sexuality. School officials no longer can reasonably blame evasive or nonexistent approaches to sex education on religious organizations.

[5] © 1971 by The New York Times Company. Reprinted by permission.

How can the churches respond to the needs of youth? Although we explore this issue elsewhere (chapter 10, "Current Innovations and Suggestions for Creative Action"), probably the most important action religious groups can take is to form alliances with local civic groups interested in responsible sex education for their youngsters and to urge repeal of legislation against sex education.

Conclusion

A sampling of religious viewpoints has been presented. Some of the pamphlets and books prepared by major religious denominations are included in the "Selected List of Resources" for readers who wish to pursue a more comprehensive study.

Sex, in and of itself, is not moral or immoral. Significant divergences of opinion about sex education however should be discussed, for it is the responsibility of individuals, their families, and their religious groups to interpret the moral issues involved. It is one thing to be moral—it is another to be moralistic, which we see as an attempt to impose one's own view on everyone. More specifically, it is society's responsibility to discuss vital information along with theological tenets. In this context, we support the Methodist statement: "All children have the right to a full sexual education, appropriate to their state of development that utilizes the best educational techniques and insights" (Social Principles, 1972).

References A compendium of statements on abortion by denominations and church-related agencies. Compiled by the Coordinator of Family Ministries, National Council of Churches, 475 Riverside Drive, New York, N.Y. 10027.

A synoptic of recent denomination statements on sexuality, by William Genné, Coordinator of Family Ministries, National Council of Churches, Department of Educational Development, 475 Riverside Drive, New York, N.Y. 10027.

Abortion foes press drive, buoyed by growing support. *New York Times,* 23 October 1971, 1.

Calderone, M. S. *Sexuality and human values.* New York: Association Press, 1974.

Christian Life Commission of the Southern Baptist Convention. *Issues and answers—population explosion.* Nashville: Christian Life Commission, 1970.

Ellzey, W. C. *Approaching Christian marriage.* St. Louis: United Church Press, 1964.

Gittelsohn, R. B. *Consecrated unto me.* New York: Union of Hebrew Congregations, 1965.

Gordis, R. *Love and sex: A modern Jewish perspective.* New York: Farrar, Straus, and Giroux, 1978.

Graham, B. What the Bible says about sex. *Readers Digest,* May 1970.

Human sexuality: A preliminary study. New York: United Church Press, 1977.

Human sexuality—New directions in American Catholic thought. New York: Paulist Press, 1977.

Interfaith statement on sex education. Released by the National Council of Churches, Commission on Marriage and Family; the Synagogue Council of America, Committee on Family; and the United States Catholic Conference, Family Life Bureau. New York: National Council of Churches, 1968.

Kennedy, E. *What a modern Catholic believes about sex.* Chicago: The Thomas More Press, 1971.

Mace, D. *The Christian response to the sexual revolution.* Nashville: Abingdon Press, 1970.

McNeill, J. *The church and the homosexual.* Kansas City: Sheed, Andrews, and McMeel, 1976.

Minor, H. W., Myskens, J. B., & Alexander, M. N. *Sex education—the schools and the churches.* Richmond: John Knox Press, 1971.

National Abortion Rights Action League, 825 Fifteenth St., N.W., Washington, D.C. 20005.

Pope Paul VI. *Humanae vitae.* Rome: The Vatican, 25 July 1968.

Presbyterian Church in Canada. *Marriage and divorce.* Ontario, Canada: Presbyterian Church, 50 Wynford Dr., Don Mills, M3C 1J7, 1972.

Responsible parenthood. A statement adopted by the General Conference Meeting of the United Methodist Church, Atlanta, April 1972.

Sex is aweful. *Journal of Current Social Issues,* 1978, *15* (1), (entire issue).

Sexuality and the human community. New York: Office of the General Assembly, 475 Riverside Dr., New York, N.Y. 10027, 1970.

Social principles of the United Methodist Church. Presented to the General Conference Meeting, Atlanta, April 1972.

Steinem, G. Abortion alert. *Ms.,* 1977, *6* (5), 118.

United Church of Christ. *Human sexuality: A preliminary study.* New York, 1977, 103–105.

Westoff, C. F., & Jones, E. F. The secularization of U.S. Catholic birth control practices. *Family Planning Perspectives,* 1977, *9* (5), 203–207.

141

Eight

Sex Education
for Youth
with Handicaps

People with disabilities often have problems expressing their sexuality. Sex education is important for them because handicapped youth are especially vulnerable and easily exploited. Exceptional children, whether retarded, handicapped, emotionally disturbed, or learning disabled, have normal impulses and desires. These children need sex education as much as, if not more than, any other group.

As Medora S. Bass (1970) states:

> Today 95 percent of the retarded are living in the community, and they are often the most difficult to reach with birth control services and sex education programs. Many of the teenage retarded are dropping out of school, pregnant. . . . Society expects the retarded to adopt socially acceptable behavior and to control their sexual impulses, yet society offers them almost no training to handle sex in a responsible manner. Few schools have family-life sex education for the special class student, and it is particularly difficult for parents of the retarded to tell their children about "the facts of life."

In our many years of experience with handicapped children, we have learned to listen very carefully to the messages of both parents and children and not to be overly reassuring about permanently handicapping conditions. Retardation, blindness, or neurological impairment represent permanent life-long strains and tensions in families.

It is insensitive to "preach" to handicapped youth and their parents that we all have handicaps and then point to Einstein, Edison, and Churchill as leading examples of those who made good. The plain fact is that a few will successfully cope with their disabilities, no matter what we do. We must address ourselves to the millions of parents and individuals with handicaps who suffer a great deal. What we have learned is that it is compassionate and sensitive to discourage people from being heroic in somebody else's situation.

This chapter was written in collaboration with Leslie Weiser, who has worked with handicapped children and their families as a school psychologist in Massachusetts. He is currently a doctoral candidate at Syracuse University.

Sex Education Is Important for Persons with Disabilities Too

Parents and professionals do not have to be convinced that young people with disabilities need more opportunities to meet people and make friends. These young people can miss a great deal if their disability limits opportunities for social interaction.

For instance, being unfamiliar with the ordinary obscenities that young people use can make a disabled person the brunt of coarse jokes. People with disabilities have trouble enough without additionally having to suffer the consequences of not being well informed.

Development of Sexual Identity

Sexuality is a part of every person's life. The youngest infants are sexual beings who delight in their own bodies and respond with great pleasure to the closeness and caresses of parents and siblings. As they continue to grow and to learn, children begin to develop a more detailed sexual identity which encompasses not only the physical attributes of their gender, but a broader appreciation of human relationships, including the right of each individual to healthy, nonexploitative sexual expression.

It is not easy to come of age today in America, and it is particularly difficult for children and young people who have handicaps or disabilities. If disabled youngsters are thought not to have sexual needs or desires, or if the idea that they do is intolerable to the larger society, information about sexuality will become increasingly restricted for them. Why tell them what they need not know or must not find out? And what ignorance cannot prevent, negative attitudes and vastly limited opportunities for performance ultimately will. Children from whom sexual information is kept secret, who are discouraged from asking questions, scolded for experimentation, shamed for being found out, and denied both the privacy and the social opportunities to explore their natural sexuality, will probably suffer more than normal adolescents under the same circumstances. In sum, to deny the sexuality of handicapped youth is to burden them further. It is not a kindness to structure their lives so as to close off the entire area of sexuality; it is handicapping them a second time.

Sexuality for Handicapped Persons

In her excellent book, *Entitled to Love—The Sexual and Emotional Needs of the Handicapped,* Wendy Greengross (1976) writes:

> Today we are living in an almost totally sex-oriented world . . . but if you are permanently disabled, physically or mentally, partially or severely, then to a greater or lesser degree you find yourself rejected as a nonparticipant. Society, by and large, just cannot cope with the idea of the disabled having the same emotional needs and desires as the rest of the population. And by society I do not mean just the ordinary able-bodied person who has little or no contact

144

with his handicapped neighbor: what is more shocking and more serious is to find this attitude widespread amongst those who are intimately involved through their treatment and care of the disabled in their homes or in residential situations.

In our society you score no points for being handicapped. Every person who is handicapped has to struggle in order to make it, and making it means having friends, leisure interests, and working toward or at a job you want to do later in adult life. Making it is also feeling loved, lovable, sexual, and marriageable.

We strongly encourage those who work with handicapped adolescents to include in their treatment programs information and skills that will encourage them to accept responsibility for their lives and their sexual activities. Sexual health is inseparable from total health. The first step is to recognize the universal right to full and responsible sexual expression commensurate with an individual's age, development, and capabilities. For a young child, exploration of his own body and the discovery of pleasurable sensation are appropriate and healthful expressions of sexuality. For a seriously disabled adult who could not cope with pregnancy and childrearing, having a child would be inappropriate.

What most commonly stands in the way of a disabled individual's successful social and sexual adjustment is not so much the nature of the handicap, as it is his or her self-image, which reflects his or her ability to socialize and to be productive. To this end, information is a first and most powerful ally. It is a sad and dangerous mistake to protest that disabled youngsters have enough to do to learn to read and do arithmetic. Perhaps more than their normal peers, disabled adolescents need to understand that with or without arithmetic, they are important and valued members of the larger society and, among a smaller group, considered attractive, interesting, and desirable individuals.

For those whose access to certain kinds of success has been arbitrarily and permanently blocked, for those whose learning skills will never carry them into law, medicine, music, or science, for those whose uncooperative bodies will never accept discipline or grace, success and satisfaction in personal relationships takes on heightened importance. There is little left for one who has cause to feel permanently outside the circle of things that matter. In its broadest sense, sexuality has to do with the full range of personal relationships, with physical and emotional ties and the problems involved therein. Education for sexuality is vital for all youth, but particularly for the disabled, who may be less adept at separating out fact from nonsense in the highly charged sexual messages in the media and other unreliable sources of sex information.

Their true need is for knowledge, not for protection, and for as much freedom and independence as their impairment permits. The disabled or handicapped also must be taught about love, conception, contraception, and

145

venereal disease. They must also learn to take chances and play the odds like everyone else (Gordon, 1976; 1977).

Just What Is Sex Education?

Definitions, statements, or descriptions of "sex education" vary extensively. Parents, teachers, counselors, and other educators need to be aware of their own, as well as other, definitions. In its broadest sense, "sex education" can be viewed as an exploration process involving a dialogue with people concerning their relationship with other human beings.

Every handicapped individual has a self-concept that is, to varying degrees, fused to his or her sex and consequently important to their development as a man or a woman. The sex of an individual is related not so much to what a person does, but to what they are and the totality of being human.

Winifred Kempton (1973) expands the dimensions of this definition by three categories. The first category involves relationships and "how we feel about ourselves in relation to family, friends, lovers, spouses, etc., and how we act according to these feelings." The second involves the learning of the physiology of the human body: "the respective male and female roles in human reproduction, and the activity involved." The third category consists of the "understanding of sexual impulses or body feelings and how they are aroused and controlled" (p. 30).

For many people, a disability prevents their experiencing the games and social activities of nonhandicapped teenagers. Disabled young people's needs for assistance may force them to be observers rather than participants. Their feelings of self-worth decrease or become distorted; they become frustrated, angry, and compound their disability with emotional difficulties.

Denial and sexual alienation apply more to the handicapped than to others. Consider, for example, the adolescent youth with a congenital brain injury who "lies on the examining table in the doctor's office, where attention is directed toward physical restoration of the hand, the leg, or speech, but seldom toward sexual development. Major treatment facilities for disabled children continue to overlook the sexuality of their clients and, when asked to do something, react in anger and dismay" *(SIECUS Report,* 1976).

The Home Climate and Parental Roles in Dealing with Sexuality in Their Children

It is understandable if a parent discourages a disabled teenager from dating or going to school dances or parties for fear the child will be hurt or rebuffed. But the child denied an opportunity to try, to get dressed up and go out and take a chance, to risk getting hurt and feeling heartbroken is also denied a major part of living, one that none of us ourselves would ever agree to do without.

For all children, healthy and handicapped alike, many sexual feelings and attitudes are determined before the age of five, and this is so whether or

146

not the parents make any special effort to transmit values or to explain particular aspects of sexuality. Children learn by seeing what happens and noticing what does not occur, by hearing what is said and noting what is left unspoken.

Parents can do their preschool children a considerable service by always using the correct words for bodily parts and functions. Males have penises; females have vaginas; the toilet is used for urinating or for bowel movements. It is no kindness to any child, least of all one who already has cause to feel different, apart, or inferior, to send him or her out into the world with a babyish and embarrassing substitute for a proper sexual vocabulary.

Emphasis in Institutional Climates and the Role of the Staff

We would like to include an aside on some problems people with handicaps face in institutions. In one such institution for the mentally retarded where the senior author addressed the staff about sex education, aides and nurses were invited to submit questions in advance of the presentation. The majority of the questions could be summarized as follows: How can we stop masturbation? A considerable amount of staff energy was devoted to catching or curbing the masturbators.

In addition, great emphasis was put on discouraging sexual behavior. When this institution was composed of only male residents, much energy was spent in punishing or curbing homosexual behavior, but now with female residents added, the main thrust is against any expression of heterosexuality.

Administrators, school officials, and others blame the staff. Staff is everywhere said to be conservative; yet it is the administrators who select the staff. There are also numerous examples of staff being fired for not maintaining the traditional standards of conservatism.

The fact is that the retarded (and, in many respects, the nonretarded) do not need to know many facts about sex. The information that needs to be imparted can be given in a few minutes, then repeated at different levels and different times.

Implications for Professionals (What Needs To Be Done?)

If one accepts the relationship between sexuality and the adjustment of the handicapped teenager to other aspects of his or her life, then certain steps must be taken. First, parents, teachers, and other involved individuals cannot disregard sexuality. They need to deal with the handicapped person's sexuality as well as their own. Second, they need to integrate sexual health in the overall health support system of the handicapped individual. Health care professionals must make use of available sex education programs for themselves so that a better understanding of their own sexuality might then affect their awareness in the treatment of others.

One method used to help health care professionals understand the sexuality of the handicapped is to allow them to fantasize their "own" handicap or physical disability. This exercise can facilitate a willingness to consider the sexuality of others. Take a moment and have a fantasy. Imagine yourself as having a colostomy, an amputated leg or arm, poor gross motor control, or even a mental disability. Now superimpose one of the handicaps upon a sexual experience that you recall from adolescence. This will help you acknowledge the importance that health plays with regards to the sexuality of a disabled adolescent and the potential negative impact that avoidance of sexuality can have on self-esteem. The point is simply that professional sex educators, teachers, or parents should try to cultivate attitudes, information, and skills that incorporate the problems of the handicapped.

Some thoughts for helping health practitioners and the handicapped in learning about their sexuality (as suggested by Cole and Cole, 1976):

1 Urinary incontinence does not mean genital incompetence.
2 Absence of sensation does not mean absence of feelings.
3 The presence of deformities does not mean the absence of desire.
4 Inability to move does not mean inability to please.
5 Loss of genitals does not mean loss of sexuality.

The main problem many people with handicaps have is that they feel inferior. We can make this point clearer and influence youth in a very special way, if we declare that no one can make you feel inferior without your consent. Not long ago when the senior author made that statement at a dramatic meeting with several hundred severely handicapped people, with their parents and teachers present, there was an emotional outburst from a workshop leader who was responsible for a group of severely cerebral-palsied adults in wheelchairs. She shouted, "How can you say things like that when you see before you people who only need to look at themselves in the mirror to know what you say represents empty promises of a future that is not possible for any of them." The answer came from a beautiful woman confined to a wheelchair. She said, "You know, when I look only at myself, I feel depressed. When I take in the world I live in, I'm impressed. And when I allow God to touch me, I feel blessed." Pandemonium broke out, and what was an unreceptive, silent, almost sullen group of handicapped adults turned out to be a group of people wanting desperately to talk about their hidden aspirations—mainly in terms of their desperate desire for love, companionship, and sexual expression.

The meeting was an inspiration as nothing else had ever been for those young people. There are very few limitations that people with handicaps, their parents, their teachers, and the general public can't overcome.

Here are the highlights of some messages we would like to offer the handicapped. (Further readings on these points are contained in the selected bibliography.)

1 If you have an interest (hobbies, work, talents, passions) someone will be interested in you.
2 If you are bored, you are boring to be with.

148

3 If you don't have a sense of humor, develop one. If you can't develop a sense of humor, you can always become a supervisor!

4 Organize. Join an advocacy group for the handicapped and their parents.

5 Work toward being a realist. (Remember, every busybody is a hero in somebody else's situation.)

6 Don't dwell on the meaning of life. Life is not a meaning. Life is an opportunity for any number of meaningful experiences.

7 All thoughts, all desires, all impulses are normal. Behavior can be immoral or abnormal, but not thoughts. If you are preoccupied with thoughts that are unenjoyable to you, it is only because you feel guilty. These thoughts then become obsessive (involuntary). Guilt is the energy for the repetition of thoughts that are unacceptable to us. If we all realize that whatever thoughts we have—whether they be sexual, sadomasochistic, lustful—are normal, then they pass, they don't last, and they do no harm. Only what we do counts, not what we think about.

8 Read. Discover as much as you can about yourself in the world. For heaven's sake, don't watch more than an hour or so of television each day. Haven't you noticed that the more television you watch, the more exhausted you are?

9 Operate on the assumption that the so-called general public is uncomfortable with you. Most people are uncomfortable in the presence of severely handicapped people. And if we announce that they don't have to feel guilty about being uncomfortable, then they don't have to respond by withdrawing from you or having pity. Take the initiative and tell them what you'd like them to do. And in some subtle way, convey to them that it's okay to feel uncomfortable.

These "rules" are the basic steps toward realizing goals in the area of sexual expression and marriage. If you haven't gotten the message, let us say it another way. Socialization skills and opportunities are more important than anything else. If you feel good about yourself, someone will feel good about you. If you feel friendly, someone will be friendly to you. If you are open to sexual expression, someone will want to be sexual with you. The ethical, moral rules also apply to the handicapped. This means, of course, that we are opposed to any form of exploitation or behavior that is not consensual.

Nothing we have suggested is easy. In fact, all really meaningful experiences in life involve risk, hard work, and the ability to postpone momentary gratification for long-range satisfaction.

Key Facts for Parents, Teenagers, Social Service Professionals, and Institutional Personnel

While the precise nature of discussion about sexuality will vary from one household to the next or from one institution to the next, certain key facts need to be communicated to handicapped adolescents.

1. There is always a risk of pregnancy in unprotected intercourse between physically mature persons. While the risk is not as great during menstruation and on the days just before and after, proximity to menstruation is still no guarantee against pregnancy.

2. The rhythm method of birth control is not dependable. Effective methods include the pill, the IUD, the diaphragm, contraceptive foam, and the condom, which has the additional benefit of providing protection against venereal disease. Each method has particular advantages and drawbacks. No method improperly used is worth the money. Pills do not work unless taken exactly according to directions. Foam doesn't work unless it is applied before intercourse. A diaphragm wrongly inserted or used without contraceptive cream is useless.

3. Teenage pregnancy and childbirth is almost always unwise from a number of standpoints: medical, moral, and psychological. Abortion is one alternative for pregnant teenagers, but it may violate deeply held religious beliefs. Surrendering an infant for adoption or keeping a baby when one is emotionally and practically unprepared to raise it presents equally painful problems. It is always preferable to take effective precautions *before* the fact.

4. Masturbation is a normal expression of sexuality at any time of life, and especially during adolescence, when it serves as a healthy alternative to direct sexual activity. Like all other sexual behavior, it should be private. It is cause for worry only if and when it becomes compulsive or is closely associated with feelings of guilt or anxiety.

5. Genital sex is not a requisite for good health. Our society, especially its advertising, has consistently exaggerated the meaning and importance of sexual intercourse for an individual's health and well-being. Adolescents in particular who are otherwise healthy and occupied need not fear feeling indifferent about sex. And should they experience some interest several months or years hence, that's healthy too. No adolescent need worry that his or her timetable lags behind that of everyone else at school. Interest and desire are normal to the extent that they develop naturally. But a fifteen- or sixteen-year-old with other strong interests should not be labeled or badgered.

6. Our definition of homosexuality is having and preferring sexual behavior with members of one's same sex. Thoughts about homosexuality do not make one a homosexual. Nor do isolated homosexual experiences. Some 4 to 10 percent of the total population may be described as exclusively homosexual, and as a form of sexual behavior between consenting adults it should not be anyone else's business. It is not possible to predict an individual's subse-

quent choice of homosexuality on the basis of childhood behavior or family circumstances.

7. There is nothing inherently wrong with any adult nonexploitative sexual behavior. Each individual has the right to accept or reject particular forms of sexual expression on the basis of personal preference. But anyone disturbed by the knowledge that others enjoy certain sexual practices has a problem.

8. There is nothing shameful or abnormal about the male wet dream. There is nothing dirty or insidious about female menstruation. There is no value for any child in being shocked or startled by these experiences. They should be prepared to recognize them as normal aspects of sexual development.

9. Venereal disease is epidemic. When the original symptoms disappear it is not a sign that the disease has cured itself. Venereal disease does not mysteriously go away; it always requires prompt medical attention. Girls in particular should be aware that with certain forms of venereal disease females exhibit no symptoms whatsoever.

10. All things considered, pornography is a minor matter. It is neither educational nor harmful. It is usually boring to those properly educated about sex.

11. There is a correct and dignified word for everything. Little is gained by the use of self-consciously puerile substitutes.

12. Genital size has nothing to do with a man's sexual pleasure or performance. Time spent worrying over it is wasted. The size of a woman's breasts is equally irrelevant to sexual pleasure and secure gender identity. Furthermore, breast size in no way affects the ability to breast feed. Any healthy woman can successfully nurse her infant.

13. Sexual abuse, rape, and incest are crimes. Children can and must be made to understand that while they need not be in a state of perpetual fear, they must be alert to unseemly sexual advances by any adult of either sex. Disabled children are particularly vulnerable targets for disturbed people. Children must be taught to reject sexual advances as firmly and quickly as possible. They must also know that in the majority of abuse cases, the aggressor is someone familiar to the child—a relative, neighbor, or caretaker. Should a parent suspect that a child has been molested, or if a child tells a parent of sexual abuse, the parent has two crucial responsibilities. The first is to find out as much as possible about the incident. Children, who under pressure and in the terror of the moment promised never to reveal a word, must be told that promises made under such circumstances are not meant to be kept. Having learned the details, parents must then in no way imply that the child was at fault. Sexual abuse is always the fault of the adult aggressor. Such careless remarks as "Why did you let him do this to you?" can be devastating. Children must be assured over and again that nobody blames

151

them for what has happened. It has been found that many adults who suffer acute psychological distress as a result of having been molested during childhood are less disturbed by memories of the incident itself than by the possibility that they were somehow responsible for provoking it (Gordon & Dickman, 1977).

14. Self-acceptance is a key to successful relationships. People who feel good about themselves and who are interested in life will find that others become interested in them. Mature relationships are difficult for people who feel inferior or inadequate. Marriage in itself is no cure for pervasive feelings of inferiority. On the contrary, such feelings work against a successful marriage or adult relationships.

15. Love can be mature and genuine, or it can be immature and destructive. From mature love one can take comfort and strength. Healthy relationships are energizing. There is plenty of time in the context of a loving relationship to get everything done. Immature love is exhausting and unpleasant. It makes people tired and quarrelsome. It needs constant affirmation. Mature love means that it isn't necessary to be forever claiming it's true. The partners simply know it is.

16. Knowledge is not harmful. Mistakes are not fatal. The more a child knows, and the more he feels encouraged to learn, the better for everyone.

Marriage and Parenthood for the Handicapped

Social Appearance

Most disabled adolescents will want to socialize as much as other teenagers. Since adolescents generally have far more social experience with members of their own sex, they tend to feel nervous and anxious about their first dating experiences. This is especially true for those with obvious physical impairments, whose braces, wheelchairs, awkward movements, or unusual speech often make them feel ugly and fear rejection. For this reason, double-dating or group activities are often preferable and easier in the beginning.

A young girl worried about her appearance, for example, would feel more comfortable in a mixed group. When all the girls excuse themselves for a conference in the bathroom, she could join them and share in the general concern over hairstyles and lipstick. It may give her renewed confidence to see that the other girls have just as many uncertainties and dissatisfactions as she.

There are, of course, some things everyone can and should do to keep in shape and look one's best; grooming, manners, and appropriate clothing all help. Beyond these, there is a psychology of feeling attractive. Disabled youth should realize that no matter what they do, some people will find them ugly, others won't seem to care, and still others will find in them a singular beauty. The point is that if one looks and feels one's best, one will almost certainly, eventually, meet somebody else who couldn't agree more.

Beating All the Odds: Getting Married

As teenagers mature in their social relationships, they may begin to think seriously about marriage. Popular mythology notwithstanding, many disabled persons do marry and adjust quite successfully. Others simply prefer to remain single. The problem is with those remaining single who would very much like to marry but who fear that their particular impairment makes them ineligible. This group might gain renewed hope and confidence from seeing the film *Like Other People,* (Perennial Education, see "References"), the story of a young man and woman, both with cerebral palsy, who fall in love and marry, beating all the odds.

Sometimes a disabled youth becomes so immersed in self-pity that he or she decides far in advance that nobody will ever come to love them or want to marry them. The alternative to making grim prophecies and waiting for time to bear them out is to find or create new reasons to love and respect oneself. Self-regard is in itself a form of true beauty. If I look like I am mightily enjoying my own company, chances are somebody else will soon be along wishing to share it. I have then only to decide whether or not to encourage this newcomer's attention.

Financial Considerations

Some parents insist that their sons and daughters be able to demonstrate financial independence as an absolute prerequisite to their considering marriage. From the parents' point of view, this is a key consideration, for they may quite understandably resist the prospect of a new financial burden coinciding with their own retirement years. Parents who have already accepted permanent financial responsibility for a disabled child may find, however, that with the help of a second set of parents, supporting a disabled couple is not more burdensome but less. There will be others to share shopping and laundry and chauffering not to mention rent and utilities and telephone bills. Moreover, with new feelings of independence, and with the energy generated by the loving relationship, the disabled partners may well become less emotionally dependent upon their respective parents. Feeling needed and loved and more confident now, than in years past, they may each rise to the occasion, daring to do for themselves and each other what would have previously been unthinkable, taking real pride in new challenges met and mastered.

Running a Household

While adequate finances certainly help a marriage, other factors are no less important to its ultimate success. Both partners need the emotional maturity to deal with the problems they face together and individually. There must be some arrangements made about household work—cleaning, shopping, cooking, repairs, etc. It would be a mistake to dismiss such matters as trivial, for when two people live with each other, washing the dishes can become a focus

153

of major disagreement. In this, a disabled couple is no different from anyone else. Much of married life is a sharing of unexciting routine.

Parents should be aware of their reasons for encouraging their disabled children to marry. Is it to get the son out of the house once and for all so that some semblance of "normal" family life can again be restored? If so, they must think again. Pushing a daughter out, even when she wants to go, can prove disastrous. Perhaps a son has expressed a desire to marry only because it seems to coincide with his parents' unspoken wishes. Everyone in such a situation must examine motivations closely. Hasty decisions made in the wrong spirit and for the wrong reasons may bring temporary relief, but the situation itself will grow worse with time.

Does the Marriage Include Having Children?

For most people, the decision to have children is simply a matter of preference. For others, however, there are other important considerations. Disabled persons who want to have children may be confronted with furious objections from doctors and parents and less able to counter effectively with their own views. There can be fear that the child of such a marriage wouldn't have proper care, and anxiety lest the child be born disabled, thus placing severe additional strain on the marital relationship.

As with love and marriage, there are a great many romantic fantasies about parenthood: cuddling sweet sleeping infants, feeding them and dressing them while they gurgle delightedly, and generally loving them to pieces with never a scream in the middle of the night, or rashes, allergies, emergencies, indigestion, two weeks of diarrhea, or a broken washing machine and not a dime in the house.

It is natural to look forward to nurturing children, but the process is far from smooth even for the healthiest among us. All parents go through periods of intense frustration and exhaustion, not to mention worrying about the staggering costs of raising a child. In fact, one very popular book on the subject of child care devotes a small section to a problem called "wanting to throw the baby out of the window." The point is that it is natural to have such feelings from time to time.

Some adults, disabled or not, are simply unsuited, emotionally or physically, for raising a family. Those who think they would like to have a child but aren't sure about their own ability to manage might volunteer to work in a nursery or day-care center for a while to get an idea of what is involved. It's not foolproof, but it can be instructive.

It has been shown that marriage for the disabled is often more successful without children, without the inevitable disruption and strain involved in childrearing. Other drawbacks include the possibility that a normal child born of mentally retarded parents may subsequently become retarded as a consequence of inferior care and insufficient stimulation during the formative years. It is difficult for even a mildly retarded or learning disabled couple to under-

154

stand the future implications of having a child and providing years of care and nurture; more commonly an emotionally disabled husband and wife will tend to focus on the present, the pleasures and satisfactions of the moment, at the expense of hard thinking about tomorrow's consequences and responsibilities.

In some cases, voluntary sterilization (vasectomy for the male; tubal ligation for the female) may be the best answer for seriously disabled couples, for those who couldn't possibly expect to cope with parenthood, or for those who are certain that they do not, and never will, wish to have children. Although reversal is sometimes possible with surgery, this is exceedingly rare, and sterilization should thus be considered as permanent and therefore inappropriate for anyone uncertain about choosing a childless life-style.

An unplanned or unwanted pregnancy can mean exceptional hardship for the disabled, from coping with the rigors of pregnancy to caring for the child after it is born. In such cases abortion may be a solution.

Parents of Handicapped Children Need Time Off for Good Behavior

Lest the foregoing seem to stress parental responsibilities at the expense of parental rights to "live a little" too, let it be understood that parents owe it to themselves and to their children to find time to live. Totally selfless devotion is neither possible nor desirable. Moreover, it is dreadfully boring to all who must live with it. Guilt is no excuse for directing every thought and every last bit of energy to a life other than one's own life. All parents, not the least those who most vigorously deny it, need time off for good behavior and for good emotional health. Parents of handicapped children frequently err in thinking that they are somehow to blame for their child's affliction. Unable to relieve themselves of such misplaced guilt, they compound matters by subconsciously resolving to punish themselves by reorganizing their lives so that the disabled child is always and forever at the center. There are many consequences of such sadly convoluted thinking, and all of them are negative. Storybook perfection is fine for storybook people. Real children, whether disabled or not, need their mothers and fathers to know when it is time to stop sacrificing and be unafraid to say so.

Thus, as a Bill of Rights for the parents of disabled children we suggest the following freedoms:

> To feel that you have done the best you can.
>
> To love, care for, and enjoy your child.
>
> To be depressed or angry from time to time without feeling guilty.
>
> To enjoy life as intensely as possible.
>
> To be busy with a variety of things you yourself find interesting.

155

To let your child have privacy, and to take personal advantage of that time yourself.

To let yourself have privacy and learn to enjoy it.

To get away each year for at least a two-week vacation without your child.

To put aside special and regular times for adults only; to have and enjoy dates, celebrations, weekends away with your husband, wife, or companion.

To have a sense of humor and feel free to let it show even in the presence of those who will never see anything to laugh about.

To feel that spending extra time with a child who needs it is not saying you love the rest of the family less than this child.

To decline even the kindest offers to talk about your problems or "bare your soul."

To boast about your child's progress and accomplishments.

To let the brave mask drop once in a while.

To assert yourself among professionals and educators; to remember that your views have merit by virtue of being your own.

To criticize and correct your child when you feel it is necessary.

To withhold unearned praise.

To spend some money just for yourself.

To honor your own special interests; to claim your regular hour or afternoon and use it as you would if there were no other demands on your time.

To define who you are without reference to husband, wife, or children.

The Outside Climate: A Help or a Hindrance?

Many parents feel very uncomfortable or, in fact, are unable to discuss sexuality with their children. Since school is a compulsory and universal system for children, it would seem logical to pass the "education problem" over to the schools for resolution. Unfortunately, we are beginning to have strong reasons to doubt the effectiveness of such school-based sex education programs in their ability to significantly decrease ignorance about sex or the consequences of it.

Sex Education Programs for Handicapped Persons

The basic principles that apply to a well-structured sex education program for the "normal" child apply also for the handicapped child: the goals are the same. The disabled teenager is equally curious about "where he or she came from," differences between the sexes, changes at puberty, mate selection, dating, premarital sex, marriage, homosexual relations, masturbation, and contraception.

How then does sex education programming for the handicapped differ:

> A handicapped teenager will probably have less information and greater misinformation (Bloom, 1969).

> Due to isolation and overprotection, the handicapped are usually lacking in social skills and are more acceptant of authority than others (excepting the behaviorally disordered, emotionally disturbed, and culturally deprived).

> Individuals with severe handicaps are probably less likely to be married. They need to be helped to understand that happiness can be obtained without marriage, and that there are many alternative life-styles that might work better for them.

> Information on genetic factors needs to be included so that there is an understanding of the consequences if they decide to have children.

> The curriculum must be adapted to take into account how their particular handicap inhibits comprehensive understanding.

More specifically, a curriculum for the retarded is best presented in simple terms with considerable repetition (Kempton, 1973).

For the blind, more emphasis is placed on tactility: the use of dolls with genitals is preferable to neuter dolls. As far as it is comfortable for parent and child alike, parents with a blind child should allow the child to explore his body. For the blind teenager, rubber models are available similar to those used by medical schools. Several helpful books printed in Braille include Evelyn Duvall's *Fact of Life and Love for Teenagers* (1963), and Eric Johnson's *Sex: Telling It Straight* (1967). A course curriculum developed by the Oregon School for the Blind (1968) and other materials are available from the Sex Information and Education Council of the United States (SIECUS).

For the deaf, a visual mode emphasis is most beneficial. Materials with detailed drawings of male and female anatomies, prenatal development, birth, and contraceptive information is necessary (Gordon, 1978).

Lastly, with the physically and neurologically handicapped, one must be particularly concerned with their lack of information and available misinformation. Bloom (1969) found that physically and neurologically handicapped adolescents exhibited less information about sex than a control group of normal youths. The overprotection commonly experienced by this group has blocked an exchange of information with peers, making them feel isolated, misinformed, and, most of all, giving them exaggerated feelings of being different. Film presentations portraying disabled people and their need to give and receive affection are available.

The handicapped adolescent, along with his family and other pertinent persons, might have to consider decisions concerning such matters as voluntary sterilization and contraception. Constantly improving methods of birth control, in combination with progressive acceptance of sterilization by both nonimpaired and hereditarily impaired couples, have made the child-free marriage a possibility. Thus, for those handicapped individuals capable of a stable intimate relationship who either fear passing genetic defects on to their children or fear they would be incapable of parenting, the childless marriage presents a viable life-style.

Two renowned authorities, Robert W. Laidlow and Medora S. Bass, summarized sterilization in this manner (1964):

> Voluntary sterilization can and does contribute to mental health; by helping to keep the population increase in line with developing resources; by reducing the anxiety caused by fear of unwanted pregnancies; by preventing children from being born to irresponsible parents with resultant neglect and social ills; by allowing the retarded to marry and lead more normal lives; by preventing some hereditary abnormalities. All this can be accomplished without unfavorable psychological effects and with a high ratio of satisfaction.

Mainstreaming: A Benefit to Sex Education

In a world becoming more complex with each year, the difficulties experienced by disabled teenagers have grown more traumatic. Frequently teenagers find themselves neglected, isolated from the mainstream of events, and inappropriately educated in useless skills. Moreover, the experience of the handicap itself can be minimal when compared to the overpowering feelings of uselessness and despair.

No educational system can be effective if it supports an environment where a handicapped youth is separated from other students by not only the physical barriers of specialized classrooms, but also by the invisible barriers of fear and ignorance. The opportunity to learn in the least restrictive environment "means more simply the right to a formal education; it implies the right to participate in ordinary school life, to have friends and activities as nearly typical as possible" (Bookbinder, 1977).

To make the social aspects of mainstreaming (integrating the handicapped into regular classrooms) work, all schoolchildren, administrators, teachers, employers, and other involved people need to know that it is not unusual for them to sometimes feel uncomfortable with a handicapped person. If people can acknowledge their discomfort, they can relate in a mature way to people who are handicapped—not by pity or rejection, which often accompany feelings of guilt in response to being uncomfortable. Even if we are uncomfortable, we can still go out of our way to be helpful. There is nothing wrong with being empathic, useful, and doing something for another human being.

We have to be able to say in advance that there is something wrong with the "climate" of a school (with administrators at fault) when a principal or a teacher says, in response to a parent's complaint that the other children are making fun of their handicapped child: "Well, I am sorry Mrs. Jones, but I can't control what children feel" or "I can't monitor every child." It simply means that the principal is not fulfilling his or her job responsibilities (or hasn't been prepared to do so). There are plenty of schools where teenagers with handicaps are treated with respect. In those schools where mainstreaming is unpopular, a disabled person is more likely to experience school as an unfriendly, lonely place where he or she is teased, ridiculed, and ignored by others.

It must be understood that mainstreaming requires considerable preparation, readiness, and a transition period leading from segregation to integration. Also, to be realistic, we are not suggesting that a facility not remain homogenous, but rather that the disabled be given every opportunity to function in the most normalized fashion. The implementation for such needed programs must come from the schools, rehabilitation services, and public assistance agencies in all communities.

It should be acknowledged that for a small minority of disabled individuals, segregated activities might be considered an acceptable life-style. However, we find it almost incomprehensible that such a person could not normalize at least *some* components of his or her life. It is our experience that feelings of being involved, included, and just being a part of "what's happening" are necessary for optimum mental health for all individuals, and perhaps teenagers in particular, because of the development that takes place during those years.

Let's "Mainstream" Ourselves

In many parts of our country, efforts to establish halfway houses or residential living centers for the mentally retarded in "good" neighborhoods are meeting with intense opposition from "respectable" neighbors. (When this happened to ex-residents of mental hospitals, advocates for the retarded, as well as most of the rest of us, didn't see it as our business and offered no support.)

Hundreds, perhaps thousands, of "Marys"—released from institutions against the advice of superintendents as not being ready, but under pressure from "advocates"—are pregnant. They are no more ready to bear and take care of a child than they are able, because of institutional neglect, to educate them.

159

But where are the voices demanding sex education during all the time Mary was institutionalized? And what did the superintendent do? (He ignored the whole thing and did little to prepare Mary for life.)

All people, handicapped or not, must have opportunities to express their highest potential. But let's face it, we, the controlling society of mainly non-handicapped people, with power and influence, have a lot of groundwork to do.

First and foremost, the struggle for equal rights of handicapped people is *no* different than the struggle of all depressed and deprived groups. Together we need to champion the rights of homosexuals, women, the mentally ill, and blacks. Just as women and blacks needed to receive legislation or Supreme Court decisions first, so do the handicapped. We can't count on good-will; good-will comes later with education.

We need to prepare the general public with a few facts. For example, it is not the retarded who are sexually dangerous (the common fear); the retarded are the victims of so-called normals in more than 95 percent of the cases. This is the same kind of education the public needs regarding gay people. Ninety percent of the victims of child molestation involve heterosexual men attacking female children. Does this mean no heterosexual male should be permitted to teach in the public schools?

Obviously, we've just scratched the surface, but we want to leave you with one message: We are all in this together. Blacks not too long ago learned that without coalitions, such as those created during the civil rights movement, very little could be accomplished. Thus, little can be expected unless we work together for this cause in relation to all the other causes involving the rights of every person.

References   Bass, Medora S. *Developing community acceptance of sex education for the mentally retarded.* New York: SIECUS, 1970.

Bloom, Jean L. Sex education for handicapped adolescents. *Journal of School Health,* 1969, *39,* 363–367.

Bookbinder, S. What every child needs to know. *The Exceptional Parent.* 1977, *7* (4), 31–34.

Cole, T. M., & Cole, S. S. The handicapped and sexual health. *SIECUS Report, Special Issue on the Handicapped,* 1976, 1–2; 12.

Duvall, E. M. *The facts of life and love for teenagers.* New York: Associated Press, 1963.

Gordon, S. *Facts about sex.* Charlottesville, Va.: Ed-U Press, 1978.

Gordon, S. Love, sex and marriage for people who have disabilities. *The Exceptional Parent,* 1976, *6* (4), 18–21.

Gordon, S. Is parenting for everybody? *The Exceptional Parent,* 1977, *7* (2), 8–10.

Gordon, S., & Dickman, I. R. *Sex education: The parents' role.* New York: Public Affairs Pamphlets, 1977.

Greengross, W. *Entitled to love: The sexual and emotional needs of the handicapped.* London: Malaby Press Ltd., 1976.

Johnson, E. W. Sex: Telling it straight. *Braille.* Philadelphia: J.B. Lippincott, 1967.

Kempton, W. *Guidelines for planning a training course on human sexuality and the retarded.* Philadelphia: Planned Parenthood of Southeastern Pennsylvania, 1973.

SIECUS Report, Special Issue on the Handicapped. New York: Sex Information and Education Council of the United States, 1976.

161

Nine

The Effects of
Sex Education:
A Review
and Critique
of the Literature

Opposition to sex education has generally been fueled by two beliefs: knowledge about sex stimulates irresponsible sexual behavior; and, in any case, sex education does not promote responsible behavior. It has become almost fashionable to mock sex education. Inadvertently, some professionals have added legitimacy to the controversy by simply reporting, without deeper analysis, that differences in sexual and contraceptive behavior between those who have taken a sex education course and those who have not are "insignificant." Notably absent in these reports are such critical factors as whether the course was interesting or boring, whether the teacher was adequately trained, whether the course gave a comprehensive, semester-long treatment or a single hurried lecture, whether "communication," "responsibility," "sexual attractiveness," "love" and other concepts were discussed or whether only "the facts" were presented.

The argument that knowledge stimulates sexual "experimentation" is raised by a few parents and cited by school boards in defense of a sexless curriculum; it is raised by some clergy and physicians and then cited by parents in support of their own fears. For instance, in New York, a state senator objected to our distributing the comic book *Ten Heavy Facts About Sex* (Gordon, 1971) at the New York State Fair. His reason? The book would put "ideas" into the minds of young people who didn't have the "ideas" already. Magazines such as *Playgirl, Viva, Penthouse,* etc., are made more titillating by being displayed with the front cover diagonally folded back to hide "offending" breasts or pubic hairs. In Tallahassee, Florida, a local minister who had read that 984 out of 1,000 girls had "committed fornication" while rock music was being played began collecting and destroying such records in order to "protect the moral decency of youth" (Cvetkovich & Grote, 1976).

A *New York Times* article (Powledge, 1977) questioned whether sex education has *any* effects, stating, "No one has the slightest idea of what the effects of sex education are, or can be." In that one sentence, the author managed to dismiss a volume of research so vast that we have taken nearly a year to review it and reach some tentative conclusions. The most recent nationally representative study of teenage women in the U.S. also concluded, "The transfer of knowledge in formal settings may be likened to carrying water in a basket" (Zelnik & Kantner, 1977, p. 59). In another book that sup-

163

posedly contained the most up-to-date "advice," based on modern research about childrearing, the authors stated, "Studies do not indicate that children who receive detailed sexual instruction from their parents arrive at any better long-term sexual adaptation than children who receive their instruction from other sources" (Fisher & Fisher, 1977, pp. 105–106). Our review of the literature, however, has consistently indicated that children whose parents talk to them about sex do in fact delay their first intercourse longer than children whose parents avoid sex education, and these children tend to use contraception when they do have intercourse.

Is There a Direct Relationship Between Education and Behavior?

There are both educational and social causes for the lack of a more direct relationship between education and "responsible" sexuality. For example, with greater percentages of sexually experienced females waiting longer to get married (in part because of dramatically increased numbers of women in college—see Glick, 1975) and greater percentages of young people having intercourse at earlier ages (Zelnik & Kantner, 1977; 1972) in a wider variety of relationships (Bell & Chaskes, 1970; Hunt, 1974; Zelnik & Kantner, 1977), unwanted births to unmarried women are likely to increase (Westoff, 1975). Cutright pointed out that "improved health conditions appear to have increased the chances that an out-of-wedlock conception will be carried to term (hence, become visible, and a problem) and have also increased the capacity of sexually active young girls to conceive" (1972). Also, with increased educational efforts and staffing of neighborhood health centers, venereal disease statistics may show a rise owing to improved reporting, regardless of the "absolute" level of cases.

In another instance, Glick (1975) reported that cohabitation is the fastest growing life-style among young people in the United States. While his figures may have only limited current application to the teenage years, they do include eighteen- and nineteen-year-olds. Glick estimated that the 1960s saw an increase in cohabitation 23 percent greater than that of young adults living with a spouse. By offering increasing opportunities for intercourse and lessening the necessity of marriage in order to live with someone, these changes may have already had some influence on "illegitimacy." Interestingly, although such patterns may increase illegitimacy (for instance, in 1975, "illegitimacy" among twenty-to-twenty-four-year-olds rose for the first time since 1970), the stability and commitment to a partner over time implicit in living together may also help to decrease the percentage of pregnancies that could properly be called "unwanted." Clearly, so many factors are at work that no one force by itself directly influences contemporary patterns of behavior.

Although research shows that most teenagers do *not* want to get pregnant (Alan Guttmacher Institute, 1976; Diamond et al., 1973; Presser, 1974; Zelnik & Kantner, 1972), the birth rate for younger teens (under seventeen) has *increased* in the last ten years, while across the ages fifteen to forty-four, it has *decreased* 27 percent. The "illegitimacy" rate among the young has also jumped 50 percent in that period. These birth increases are primarily due to a 6 percent increase in the white birth rate among fifteen-to-seventeen-year-olds. Ten years ago, the black birth rate was four times that of whites. Now the rate is three times that of whites, with births to young blacks dropping 12 percent in the period that white rates have risen (National Center for Health Statistics, 1977).

Additional clouding effects are contributed by variables such as welfare status and different racial access to pregnancy termination or marriage as a post hoc "legitimizer." Janowitz (1976) reported a study of AFDC recipients in fifty-eight Standard Metropolitan Statistical Areas for which population and illegitimate birth data were available by race and age. The major finding of the study was that "socioeconomic factors affect illegitimacy by affecting *legitimacy* rather than by adding to total births" (p. 489, emphasis added). Janowitz concluded that the high illegitimacy rate among young nonwhite women is associated with the welfare system's failure to include poor, male-headed households. In addition, white females' use of abortion and marriage after premarital conception has tended, until recently, to maintain racial differences in illegitimacy rates. For example, Moore and Caldwell (1976) of the Urban Institute compared Zelnik and Kantner's 1971 national study of fifteen-to-nineteen-year-old women with state-level data and found that illegitimate black births are substantially reduced in states with subsidized birth control services while illegitimate white births are reduced by the availability of abortion. Welfare benefits were found *not* to encourage illegitimacy.

In addition, direct relationships between "sex education" and measures of responsible sexuality are rarely observed because society's approach toward preparing youth to deal with their sexuality has been based on guilt, innuendo, and at times an outright denial that young people are sexual: "We offer religions thick with the dust of a past era, parental counsel that is vague, timid, false, irrelevant, or negligible, and teachers who, on the subject of contraception, are silenced by rule of law" (Konner, 1977). Michigan, for instance, prohibited teaching about contraception until late 1977, even though "sex education" was in the schools (Scales, 1977b). Furthermore, only two states *require* that sex education of some sort be taught (Kirby and Scales, 1979), and three-fourths of "comprehensive" programs for already pregnant women don't teach the birth control that would help prevent a second unwanted, and usually disastrous, pregnancy (Alan Guttmacher Institute, 1976).

Organization of the Review

Research on the effects of sex education can be grouped into several categories: inservice training in sex education for professionals; college, high school, and junior high school class studies; studies of general parent education programs without a specific focus on sex education; and parent education programs specifically concerned with sex education. The last category is the least represented in the literature. There is a fifth category comprised of studies generally concerning the relationship of knowledge about sex to behavior, but these are not typically studies of formal sex education classes or courses.

It is difficult to extract significant relationships from research on the effects of sex education. Methodologically, sex education studies are in their infancy as sociological research. The sophistication of instruments and appropriateness of statistical techniques, adherence to rigid standards of experimentation, and completeness of reporting results are far less developed than in other subfields of sociology, and even less than the standards of family sociology in general, a field not much past its own infancy. Scales and Everly (1975) have noted:

> The majority of designs used in studies of sex education program effects have been pre-experimental; few have used control groups; even fewer have reported attempts at random assignment of subjects to treatment and control conditions; and reported reliability and validity of measures vary widely from study to study (p. 10).

Wilson (1974) stated the problem of definition common to all educational studies and even more prevalent in sex education than in many other fields.

> Sex education programs are difficult to evaluate because there have been no agreements reached as to what "sex education" is. There are no clearly defined goals or objectives, few tried and tested approaches. Because much of sex education deals with sensitive, personal issues, few programs resemble any others. The approach to the topic tends to depend on the instructor, the kind of group to whom the course is being offered, and the goals and objectives. Therefore, any findings which may be reported tend to apply only to the group from which the findings were compiled (p. 31).

Somerville (1971) raised a similar point: "Most family life and sex education programs have not been open to outside observation and evaluation, and as a result there has been almost complete dependence on self-report of those involved in the given program" (p. 231). Somerville also mentioned a key qualification to studies of the effects of sex education: the need to realize that sex education remains a sensitive, political issue in many communities, and that any evaluation of programs should take into account how well communities are "able to withstand the organized attacks on family life and sex education" (p. 221).

Given these caveats regarding the general state of the art in evaluating sex education, we wanted to answer the following questions:

1 Can "sex education" increase people's knowledge about sex?
2 Can "sex education" alter attitudes?
3 Does "sex education" contribute to "responsible" expression of sexuality?

We reviewed studies that most directly concern "sex education" and "sex information." Samples ranged from grade school to middle-age professionals. Where reliability and validity coefficients or estimates were provided, we included them in our discussion. Family planning programs in developing and developed countries are minimally covered in this review. Research, however, does show that such programs do dramatically contribute to a lower birth rate in both developing and developed countries (Population Crisis Committee, 1976; and Freedman & Berelson, 1976, for detailed discussions). Other KAP (knowledge-attitude-practice) studies that have a more indirect bearing on this chapter were also not included. (See Fawcett, 1970; Population Council, 1970; and Rogers, 1973 for extended treatment of these studies.) We make no claim to have reviewed every study in the field. We have reviewed scores of research reports, the majority of which have been published since 1972. Rather than provide detailed discussion of all the studies reviewed, this chapter presents examples of the most important in order to illustrate the kind of data on which our conclusions are based.

What Is "Irresponsible" Sexuality?

For purposes of definition, we use "irresponsible" to mean having sexual intercourse exploitatively, coercively, or compulsively, often unprotected by contraception, spreading venereal disease, or committing sex crimes, such as rape or child molestation. Other behaviors are clearly "irresponsible" such as using "lines" to get someone to have sex, but virtually no sex education course raises consciousness in this area. Thus, we cannot justifiably expect changes in use of "lines" as a result of sex education. This area, in addition, is only now beginning to be researched (Carrera, 1978; Gordon, 1978).

Research on the Effects of Sex Education

Knowledge

Studies on the relationship between sex education and performance on selected knowledge items, involving a range in the rigor of designs and the use of largely noncomparable measures, indicate that knowledge performance *can* be improved by participation in a sex education class or program. Nearly all of these studies are of school-age and college-age people, with a few scattered

167

studies reporting on professionals who participated in an inservice course or program.[1]

It is worth stressing that it is difficult to predict levels of knowledge increase due to sex education because studies are rarely comparable in either the instruments used to measure change or the content of the various sex education courses under investigation. As an example of the latter, Goldsmith et al. (1972) reported that the thirteen-to-seventeen-year-old females in their comparative study of a "contraceptor" group, an "abortion" group, and a "maternity" group showed no relationship between level of knowledge on a "group of questions" developed by the authors (no reliability given) and previous exposure to sex education or to discussions with parents. The authors pointed out that knowledge was related directly to age, and speculated that the type of "direct, applied questions" they asked were not usually discussed in school or with parents, but were possibly the kind of content discussed with friends. Although their questionnaire was itself suspect, Goldsmith's explanation for their findings is compelling: The sexual myths that circulate in the school, in the home, and in the media are not easily overcome by current education. Most destructive is the myth that in the area of sexuality, knowledge is harmful and ignorance is bliss. However, young people are exposed to such myths and often get the message that they are not supposed to know anything about sex. In view of this, even minimal increases in knowledge are encouraging.

Examples of Knowledge Gain Studies

Reichelt and Werley (1975) reported a study of Detroit teenage clients at a Planned Parenthood center. Data were collected on 1,190 clients (nearly 90 percent females) prior to their participation in a required "rap" session. Ten weeks later, 367 females aged fourteen to seventeen who had selected the pill and were returning for supplies were given a postadministration of the questionnaire. No reliability figures were reported. It was stated that both groups of subjects were similar on their pretest level of knowledge. The authors reported "striking improvement in knowledge in all areas subsequent to the rap sessions."

Wilson (1974) studied 100 males and 100 females in a control group design in order to assess the effects of a college sex education class. Using the Sex Knowledge and Attitudes Inventory that he developed (Kuder-Richardson 20 reliability of .81 for the knowledge section), Wilson found that students participating in the course gained significantly in knowledge when compared with students who had not taken the class. Crosby (1971) used a

---

[1] Other studies of knowledge gain reviewed but not discussed here were: Adams (1971), Battista (1972), Hoch (1968), Board of Education, Flint, (1976), Mims, et al. (1974), Perkins (1959), and Woods & Mandetta (1975).

three-experimental-group, three-control-group design to study twenty-nine males and twenty-nine females in grades 8–12. A major caution in interpreting his results is that twenty-four of the twenty-nine males were students in a military school, grades 10–12. No attempt was reported to study this subgroup in order to determine whether the possibility of an indoctrination atmosphere in the military school might have been a strong enough variable to warrant efforts at control. Experimental students showed greater gains in knowledge on a questionnaire developed by the author. Crosby reported reliability in the .80s, but discussed only "face" validity.

Miller (1973), in a study of two San Francisco area high schools, reported that the effects of sex education are apparently related to the student's motivation to use the information and the extent to which the information is relevant to the student's personal situation. In his study, only about one-third of all respondents knew when the fertile period occurs during the menstrual cycle, but the females in the "middle-class" school showed a difference depending on whether they were sexually active or not. The sexually experienced females were significantly more informed about the cycle, with three-fourths knowing the timing of the fertile period. Although the middle-class school was the only one offering a course in sex education, only the sexually active females scored well on this indicator of knowledge. What could not be determined was whether their knowledge preceded or followed their sexual activity.

What Kind of "Knowledge" Is Important?

It is obvious that the *type* of knowledge a person has is a critical variable. Research indicates that there are widespread inaccuracies, distortions, and myths about reproduction, pregnancy, and contraception (Driscoll & Davis, 1971; Goldsmith et al., 1972; Presser, 1974; Shah, Zelnik, & Kantner, 1975; Sorensen, 1973; Zelnik & Kantner, 1972). Sorensen (1973) found that nearly half of his teenage females with recent intercourse who didn't always use contraception believed they could not become pregnant if they really didn't want to. Seventy percent of Zelnik and Kantner's (1972) teenage girls failed to use contraception because they believed they could not become pregnant; blacks tended toward mythical beliefs, such as that not wanting pregnancy or having intercourse standing up were effective methods of birth control; whites held inaccurate beliefs about "safe" and "fertile" periods. In Finkel and Finkel's (1975) purposive sample of four hundred urban high school males, only 32 percent knew that a female could get pregnant even if the male withdrew "before coming."

It is apparent that some kinds of knowledge are more motivationally useful than others. It may make no difference in a woman's behavior if she knows that contraceptives are available at a local Planned Parenthood center, but does not also know that they may be given away free. A young male can score 100 on a test of anatomical knowledge, but still spread venereal disease or impregnate his partner if he finds it difficult to talk about sexuality or to

169

turn down a sexual opportunity without fear of appearing disinterested or asexual.

Theoretical knowledge alone is not enough to guarantee use of birth control or preventative measures against VD. Several studies have shown that knowledge and awareness of methods can be high without a concomitant use of the methods (Brown, Lieberman, & Miller, 1975; Cobliner, 1974; Gilbert & Matthews, 1974; Zelnik & Kantner, 1972). Hertoft (1974) found the same pattern in a sample of four hundred Danish men, aged eighteen to nineteen. The majority knew most of the common contraceptives, but only about half of the sexually experienced used contraception regularly. Furstenberg (1976) reported that only 6 percent of his adolescent mothers could not *identify* any method of birth control, but their knowledge tended to be superficial and of limited practical value: The young mothers were most aware of methods, such as the pill, to which they had the least access.

People need another kind of knowledge, including the knowledge of how to use contraceptives, how to raise the issue of contraception in relationships, how to comfortably include sex in their lives without being dominated or swept away by it, or how to use the local VD clinic. If education fails to provide such knowledge, it is unlikely that more powerful relationships between "knowledge" and responsible behavior will be observed. The difficulty, of course, is that these are just the areas that many teachers avoid and many overly sensitive school boards forbid, preferring instead to use a "scientific" approach limited to biological facts. For instance, a curriculum suggested for Fairfax County, Virginia, schools would not promote "any particular set of values." Nevertheless, values need to be discussed. The exploration of values of all kinds would create a young population with knowledge they can *use* in their sexual lives.

Attitudes

Many of the studies of knowledge and its relation to sex education also investigated attitude change as a possible effect. Again, in most studies a variety of measures have been used with no reliability values reported. These studies usually consist of "convenience" groups (rather than "samples") of college and school-age subjects.[2]

Attitude literature is usually concerned with whether subjects are "liberal" or "conservative" following a sex education course. We use these terms as they are used in the studies, but do not suggest that a person is consistently "liberal" or "conservative" across all attitude issues. Since attitudes measured vary with difference in items used among studies, it is likely that

---

[2] Other studies of attitude change reviewed but not discussed here were: Adams (1971), Battista (1972), Carton & Carton (1971), Fassbender (1971), Hoch (1968), Insko (1971), Price (1971), Scales (1976), Wilson (1974), and Woods & Mandetta (1975).

there are several dimensions of "liberalism" or "conservatism" being measured. While the usefulness of these terms in sex education is questionable (Scales & Everly, 1977), the fear of encouraging rampant permissiveness and liberalism is frequently used to oppose sex education. Therefore, it is appropriate to ask whether such increases in permissiveness/liberalism are typical effects of sex education.

The summary of research on the contribution of sex education to attitude change is less clear than the corresponding work on knowledge acquisition. Overall, it does appear that participation in a sex education course or program may be associated with more "favorable" attitudes toward particular content areas, although people do not seem to become more predictably "liberal" in their attitudes. Although the distinction between these two terms is rarely discussed, the clearest expectation justified by previous research is that people may become more accepting of particular sexual behaviors, even if they would not engage in the behaviors themselves (Howard et al., 1970).

The "attitudes" studied in most research, however, have little to do with how one behaves sexually. More important than measuring attitudes toward "premarital" sex, for example, is the study of how sex education affects people's attitudes about their *own* sexuality. For example, research consistently demonstrates the positive relationship between "acceptance" of oneself as a sexual person and the use of birth control. In these research reports, "acceptance of sexuality" has been defined as a willingness to admit that one behaves sexually, a relative absence of guilt about sexual feelings and experiences, a belief that one is sexually attractive to some people, and a realistic (i.e., not exaggerated) view of one's own level of sexual activity compared to others. Sorensen's study (1973) offers additional support for the relationship between acceptance of sexuality and use of birth control, such as the young woman who said, "I was trying so hard to think I wasn't fucking that the thought I might get pregnant never entered my mind" (p. 324). It is reasonable to ask how an "acceptance" of sexuality can be communicated if sex education teachers are often untrained and even more frequently unsupported by their administrators.

Examples of Attitude Change Studies

Olson and Gravatt (1968) administered their Premarital Attitude Scale (test-retest reliability reported as .85 with no time interval indicated) to an experimental group of ninety-seven undergraduates taking a "marriage and family" course and to a control group of forty-seven students taking a one-credit course in the same department. The researchers found that both groups showed some attitude change at the conclusion of the semester, but that the experimental group showed significantly more changes in the direction of more positive acceptance of sexuality. Humphrey, Libby, and Nass (1969) studied the effects of a six-week, inservice, family-life education institute with an emphasis on sex education. Using the Sex Education Liberalism Scale

171

(Libby, 1970—Spearman-Brown reliability of .64), the authors concluded, "The data reveal a rather consistent change toward increased openness and a willingness to accept a more liberal view of high school sex education upon completion of the institute." However, there was no control group with which to compare the responses of the sixty-two institute participants.

Crosby (1971) reported that experimental students in his study showed greater gains in self-concept at the conclusion of the course than did the control students, but that there was no difference between experimental and control group "attitudes toward family life." Lance (1975) reported a study of 150 students enrolled in a college human sexuality course. Most (103) were graduate students, and over half were married. Lance did not discuss the instrument or report any reliability figures for the attitude section, but covered four topics in this report: attitudes toward premarital intercourse, homosexuality, oral-genital sex, and extramarital sex. Approximately half of the students demonstrated a change in attitude across these four topics, most toward greater acceptance of the behavior, except for extramarital sex, which became less acceptable. There was no discussion of whether there was overlap among the groups reporting change on each of the items.

Behavior

Researchers should be wary of presuming that a simple linear concept relates knowledge and attitude change to behavior change. A recent reminder of the complexity of behavior change is provided by Arrey and Tresher (1976), who discuss changes in abortion attitudes from 1972 to 1975. They point out that the January 1973 Supreme Court ruling "apparently caused a rapid shift in abortion attitude," with very little change in attitudes occurring since that time, despite the fact that several million U.S. women have had legal abortions. This suggests that "behavioral changes . . . may take considerable time *before* they are reflected in changed attitudes" (p. 124, emphasis added).

Another problem is exactly how to measure "behavior." Liska (1974) looked at studies in which behavior was measured in terms of behavioral intentions, self-reports of past behavior, and observation of actual behavior. While Liska's review was comprised of nonfamily studies, and thus probably overstates the case for nonobservational substitutes for behavior, he did conclude:

> While there is evidence to consider the relationship between overt behavior and questionnaire measures as problematic, the evidence . . . does not suggest that alternate measures of behavior would significantly increase the observed attitude-behavior relationship (p. 263).

Liska suggests that current approaches to studying these social phenomena *may* be capable of achieving moderate degrees of predictive power if designs and instrumentation are improved. Schuman and Johnson (1976), however, disagree with Liska's suggestion that self-report may be an adequate way to measure behavior.

The majority of studies on the effects of sex education consist of behavioral intentions and self-reports, although some investigate "actual" behavior. Few studies, however, use "behavioral intentions" within a sophisticated "expectancy-value" model, as used by Cohen (1976) and Fishbein (1967).[3]

Is Knowledge a Stimulus for "Responsible Behavior?"

An assumption of a substantial proportion of American adults is that provision of sex information will lead to sexual promiscuity and perhaps even to sex crime, such as rape (Abelson et al., 1970; Hoyman, 1968). Lipson and Wolman (1972) described a national probability interview study conducted with over 1,700 males and females sixteen and older. One-third of the respondents agreed that "sex education in schools will encourage more teenage sex before marriage."

In the Abelson et al. (1970) national probability study of 2,486 adults undertaken for the Commission on Obscenity and Pornography, interviewers asked subjects to read a list of possible effects of "looking at or reading sexual materials." Fifty-six percent of the respondents thought such behavior leads to a "breakdown of morals," and 49 percent believed such behavior leads "people to commit rape." (Forty-seven percent of the males and 51 percent of the females believed this statement about rape.) The commission reported that 35 percent of the respondents would oppose the availability of sexual materials even it if were shown that the materials were not harmful. Those respondents who thought undesirable effects followed exposure to sexual materials "rarely or never report having personally experienced them, are more likely to say they occurred to someone else, and are most likely simply to believe in the effect occurring without reference either to themselves or to anyone they personally know" (Report of the Commission, 1970, p. 193).

In a 1974 random telephone survey conducted in Syracuse, one of the nation's leading test markets (Institute for Family Research and Education, 1977), it was found that 18 percent of over nine hundred adult respondents felt that "providing factual information" about sexuality to teenagers would stimulate "experimentation" with sex.

The research we reviewed suggests that sex education course experience is *not* associated with increases in petting, oral-genital sex, homosexuality, extramarital sex, or intercourse. It is important to emphasize that most studies of courses or classes do not include information on the nature of the content

---

[3] Other studies on behavior change reviewed but not discussed here were: Carton & Carton (1971), Crawley et al. (1974), Crosby (1971), Luckey & Bain (1970), Sarrel & Sarrel (1967); Quality Educational Development (1970); and Weichmann & Ellis (1969).

or the teaching style used, and rarely indicate whether the class was well received or was considered boring. It may be unrealistic to expect the same school that cannot effectively teach reading to effectively teach sex education. (Of course, the particular teacher involved could make the difference.)

There is evidence to suggest that education may be helpful in reducing the incidence of venereal disease. There is also evidence indicating that sex education and knowledge are associated with lower rates of unwanted pregnancy and births among unmarried women, but findings are somewhat unclear from study to study because of differences in program comprehensiveness and attention to factors such as the sexual life-style of subjects and the regularity of repeated contacts with program staff.

In addition, our review of the research has indicated that sex education is unlikely to change either the variety or the frequency of a person's patterns of usual sexual behaviors. That is, a person who usually does not enjoy oral sex is unlikely to change the frequency of this behavior after a sex education course, and a person who has frequent intercourse is unlikely to change that frequency because of the course.

Examples of Behavior Change Studies

Levine (1967) reported a study of sex education's association with venereal disease decrease in a Washington, D.C. high school with a high rate of VD. Using another school with no sex education program as a control school, Levine reported that after one year the incidence of gonorrhea in the experimental school had dropped, while the rate in the control school was unchanged. When the control school offered a course, its incidence of gonorrhea also dropped.

Furstenberg et al. (1972) reported a study of the effects of a post partum program designed to encourage the use of contraception and prevent repeat pregnancies among adolescents. Approximately 350 females (85 percent between the ages of fifteen and seventeen) participated in the study, with about 200 in the post partum program and about 150 in a regular prenatal program in which no extra or intensified efforts were made after birth to encourage contraceptive use. (These subjects represented those from the original sample of 404 who were successfully followed up two years after delivery.) The authors reported that the effect of the special program was "visible almost immediately." The difference in repeat pregnancy rates favored the special group from the start and reached a peak at fifteen months after the delivery of the first child, when 36 percent of the regular group and 25 percent of the special group had repeats. Thereafter, differences diminished to the point where, after three years, about 50 percent of both groups had become pregnant again. Rather than taking the early difference in group rates as evidence of success, albeit warranted statistically, the authors pointed out that the figures revealed the inadequacy of care offered in both programs. More repeated contacts with staff may have alleviated the basic problem of inefficient contraceptive use due to sporadic sexual activity.

In his study of 150 college students, Lance (1975) investigated both attitude and behavior change on premarital intercourse, homosexuality, oral-genital sex, and extramarital sex. Lance reported, "None of the single students not having experienced sexual intercourse before the course were engaging in sexual intercourse following the course." He found the same result with regard to homosexuality and oral-genital sex and reported that only one student who had not engaged in extramarital sex before the course was engaging in it following the course. Goodman and Goodman (1976) discussed a program involving required sex education for eleventh-graders, and a Parent Orientation series for parents of the participating students. Unfortunately, the study's methodology renders nearly meaningless the conclusion that parents taking the program showed greater improvement in communicating with their children than parents not in the program. All that is known of their pre/post questionnaire is that it was "simple" and that both the pre- and the post-administrations were mailed to the participating parents. The refusal rate, possible differences between those refusing and those participating in the questionnaire, and reliability for the "attitudes and communication" questionnaire were not reported.

Spanier (1976) reported a national probability study concerning the relationship between premarital sexual behavior and *perceived* sex knowledge among college students. The 1,177 students represented a 70 percent completion rate, with no data available on those who refused participation. "Perceived sex knowledge" was a measure of the respondent's self-reported amount of relevant material obtained, amount of scientific or technical material read, and knowledge relative to friends. The three-item scale had an alpha reliability of .51. Although Spanier concluded his report by stating that it was "not possible to conclude causality one way or another from these data" and that his "findings would best be explained by looking for intervening variables," his discussion of the knowledge-behavior data implies that sex knowledge, especially when received from peers, is antecedent to sexual behavior. (See Lewis's similar conclusion, 1973.) However, Spanier did not distinguish the *kinds of knowledge that are necessary antecedents* for almost all individuals' sexual behavior (e.g., the simple awareness that there is such a thing as intercourse) from those kinds of knowledge that are often thought to be *"stimulators"* of premarital sexual behavior (e.g., sex education that discusses contraception, thereby supposedly "condoning" or "encouraging" intercourse). Unfortunately, and more important, we only know what respondents say they have been exposed to rather than what they actually *know*. The low gamma coefficients describing the relationship and the poor reliability of the perceived knowledge scale suggest caution in drawing any conclusions from the data.

175

Scales (1976) found in his exploratory study of fourteen "treatment" and thirteen "control" families that mothers who had taken a parent sex education course, as compared to mothers who had not, reported significant increases in several variables of communication, including comfort in talking about sex and frequency of initiating conversations with their children about sexuality. In similar research, where parents and children talking about sexuality were videotaped (Institute for Family Research and Education, 1977), families in which a parent had participated in a sex education program, as compared to those who had not, were more likely to be rated "facilitative" rather than "inhibitive" in their communication.

Oskamp et al. (1975) reported on the mid-project results of a longitudinal study on the success and failure of contraceptive planning. New birth control clinic patients in the Los Angeles area had been followed up for one year at the time of the report. A research group of 646 patients was randomly selected, specially interviewed, and sent a follow-up reminder letter (to non-returnees) two months after the usual clinic letter had been sent. A control group of 431 patients received only the usual clinic intake and reminder letter. Using three primary criterion measures (regularity of return to clinic, incidence of unwanted pregnancy, and attrition at the one-year point), Oskamp reported that the use of Miller and Fisk's (1972) Sexual and Contraceptive Knowledge Questionnaire explained 31 percent of the variance on the criterion of "attrition" (multiple $R = .56$), 25 percent of the variance on the criterion "regularity of return" (multiple $R = .50$), and 18 percent of the variance on the criterion "unwanted pregnancy" (multiple $R = .43$). These figures represented the greatest predictive value of any of the single personality, attitude, and knowledge tests used in the study. In addition, two subgroups of the research group were studied: a pregnancy group, who had experienced an unwanted pregnancy after beginning a contraceptive clinic program; and a regular returnee group, who had a perfect record of prompt returns over the one-year study period. The authors found that a "Sex Knowledge" measure (adapted from Goldsmith et al., 1972) revealed that the poor contraceptors had less knowledge about sex.

The technical volumes of the U.S. Commission on Obscenity and Pornography (1970a) contain reports of many studies broadly investigating the relationship between sex knowledge and behavior, including criminal behavior.[4] The commission's studies, though sometimes flawed, uniformly pointed to the conclusion that exposure to erotica does not appear to be related in a significant, causal way to sex crime, either among adults or adoles-

---

[4] The scope of the commission's review of research is currently limited: Few of the studies reviewed in the present paper had been completed in time to be included in the commission's review. That the commission's review may have been limited in any case is indicated by Keating's critique of the research (part of the minority statement issued by three of the commission's nineteen members). (See U.S. Commission on Obscenity and Pornography, 1970b.) (See also Wills, 1977.)

cents. Research reviewed by the commission indicated that sex offenders have *less* exposure to erotica than nonoffenders. Overall, the commission wrote in its summary, research suggests that "childhood experiences which encourage *sexual repression and inhibition of sexual curiosity are associated with psychosexual maladjustment and antisocial sexual behavior"* (1970, p. 286, emphasis added). [5]

Finally, the possible effect of increasing public access to information is illustrated by studying demographic data of the last thirty years in Denmark. In 1940, there were 28 illegitimate births per 1,000 fifteen-to-nineteen-year-olds, and by 1965, the rate had increased to 48 per 1,000. In 1966, however, the Pregnancy Hygiene Act was passed. The two main provisions of the act were: a doctor *must* discuss planning the next child with new mothers, and everyone about fifteen years of age is allowed to seek contraceptive advice and guidance without the consent of parents. While we cannot presume that passage of this act "caused" any change in the illegitimacy rate, the dramatic drop in teenage illegitimacy to a rate of 33 per 1,000 by 1970 could not be explained either by abortion or increased marriage (Braestrup, 1975; 1974).

A more recent development in Denmark is that sex education has been obligatory in all schools since 1971; even in the early 1960s, about half of Denmark's school-age children were estimated to have received sex education. Although the full impact of this curriculum change will not be known for some time, it is important to note that few American states require sex education, and 60 percent of those U.S. school districts that include "sex education" *exclude* birth control as a topic (Alan Guttmacher Institute, 1976). Given this lack of comprehensiveness, it is not surprising that most studies conclude that "sex education" makes little difference in measures of sexual responsibility. Our review has suggested, however, that those with more of the right kinds of "knowledge" about sexuality do tend to behave more responsibly.

Variables That Intervene Between "Sex Education" and "Responsible Sexual Behavior"

While we believe that the search for a direct, causal relationship between current forms of sex education and "responsible" sexuality is probably illusory, one of the reasons for the lack of greater predictive power may be a theoretical and educational neglect of some important variables that intermediate between knowledge acquisition and the manner in which sexual behavior is expressed.

Some of the crucial variables related to responsible sexual behavior which we have not yet treated are: the source of a person's sex education; the type of relationship in which sexual behavior occurs; the person's relative level

---

[5] For an extended historical discussion of pornography, obscenity and the commission, see W. Cody Wilson, 1973.

of literacy; and the extent to which the sexual partners communicate before having intercourse.

Parents and Friends

Parents emerge as important, albeit infrequent, sex educators of children. Several studies have reported that children who confide in or talk frequently with their parents about sex tend to follow more "traditional" norms of sexual behavior by delaying and/or having less frequent intercourse (Cahn, 1975; Fox, 1978; Furstenberg, 1976; Lewis, 1973; Miller & Simon, 1974; Zelnik & Kantner, 1972). And one nationally representative study has indicated that teenage women who confide in their parents about sex are more effective users of contraception (Kantner & Zelnik, 1973).

Research consistently indicates, however, that parents do not frequently assume the responsibility for the sex education of their children, and that when they do, the sex education tends to be limited, especially for males (see review in Scales, 1976). Most young people report that their information was given primarily by friends. Lewis (1973) concluded that sex education received from friends "seems to be associated with more permissive sexual behavior." Especially for males, acceptance by peers may be a crucial contextual variable affecting moral standards (Libby, 1974; Spanier, 1975; Teevan, 1972). While some gross indicators suggest that fewer people currently assent to a double standard, it is obvious that both peers and parents still contribute significantly to a persisting double standard (Scales, 1977a; Buder, Scales, & Sherman, 1977).

Furstenberg (1971; 1976) studied 337 unmarried black teenagers attending a prenatal clinic. He found that girls were much more likely to have used contraception if both they and their mothers reported they had discussed birth control. In addition, birth control use was highest when the teenager said, and the mother confirmed, that the mother was aware of the daughter's sexual activity. Further, girls were much *less* likely to have used birth control if their mothers "strongly disapproved of premarital sexual relations." Cahn (1975) also studied a clinic group of 242 teenagers on their first visit to a Planned Parenthood center. He concluded, "Adolescents who expected a positive reaction from their parents were not only more likely to discuss their family planning needs with their parents, but also were more likely to actually use contraceptive methods in the past" (p. 8). Support for educational efforts intended for parents seems most advisable in light of these research findings. (See Scales & Everly [1977] and The Institute for Family Research and Education [1977] for a discussion of one such program.)

Intimacy and Marital Status

At least two aspects of a couple's relationship seem to affect their level of responsibility in use of birth control: intimacy and marital status. Marriage, for example, is a socially acceptable context in which to view oneself as behaving sexually, and in which one can then take the necessary precautions in order to avoid negatively valued consequences of unprotected intercourse. Pregnant teenagers are increasingly likely, however, to delay marriage and to carry their pregnancies to term. The practical significance of marriage as a contextual aid to responsible sexual behavior among teenagers is further diminished by Presser's (1974) study of New York City mothers. More than 40 percent of the four hundred mothers indicated that they did not speak with their husbands about ways of avoiding birth before their first child was born, and about one-fourth who had already given birth still had not discussed birth control with their husband. These figure dampen the optimism of Westoff's (1976) conclusion that the decline of unplanned births accounted for 95 percent of the 1965–70 reduction in marital fertility. As Westoff pointed out, however, 39 percent of marital fertility remained unplanned, "offering considerable room for decline." Certainly, most teenagers do not have the benefit of a socially sanctioned relationship in which to be consciously prepared, and even the sanctioned relationship of marriage does not solve the problem for sizable percentages of people (Alan Guttmacher Institute, 1977).

As might be expected, the degree of intimacy in a relationship has some effect on the use of contraception to avoid pregnancy, but even these findings are not without qualifications. Research indicates that contraceptive use is positively related to the stability of a relationship (Diamond et al., 1973; Furstenberg, 1971) and to the degree of dyadic commitment, expressed as intentions to marry (Reiss et al., 1975). In Kirkendall and McDermott's (1970) study of U.S. college males, however, birth control did not rate highly as a preintercourse discussion topic, regardless of the affection between the partners. It would also appear that conventional affectional contexts for first sexual relationships have persisted for substantial percentages of adolescents. More teenage females than males tend to have their early sexual experiences within a loving and long-term relationship. It also seems that between 33 to 50 percent of teenage males may not be concerned enough about the possibility of pregnancy to think about using contraception or about raising the issue for discussion (Scales, 1977a; Buder, Scales, & Sherman, 1977). There is also evidence that sweeping changes in *some* sex-role attitudes have not taken place even among college students. Sizable percentages of both sexes assent to a sexual division of labor within the family, although females tend to be more "egalitarian" in their attitudes than males (Osmond & Martin, 1975; Parelius, 1975; Scanzoni, 1976).

Sexual intercourse is increasing among young people (Cannon & Long, 1971; Hunt, 1974; Juhasz, 1976; Sorensen, 1973; Zelnik & Kantner, 1972, 1977), and the relationships in which intercourse is considered acceptable are broadening among high school and college students (Bell & Chaskes, 1970; Hunt, 1974; Zelnik & Kantner, 1977). In view of this, it is important for educational efforts to focus on how to encourage responsible decisions within *any* relationship, regardless of marital status and/or the level of intimacy between the partners.

179

A case in point is the "James at 15" TV show in early 1978, in which the NBC censors decided James could not even euphemistically ask his girlfriend if she was "responsible." It was ironic that with all the fuss raised over the show, a group of teenagers who watched it were uniformly more disappointed at, and critical of, what they thought was a questionable pairing of the barely pubescent James with a girl "at least eighteen or nineteen" and "obviously experienced." To a person, they were angered at the network's censorship of James's attempt to behave responsibly; but they were even more concerned that the *relationship being portrayed didn't seem credible.*

This should be a tremendous lesson: those young people saw that, on the surface of it at least, these two might better not have been sexual partners. We should encourage more of this ability to critique their own relationships, for then young people will be more equipped to say "No" when they want to; and when they say "Yes," it will be with carefully chosen partners, with respect for themselves and their partners which will require them to be prepared. We must help young people select their sexual and reproductive destinies rather than allow them to back into experiences because we simultaneously elevate the importance of sex while trying to keep them from it.

Educational Level and Literacy

The role played by educational level and literacy is critical and is clearly illustrated in a comparison between developing and developed countries. Although traditional roles may be changing in some developing countries, the typical pattern in Islamic society, for instance, has been for nearly all females to be illiterate and eager for marriage and the increase in status that accompanies high fertility, especially of male offspring (Farman-Farmaian, 1975). A similar pattern has existed in Indonesia (Soewondo, 1975); new marriage laws intended to change this pattern only recently have been implemented. As described by a 1973 regional Asian conference on the status of women and family planning, there has been a "close relationship between the low status of women, early and universal marriage of girls, and a high fertility" (Soewondo, 1975, p. 19).

The difference between tradition in the developing countries and current reality in developed countries is dramatic. Illiteracy is common in the developing countries, with early marriage a common means of avoiding temptation to violate religious law prohibiting sex outside of marriage. Thus, conception usually follows marriage. The female fifteen-to-nineteen-year-old population in the United States tends to be more literate than the same age group in developing countries, yet 76 percent of all first births to teenagers are conceived prior to marriage (Kantner & Zelnik, 1975).

Within the relatively more literate United States population, however, differences in illegitimacy by race and socioeconomic status are dramatic. Westoff and Westoff (1971) stated that the 1965 National Fertility Study showed "the poor of both races use contraception less." Among married couples under forty-five, blacks were significantly less likely to have ever used contraception. Part of the reason for this difference is that only 22 percent of black women, as compared to 50 percent of white women, correctly knew when during their periods they could become pregnant. Low- and marginal-income women were also more likely to continue their significantly higher fertility rates than high-income women in the 1970 National Fertility Study. The U.S. Commission on Population Growth and the American Future (1972) described the inverse relationship between education and fertility: With increased education, both planned and unplanned fertility decrease and racial differences tend to be erased. The crucial role of education in eliminating racial fertility differences is also supported in a study of the Atlanta area (Anderson & Smith, 1975). In addition, Weller (1976) reports that in the 1972 National Natality Survey, mothers with less schooling were more likely to say that births were unwanted.

The scope of this problem is enormous. Between 1966 and 1970, about one-third of white and two-thirds of nonwhite women of childbearing age lived in families whose income was 200 percent below the official poverty line, with about half of all U.S. children born into these families (Jaffe, 1972). Although racial differences in both legitimate and illegitimate births continue to decrease, the illegitimacy rate of nonwhite fifteen-to-nineteen-year-olds is still eight times higher than that of white fifteen-to-nineteen-year-olds (National Center for Health Statistics, 1976). Classified by educational attainment, about 47 percent of 1974 live nonwhite births were to women with less than twelve years of schooling; by comparison, only 25 percent of white births were to women with less than twelve years of schooling (National Center for Health Statistics, 1975).

A study reported by Jekel et al. (1973) underscores the importance of these statistics. They studied a group of 180 unmarried black women under eighteen who had entered Yale University's Young Mothers Clinic program, part of which entailed attendance at a special school for pregnant students. At fifteen months post partum, over three-quarters of those still in school or graduated were using contraception, as compared with less than one-third of those who had dropped out. Predictably, only 8 percent of the in-school group had another pregnancy, as compared with 44 percent of the dropouts.

Furstenberg (1976) and Presser (1975) have also demonstrated the complicated, inverse relationship between educational attainment and unwanted fertility. Furstenberg (1976) conducted a five-year study in Baltimore of about four hundred adolescent mothers and their classmates who avoided early parenthood. Forty percent of the women who left school after their first child was born had two more pregnancies, while only 25 percent of the women who returned to school had an equal rate of reconception. At the five-year follow-up, 90 percent of the returnees had completed high school, while only about half of the young mothers had finished school. On the average, the young mothers had about two fewer years of schooling at the five-year follow-up than the nonparent classmates. About 80 percent of pregnant teens will never return to school (Alan Guttmacher Institute, 1976).

Throughout the world, illiteracy and low educational levels tend to be most common in areas of high population growth. Brown et al. (1976) have summarized the demographic problems of nations with high illiteracy rates with its implications for fertility, understood best by noting that *women* comprise nearly two-thirds of the world's 800 million illiterate adults. Not only are funds in short supply, but "the pyramidal distribution of age groups in a rapidly growing population also means that the ratio of trained teachers to school-age children is also decreasing" (p. 9). The continued illiteracy and low status of women ensures, in most cultures, that their fertility will be high and will serve to prevent women from having control over their own lives (Newland, 1977).

These changes have legal, economic, and political consequences in addition to the manifest social ones. Legally, questions must be raised in developed countries about: laws requiring parental consent for sexuality-related health care; definitions of "social union," and hence, definitions of property ownership, taxation, and inheritance rights of those born outside marriage; and the necessity of mandatory or voluntary sex education of children by formal social groups and institutions. Economic implications arise from increased needs and decreased earning power of young mothers. The lack of child-care services makes it even more difficult for young women to get jobs.

Fawcett (1970) provided a cautionary note to any discussion or explanation for these trends: "Mistakes may be made in deducing from behavior that certain motives are primary, when in fact the behavior in question is the result of a compromise among many motives" (1970, p. 77). It is necessary, however, to try to place these phenomena in some rational framework in order to plan effective social action. The irony, of course, is that decisions about sexual and contraceptive behavior are typically "irrational" for most young people, and attempts at "rational" explanation of motives may fall into the trap described by Fawcett. Decision making about sexuality among adolescents in Western society seems to be a result of compromise among uncertain degrees of commitment, continued belief in the sexual double standard, and combinations of legal obstacles, factual ignorance, and behavioral discomfort in talking about feelings. These dynamics appear to affect most young people regardless of demographic characteristics, but their effect on the relatively less literate is even more dramatic.

Literacy may have two faces: in the developing countries, a lack of it helps to perpetuate population-related problems; in the developed countries, a lack of it has the same effect, but so perhaps does the presence of literacy. With some minimal literacy and exposure to the basic media of industrialized society (books, magazines, newspapers, records, television, radio, and movies), the effect of this greater literacy (relative to the nonindustrialized countries) might be to reinforce even more insidiously beliefs that knowledge is harmful, that sex must be spontaneous, or that females who get pregnant really wanted to anyway. Cohen's (1976) previously cited work is provocative in this regard. He found that normative standards were more highly associated with behavioral intentions to use a particular contraceptive than were attitudes about that contraceptive. That is, other sources, such as doctors, were powerful influences on behavioral choice.

In addition, the relatively more literate person who holds some mythological beliefs may also be a more difficult target of sex education. For instance, in a probability study of a large urban area in Venezuela, McNelly et al. (1975) found that respondents above the median on a composite indicator of socioeconomic status (including years of education) were more internally consistent and demonstrated higher degrees of organization in their belief systems than respondents below the SES median.

Thus, literacy and the manner in which the symbols of mass communication are manipulated may have an intermediating effect on the sex education–observed/reported behavior relationship. In this regard, attention has recently been directed toward how to best market family planning ideas and technology in developed countries. How to increase condom use, best techniques for getting people to use a birth control clinic, and testing the effectiveness of slogans and attractive packaging are some examples of this effort.

Communication

A major part of instruction involves helping people to communicate verbally about sex with each other. Research consistently indicates that young, unmarried people do not talk with each other frequently or in great depth about contraception and venereal disease (Arnold, 1972; Goldsmith et al., 1972; Gordon & Scales, 1977; Kirkendall & McDermott, 1970; Sorensen, 1973). A great deal of sexual expression occurs interpersonally, but few people learn how to communicate honestly with others until they are in a pressurized situation demanding decisions. Part of this essential instruction in communication might involve discussion and demonstration of how sex-role teachings perpetuate miscommunication and ignorance in sexual relationships. Males might examine, for instance, the feelings they had when they honestly wanted to refuse sexual intercourse, but did not because of a deep-seated notion that they *should always* want sex. Hatcher (1978) reports, for instance, that the most popular chapter in Emory University's *What's Happening* magazine is "How to Say No."

Educators cannot, of course, simply tell young people it's all right to say "No." A more prevalent concern is how to say "No" without turning off the partner. The counselor or educator might respond that there is risk involved, and that no guarantee over the partner's reactions can be made. Young people appreciate honesty and also appreciate the further observation "If your partner threatens to leave if you say 'No,' it might be, as the old blue-grass song says, 'the best thing that's happened yet.' "

Finally, both sexes might benefit from creative instruction in the area of fantasy. Learning that fantasies are "normal" and that you do not always have to act on them can have a very liberating effect and could help people more easily accept themselves as sexual beings. As we have already noted, acceptance of sexuality has been consistently related to increased use of contraception (Hacker, 1976; Reiss et al., 1975; Kantner & Zelnik, 1973; Shah, Zelnik, & Kantner, 1975). However, parents, counselors, educators, and social planners can expect little responsible sexuality if young people are admonished to be responsible but also taught to feel guilty and secretive about their sexual experiences. The only credible way to help young people say, "No" is to provide an environment in which it is also possible to say, "Yes." And saying "Yes" need not necessarily (or at all) mean sexual intercourse. There are many ways to express one's sexual feelings and impulses—petting, kissing, mutual masturbation, caressing, to say nothing of the ancient erotic and delectable art of massage. The book that in our judgment most sensibly treats this subject is Eleanor Hamilton's *Sex With Love* (See "Selected List of Resources").

References Abelson, H., Cohen, R., Heaton, E., & Slider, C. Public attitudes toward and experience with erotic materials. In U.S. Commission on Obscenity and Pornography, *Technical Reports of the Commission.* Washington, D.C.: U.S. Government Printing Office, 1970, *6.*

Adams, W. J. Sex composition in family life courses: How important is this? *Family Coordinator,* 1971, *20,* 55–61.

Alan Guttmacher Institute. *Planned births, the future of the family, and the quality of American life.* New York: Planned Parenthood Federation of America, June 1977.

Alan Guttmacher Institute. *11 million teenagers.* New York: Planned Parenthood Federation of America, 1976.

Anderson, J. E., & Smith, J. C. Planned and unplanned fertility in a metropolitan area: Black and white differences. *Family Planning Perspectives,* 1975, *7* (6), 281–286.

Arnold, C. B. The sexual behavior of inner city adolescent condom users. *Journal of Sex Research,* 1972, *8* (4), 298–309.

Arrey, W. R., & Tresher, W. H. Trends in attitudes toward abortion, 1972–1975. *Family Planning Perspectives,* 1976, *8* (3), 117–124.

Battista, A. *An exploration of factors associated with the effectiveness of training health education teachers: An evaluation of New York University's experienced teacher fellowship program in sex education for the elementary school. . . .* Disseration, New York University, 1972.

Bell, R. R., & Chaskes, J. B. Premarital sexual experience among coeds, 1958 and 1968. *Journal of Marriage and the Family,* 1970, *32,* 81–84.

Board of Education, Flint, Michigan. *Evaluation of the family life education program.* Flint, Michigan, 1975.

Braestrup, A. *Sex education in Denmark.* Paper presented at seminar on Population and Family Planning Education, Scandinavian Seminar College, Denmark, June 22–July 19, 1975.

Braestrup, A. Teenage pregnancies in Denmark. *Journal of Biosocial Science,* 1974, *6,* 471–475.

Brown, L. R., McGrath, P. L., & Stokes, B. *Twenty-two dimensions of the population problem.* Worldwatch paper 5, March 1976. Washington, D.C.: Worldwatch Institute.

Brown, S., Lieberman, E. J., & Miller, W. B. *Young adults as partners and planners.* Paper presented at annual meeting of the American Public Health Association, Chicago, Illinois, November 16–20, 1975.

Buder, J., Scales, P., & Sherman, L. Virgins may be vanishing, but the double standard persists. Unpublished paper, 1977.

Cahn, J. *Adolescents' needs regarding family planning services.* Paper presented at World Population Society Conference, Washington, D.C., November 19–21, 1975.

Cannon, K. L., & Long, R. Premarital sexual behavior in the sixties. In C. Broderick (ed.), *A decade review of family research and action.* Minneapolis: National Council on Family Relations, 1971, 25–38.

Carrera, M. A. A sex education program that works. *SIECUS Report,* 1978, *6* (4), 6.

Carton, J., & Carton, J. Evaluation of a sex education program for children and their parents: Attitude and interactional changes. *Family Coordinator, 23* (4), 359–364.

Cobliner, W. G. Pregnancy in the single adolescent girl: The role of cognitive functions. *Journal of Youth and Adolescence,* 1974, *3,* 17–29.

Cohen, J. *A study of attitudinal and normative factors leading to partners' contraceptive decisions.* Final Report, NICHD Contract #N01-HD-52805. University of Florida: Center for Consumer Research, 1976.

Crawley, L. W., Malfetti, J. L., & Bartholomew, F. E. Sex education for school physicians: Follow-up of an in-service training course. *Family Coordinator, 23* (4), 359–364.

Crosby, J. F. The effects of family life education on the values and attitudes of adolescents. *Family Coordinator,* 1971, *20* (2), 137–140.

Cutright, P. The teen-age sexual revolution and the myth of an abstinent past. *Family Planning Perspectives,* 1972, *4* (1), 24–31.

Cvetkovich, G., & Grote, B. *Psychosocial development and the social problem of teenage illegitimacy.* Paper presented at Conference on Determinants of Adolescent Pregnancy and Childbearing, Washington, D.C., May 3–5, 1976.

Diamond, M., Steinhoff, P. G., Palmore, J. A., & Smith, R. G. Sexuality, birth control, and abortion: A decision making sequence. *Journal of Biosocial Science,* 1973, *5,* 347.

Driscoll, R. H., & Davis, K. W. Sexual restraints: A comparison of perceived and self-reported reasons for college students. *The Journal of Sex Research,* 1971, *9* (2), 253–262.

Farman-Farmaian, S. Early marriage and pregnancy in traditional Islamic society. In P. Piotrow (ed.), *Draper World Population Fund Report, 1,* Autumn 1975, 6–9. Washington, D.C.: Population Crisis Committee.

Fassbender, W. V. *The sex knowledge of health and physical educators as it relates to attitudes toward sex and sex education, patterns of professional preparation and practice, and selected personal factors.* Dissertation, Temple University, 1971.

186

Fawcett, J. T. *Psychology and population.* New York: The Population Council, 1970.

Finkel, M. L., & Finkel, D. J. Sexual and contraceptive knowledge, attitudes, and behavior of male adolescents. *Family Planning Perspectives,* 1975, *7* (6), 256–260.

Fishbein, M. Attitude and the prediction of behavior. In M. Fishbein (ed.), *Readings in attitude theory and measurement.* New York: Wiley, 1967.

Fisher, D., & Fisher, R. L. *What we really know about childbearing.* New York: Basic Books, 1976.

Freedman, R., & Berelson, B. The record of family planning programs. *Studies in Family Planning,* 1976, *7* (1).

Furstenberg, F. F. *Unplanned parenthood: The social consequences of teenage childbearing.* New York: The Free Press, 1976.

Furstenberg, F. F., Jr., Masnick, G. S., & Ricketts, S. How can family planning programs delay repeat teenage pregnancies? *Family Planning Perspectives,* 1972, *4* (3), 54–60.

Furstenberg, F. F. Birth control experience among pregnant adolescents: The process of unplanned parenthood. *Social Problems,* 1971, *19* (2), 192–203.

Geyer, G. S. *The young Russians.* Homewood, Ill.: ETC Publications, 1975.

Gilbert, R., & Matthews, V. G. Young males' attitudes toward condom use. In M. A. Redford, G. W. Duncan, & D. J. Prager (eds.), *The condom: Increasing utilization in the United States.* San Francisco: San Francisco Press, Inc., 1974.

Glick, P. Some recent changes in American families. U.S. Bureau of the Census, *Current Population Reports,* July 1975, Series P-23, *52,* 1–17.

Goldsmith, S., Gabrielson, M. O., Matthews, V. G. & Potts, L. Teenagers, sex, and contraception. *Family Planning Perspectives,* 1972, *4* (1), 32–38.

Goodman, B., & Goodman, N. Effects of parent orientation meetings on parent-child communication about sexuality and family life. *The Family Coordinator,* 1976, *25* (3), 285–290.

Gordon, S. *You would if you loved me.* New York: Bantam, 1978.

Gordon, S. *Ten heavy facts about sex.* Charlottesville, Va.: Ed-U Press, 1971.

Gordon, S., & Scales, P. Sexual communication among college undergraduates. Unpublished data, 1977.

Hacker, S. *The effect of situational and interactional aspects of sexual encounters on premarital contraceptive behavior.* Paper available from the University of Michigan, Dept. of Population Planning, School of Public Health, Ann Arbor, 1976.

Hatcher, R. Remarks made at Second Annual Conference of the Florida Alliance for Responsible Adolescent Parenting, Orlando, April 1978.

Hertoft, P. *Some remarks on sex education in the schools.* Paper presented at Congress International de Sexologies Medicale, Paris, Charlottsville, Va.: Ed-U Press, 1977.

Hoch, L. *Attitude change as a function of sex education in a high school general biology class.* Dissertation, Indiana University, 1968.

Howard, F. W., Riefler, C. B., & Liptzin, M. B. Effects of exposure to pornography. *Technical Reports of the Commission on Obscenity and Pornography, 8,* Washington, D.C.: U.S. Government Printing Office, 1970.

Humphrey, F. G., Libby, R. W., & Nass, G. O. Attitude change among professionals toward sex education for adolescents. *Family Coordinator,* 1969, *18* (4), 332–339.

Hunt, M. *Sexual behavior in the 1970's.* Chicago: Playboy Press, 1974.

Insko, R. W. Developing family actualization: The Frankfort Project. *Family Coordinator,* 1971, *20,* 17–22.

Institute for Family Research and Education. *A training manual for organizers of community sex education programs for parents.* Charlottesville, Va.: Ed-U Press, 1977.

Jaffe, F. S. Low-income families: Fertility changes in the 1960's. *Family Planning Perspectives,* 1972, *4* (1), 43–47.

Janowitz, B. S. The impact of AFDC on illegitimate birth rates. *Journal of Marriage and the Family,* 1976, *38* (3), 485–494.

Jekel, J. F., Klerman, L. V., & Bancroft, D. R. E. Factors associated with rapid subsequent pregnancies among school-age mothers. *American Journal of Public Health,* 1973, *63* (9), 769–773.

Juhasz, A. M. Changing patterns of premarital sexual behavior. *Intellect,* 1976 (May), 511–514.

Kantner, J. F., & Zelnik, M. Sex and reproduction among U.S. teenage women. *The Draper World Population Fund Report.* Washington, D.C.: Population Crisis Committee, 1975, 13–15.

Kantner, J. F., & Zelnik, M. Contraception and pregnancy: Experience of young, unmarried women in the United States. *Family Planning Perspectives,* 1973, *5* (2), 21.

Kirkendall, L. A. & McDermott, R. J. Premarital intercourse. In J. P. Semmens and K. E. Krantz (eds.), *The adolescent experience.* London: The Macmillan Co., 1970.

Konner, M. J. Adolescent pregnancy. *New York Times,* 24 September 1977.

Lance, L. M. Human sexuality course socialization: An analysis of changes in sexual attitudes and sexual behavior. *Journal of Sex Education and Therapy,* 1975, *2,* 8–14.

Levine, M. I. Sex education in the public elementary and high school curriculum. *Journal of School Health,* 1967, *37,* 30–39.

Lewis, R. A. Parents and peers: Socialization agents in the coital behavior of young adults. *Journal of Sex Research,* 1973, *9* (2), 156–170.

Libby, R. W. Adolescent sexual attitudes and behavior. *Journal of Clinical Child Psychology,* 1974, *3* (3), 36–42.

Libby, R. W. Parental attitudes toward high school sex education programs. *Family Coordinator,* 1970, *19* (3), 234–247.

Lipson, G., & Wolman, D. Polling Americans on birth control and population. *Family Planning Perspectives,* 1972, *4* (1), 39–42.

Liska, A. E. Emergent issues in the attitude-behavior consistency controversy. *American Sociological Review,* 1974, *39* (2), 261–272.

Luckey, E. B., & Bain, J. K. A follow-up study on in-service training in family life education. *Family Coordinator,* 1970, *19,* 88–94.

McNelly, J. T., Martin, R., Izcaray, F., & Khampitoon, B. Cognitive organization and socioeconomic status: Belief systems about population and family planning in Barquisimeto, Venezuela. Madison: University of Wisconsin, August 1975.

Miller, P. Y., & Simon, W. Adolescent sexual behavior: Context and change. *Social Problems,* 1974, *22* (1), 58–76.

Miller, W. B. Sexuality, contraception, and pregnancy in a high school population. *California Medicine,* 1973, *119* (2), 14–21.

Miller, W. B., & Fisk, M. M. *Sexual knowledge questionnaire.* Stanford: Stanford University School of Medicine, 1972.

Mims, F. Effectiveness of an interdisciplinary course in human sexuality. *Nursing Research,* 1974, *23,* 248–253.

Moore, K., & Caldwell, S. Out of wedlock pregnancy and childbearing, working paper 992-02. Washington, D.C.: The Urban Institute, September 1976.

National Center for Health Statistics. *Teenage childbearing: United*

States, 1966–1975. Monthly Vital Statistics Report, (HRA) 77–1120, *26* (5), Supplement, September 8, 1977.

National Center for Health Statistics. *Advance report, final natality statistics, 1975.* Rockville, Md.: U.S. Department of Health, Education and Welfare, *25* (10), December 30, 1976.

National Center for Health Statistics. Final natality statistics, 1974. *Monthly Vital Statistics Report,* 1975, *24* (11), (supp. 2, HRA 76–1120).

Newland, K. *Women and population growth: Choice beyond childbearing.* Washington, D.C.: Worldwatch Institute (paper no. 16), December 1977.

Olson, D., & Gravatt, A. Attitude change in a functional marriage course. *Family Coordinator,* 1968, *17* (2), 99–104.

Oskamp, S., Mindick, B., & Berger, D. *Longitudinal study of success versus failure in contraceptive planning.* Paper presented at annual meeting of the American Psychological Association, Chicago, September 1975.

Osmond, M. W., & Martin, P. Y. Sex and sexism: A comparison of male and female sex role attitudes. *Journal of Marriage and the Family,* 1975, *37* (4), 744–759.

Parelius, A. P. Emerging sex role attitudes, expectations, and strains among college women. *Journal of Marriage and the Family,* 1975, *37* (1), 146–154.

Perkins, E. V. Reproductive education in a college general biology course. *Marriage and Family Living,* 1959, *21* (1), 41–42.

Population Council. *A manual for surveys of fertility and family planning: Knowledge, attitudes, and practice.* New York: The Population Council, 1970.

Population Crisis Committee. Family planning programs do work. *Population,* 1976, *4,* 1.

Powledge, R. M. What schools teach of sex is still controversial. *New York Times,* 27 February 1977.

Presser, H. B. *Social consequences of teenage childbearing.* Paper presented at NICHD Conference on the Consequences of Adolescent Pregnancy and Childbearing. Bethesda, Maryland, October 1975.

Presser, H. B. Early motherhood: Ignorance or bliss? *Family Planning Perspectives, 1974, 6* (1), 8–14.

Price, Q. L. E. *Influence of sex and family life education on student attitude toward traditional family ideology and sex knowledge.* Dissertation, United States International University, Ann Arbor: University Microfilms, 1971. No. 71-7881.

Quality Educational Development, Inc. Sex education programs in the public schools of the United States. *Technical Reports of the Commission on Obscenity and Pornography, 10.* Washington, D.C.: U.S. Government Printing Office, 1970.

Reichelt, P. A., & Werley, H. H. Contraception, abortion, and venereal disease: Teenagers' knowledge and the effect of education. *Family Planning Perspectives,* 1975, *7* (2), 83–88.

Reiss, I. L., Banwart, A., & Foreman, H. Premarital contraceptive usage: A study and some theoretical explorations. *Journal of Marriage and the Family,* 1975, *37* (3), 619–630.

Rogers, E. M. *Communication strategies for family planning.* Glencoe, Ill.: Free Press, 1973.

Sarrel, P., & Sarrel, L. J. The university hospital and the teenage unwed mother. *American Journal of Public Health,* 1967, *57* (3), 1308–1313.

Scales, P. *Sex education policies and the primary prevention of teenage pregnancy: Toward a family impact perspective.* Paper presented at Family Impact Seminar Conference on Family Policy and Teenage Pregnancy, Washington, D.C., October 1978.

Scales, P. Males and morals: Teenage contraceptive behavior amid the double standard. *Family Coordinator,* 1977a, *26* (3), 210–222.

Scales, P. *Youth and the future of ignorance.* Paper presented at annual meeting of American Association of Psychiatric Services for Children, Washington, D.C., November 18, 1977b.

Scales, P. *A quasi-experimental evaluation of sex education programs for parents.* Dissertation, Syracuse University, 1976.

Scales, P., & Everly, K. A community sex education program for parents. *The Family Coordinator,* 1977, *26* (1), 37–45.

Scales, P., & Everly, K. *Preparing community leaders to be sex educators of parents.* Paper presented at annual meeting of Society for Scientific Study of Sex, New York City, November 2, 1975.

Scanzoni, J. Sex role change and influences on birth intentions. *Journal of Marriage and the Family,* 1976, *38* (1), 43–60.

Schuman, H., & Johnson, M. P. Attitudes and behavior. In A. Inkeles, J. Coleman, & N. Smelser (eds.), *Annual Review of Sociology.* Palo Alto, Calif.: Annual Reviews, Inc., 1976, *2,* 161–207.

Shah, F., Zelnik, M., & Kantner, J. F. Unprotected intercourse among unwed teenagers. *Family Planning Perspectives,* 1975, *1,* 39–44.

Soewondo, N. Marriage law reform in Indonesia. In P. Piotrow (ed.), *Draper World Population Fund Report, 1,* Autumn 1975, 18–19. Washington, D.C.: Population Crisis Committee.

Somerville, R. Family life and sex education in the turbulent sixties. In C. R. Broderick (ed.), *A decade of family research and action.* Minneapolis: National Council on Family Relations, 1971.

Sorensen, R. C. *Adolescent sexuality in contemporary America.* New York: World Publishing Co., 1973.

Spanier, G. B. Perceived sex knowledge, exposure to eroticism, and premarital sexual behavior: The impact of dating. *Sociological Quarterly,* 1976, *17,* 247–261.

Spanier, G. B. Sexualization and premarital sexual behavior. *Family Coordinator,* 1975, *24* (1), 33–41.

Teevan, J. J. Reference groups and premarital sexual behavior. *Journal of Marriage and the Family,* 1972, *34* (2), 283–291.

U.S. Commission on Population Growth and the American Future. *Population and the American future.* New York: New American Library, 1972.

U.S. Commission on Obscenity and Pornography. *Technical report of the commission, VI.* Washington, D.C.: U.S. Government Printing Office, 1970a.

U.S. Commission on Obscenity and Pornography. Report of Commissioner Charles H. Keating. *Report of the commission.* New York: Bantam Books, 1970b, 578–700.

Weichmann, G., & Ellis, A. A study of the effects of sex education and premarital petting and coital behavior. *Family Coordinator,* 1969, *18* (3), 231–234.

Weller, R. H. Number and timing failures among legitimate births in the United States: 1968, 1969, and 1972. *Family Planning Perspectives,* 1976, *8* (3), 111–116.

Westoff, C. F. The decline of unplanned births in the United States. *Science,* 1976, 191, 38ff.

Westoff, L. A. Two-time winners. *New York Times Magazine,* 10 August 1975.

Westoff, L. A., & Westoff, C. F. *From now to zero.* Boston: Little, Brown, 1971.

Wicker, A. W. Attitudes versus actions: The relationship of verbal and overt behavioral responses to attitude objects. *The Journal of Social Issues,* Autumn 1969, *25,* 41–78.

Wills, G. Measuring the impact of erotica. *Psychology Today,* August 1977, 30–34; 74–76.

Wilson, E. R. *An intervention strategy to improve information about human sexuality among undergraduate students.* Dissertation, Syracuse University, 1974.

Wilson, W. C. Pornography: The emergence of a social issue and the beginning of psychology study. *Journal of Social Issues,* 1973, *29* (3), 7–17.

Woods, N. F., & Mandetta, A. F. Changes in students' knowledge and attitude following a course in human sexuality: A case control comparison. *Journal of Sex Education and Therapy,* 1975, *2,* 47–59.

Zelnik, M., & Kantner, J. F. Sexual and contraceptive experience of young, unmarried women in the United States, 1976 and 1971. *Family Planning Perspectives,* 1977, *9* (2), 55–71.

Zelnik, M., & Kantner, J. F. The probability of premarital intercourse. *Social Science Research,* 1972, *1,* 335–341.

Ten

Current Innovations and Suggestions for Creative Action

The turnaround on the issue of teenage sexuality and pregnancy is amazing. It is now one of the most fashionable of social causes. The level of public discourse has improved in quality and is reaching a broader constituency, with TV specials such as "Guess Who's Pregnant?" and "And Baby Makes Two," articles in everything from *Psychology Today, Teen,* and *Family Health* to the *Reader's Digest,* and projects such as New York's Door, the Youth Values Project of the Population Institute, Rochester (NY) Planned Parenthood's "Man '78," the Rock Stars Project of San Francisco Population Institute, Zero Population Growth's "Love Carefully Day," and National Family Sex Education Week of the Institute for Family Research and Education. The National Alliance for Optional Parenthood sponsored a contest to pick the best article on teenage sexuality written for a high school newspaper. Hundreds of communities have held health fairs, workshops, and professional meetings.

Suggestions for Creative Action

For Adolescents

Laws and hospital practices that require adolescents to have parental consent to obtain contraceptives and medical aid for pregnancy or its termination should be repealed. The courts have consistently held in the last several years that most parental consent and notification statutes are an unconstitutional infringement of adolescents' rights, even "underage" adolescents. The confidentiality of the adolescent-physician relationship must be protected by law.

A national network of youth clinics associated with general hospitals and county health departments and Planned Parenthood agencies, where adolescents can receive free birth control and abortion services as well as general medical treatment, should be developed.

Adolescent clinics with specially trained counselors and medical staff should be added to existing community family planning agencies and Planned Parenthood centers.

Laws that restrict where and to whom nonprescriptive contraceptives can be sold should be repealed. Moreover, open display of contraceptives in drugstores is essential.

195

More quality programs are needed in sex education and family planning in professional schools. Medical, nursing, social work, psychology, and teacher-training departments and institutions, which need these programs the most, often deal with human sexuality in a perfunctory way.

Organized religious groups can be encouraged to translate their generally progressive and ethical positions on adolescent sexuality into active support for birth control centers for youth and into programs for disseminating sex information through their own youth-sponsored groups.

Basic facts about ovulation, pregnancy, and the correct uses of contraceptives can be disseminated through the popular media, student newspapers, magazines, community agencies, and youth groups.

It is essential to produce films and publications that meet the needs of the vast majority of adolescents, who are not intellectuals, and of such neglected groups as adolescents with learning disabilities, the physically handicapped, and the mentally retarded.

Hot lines for teenagers seeking sex information can be staffed by collaborative efforts of mental health clinics, social service agencies, and other sophisticated community health groups, which have had virtually no role in sex education and are seeking a way of offering a community service.

Health care and straightforward information about contraception, prevention of unwanted pregnancy, and venereal disease can be provided for the several hundred thousand adolescents incarcerated in detention centers, homes for the emotionally disturbed, prisons, or schools for delinquents.

The use of nonprescription contraception for adolescents should be emphasized by encouraging newspapers and magazines to accept advertisements from manufacturers of condoms and foams. Private enterprise will find a discreet way of popularizing and letting adolescents know about the appropriate use of these contraceptives. Some changes are underway. KNTC, San Jose, California's ABC affiliate, has been airing a Trojan advertisement with some initial negative response yielding to a five times greater favorable viewer response. The June 1977 Supreme Court ruling that it is unconstitutional to prohibit advertising or display of contraception is expected to encourage more widespread publicity of contraception (Brozan, 1977).

Antivenereal disease propaganda makes more sense when the condom is emphasized as a means of prevention.

Research is needed on adolescent myths about sex and the lines adolescents use for exploitation and seduction ("If you love me, you'll sleep with me"). These can be appropriately dispelled or neutralized by publicity in the youth newspapers, recordings, magazines, and television.

The Role of the School

Following informal discussions involving the effectiveness of sex education programs in the schools, we are usually asked to give several examples of what we consider a model program. At this point, we know of no program that can be considered a proven model. We are still working on it! A successful sex education program, however, should have the support and encouragement of teachers, parents, administrators, politicians, and the community as a whole.

The Sex Education Committee of the New York State Coalition for Family Planning (1975) suggests, "The effective sex education program concerns itself with the biological, sociological, and the psychological variables which affect personality development and interpersonal relations." Such a program is based on three interrelated components:

1 Cognitive: dealing with factual information, research findings, and other authoritative materials which will provide one with a sound and comprehensive informational base about sexuality.

2 Affective: activities leading to the development of insights and understandings of one's own sexuality and the implications of this knowledge for personal relationships.

3 Skill: learning to make decisions, determine values and behaviors dealing with issues of sexuality.

The committee suggests that a program begin by first presenting a core of sexual facts and research that hopefully will stimulate discussion of attitudes, feelings, and values concerning human sexual behavior. "An increased understanding of self, others, and relationships can occur with sound information, discussion, and appraisal. Sexuality is then viewed in its totality and in relation to each individual's needs and desired lifestyle."

Other specific goals provided by the Sex Education Committee include:

To provide for individuals an adequate knowledge of their own physical, mental, and emotional maturation process as related to sex.

To eliminate fears and anxieties relative to individual sexual development and adjustments.

To develop objective and understanding attitudes toward sex in all of its various manifestations—in the individual and in others.

To give individuals insight concerning their relationships to members of both sexes and to help them understand their obligations and responsibilities.

To provide an appreciation of the positive satisfaction that wholesome human relations can bring in both individuals and family living.

To build an understanding of the need for moral values that are essential to provide rational bases for making decisions.

Although not a "proven" model, one of the best school-based programs to date is the Family Life Education Program initiated by the Community Schools of Flint, Michigan. The basic aim of their sex education program is to assist a youth in achieving his or her fullest capacity for a healthy personality through a planned program designed to help growing persons understand all aspects of the human growth process. These schools view sex education as an important facet of any family life education program, with the facts of human reproduction comprising only one segment of sex education.

The Flint program has focused on three stages of human development. The primary focus during the preadolescent program (grades 4–6) is on concepts involving the facts of reproduction, with greater emphasis placed on psychosocial and psychosexual concepts during adolescence (grades 10–12). The choice of grade levels 5, 8, 10, and 12 is based on prior community experience, which indicated that "these levels best meet the needs of children and parents. Also, the practical requirements of training teachers and developing suitable materials for use in the classroom have influenced the selection of these specific levels" (Dale & Chamis, 1971).

Throughout the program there is an emphasis on helping students build a system of values to guide their behavior as they encounter decisions that will significantly affect their lives. Philosophically, the sex education program provides the student not only with facts, but with "the opportunity to explore, test, and retest his opinions and attitudes with the teacher and with his fellow students."

Of particular interest is their list of "Common Misconceptions of a Sex Education Program" and an explanation:

Common Misconceptions of a Sex Education Program

That it will relieve the parent of responsibility for guiding children and adolescents.

That it will relieve the church of responsibility for helping individuals build sound values.

That it will lessen sexual promiscuity or increase it through the stimulation of natural curiosity.

That it will automatically reduce the incidence of venereal disease.

That it will eliminate unwanted pregnancies.

That it will prevent hasty, ill-advised marriages.

Any school program that sets as its goals any of these misconceptions is idealistic and unrealistic. This is the kind of negative thinking that characterizes many school administrators and parents. It cannot form the basis for the development of a sound educational program. Sex education in

> the schools cannot be equated with moral indoctrination; it should seek to equip young people with the skills, knowledge, and attitudes that will enable them to make intelligent choices and decisions (Dale and Chamis, 1971).

The Flint plan also includes discussions with parents of participating students. Many of the parents revealed inaccurate information, inadequate vocabularies, and generally had difficulty communicating with their children. A letter is sent home inviting parents to a "special meeting" in which the objectives and content of presentations to their children are examined. According to Dale and Chamis (1971), "Parents need to understand the normalcy of sexual interest in children, and be able to accept growth changes as they occur." They need to be reassured that their standards of family living and values will be supported. They need to hear that they, as parents, play the most important role as sex educators of their own children, and that the school program is only supplementary.

Until schools can improve their image with adolescents, however, the best they can do is to improve the teaching of the human reproduction sequence in biology and the venereal disease component in health. For those able to teach more, one of the best teaching guides we know of is Canada's *Sex Education—A Teacher's Guide* (1977), which includes five pamphlets on sexual activities, family planning, birth control and abortion, misuse of contraception/VD, and population. Included in the sixth pamphlet, the "Introduction," is the following message for teachers:

> Teaching sexuality implies that the person teaching knows enough about the subject to communicate sound information, and feels sufficiently comfortable to do this without the red-faced embarrassment and nervous giggles that have accompanied many former attempts at sex education. In our society, which has had such a long history of sexual repression, especially of the female's sexuality, such a person is indeed unusual. The present flux of standards, morals, and attitudes makes the teacher's job even more difficult, for in addition to factual information, the teacher must communicate the need for some structure, some sense of values.
>
> Perhaps the information adolescents are searching for most is how sex fits into their lives. Our society for the last two hundred years has operated on the basis that one falls in love, gets married, and then has sex as an expression of the marital love. Love here is the pivotal concept—if one is in love, then one gets married; if one is in love, then one can have sex with the loved partner; if one is having sex, then one must be in love (this applies much more to females than males at the present time). If love makes all this all right, then all that is necessary is to figure out what love is, and find out

how to tell if one is "in love." Every day, we are assaulted by love—from magazines, television, commercials, music, art. Love, we are led to believe, is any emotion ranging from passion to romance, friendship, affection, "feeling good." Very rarely is there any mention of the courage, initiative, patience, risk, hard work, flexibility, and persistence that are often required in a love relationship. Thus adolescents are often doubly disadvantaged—not only do they lack a good understanding about their bodies and sexual functioning, but they do not understand love—the conflict and resolution, the give and take that it involves.

Sexuality education is not just reproductive biology or contraception, though these subjects are intrinsically involved. Rather it is the communication of the responsibility, the humour, the pleasure, the place and function of love, sex and sexual expression in our lives. It is basically communication of intangibles, of feelings in addition to facts. We do not want to provide our adolescents with just factual information on how their bodies work, or how to "do it"; rather, the goal is to provide some guide to this confusing and important part of life. Hopefully, sexuality education will help our teen-agers communicate with each other, and with the adult society in which they live. It should have the effect of opening up this area to discussion, of making it possible for adolescents (and teachers) to ask questions and get informative answers, and to eventually be more comfortable with their bodies and themselves.[1]

Schools might also communicate directly a few facts about contraception and birth control in articles in the school newspapers or in an advice column, or refer students to better-informed sources. There has recently been progress in students' rights to publish sex-related articles in their school newspapers. Cases in Fairfax, Virginia, among others, have resulted in court decisions upholding the right to publish articles about sex and contraception. Some survey questions that sparked a New York controversy were: "What are your attitudes toward the traditional dating situation?" "Do you approve of contraception?" and "How would you react to homosexuality if it occurred among your peers?" (Donovan, 1977). *Circus* regularly runs articles on VD, sexual behavior, and birth control, and its May 26, 1977 issue contained "Sex and Today's Teenager," including the magazine's own sex survey.

Some "advanced" schools could conduct forums on sex and morality, while recognizing that it is a controversial issue. The main focus now should be on in-service training of teachers.

---

[1] Reprinted with permission from the Department of National Health and Welfare, Ottawa, Ontario, Canada.

The role of home economics teachers as a significant force in the sex education of adolescents should be stressed. Priority should be given to in-service training of home economics teachers and leaders of Future Homemaker groups in preparing adolescents as future parents so they can provide healthy sex education for the children they may decide to have, and in this context become better informed themselves. Again, this would not be a separate course but would be woven into the curriculum of "parenting," as is already being done by outstanding home economics teachers throughout the country. An example of the kind of information which could easily be incorporated into high school family life courses is the following article, which served as the basis for the article entitled "10 Most Important Things in a Marriage," in the April 1978 issue of *Good Housekeeping* magazine (Gordon, 1978a).

Preparing Today's Youth for Tomorrow's Family

Ninety-three percent of Americans marry at some time in their lives. There are indications that the current one-in-three divorce rate may be leveling off. Even so, four out of every five divorced adults eventually remarry. Despite statistics, theories, and pressures from within and without, millions of us, trusting our hearts and our hopes, simply refuse to let marriage die. The problem today is how to think about marriage, how to prepare for it and behave within it so as to enhance the promise of our lives.

The clear trend today is in the direction of egalitarian marriages in which both partners tend to find greater stability, more excitement, and a heightened sense of worth in themselves and in each other.

To the family of tomorrow, husband and wife will bring comparable education. Both will work outside the home for the great portion of their adult lives. Of those who consciously decide to have children, a majority will stop at two. Parenthood will be a shared experience, with both partners taking major responsibility for child care.

People will marry because they love and care for each other. They will have children because they want to. They will not allow the desire for money or prestige to push them into ill-considered alliances. They will not marry to legitimize unplanned pregnancies. They will not subordinate their own feelings and preferences in a futile quest for parental approval. Without all that excess baggage, without the guilt, fear, and uncertainty that return to haunt so many relationships today, tomorrow's parents will be far better able to meet and enjoy the challenge of marriage, childrearing, and work.

Why do so many of today's families break apart? Most of the time it has very little to do with sexual maladjustments or with the presumed emergent aggressiveness on the part of women. It is much the same reason that other old relationships disintegrate: boredom and inequality.

People who marry for the wrong reasons, whose expectations are unrealistic and immature, will sooner or later grow terribly bored with each other. What—when two people live in the same house, sleep in the same bed, and eat at the same table every day—could possibly be worse? An occasional episode of impotence? A redistribution of a few household chores? These and similar disruptions do not threaten the bond between two people who love each other. But boredom not only threatens a relationship, it can destroy it.

There are those who cry for a return to traditional values, and others who claim that successful pursuit of the ultimate multiple simultaneous orgasm will solve everything. But such "remedies" for marital distress are bankrupt and unworkable. They fail to address the fundamental questions: Do we love and care about each other? Do we *interest* each other?

Some of the harshest critics of the women's liberation movement are forever warning us about the dangers of a generation of "aggressive women." A far more serious danger awaits those who accept such scare talk and creep back inside their houses. Of course women *are* becoming more assertive. But assertiveness is nothing more than the pursuit of self-respect. It does not suggest a particular style of clothing or tone of voice or political orientation. Think about it. Have you ever done something that made you feel good about yourself and then worried lest in the process you lost respect in the eyes of other people? True assertive behavior increases self-esteem; and the more you have cause to respect yourself, the more other people have cause to agree.

Assertive women (and men) can protect their interests without resorting to aggressive or "pushy" behavior. In caricature, the aggressive woman dressed in heavy overalls punches her boss in the face and demands a raise. In truth, the assertive woman dressed attractively in her own style confronts her boss with a statement of fact and purpose: "I am here to ask for a raise for the following reasons." Women whose legitimate rights are not realized have every reason to become aggressive.

To illustrate from my own marriage, I hate doing any kind of housework but I do it now because I have an assertive wife. I didn't want her to become aggressive. (Incidentally, I was quite surprised to get her message that she dislikes housework every bit as much as I do.)

Men today are said to be impotent with aggressive women. For obvious reasons, this is a difficult statement to test. Even if it has some truth, I say that for every case of impotence, ten thousand of us have become liberated. Where did I get those statistics? I made them up! They make up theirs and I'll make up mine.

What exactly does it mean to say that men have become liberated? Again, it has nothing to do with dress, manner, or politics. It is that state of mind in which a man is not threatened by his partner's growing self-respect or legitimate ambition. It is mature and accommodating; in large part it is what makes healthy relationships work.

Before turning specifically to the qualities that characterize dynamic and exciting marriages, relationships between liberated and assertive partners, I offer, first, a few ground rules, but not in any particular order.

1. The *quality* of marriage need not be in any major way affected by a couple's decision about children. The important thing is for two people to develop their relationship with each other first, before children are born or even contemplated, and to reassess and reaffirm that relationship often through the years whatever the decision about children has been. Thus, my list will make no references to children.

2. There is no end to new beginnings. Even the most tiresome marriage can be salvaged. To be sure, the passage of time in itself does very little except to make us older. But it's amazing how time *and* effort *and* genuine mutual desire for change can bring new happiness and interest into a relationship.

3. One "sure" test of marital happiness is your energy level. Good marriages are energizing. There is time for everything—or almost everything. Happily married people do not scurry about all day long in a hyperactive frenzy, but they do have the will and energy to be creative and productive. Bad marriages, immature relationships, are exhausting for both partners.

4. For all the screeching about so-called liberated women, the fact is that liberation in its truest sense becomes and enhances those who embrace it. What best distinguishes liberated adults of both sexes from their unliberated neighbors is their freedom to behave, and to behave *well,* to be interesting and interested, to be alternately warm and businesslike, dependent and daring, needed and in need. Liberated men and women have dignity. They do not feel inferior to others; they will not let themselves be made to feel inferior. At the same time, they are delighted to praise the real achievements of other people.

Liberated people have—or make—equal opportunities to develop careers and to make the decisions which most closely affect the course of their lives. They need make no excuses to anyone for spending their days however it is that they do—be it keeping house, designing aircraft, painting portraits, or mining for coal. The point is not what they do, but why they do it. Quite understandably, liberated women will perceive unliberated men as boorish, boring, unhelpful, and unsympathetic.

Those who do not assert their rights will inevitably find their husbands and wives spending less and less time with them. Nobody wants to be bored. To avoid it we drag ourselves bowling on Mondays, play cards on Tuesday, watch movies all night on Wednesdays, hit the bars on Fridays. . . .

5. Marriage without passion is admittedly dull, but without friendship it is devastating.

6. Conspicuous by their absence from this list are offerings to such familiar goddesses as fidelity, exclusivity, total honesty, owning, belonging, total sharing, and "meant for each other."

7. I believe in love but not when it becomes a burden, in priority not exclusivity, in sharing not soul purges, in deeds not promises. There has to be

space within the context of commitment; without it, self-indulgence and ex-ploitation will take root and grow.

Fair enough, you say, but what do all these words look like in real life?

The Big Ten (in order of importance)

1. Love—caring, intimacy, loyalty, and trust during good times and bad, holding strong in the face of illness or stress. It includes such simple things as remembering birthdays and anniversaries and ordinary courtesies like offer-ing help without being asked, saying, "I love you."

2. Learning how and when to laugh—having a sense of humor and keeping it tuned. You had one when you were little. Where did it go? If living were a series of traumatic episodes, laughter wouldn't be practical. But there are very few real traumas in life. It isn't necessary to be downcast so much of the time. Learn to laugh. Practice.

3. Making interesting conversation—being sensitive to the interests of your partner, sparing him the office gossip, sparing her the traffic situation on Interstate 80. The key here is the willingness to communicate. Don't be afraid of hurting your partner's feelings or of revealing your own. Express your own point of view. If your partner doesn't share it, nothing is lost. If he or she ex-plains why, so much the better.

4. Together, a passionate sense of mission or purpose about something(s)—an involvement with other people's lives as means of enhancing your own. It can be anything—a "cause," your religion, the environment, politics.

5. Friends together and separately—sharing time and talk with people you both enjoy, being sensitive to the negative chemistry between your partner and some of your dearest friends. Learn to cherish some space, privacy, inter-ests, hobbies, and even an occasional vacation of your own.

6. A promise—you will not compromise the person you want to be. You are not negotiable. Do what it pleases you to do (this category may be nowhere near as large as you might at first think). If you want to have children and stay home with them while they're small, if you'd rather work away from home, or if you want to balance work and family, *do it* and with no apologies. If someone expresses disapproval or says you're wasting your time, it's not your problem unless you agree. In this respect it might not be a bad idea to declare a moratorium on analyzing. If you're reasonably happy with whatever it is you do, why look for reasons to reconsider?

7. Tolerance—for occasional craziness, irritableness, tiredness, clum-siness, memory lapses, human error, disagreement, argument, and very con-trary points of view.

8. Willingness to accept each other's style—active in some respects, passive in others. Don't be bound by fixed or predetermined notions that X is always a female prerogative or Y always a male imperative. A man can change diapers, tend sick children, respond with pleasure to a woman's sexual in-

itiatives. A woman can change a tire, bring home the biggest paycheck, get the first (or only) Ph.D. in the house.

9. Sexual fulfillment—not measured in terms of orgasmic frequency or quality, but as an abiding expression of shared intimacy. It is possible for people who hate each other to have good mechanical sex. And there are loving, devoted couples whose coital positionings leave much to be desired. While the sex machines may never learn to like each other, the caring partners can learn to overcome their sexual difficulties—by relaxing and by foregoing intercourse for a while in favor of simple touching, truthful talk about what gives pleasure, a shower for two, listening to music.

Sex is the most grossly overstated "privilege" of marriage. Even today we still hear righteous warnings that sex before marriage leaves nothing to look forward to. I'd advise those who perceive sex as the main benefit of marriage not to marry. It's not worth it.

10. Sharing household tasks—I clean, you cook; I fold, you iron; I mow, you rake. Next week reverse it, or not, as it suits you both.

Of course, very few marriages are in an optimal state all or even most of the time. Ebbs and flows, ups and downs, are part of the human condition. But the partners in good marriages find happiness in striving toward it. This isn't Pollyanna-style gaiety, all sweetness and light with never a blessed break, but a sensible optimism, buoyant and energetic, for at least a part of every day. After all, most meaningful peak experiences are of brief duration—a certain look in someone's eyes, a sunset, a baby's first cry. The rest of the time most of us are just too busy to be analyzing ourselves.

Marriage might best be seen as a journey in which two people together, and at times separately, discover all the other things that are still missing in their lives. There is a growing sense that the past is past and that life is not a meaning but an opportunity for meaningful experiences. While children, traditions, rituals, and observances can give marriage structure, they can never substitute for loving, caring, kindness, loyalty and having fun together.

Additional Recommendations

Schools should encourage pregnant girls to finish high school by providing special programs for them within the schools, including birth control counseling in how to avoid a second unintended pregnancy.

Introduction of women's studies into the high schools could enhance the respect of males and females for each other.

Pilot studies in a few schools which have high rates of teenage pregnancy could focus on a massive program of health care. Teenagers respond to challenges such as "How healthy am I?" This would be an opportunity for a full-scale health prevention and intervention program.

A national study of high school students' basic competence in sexual health should be undertaken, similar to those conducted on reading comprehension, science skills, and political awareness by National Assessment of Educational Progress (1977). Another recent survey that could easily be extended in scope was conducted by *Who's Who Among American High School Students* in the fall of 1976. Opinions were asked on the appropriateness of premarital sex, marriage, sources of sex information, the feminist movement, etc. As this particular study covered only the top 4 percent of achievers in the country, it does not represent the sexual attitudes and behaviors of youth in general (for example, three-fourths of the 24,000 said they had *never* had intercourse; since over 80 percent were seventeen-years old, we would have expected about twice as many—roughly 50 percent—to have had intercourse). However, the type of questions and the results are provocative and are in need of further exploration. For instance, only 2 percent of these student leaders felt "women's rights" should be among the nation's top priorities, and only 2 percent felt that "discrimination" was an important issue.

Research is urgently needed to determine the impact of different models of formal school sex education programs upon the attitudes and behavior of adolescents. Although a great deal of research bears on this issue and is reviewed in the previous chapter, most studies are still designed poorly, utilize unreliable questionnaires or inappropriate indicators of "success" or "failure," and lack experimental control to rule out alternative explanations for findings.

For the Community

The following recommendations are not specific to adolescents. Nevertheless, they contribute to creating a community acceptance of family planning in general by suggesting ways that existing community groups can develop new sex education programs and implement current programs.

Health and Social Services

Family planning education would be beneficial in all programs that train professionals and paraprofessionals in the areas of child care, practical nursing, home visitation, and welfare. In addition, family planning training programs should be developed for community aides who serve in hospitals and in outpatient and well-baby clinics.

Government

The role of the government in family planning is becoming increasingly important and constructive. Government agencies, notably the Department of Health, Education and Welfare, fund numerous scientific inquiries in social research and the medical profession. Smaller and recently founded family planning centers and street clinics can be instructed in how to take advantage of these grants via funding proposals and program designs.

As national comprehensive health coverage gains momentum, qualified medical care should be made more readily available to those least able to afford it (the young, the poor). Some experts fear this will result in poorer care once free enterprise is replaced by some form of socialized medicine, but it is generally agreed that with public support, the programs could succeed.

An Example of Government's Contribution

Senate bill 2910, introduced in the spring of 1978, provides an additional $50 million in 1979 funds for teen pregnancy programs through HEW (and $60–70 million in 1980 and 1981). This bill was the first legislation of the Carter administration's "teen pregnancy initiative." Although the title gives lip service to prevention, the bill and its supporting documents emphasize "comprehensive" adolescent pregnancy services, concentrating on the *management* of pregnancy.

Senator Kennedy, who introduced the bill, had inserted in the *Congressional Record* an outline of "essential" components of such a comprehensive center, as prepared by the Joseph P. Kennedy, Jr. Foundation. Most telling is that, out of fifteen components, "prevention of adolescent pregnancy" comes in at number fourteen, beating out only the lowly "evaluation," a program category habitually left to scramble for the leftover crumbs.

Predictably, the bill also limits teenagers' options if primary prevention efforts fail. Their choice is either never to get pregnant (though one out of ten do, year after year), or to adjust to a pregnancy by carrying to term and keeping the baby or giving it up for adoption. Use of funds for abortion is prohibited, although counseling pregnant teenagers on "all options" is permitted.

The bill has several good points, as well as the obvious weaknesses. The mere fact of developing an initiative on teenage pregnancy has helped raise the visibility of prevention efforts, and the infusion of extra funds, though still not enough (are the funds authorized ever enough for your favorite causes?), is a first step that may help make succeeding efforts for increased funding more politically palatable. The bill calls for involving teenagers and their families in the planning and conduct of funded projects and recognizes the importance of outreach in working with teenagers. And the attempt to coordinate services and provide increased training for service providers is an admirable tightening-up effort.

But whatever the bill's merits, it has an inherent structural flaw: The love of things "comprehensive" has resulted in too much being mandated under one authorization, everything from primary prevention, to care for pregnant teenagers, to helping "adolescents become productive independent contributors to family and community life." A greater service could be done both teenagers and society's resources by allowing the primary prevention effort its own arena and funds. Here are a few steps that could greatly strengthen this and other efforts for primary prevention:

1 Prevention should be clearly separated from postpregnancy management in both concept and funding.
2 Encouragement of communication-based sex education that deals with relationships should be explicit.
3 More funds should be under the HEW secretary's discretion for evaluation of new programs.
4 Funds authorized and appropriated for postpregnancy management should support the choice of abortion as well as childbearing and adoption.
5 Funds need to be provided to enable the federal government to become more familiar with many current innovative programs and projects which are not based on postpregnancy management, but on prevention.
6 A greater total outlay of funds is needed. The PHS Title X extension of 1978, for instance (HR 11925), would provide $35 million just for reaching *one-third* of the remaining 2 million teenage women at risk of unintended pregnancy, in contrast to S. 2910's total first-year amount of $50 million.

Government need not "force" prevention to compete for the same funds as postpregnancy management. It should be putting its greatest effort into preventing the pregnancies in the first place. More details on recent federal efforts are described in Scales (1978b; 1978c).

Parent Education

The most obvious resource in teaching youth about sex is the one most often neglected. The leaders of religious and public adult education programs need to take a new look at their priorities and seriously consider their obligation to provide courses, seminars, and lectures designed to prepare parents for their role as the primary source of sex education for their own children. Parents in community sex education programs want to talk about questions like:

"How do I start talking with my children about sex when I've been embarrassed to do so in the past?"

"How much should a nine-year-old know about VD and pornography?"

"What do I talk about first—what's been bothering me, or the basic facts so my kids know what I'm talking about?"

"Is too much masturbation harmful?"

"What can I do to keep my child from becoming homosexual?"

These and other questions, as well as a self-help quiz, "Are You An Askable Parent?" are included in the training manual for organizers of parent sex education courses that grew out of our three-year NIMH-supported program for parents (Institute for Family Research and Education, 1977).

Current Innovations

It is obvious from the previous chapter that current attempts to reach young people through school courses have a limited chance of success; so do clinics and family planning agencies that exclude males, provide only lists of birth control methods, and generally fail to deal with the difficult questions about caring and relationships as factors in sexual responsibility; so do parents who think a moralistic "don't" or threatening "you'll be sorry" approach will deter youth from having sexual experiences.

In the past few years, a number of projects have begun which use innovative means of communicating, imaginative resources, and a non-moralistic, sometimes humorous way of presenting not just the "facts," but also information that adolescents need to know about relationships, about interpersonal communication, and about feelings. Some of these have already been described. The following are some other examples. Many readers will no doubt know of other resources and projects, and omission of these is not intended as a judgment of their significance.

The Institute for Family Research and Education was established in 1970 for the purpose of strengthening the American family and reducing unwanted pregnancy and venereal disease. The institute is extensively involved in all aspects of the field of adolescent sexuality, including research, speaking engagements, community workshops, production of media educational products, and extensive publishing within the professional community and for the popular consumer.

For the past eight years the institute has held a summer workshop on adolescent and parent sex education. The recent emphasis of the workshop has been the training of professionals in preparing youth for future parenthood and improving skills and ability to utilize resources and knowledge about human sexuality. The specific objectives are to experience and integrate an effective model for sex education; to develop skills through practice in planning and leading educational programs, and to enhance the competence and confidence of professionals in the area of human sexuality. In order to meet these goals, the workshop includes lectures, seminars, discussion groups, films, and specialty workshops on such topics as family life education in the schools, preparing parents to be sex educators of their children, sexuality and the role of organized religion, sexuality and the handicapped, designing and resourcing sex education programs. A Sexual Attitude Reassessment (SAR) is also available for those interested in becoming more aware of their own attitudes, values, and feelings about sexuality in order to make communication about sexuality more comfortable.

Other professional workshops have included two major conferences devoted to "Organized Religion and Sexuality" with the goal of presenting a sex education model that could be used throughout the country for initiating and further developing programs in churches and synagogues. Such workshops are important, because organized religion has developed sensitive and committed statements supporting the basic parental prerogative for the sex education of their children. Not only do religious organizations represent a vital force in bridging the critical gap in communication between parent and child, but they also have a major role in preparing parents to serve as the sex educators of their children in the broadest context of moral and value development.

In 1974, the institute initiated a national Wingspread Conference entitled "Adolescent Sexuality and Health Care." The conference, through the auspices of the Johnson Foundation, brought together recognized authorities on sex education and adolescent behavior; health care professionals; sex educators and counselors; representatives of national youth-serving, religious, population and family planning organizations; and foundation and media representatives. The purpose of the three-day conference was to: examine the legal, moral, and medical ramifications of adolescent sexual behavior; discuss existing and new program approaches in dealing with the problems of unwanted pregnancies and venereal disease in adolescents; and to develop coalition approaches to deal with problems related to adolescent sexuality. The position statements, specific goals, and methods of implementation arising from this conference were distributed nationwide, in addition to becoming part of a special *Journal of Clinical Child Psychology* issue entitled "Adolescent Sexuality" (see "A Selected List of Resources"). The interdisciplinary conference followed by mass dissemination of its findings, is a vital part of presenting a coherent, well-organized statement on adolescent sexuality to the lay public as well as to professionals.

Ongoing efforts in this direction include testimony to the Commission on Population Growth and the American Future in 1971 (Gordon, 1972) and to the HEW Intra-Departmental Work Group on Sexually Transmitted Diseases in 1978. The purpose of this latter group was to stimulate discussion and criticism and to generate ideas that will enable the formulation of a comprehensive and effective federal policy with regard to the problem of sexually transmitted diseases. In July 1978, testimony was presented to the Senate Committee on Human Resources, which was the basis of the article entitled "Sex Education and the Role of the Federal Government" (see Scales, 1978b).

Although such efforts assist the formulation of federal policy, there is a continuing need to check research assumptions in the area of sexuality. With this focus in mind, the Institute for Family Research and Education received a grant from the National Institute for Mental Health in 1974 to conduct a three-year research and demonstration project entitled "Community Family Life Education Program for Parents." The primary focus of the project was to train key leadership in central New York to conduct parent sex education programs. As a result of five eight-week training sessions for community leaders, over 1,000 parents were reached in this area alone. As part of the institute's goal to disseminate information on how to facilitate communication in the area of sexuality, a manual for organizers was also developed: "Community Sex Education Programs for Parents." The manual details basic assumptions about sex education program rationale, outlines how to plan and organize training programs, and provides references, questions parents ask, and articles that could be incorporated into parent programs.

The institute has also been instrumental in disseminating information to youth in formats they appreciate. Examples include distribution of over 3 million comic books entitled: *Ten Heavy Facts About Sex, Protect Yourself From Becoming An Unwanted Parent, VD Claptrap, Juice Use, Gut News,* and *Drug Doubt?;* the film *About Sex,* which was awarded the 1973 Blue Ribbon Award by the American Film Festival in New York; a ten-minute audiotape filmstrip called "Getting It Together is Life Itself," and a one-hour cassette tape entitled "Coming To Terms With Your Own Sexuality." (See "A Selected List of Resources.")

The Institute for Family Research and Education has emphasized male involvement in its adolescent project. The institute has completed a comprehensive review of the literature and concluded that the double standard is still very much with us (Scales, 1977). The institute also conducted a participant-observation study in Syracuse, New York, birth control clinics to gain a systematic view of whether males were being excluded. The results showed that the birth control counselors studied were "mildly unreceptive" to male involvement (Scales, Etelis, & Levitz, 1977). Based on these findings, the institute developed a prototype two-minute film, "What If It Was *You* Who Got Pregnant?" in which the male gets pregnant.

Another project concerned specifically with the male role is the lines project. For years, boys have been using lines to get sex: "If you really loved me . . ."; "What's the matter, you frigid?"; etc. Girls need to know not just typical lines, but possible responses to those lines. For many young people, sexual behavior is something that happens, but is not discussed very much beforehand. In one of the institute's college studies (the students' mean age was just over nineteen), over one-third of the more than four hundred students said the first time or two they have sex with someone, it "just seems to happen without talking" (Gordon & Scales, in progress). Using the lines, the goal is to give teenagers a tool with which to stop or slow down a situation that frequently develops a momentum of its own.

For those who object that "lines" went out of style with "want to see my etchings," we point to Ann Landers's column. When asked to invite readers to send in the lines they had experienced, she was swamped with over 18,000 replies! Here is one of the most interesting:

Dear Ann Landers:
You asked teenage girls to write and tell you the "lines" that

211

Reprinted with permission from Pharmacists Planning Services, Inc., Sausalito, California 94965.

212

were used on them by boys who were after sex. What a great idea!

I'm no teenager (I'm 22) but I thought you might be interested in the approaches made to me over the past several years. Some of them were hilarious, others downright pathetic.

The adolescent, non-serious passes started in the seventh grade with games like spin-the-bottle and post office. Then there were those unforgettable scavenger hunts—with kids pairing off and wandering around in search of pink toilet paper and vegetable sieves.

The serious, for-real lines started in the ninth grade. My favorite boy friend was best pals with a guy who dated the most popular girl in school. He told me she "did it." That, of course, meant "it" was the thing to do. When he discovered that strategy didn't work, he promptly switched to: "If you loved me you'd prove it." I told him if he loved *me* he wouldn't make such demands on me.

Finally, he became adamant and said I *had* to give in because my stubbornness was lousing up his maturing process and giving him pimples. When I told him to buzz off he threatened to kill himself. The threat turned out to be as ridiculous as the rest of his garbage.

Then I started to date a fellow who was extremely considerate of my feelings, but also very affectionate. When I made my position clear, he didn't pester me about sex. We necked a little but he never tried to step beyond the boundaries I set up. After a few blissful months, Mr. Well-Behaved informed me I was going to have to share him with Winnie (a hot number) who wrote notes which made it plain she was ready, willing and able to fulfill him.

Off I went to college—still intact but getting curiouser and curiouser. The second day on campus I met Claude. He told me on our second date that dozens of girls had followed him from the swimming pool to his apartment, lusting after his body. Others were so aggressive (and hungry) they knocked on his door with bottles they couldn't open, dresses that needed to be zipped, furniture they couldn't move—anything to get past his front door and hopefully into his bed.

Then there was Horace, two years my junior, who wanted me to teach him and Bernie, who was dying to know if a political science major had anything that worked besides her brain. And Orval, a religious nut who had been instructed by God to "show me the way."

Funny thing, nothing wore down my resistance. The lines just made me run in the other direction. No girl wants to feel used, fooled or easy.

When I finally said yes, it was because a sensitive and

> caring young man made me feel valuable as a human being. He applied no gimmicks, no hogwash, no sales talk. I made up my own mind. It was beautiful. I'm glad I waited.[2]

In the course of ten years enough lines have been collected to fill a book entitled *You Would if You Loved Me* . . . (Gordon, 1978b), and here are some of its "gems":

> "I promise I won't touch you. We will just sleep together."
>
> "You'll never get to know me any better any other way."
>
> "Let's do it so I'll have something to remember you by after you've gone."
>
> "Why don't you relax?"
>
> "A man has got to have it."
>
> *He:* Wanna go to bed?
> *She:* No thanks—I just got up.
>
> *Male:* Do you play games?
> *Female:* Let's play house and you're all alone.
>
> "I promise you won't get pregnant."

Although the institute's efforts to directly reach youth, parents, and community leaders have been widely recognized, perhaps the most successful project has been the National Family Sex Education Week. The intent of the week, held annually since 1975, is to promote through its newsletter, *Impact,* the idea that parents are the main sex educators of their children. *Impact* (see "Selected List of Resources" in the appendix), which is disseminated annually to over 50,000 organizations and individuals directly involved in sex education, includes a statement of philosophy, summaries of previously successful projects, and suggestions for promoting National Family Sex Education Week. Such efforts have resulted in hundreds of communities across the nation implementing parent workshops, seminars, bookstore displays, and TV and radio talks, in addition to an annual increase in the number of endorsements from governors and mayors. The week has prompted a variety of interesting projects. In Old Westbury, New York, the Association for Identity Development sponsored a poster and slogan contest for young people on the theme of family sex education. The Sex Health Education Center in Dade County, Florida, which was developed by Lynn Leight as a result of National Family Sex Education Week in 1975, offered a "sex symposium" in 1977.

---

[2] *Chicago Daily News,* December 6, 1976. Dist. Field Newspaper Syndicate. Reproduced by permission.

Over eight hundred teens attended a series of workshops on birth control, love and marriage, teenage pregnancy, etc. The response was so enthusiastic that 97 percent of those who attended the symposium requested that NFSEW be celebrated as an annual event.

Media coverage in the Dade County areas included a Sunday Supplement in the *Miami Herald* entitled "What Happens When Children Have Children." The *Miami News* ran a four-part investigative series on "Sex and Teenagers," in addition to an opinion poll that revealed that 72 percent of the readers favored sex education in their schools. The radio and TV coverage were equally responsive, with WKAT radio's opinion poll revealing that 76 percent of the callers favored a mandated school sex education curriculum.

The City-County Health Department of Eau Claire, Wisconsin, aired a videotape on the theme "Family Sex Education: Are You An Askable Parent?" on their regional public TV. The tape included discussions of sex questions and problems between youth, parents, and professionals.

Planned Parenthood of Waterbury, Connecticut, introduced its community to "Sigmund the Stork." The giant feathered bird stood proudly in the lobby of the Waterbury Library along with a selection of resource material for young people and parents on sex education. "Sigmund the Stork" then moved on for a visit at the YWCA, accompanied with the poster explaining his presence and reminding parents of their responsibility in giving accurate information, not perpetuating myths. The local newspaper carried a picture story of "Sigmund," and the community college cosponsored an educational seminar on "Being Askable."

Publicity for National Family Sex Education Week included the following statement of position regarding the preparation of youth for tomorrow's family:

> We need to prepare today's youth for tomorrow's family. In order to communicate mature and responsible attitudes, parents must become the primary sex educators of their own children. We know that silence and evasiveness are just as powerful teachers as are the facts.
>
> Everybody says that parents should be the primary sex educators, but who is preparing the parents for this role? Indeed, in terms of the values and spiritual life of the child, no outside group or agency could replace the family. Thus, we see education for sexuality taking place within the context of the family's value system which hopefully strives toward a family life free of racism, sexism and prejudices against people with other values. Most churches and educators officially support this position, but few are doing anything about it.
>
> Studies consistently have revealed that children do not acquire the information they need from parents. It is time for parents to assume this responsibility. Parents, of course, cannot be the sole educators; if they wanted to be, they

215

would have to prevent their children from reading books, newspapers and magazines, keep them away from television, movies and public bathrooms, and certainly prohibit them from having any friends at all. Parents are *the main* educators, with schools, religious and community groups as partners in a life long process.

Society consistently underestimates the capabilities of parents and their children. You can't tell a child too much: Knowledge doesn't stimulate inappropriate behavior; ignorance does. If you tell children more than they can understand, they will ask another question or turn you off. Parents must work toward being *askable.* We know most parents want to educate their children, but they are often uncomfortable and don't know how. Obviously, parents who find it difficult to talk to their children about any important issue will not be ready to talk about sex. However, it seems that most parents are ready, but want some support.

It is essential for parents to be alert to extremist propaganda and political maneuvering, especially by those groups claiming to have a monopoly on the Judeo-Christian ethic. Censorship in the schools and media is one method used by extremist groups who want to impose their views on everybody. Parents should not be intimidated by scare tactics used as subterfuges for acquiring power on school boards or in churches. In support of these principles, PTAs, foundations, church and synagogue related groups and community organizations can develop ongoing institutes, workshops, seminars, and media presentations, and put together bibliographies and library and bookstore displays, to get the public involved (continuing education is more effective than one-shot lectures). It is expected that religious groups in particular will develop programs based on their own moral beliefs. Community-minded groups should discover opportunities for getting their message heard via public service options on TV and radio, as well as in newspapers and magazines. We must counter the propaganda that information is harmful or constitutes license for irresponsible behavior. It's time that the "silent" majority expressed itself vigorously, visibly and vocally.

The Population Institute is significantly involved in several projects for teenagers. A provocative idea, begun in Los Angeles in 1975, is advertising contraceptive services in high school yearbooks. Starting out by publicizing the Los Angeles Regional Family Planning Council's hot-line number in sixteen yearbooks in 1976, the technique successfully placed advertisements in eighty yearbooks for 1977. The council attempted a cost-benefit analysis of this approach and concluded that it cost $600, about 4¢ per each of the 16,500 teenagers who bought yearbooks in 1976. Yearbook advertising can be especially useful as a means of getting started in previously hesitant schools. Even schools reluctant to promote "sex education" are faced with hard economic facts in developing yearbooks, and because each page of advertising pays for about five pages of pictures, they will think twice before refusing a potentially controversial ad (Getting It Together, 1977). A similar approach is used by Planned Parenthood of New York City. Early in 1977, they reached agreement with the telephone company on running advertisements in the yellow pages: Advertisements now may state not simply that information is offered about sterilization, infertility, and abortion, but that these services are actually *provided.*

In New York City, the "Youth Values Project" (1978) has conducted extensive questioning of one thousand young people. A ten-person teenage advisory group worked on the project to determine what media young people are exposed to. Using information collected from their questionnaire, the project made contacts with city television and radio program managers and disc jockeys, conducted workshops in various teen centers, and developed advertising for subways and buses (Ross, 1978). On the West Coast, the institute has begun a "Rock Stars" project, the basic goal of which is to use rock musicians to communicate messages of responsible sexuality and parenthood. As expressed by Rick Sadle, coproducer of the thirty- and sixty-second radio spots, "Our problem was to get people who don't want to be preached at to listen to our message." The spots use clips from the musician's records interspersed with segments of often humorous interviews about parenthood and sex to communicate the message that "becoming pregnant as unmarried teenagers is not in their best interests." After the spots are aired, there is provision for a local family planning service number to be read. In addition, the project also publishes *Pregnant Pause,* a newsletter of its activities, and has developed a "trigger-tape" package with the spots and discussion questions based on them. Any of the materials can be obtained through the Population Institute (Kamen, 1978).

In conjunction with these efforts, more attempts are being made to raise consciousness among record producers, songwriters, and artists about the effects which certain songs can have (from "Shake Your Booty" to "Having My Baby"). Reverend Jesse Jackson and People United to Save Humanity, as well as the Population Institute, have met in over a dozen cities with record company executives for this purpose. That the task is not easy is indicated by the comments of one music director from a Detroit station: "I think they have good intentions, but when we see records on the charts and selling, we have to put them on in order to compete" (Stewart, 1977). The object, of course, is to produce records with responsible messages which are commercially competitive—simply asking station managers to drop offensive records will not work unless production and publicity money is slated for records that can fill the economic gap.

217

A 1978 project of the Population Institute is to involve popular sports heroes in programs to encourage responsible sexuality among young people.

Significant contributions are the short 16 mm color "trigger" films produced by East Central Georgia Planned Parenthood. Their three-minute films depict crisis situations in human sexuality and are intended for group use as discussion prompters.

Chicago area Planned Parenthood used a "Teen Scene Update" idea. Short, two-to-three sentence "fillers" about sexuality, dating, and the psychology of love were prepared for DJs in an easy-to-read format so that they could be read on the air. Radio and film skits dramatizing myths about sexuality were developed as well.

Chicago area Planned Parenthood has an active program of teen-oriented projects. One recent development is their "audio-magazine," a ninety-minute tape of rock music, interspersed every few minutes with just one or two lines of "fairy tales" and "facts," such as "If you have sex standing up, you won't get pregnant. Wrong! Whether you have sex standing up, lying down, or standing on your head makes no difference. A sperm has no sense of gravity." The music then continues. This has been tested in waiting rooms and found to reduce significantly clients' perception of their waiting time, and also to improve the basic knowledge of first-time clinic visitors (Brittain-LaBrie, Menaghan, & Snyder). The groups tested, however, were about twenty-five years old, and it is likely that more positive results would be found using teenagers, for the particular music used is geared to a younger audience. Another major project for this Planned Parenthood is its male motivation program, begun in 1971. Director Darryl Hale estimates the program has reached approximately 22,000 males in Chicago and its suburbs, accounting for about 8 percent of the fifteen-to-twenty-four-year-old males in the area. The key to this program is its realization that without massive restructuring of most clinics' female-oriented atmosphere, the teenage males don't want to go to the clinic—the clinic has to go to them. So the Chicago program is almost 100 percent outreach, going to the places where young males congregate, using audiovisuals and staying away from the lecture approach, and using materials developed or adapted from existing resources intended for women (Syntex Laboratories, 1977). Both the audio-magazine and the male motivation program are part of an overall "Teen Scene" project designed to reach some youth at the clinic and some "in the streets." Planned Parenthood also provides a traveling professionally staged "folk drama" on sexuality which goes to churches, high schools, Ys, and so forth.

One of the best and most comprehensive programs for adolescents in the country is the Macomb County Teen Health Program developed by Sherry and Lannie McRill in Mount Clemens, Michigan. Some other programs also worth citing among hundreds that have sprung up in recent years are: Problems of Daily Living Clinic at Sinai Hospital in Detroit, Michigan; Choice in

Philadelphia, Pennsylvania; and the West Dallas Children and Youth Project, a comprehensive health program.

An increasing number of organizations are paying attention to the issue of male involvement in preventing unwanted pregnancy and venereal disease. Emory University Family Planning Program published a pamphlet on sex and birth control for men, "The View from Our Side"; Cleveland's Preterm Clinic has hired a counselor whose full-time job is to reach young males; and Planned Parenthoods in Marin County, California, Newark, New Jersey, and Oakland, California have developed innovative programs to involve males. The Oakland project is particularly intriguing: Two young volunteers were trained by a university video student to run a portable camera; they then visited teen hangouts to film interviews with the teenagers on their feelings about sexuality. The young males were then told they could see themselves on screen by coming to the clinic. Viewing the film led to a rap session, a self-help quiz on sexuality, and a promise by the filmmakers to return for more interviews in the following weeks. Attendance tripled at the male rap sessions after this idea was introduced (Syntex Laboratories, 1977).

Another group conducting several projects is the Los Angeles chapter of Zero Population Growth. They developed a multimedia campaign with a focus on radio and music. A two-week "saturation" campaign was arranged with the program director of KIQQ in Los Angeles, to include spots during the day, documentaries, a talk show, and call-in phone lines so teenagers could call for an informational packet to be mailed to them. The station also agreed to provide as much studio time and tape stock as ZPG needed in order to develop the spots and programs. Other stations soon joined the effort. Los Angeles's Public Advertising Council, which specializes in helping nonprofit groups with their media campaigns, arranged to fund a radio production consultant to work with ZPG for up to six months. Community organizations cooperated in the project. They also held a concert/exhibition devoted to teenagers' performing and displaying their own creative ideas based on the themes of responsible sexuality and parenthood. They received permission from the L.A. Regional Family Planning Council to use already developed posters of rock stars reduced to wallet size. On the back of these wallet size pictures are hot-line phone numbers and basic birth control information. In addition, they included the Ed-U Press series of educational comic books *(Ten Heavy Facts About Sex, VD Claptrap,* and *Protect Yourself From Becoming An Unwanted Parent)* in the informational packet, which teens could obtain by calling the radio stations.

Many of these new projects are using radio to communicate, and some are also trying to involve the songwriters, producers, and musicians who create the music young people listen to. The key is that campaign materials be developed by the organization, not the station, and that the campaign staff work closely with the station's program director to tailor the length and placement of their spots to fit the station's programming. Radio stations can help in other ways: Dr. Michael Carrera of the City University of New York set up a sex information call-in at station WMCA in New York. Begun in 1974 and still going strong as an activity of Community Sex Information, Inc., an agency organized by Dr. Carrera and Dr. Ann Welbourne, the service runs from 6:00 until 8:00 each evening, with telephone staffers using the WMCA studios to answer the more than 1,000 calls a month. Carrera reports that 95 percent of the people calling say they have never talked to anyone about their sexual concerns. With effort and a staff belief that they can make things happen, involvement of the radio and music industries seems promising.

Many new efforts are focusing on the print medium, but in newer ways. The Institute for Family Research and Education series of comics is an illustration of this approach. Planned Parenthood also has developed a comic called *The Amazing Spiderman* aimed at teaching young people about birth control and raising questions about whether they're ready for parenthood. Teenage parenting is the subject of another publication, *True to Life*. Designed and written in a slick, *True Confessions* format, this magazine offers reliable, accurate birth control and general health information in the context of a "romance" style magazine popular with many teenagers. Originally developed by the Emory University Family Planning Program and Dr. Robert Hatcher, this latest edition is published and distributed by Reproductive Health Resources, Inc. The Emory University program has developed several other noteworthy publications, including *The View From Our Side—Sex and Birth Control for Men,* a funny and accurate book.

Teen Times, the magazine of the Future Homemakers of America, published a special issue in January and February 1977 on teenage parenting. The issue includes a quiz called "Marriage—Ready . . . Or Not," intended to help teens distinguish between being a mature teenager and one mature enough for marriage. Another article covers the joint program of the Future Homemakers of America and the National Foundation March of Dimes called "Wanted: Healthy Babies." Peer education teams in all fifty states have used slide presentations, puppet shows, teaching kits, radio and TV spots, etc. to help teens make better choices about when and if to have a baby, what kind of medical care they want, whether to use drugs or not, etc. Included are actual scripts of puppet shows and numerous suggestions for other activities in which teens can participate.

The National Alliance for Optional Parenthood has published a thoughtful questionnaire for teenagers entitled "Am I Parent Material?" In a recent project, NAOP targeted the high school press. Since advertising research shows over 90 percent of high school students read their school papers, NAOP encouraged high school students to write more articles on sexuality, pregnancy, and teenage parenthood for their papers. Across the country, a potential audience of about 15 million teenagers could be reached by other teenagers in a simple extension of the peer education approach. In order to help the teenage writers, the group held a series of press conferences in seven cities just for high school reporters to give them background, discuss journalistic rights and responsibilities in covering sensitive topics, and provide them with a good look at their local resources in sexual health care (Scales, 1978d). Both NAOP and the Population Institute rock project are holding contests as well, NAOP to select the best article on sex written by a teenager, and the rock project to pick the best radio spot on sex produced by a teenager.

The National Alliance Concerned with School-Age Parents (NACSAP) is concerned with sharing information among professionals and lobbying for more comprehensive national legislation on the issue of teenage pregnancy and parenthood. They publish a newsletter containing reports of pertinent research on primary and secondary prevention programs, legislative summaries, and resources to obtain. In May 1975, they teamed with the American School Health Association to publish a special "School-Age Parents" issue of the *Journal of School Health*. Originally founded to meet the needs of pregnant teens, NACSAP voted in 1977 to include sexually active, nonpregnant youth in its constituency.

A unique resource for junior high through adult ages is the "Myth-Information" game developed by Jacqueline Reubens. The play consists of one hundred statements about sexuality, some truths and some myths. Players in teams discuss whether the statement is true and try to gain the "sexpert" buttons awarded to the team with the most correct responses. Short explanations for each statement are provided, as is a list of the references from which the truth of the statements was determined.

While television is not as responsive to sex education projects as radio and print, some outstanding programs have been developed in the last year or two which deal honestly with the problems of teenage pregnancy and with the difficulty of communicating directly about sex. The "Good Times" TV series, for example, showed (in all but two of the two hundred main markets in the country) a segment on VD. The October 14, 1978 episode of "Good Times" stressing the need for parents to sex educate their children was, in our judgment, one of the finest educational programs ever presented on commercial television. Norman Lear's "All in the Family" has aired several shows forthrightly dealing with vasectomy, unwanted pregnancy, and the human difficulties in communicating openly about sex. The American Broadcasting Company programmed "My Mom's Having a Baby" in 1977 as an afternoon special children's show. The show attracted the largest audience of any daytime special in the history of television.

In Chicago, WTTW/Chicago Public Television produced a documentary called "Guess Who's Pregnant?" for summer and autumn 1977 viewing. The show candidly dealt not simply with statistics on adolescent pregnancy, but also with the lack of success of traditional, moralistic messages from parents, teachers, and religious groups. Schools, family planning clinics, and teenagers in several areas of the country were visited to produce the documen-

221

tary. Organizations already mentioned which can provide helpful information for using the media for programs are the Population Institute, Zero Population Growth, the Institute for Family Research and Education, and the Center for Understanding Media. Other groups doing creative work are the March of Dimes, Guidance Associates, Inc., the Creative Media Group, the SHE Clinic, the Crossroads Clinic, Inc., and the Sex Education Coalition of Metropolitan Washington, D.C. (see "Selected List of Resources").

New York Medical College sponsors a Family Life Theater, which has produced "Inside/Out: A View of Teenage Life." Their hour-long series of skits is written by the teenage actors and covers alcoholism, pregnancy, sex and communications, parent relationships, and contraception. They travel to high schools and professional conferences with the show and have gotten a uniformly enthusiastic reaction because the skits are "real": "You see a little bit of yourself and your friends in it" (*New York Times,* 1977).

An important but not yet published study entitled "Programs, Services, and Approaches Toward the Reduction of Adolescent Pregnancy" was submitted by Audrey Moore (1978) to the Health Subcommittee of the Secretary's Advisory Committee on the Rights and Responsibilities of Women. The report details, perhaps for the first time, several successful programs on the national scene, among them, the Door in New York City, Center for Youth Development and Research at the University of Minnesota, the adolescent program of the Montefiore Hospital and Medical Center in Bronx, New York, the Adolescent Medical Unit at Bellevue Hospital, New York City, the Martin Luther King, Jr. Hospital in Los Angeles, and Grady Memorial Hospital in Atlanta, Ga. Additional exemplary programs have been described by MATHTECH, Inc. of Bethesda, Maryland (Scales, 1979). One of the most innovative programs to prepare young people to handle potential crisis situations related to rape was developed by O.D.N. Productions of New York City. In four superbly wrought brief films, a neglected area called "acquaintanceship rape" is illustrated so extremely well that the typical high school student could easily relate to it. The films come with excellent guides making it relatively simple for even the inexperienced but well-motivated teacher to deal with the subject. One of the best features of the program guide is a section called "A Personal Bill of Rights." Here are some of the twenty assertive statements:

> I have a right to refuse a date without feeling guilty.

> If I don't want physical closeness, I have the right to say no.

> I give myself the right not to act macho.

> I have the right to an equal relationship with the opposite sex.

The programs were developed by Oralee Wachter and the films by Christina Crowley.

There are many other creative programs for young people. It is no longer necessary to leave sex education only to watered-down courses in schools. We can give teenagers the information they need, but only if we confront the issues long enough to see sex from their perspective and have the vision and the courage to try something different.

The following statement, developed by Robert A. Hatcher, M.D., M.P.H., Director, Emory University-Grady Memorial Hospital Family Planning Program, represents a clear message and a call for action from national leaders concerned with young people:

A Statement of Concern Regarding Teenage Health Problems

We the undersigned believe that the health problems of teenagers require special attention. Adolescence is that complex and miraculous state in the transition from childhood to adulthood in which physical, mental, and emotional needs are distinct and important. Regardless of the background of teenagers, rich or poor, black or white, urban or rural, they are often medically ignored. Perhaps too old for pediatricians and not yet ready for adult services, they sometimes have no one to turn to for help.

We, as concerned members of our society, must respond to the teenage community and generate the creative approaches and financial resources necessary to confront their medical needs. We must try to see the problems from their side—by introducing services that are convenient, effective, and staffed by interested and caring professionals.

We believe there are four ways we can improve the health delivery system for adolescents:

1 by increasing private, local and federal funding specifically earmarked for teenagers in the following areas: primary care, mental health, reproductive health, and the prevention of alcohol and drug abuse

2 by providing health information and sex education in our homes, churches, and schools;

3 by encouraging self-motivation and responsibility regarding individual health care; and

4 by recognizing the rights of minors to confidentiality, while taking into consideration the advantage of consulting with understanding parents.

We recognize the important contribution teenagers make to the social fabric of American life. Our society must commit itself to finding innovative ways of meeting the health needs of teenagers.

The following individuals have signed a Statement of Concern expressing their ongoing interest and support for a vital and ongoing program of teenage health care services:

William M. McCormack, M.D.

Jack Lippes, M.D.

Harriet F. Pilpel

Andrew Maguire, U.S. Representative

Robert Packwood, U.S. Senator

Edward Asner

Edward M. Kennedy, U.S. Senator

Benjamin Spock, M.D.

Wendy Borden Morgan

Audrey Forbes Manley, M.D., F.A.A.P.

Ann F. Brunswick, Ph.D.

Cecily C. Selby, Ph.D.

T. James Trussell, Ph.D.

George H. Thoms, Ed.D.

King K. Holmes, M.D., Ph.D.

Robert L. Johnson, M.D.

Barbara Jordan, U.S. Representative

Maggie Kuhn

Toni M. Jones-Huff

Sol Gordon, Ph.D.

Frederick S. Jaffe

Kenneth R. Elwell, D.D.S., M.P.H.

Thomas E. Bryant, M.D., J.D.

John C. Cutler, M.D.

Ramsey Clark

Mary S. Calderone, M.D.

William S. Chambless, M.D.

Miriam Chambless, M.D.

Kathleen Brewer

Gail Gallaher

Toni McCown

Phyllis J. Spray

Michael R. Dursi

Alberta Wagner

Marslia Leigh

Cathy A. Cooper

Roxanne Laurey

Christy Solomon

Kathy Fuxa

Bess McNally

Leslie Arnold-Rautman

Eloise Kloifhorn

Robert A. Hatcher, M.D. M.P.H.

Beth Atkins

We would like to close this chapter by recognizing *some* of the most creative and action-oriented professionals currently working in the area of promoting mature and responsible sexual expression among teenagers. We know there are hundreds of other dedicated workers in this field. We are recording only those whose work we have observed.

Jim Achtzehn

Bill Baird

Medora S. Bass

Joan Benesch

Loren Burtt

Mary Butcher

Deryck Calderwood

Elizabeth Canfield

Harvey W. Caplan

Michael Carrera

Carol Cassell
Mary K. Chelton
Sylvia Cohen
Donald Collins
Takey Crist
Alison Deming
Robin A. Elliott
Albert Ellis
Joseph Fanelli
Norman Fleishman
Janet Forbush
Evalyn Gendel
William Genné
Sadja Goldsmith
Sylvia Hacker
Eleanore Hamilton
Robert Hatcher
Lorraine Hendricks
Adele D. Hofmann
Beverly Hotchner
Jesse Jackson
Stephen Jerrick
Eric Johnson
Warren Johnson
Kathi Kamen
Winifred Kempton
Eugene C. Kennedy
Lester A. Kirkendall
Susan Knight
Joan Kraus
Bert Kruger-Smith
Mary Lane
Miriam Leavitt

Lynn Leight
Eda Le Shan
E. James Lieberman
Harold I. Lief
Ric Loya
Angel Martinez
Ronald M. Mazur
Kathy McCoy
Brian McNaught
Sherry and Lannie McRill
Audrey Moore
Alfred F. Moran
Lonnie Myers
Maude Parker
Eve Paul
Harriet Pilpel
Wardell Pomeroy
Billie Press
Susan Procopio
Susan Ross
Charity Runden
William Ryerson
Michael Schaffer
Judith Senderowitz
Mary Lee Tatum
Sheri Tepper
Chic Thompson
George H. Thoms
Steven Viederman
Mona Wasow
Ann K. Welbourne
Judy Widdicombe
Gertrude Williams

References Alan Guttmacher Institute. *11 million teenagers.* New York: Planned Parenthood, 1976.

Brittain-LaBrie, J., Menaghan, E., & Snyder, M. R. *Testing an audio-magazine in a family planning clinic.* Paper available from Chicago Area Planned Parenthood, 55 E. Jackson Blvd.

Brozan, N. Issue and debate: Should the media accept contraceptive ads? *New York Times,* 12 August 1977.

Dale, G., & Chamis, G. C. Family life education program, Flint Community Schools. Flint, Michigan, 1971.

Donovan, P. Student newspapers and the First Amendment: Their right to publish sex-related articles. *Family Planning/Population Reporter,* 1977, *6* (2), 16–17; 23.

Getting it together. Denver: National Assessment of Educational Progress, 1977, *7* (3), 3.

Gordon, S. Family planning education for adolescents. In *Population and the American future.* Report of the Commission on Population Growth and the American Future. Washington, D.C.: Commission on Population Growth and the American Future, 1972.

Gordon, S. 10 most important things in a marriage. *Good Housekeeping,* April 1978a, 58; 61–63.

Gordon, S. *You would if you loved me.* New York: Bantam, 1978b.

Gordon, S., & Scales, P. Sexual communication, attitudes, and socialization among young people. Syracuse, N.Y.: Institute for Family Research and Education, in progress.

Institute for Family Research and Education. *Community family life education programs for parents: A training manual for organizers.* Charlottesville, Va.: Ed-U Press, 1977.

Kamen, K. Rhythm & blues: Rock 'n roll sex education from the Population Institute. In P. Scales (Ed.), *Searching for alternatives to teenage pregnancy.* Baltimore, Md.: National Alliance for Optional Parenthood, 1978, 9–10.

Moore, A. *Analysis of a field study: Programs, services, and approaches toward the reduction of adolescent pregnancy.* Final Report submitted to the Health Subcommittee of the Secretary's Advisory Committee on the Rights and Responsibilities of Women, Department of Health, Education, and Welfare. Columbia, Md., September 1977.

Reubens, J. *Myth-information.* Saluda, N.C.: Family Life Publications, Box 427, 28773.

Robertson, P., Torrance, G., & Moore, M. *Sex education—a teacher's guide.* Ottawa: Department of National Health and Welfare, 1977.

226

Scales, P. Males and morals: Teenage contraceptive behavior amid the double standard. *The Family Coordinator,* 1977, *26* (3), 210–222.

Scales, P. How to reduce teenage pregnancy. In *Fertility and contraception in America—adolescent and pre-adolescent pregnancy.* Hearings before the House Select Committee on Population, March 1978(a). *2,* 461–472.

Scales, P. Sex education and the role of the federal government. In P. Scales (Ed.), *Searching for alternatives to teenage pregnancy.* Baltimore, Md.: National Alliance for Optional Parenthood, 1978(b), 17–19.

Scales, P. *Sex education and the prevention of teenage pregnancy: An overview of policies and programs in the United States.* Paper presented at Family Impact Seminar Conference on Teenage Pregnancy and Family Impact: New Perspectives on Policy, Washington, D.C., October 1978(c).

Scales, P. The high school press covers sex. *Getting it together,* 1978(d), *8* (5), 1–2; 7.

Scales, P. *An overview of innovative non-school sex education programs for teenagers in the United States.* Bethesda, Md.: MATHTECH, Inc. (CDC contract #200-78-0804), 1979.

Scales, P., Etelis, R., & Levitz, N. Male involvement in contraceptive decision making: The role of birth control counselors. *Journal of Community Health,* 1977, *3* (1), 54–60.

Sex Education Committee, New York State Coalition for Family Planning. *Sex education, a critical concern.* Albany: NYSCFP, 1975.

Stewart, R. Curb sought on airing of records with explicit lyrics. *New York Times,* 14 April 1977, 18.

Syntex Laboratories. *The Family Planner,* 1977, *8* (2/3), 2–4.

227

Eleven

**Toward a
Politics of
Humanistic
Sexuality**

Upon signing the Declaration of Independence, Ben Franklin remarked to John Hancock, "We must indeed all hang together, or, most assuredly, we shall all hang separately." Two hundred years later, we tend to hang each other: The Equal Rights Amendment, despite the extension of ratification until 1982; may yet pass on as an historical footnote that never became law; political pussyfooting in the executive and legislative branches may replace equal access to abortion with a return to a hack butcher trade that preys upon the poor and ignorant; and homosexuals are again being denied civil liberties because of their supposed power a "role models."

We live with a confusing array of values whose inherent contradictions frequently escape us. We continue to advocate the promises of "higher education" and the value of knowledge, yet we strive to keep young people sexually ignorant by lacing their curiosity with a good dose of guilt and anxiety. We have not penetrated this last frontier with the message that knowledge is not harmful. We have not effectively responded to the vocal minority who would impose their moral convictions by prohibiting sex education in the schools, teenagers' access to birth control, elective abortion, and freedoms of occupational, marital, and sexual choice.

Over 80 percent of the parents in a recent national survey (General Mills, 1977) wanted to teach their children that "any prejudice is morally wrong," yet prejudice is still practiced in opposition to racially integrated schools and neighborhoods, in hounding homosexuals out of the pulpit and the classroom, and in maintaining the sexual double standard that oppresses women and children and distances men from both.

The struggle for humanistic sexuality is a struggle for human rights. Lewis (1977) has called it a fight to prevent the "tyranny of the majority." Certainly, while this is an apt description of antigay sentiment in the country, it is also true that the majority of U.S. citizens favor abortion rights, equal rights for men and women, and sex education of young people. We need to recognize that the anti-ERA movement, and the outcries of those who use "pornography" as an excuse to ban even worthwhile literature, are not isolated phenomena.

229

Homosexuality

The fear of homosexuality has again become a political issue after a period of abatement and movement toward equal rights. In Florida and subsequently in St. Paul, Wichita, and Eugene, Anita Bryant preyed on fear and made it a respectable motive for "saving our children"; in anonymous security, voters were able to revoke the human rights of a minority group. In a Detroit suburb, two men living together (no one asked if they were lovers as well) were prevented from renting a house in a "family" neighborhood for fear of the "example" it would set (Family Drives Out 2 Singles, 1976). In a *Circus* magazine survey of two thousand teenage readers, over a third objected to homosexuals being in positions of authority (*Circus,* 1977).

The following talk by the senior author, given at the American Library Association convention in Detroit on June 20, 1977 sums up the antigay argument and our response.

It's Not OK to be Antigay[1]

If you scratch the surface of somebody who's antigay, you're going to find an anti-ERA, anti-Jew, antiblack. That's my main message.

The Bible has been abused for a long time in history. It's been used to kill Jews, to justify slavery, to promote inequality among women. I wonder what would happen if I got up in a church or synagogue and I said, "Well, ladies and gentlemen, if God wanted black people on this earth he would have created Adam and Sheba" or "Listen, everybody, incest is not bad. It says in the Bible—don't you remember—that Lot slept with his daughters. Incest must be all right." What would happen? I would be considered an idiot because I quoted directly from the Bible.

Anita loves homosexuals—that's what she says—but I don't have a short memory. I remember when the bigots from the South would say, "We loves our blacks, our nigras; we loves them and they loves us too." With such friends, we don't need any enemies.

They're worried about gay people being teachers. If there are one hundred teachers and one might be gay, *all* the students are going to flock to the gay teacher for a role model? I don't understand. Are there no heterosexual models? If there is a gay model, is the gay person the most attractive, the most interesting, the most exciting? Don't deceive yourselves. I would like to say, to declare without *any* equivocation, that there are some people who are straight who are also models!

Part Two: I have a message for Jimmy Carter. Do you know Carter's view on homosexuality? It's not bad. He says, "I don't see homosexuality as a threat to the family." He is the first important person who has said that. Car-

---

[1] This article originally appeared in the October 1977 issue of *The Witness* magazine and is reprinted by permission of the Episcopal Church Publishing Company.

ter continues, "What has caused the highly publicized confrontation on homosexuality is the desire of homosexuals for the rest of society to approve and to add its acceptance of homosexuality as a normal sexual relationship. I don't feel it's a normal sexual relationship." But then he adds, "But at the same time I don't feel that society, through it's laws, ought to abuse or harass the homosexual." Not bad.

I would like, however, to say to Mr. Carter, to me the issue is *not* that homosexuals desire acceptance of homosexuality as a normal sexual relationship. That's *not* the main thing. The main thing that gay people are worried about and that I am worried about is the question of *rights*. If you don't think it's normal, I'm not that worried about it. There are some people who don't think that lustful thoughts are normal. I have real serious questions about celibates, but you know that the celibates are not really worried about my questions about them. They think they're normal, and, you know, they might be.

The antigays are worried about child molestation. Did it occur to anybody that 90 to 95 percent of all child molesters are heterosexual, heterosexual adults—usually a man—against a heterosexual child? But they point to statistics that of the people who are arrested a disproportionate number are homosexuals. Well, it's like the judge in Wisconsin who says that rape is normal for young men who see scantily dressed women. A lot of people think it's OK for a boyfriend or husband or stepfather to sleep with a girl, because, after all, she must have provoked it. She's five years old. You know what it is? It's heterosexual! But if it's a man with a five-year-old boy, that's sodomy! Do you know that there are thousands and thousands of cases of incest and heterosexual abuse that nobody is reporting.

We have to know that and say, "Listen, state legislature in Florida, how come you're so worried about homosexuals marrying and adopting children? Is that a really serious problem in the state of Florida?" Do you know what is really a serious problem: child abuse! There are one million cases of child abuse in the United States, thousands of them resulting in death, and you know who the parent murderers are? They're heterosexuals! Maybe we ought to worry about child-abusing parents who might adopt children. We have to say that it's not that important that you worry about homosexuals adopting children, because I have never heard a case of a homosexual parent who has abused children, but I have heard of one million heterosexual parents abusing their children.

Part Three: Some of you aren't going to like this part. A young man came to me for counseling and said, "I have to talk to somebody; I don't know how to say it." I said, "Say it, already." He said he's gay. "Do you want to be gay?" "No, definitely not; I'm terrified by the whole thing; I can't tolerate it; I don't know what to do. Can I trust you?" I said, "No." He said, "What do you mean? You're a psychologist; you're supposed to be trusted." I told him, "Me, you can't trust." "Why?" he asked. I told him, "Trust comes at the end, not at the beginning. All meaningful interactions involve risk. You have to risk the possibility that I might not like you, that I can't help you. Trust takes time."

He said, "OK, I'll risk it." I asked if he had ever had any homosexual relations. He said, "What do you take me for?" I said, "I don't know yet." I asked if he had ever had any heterosexual relations, and he said, "Of course not, are you making fun of me? I'm a homosexual." I said, "So far, you're an antisexual. Any homosexual I know is better off than you are." He said, "Oh, my God, am I that bad?" I said, "Yes. Tell me the story of your life. You have five minutes." He said, "Ever since I can remember I've had these homosexual thoughts and fantasies." I told him, "Stop, already. I know the rest of your life history. You felt guilty about these thoughts. Guilt is the energy for the repetition of unacceptable thoughts."

If there is one dynamic in all of sex education that I consider most important it is that all thoughts are normal. All thoughts, all wishes, all dreams, all fantasies are normal! If you have a thought that you're guilty about, you'll have that thought over and over again until it becomes a self-fulfilling prophecy. If I walk down the street and I see a pretty girl that captures my fancy, I have sex with her. Now, the girl doesn't know about it, my wife doesn't know about it, and it enhances my walk. I don't want you to think that's my total repertoire, because it isn't. I have all kinds of thoughts about men *and* women—and animals. *(Pronounced nervous laughter from the audience at this point.)* Why is that funny? *Who* has *never* had a thought about an animal, stand up! *(Following a pause and much more laughter, it was clear that no one intended to stand.)* That, ladies and gentlemen, is known as research. *(Applause.)* Who thinks that only Jimmy has had lustful thoughts? Gerry Ford has them; Mrs. Ford has them and some people in this audience as well. But where does an intellectually minded young man go to seek his identity? To a psychiatric textbook. And he looks up homosexuality and he finds it and it says, "Someone who has had sex with a member of the same sex . . ." and it doesn't exactly fit him because he's never had sex, so he goes to an advanced psychiatric textbook and what does he find? "Latent homosexuality." There he is, latent, and he hasn't done *anything* yet.

Well, I have messages for some of you, perhaps even for all of you. Latency is a figment of the psychiatric imagination. You might as well say, "All women are latently pregnant." We are *all* latent everything there is! We are all latent homosexuals! We are all latent heterosexuals! We are all latent bisexuals and we are all latent trisexuals. Would you like to know what a trisexual is? That's someone who tries everything!

What kind of society have we created? Some males boast, "If a faggot approaches me, I'll kill him." Why do you have to kill him? Why can't you say, "No, thank you?" Why can't you say, "Not tonight—maybe tomorrow—I'm busy—I have my period tonight." Why have we restricted ourselves to one response?

232

We live in a weird society. I'm talking to my colleagues, university professors—having this intellectual conversation—and along comes a woman, and they say, "Boy, did you see the boobs on her?" I say, "What's the matter? What kind of conversation is that?" And do you know what they say to me? "What's the matter, don't you like women?" That's the level at which we communicate in our society. We can't talk to each other the way we feel. At any point in any situation I have to somehow say, "Wow!" about somebody's ass or somebody's tits, in order to be a male, or masculine. I want to spread the *idea* that if you're going to relate to somebody, don't relate to a *part* of a person. You can't have a conversation with an ass—even a smart ass.

"People are people," and we're going to have to learn to relate to people *as* people, *not* as parts of people. And I refuse somehow to live a kind of life that says, "I can't allow myself to show any kind of intimacy with a member of my own sex for fear of being diagnosed."

I don't want to—I'm fed up—I'm sick and tired as a male of dying ten or fifteen years before women do. I don't want to do that anymore, you see. I'm fed up with the heart attacks and the ulcers. And I don't want to live in *fear*. I want to say what I feel and say what I think.

And what happens? We create delusions that hurt people. We say that somebody who is afraid of homosexuals must be a latent homosexual. I say someone who is afraid of homosexuals is afraid of homosexuals. If you are afraid of dogs, does that make you a latent dog? This whole notion of latency is barbarous. We have to accept people as they are. We are all latent.

I feel there is one preferred definition of homosexuality, and that is, "a person who in his or her adult life has and prefers relations with members of the same sex." Period. I don't know if we need a fancy explanation. Some people think it's convenient and strategic and political to consider it "constitutional." That's all right: I'm not worried about that. But after all the research that I have been able to review—I don't know why somebody wants to be gay. (You remember when you had to have a strong mother and a weak father? But now we know that there are *more* heterosexuals with that combination; everybody I knew had a strong mother and a weak father.) The only thing we know for sure about homosexuals is that they were probably brought up by heterosexual parents.

The issue is political. I'm not sure that everybody *has* to come out of the closet. And I caution some people who are contemptuous of those who remain in the closet. Until the National Gay Task Force has a fund of a billion dollars and states, "We will support anybody and their family who has been fired from their job," we should be a little cautious. Not everybody is a hero and not everybody should be a hero in everybody else's situation. People also have a right to privacy. I admire greatly the people who have come out, because they have made a political statement, and this political statement is important in our time—in just the same way that women and blacks have had to come out. And of course there are going to be some people who come out who are *not* good for the cause in just the same way that there are some women who are not good for the cause and some blacks that were in the civil rights movement who went around and said that if you don't sleep with me, you're a racist. Well, that black is not good for the cause, and there are some people who are flamboyant and provocative, and they're not good for the gay cause. But we're not responsible for everybody and everything that happens. We're just going to have to say that we believe in gay rights as a right; it's an inalienable right.

I am vitally concerned with the politics of this issue because I am a sex educator. And I want to tell you something about a sex educator. I don't get too much in the way of hate mail, but 99 percent of all the hate mail I get is anti-Semitic. There is a close, powerful relationship between the anti-sex-educators and anti-Semitism. Here is a letter I just received:

> Sex education in the schools is a filthy and obscene thing. No stranger has a right to talk about fornication to any child or teenager. To do so is to contribute to the delinquency of minors. It's just a plot on the part of Jews to first destroy the gentile family, then this gentile nation. It is succeeding only too well. May a curse be upon all of these sons of bitches.

You know this person is also antigay, also anti-ERA, and also anti-black. And the message we have to get across to people is that this is a conspiracy of bigots who hated us from the start. And they're using the symbol of Anita Bryant as a way of saying, "Now Jews are all right, blacks are OK, Cubans are OK, but gays are going to destroy us." And once they have destroyed gays, they're going to move to Jews and then to blacks and then to Cubans. We have to caution our old friends in the civil rights movement and say, "Let's stick together; let's not let these bigots deny us the unity that we all need because, if we're not going to stick together, we're going to hang separately."

That is my message to the people of this country and in particular Miami—like the blacks in Miami who forgot about the civil rights movement, the Orthodox Jews who forgot about what's happened to Jews, and the Cubans who think that there's no connection between homosexuality and the fight against communism. These are *all* connected, because freedom *is* connected, and we have to make this a political issue. If we don't stand together we're going to destroy each other.

Of course people who are in the gay part of our struggle for human rights need to give it priority, as Planned Parenthood must concentrate on birth control and, as I have to, in terms of sex education. But there are some universal concepts that must unite us all, and that is, equal rights for everybody.

Parents come to me and say, "I'm a liberal. I'm a progressive. I fought in the civil rights movement, but between you and me, I don't like to admit this, and I feel a little guilty about it, but I don't want my children to grow up gay." And I say, "Liberal, liberated, wonderful parent, it's all right." You know if a parent says to me, "I don't want my children to have sex. I want them to wait until marriage," I say, "That's all right. Tell them. It's all right for you to convey your value system and it's all right for you to want to bring up a heterosexual child. But some of you, maybe 5 or 10 percent of you, are going to have to make some decisions. Suppose that at twenty your child announces that she's gay. What are you going to do? Are you going to throw her out? Are you going to say, 'It's because I was a liberated parent? I should have told my kids that the Bible says no.' Is that what you're going to say?"

It's all right for parents to say what they want and feel, but, you know, many parents these days are having some second thoughts. They have children who are gay and creative, working, functioning. They're happy. But they have other children or they see their friends' children who are drug addicts, in jail, insane, rotten kids. I wonder if they say, "I have a rotten kid, but I'm so grateful that he's heterosexual?"

People in the gay movement need to become assertive and not allow the bigots to define the field for us. And when we don't have our rights, then we have to become aggressive. All of us. I hope that I *don't* have to say that I am gay in order to be able to say I am going to stand with you all in a common bond of solidarity. Perhaps I can say for the time being, "I am a human being and all of us must have the same rights."

ERA and Sex Roles

God, flag, and family belong to us all, but listen to the words of anti-ERA leader Phyllis Schlafly and her associates: "(We) will show them off (pro-ERA people) for the radical, anti-family pro-lesbian people they are . . . we're a pro-family, pro-American, anti-lib, anti-NOW organization" (*Newsweek,* 1977).

It seems that we are sliding back into the politics of fear. For instance, despite a proliferation of causes, demonstrations, new trends in journalism, and a new lip service to employment for women, the Equal Rights Amendment, as of late March 1979, was still three states short of being ratified. Journalist Lois Gould (1977) observed, "In politics, it matters very much whether you win or lose—which determines how you play the game." Nowhere was this more evident than in New York State, where overconfidence led to a resounding defeat for ERA at the polls in a referendum fueled by distorted literature predicting coed rest rooms and forced employment for women. A sanguine belief that the ERA is virtually assured of passage has let supporters bicker among themselves on *other* issues; while on the other hand opponents have stifled whatever internal differences they have in order to be unified lobbyists and publicists for their cause. The National Women's Political Caucus in late 1977 began a strong drive for passage including an effort to extend the

7-year ratification period, which succeeded in September 1978, along with an economic boycott of nonratified states that involved in 1978 over 150 national organizations and lost over $100 million in convention-related revenue.

Abortion

We have already discussed this issue extensively. The key to passage of the Hyde Amendment, which prohibits Medicaid support of elective abortions, has again been a failure of enough prochoice supporters to continue to fight for the Supreme Court ruling of 1973. Supporters have been placed on the defensive, while antichoice forces have lobbied effectively in the Congress. With the extensive polemical and financial support of the Catholic Church, opponents have gotten many politicians to consider that a proabortion vote is political suicide. Although three-fourths of Americans favor abortion rights, the minority in opposition has made its voice count more heavily.[2] Under the headline "Will Our Humanity Also Be Aborted," the *New York Times* (July 5, 1977) clearly illustrated the forces at work in today's sexual politics:

> Secretary Califano has been making speeches about the importance of sex education in the schools. But the same forces that oppose Medicaid abortions are apt to render such efforts meaningless; thanks to mindless pressure, the schools in Fairfax County, Va., have ruled contraception, homosexuality, masturbation and abortion to be forbidden topics of instruction.
>
> Until the forces that have been so effective at diminishing the scope of the Supreme Court's 1973 abortion decision mobilize on behalf of poor women, their children and their families, the humanity of their movement will remain in doubt. Those under severest scrutiny must be the President and his administrators. Their power is real, but their deeds have been token and their words evasive.[3]

Antisex and Censorship

People have the impression that youth today are well informed. They imagine that with all the sex education in the schools and all the sex in television and other media, the current generation of young people can't help but be informed. Many television programs, especially the soap operas, commonly use themes of violence, sadomasochism, and rape. Advertisements are plainly designed to be sexually stimulating (and sex-role reinforcing—see Erving Goffman's devastating study, "Gender Advertisements," 1977). But all of this is *antisex;* it has nothing to do with sex education. The efforts of Norman Lear to present mature sexual themes in his situation comedies, the high level of pro-

---

[2] A Harris Poll reported that a 60/37 majority of Americans support the Supreme Court decision on abortion (*Detroit Free Press,* 7 March 1979, p. 2–C).

[3] © 1977 by The New York Times Company, Reprinted by permission.

gramming evident in "The Phil Donahue Show" and programs like "My Mom's Having a Baby" (ABC-TV), "Guess Who's Pregnant?" (PBS, Chicago), "And Baby Makes Two" (KNBC-Los Angeles), as well as the recent efforts of Ann Landers, *Teen, Seventeen, Coed,* and most of the mass circulation women's magazines are notable exceptions to an overwhelming onslaught of fiercely antisexual themes. Most young people, however, still have greater access to the sexist messages in rock music, advertising, and television. Commercials and shows are full of faddish equality between the sexes—after all, almost all TV wives and mothers now have some kind of job, but when they come home, they're still worrying about the floor shine and beaming when their husband compliments the stew.

We have kept young people ignorant of alternatives to sex-role stereotypes, alternatives to taking chances with pregnancy, alternatives to pursuing a mythical notion of sexual normality that we, as educators and researchers, have created. Our own discomfort over sexuality has prevented us from communicating with young people about issues in sexual situations, which studies consistently show to be more important than background factors and theoretical "knowledge" about sex in predicting whether a couple will take unnecessary risks.

The issue of sex education, for example, is simply one of the most visible aspects of a conflict that is occurring all over the country. Censorship has resulted in Kurt Vonnegut's *Slaughterhouse Five* being burned in Drake, North Dakota; in assaults, gunfights, and bombings in Kanawah County, West Virginia, over the use of allegedly "anti-Christian" and "anti-white" materials; and the removal of the *American Heritage Dictionary* from high schools in Anchorage, Alaska, and Cedar Lake, Indiana, for giving as one of nine definitions for bed "a place for love making."

Opponents of sex education represent a small minority of the parents in any given community, but they are often the most outspoken. The defeat of school budgets, the removal from school libraries and classrooms of such books as *Down These Mean Streets* and *Catcher in the Rye,* and the elimination of family life education from health and home economics courses are typical accomplishments of this vocal minority.

Here is an example of outspokenness in reverse: parents who tell their children the truth about sexuality often warn them against telling any of their friends about it lest the neighbors take offense. And yet, parents who knowingly perpetuate misinformation about cabbage patches and storks have no fears of these stories getting around. The unfortunate result is that their children usually become the sex "mis-educators" of the neighborhood. The ridiculous notion that proponents of sex education are inspired by communism is still around too, as illustrated by an excerpt from an article in the *Kansas City Star* (Sex Education Booklets Removed, 1975). A member of the Concerned Citizens of Johnson County who thought the material was not only "pornographic" but "communist inspired" commented:

> It's educational. . . . But what are they educating them for?
> If gals want to grow up to run a house of prostitution, they'll
> know exactly what supplies are needed. I think it's a
> demoralizing promotion by communism. . . . If they get the
> young people interested in sex, they can demoralize the
> country and just walk in and take it over. That's the com-
> munistic procedure.

What possible answer can we give? Defensive poses and logical arguments often serve only to strengthen the opposition. The following example of
a completely different response is illustrative: A coalition of anti-sex-educators
once opposed the senior author's appearance at a Planned Parenthood conference in the South and almost succeeded in canceling the program. But
because the senior author made it a free speech issue, he addressed a thousand
people on schedule. He thanked the John Birch Society for making his name a
household word and for helping to sell thousands of his comic books. The
media picked up the story and headlined it, "Sol Gordon Thanks the Opposition."

The organized opposition to sex education in the public schools was
most dramatically advanced by Dr. Gordon V. Drake. His book *Blackboard
Power* (1968), published by the Christian Crusade of Tulsa, Oklahoma, at-
tacked sex education as a conspiracy to "demoralize" our young people. Dr.
Drake originated the proposition that school sex education was communist
inspired. In January 1969, the John Birch Society entered the arena as Robert
Welch wrote in the society's bulletin:

> Deep-laid plans have been carefully initiated to spread this
> subversive monstrosity over the whole American educational
> system from kindergarten to high school. But a prepon-
> derant majority of the American people are not yet even
> aware of this filthy Communist plot, of the tremendous drive
> that is behind it.

It is quite obvious that some groups in our society are extremely fearful
of values different from their own. Given their way, they would ban all books
on sex education and censor the exchange of sexual information. Schools and
public and private agencies need to proclaim loudly that such systematic discrimination is contrary to American democratic ideals, and that a community
supporting such censorship is likely to be detrimental to the individuals
residing there.

Our belief, articulated as part of the National Family Sex Education
Week campaign, is: knowledge is not harmful; no one has a monopoly on
morality; and controversy is interesting and enhancing, not threatening.

All opponents of sex education in the schools are not, however, extremists who build support for their accusations on discourteous insinuations
and misrepresentations. The anxieties of some educators and parents are
aroused by the sensational charges of the radical opposition. One hopes that

people have learned (the hard way) from such episodes as Watergate and the McCarthy hearings to be skeptical of those who claim to be protectors of morality, of those who support the silencing of ideas other than their own.

Attempts to prevent student newspapers from printing articles on sex are other signs of the power of censorship in our society. We cannot prepare youth for tomorrow's families when books are still burned and banned and when respect for other peoples' values is not encouraged. We cannot succeed when the mere words *birth control* are taboo in certain schools. We cannot succeed amid persisting fears of information and different interpretations of morality.

The furor that greeted the indictment on obscenity charges of *Hustler* publisher Larry Flynt provided a fascinating glimpse of distraught liberal minds at work, torn between belief in the First Amendment and revulsion for the man claiming its protection. But if we want young people to believe that "people are basically honest" and that "any prejudice is morally wrong," then we need to stop our own selective truth telling in the form of censorship and our own selective obedience to the law.

In judging the effects of our efforts, we need to look beyond statistics on illegitimate pregnancy and venereal disease. For instance, in Syracuse, New York, several years ago, a sculpture of two naked black boys playing soccer

"Boys Playing Soccer," (1971) by John de Andrea, American (1941–), in polyester resin and oil. Gift of Mrs. Robert C. Hosmer, Everson Museum of Art Permanent Collection.

Courtesy of Everson Museum of Art, Syracuse, N.Y.

239

caused an uproar when exhibited at the Everson museum. Now the piece is part of the permanent collection—on the first floor! Throughout the three-year period of the Institute for Family Research and Education's community project to provide sex education for parents, so-called "hate" letters to the institute have almost disappeared, and the widely publicized institute-sponsored National Family Sex Education Week prompted *no* such mail. Letters to the editor of the local newspapers opposing sex education in general and our work specifically were virtually nonexistent until a highly favorable article about the senior author appeared. A brief spate of opposition mail quickly subsided, capped by the following editorial in the morning newspaper:

> We need to educate our children. We need to point out how difficult it is to be a parent and stress that parenting is one job they can't quit. We must explain that babies grow into children who need constant love and care.
>
> We should present the facts: babies of teen-age mothers are more likely to die than those born to older women; pregnancy is cited as the major cause for dropping out of high school; pregnant teens will probably end up on welfare.
>
> We need to talk about morals and values and make youngsters understand that there are wonderful opportunities out there, and babies might limit those options. We must treat our children with respect, encourage them to make decisions on their own and guide them in making the right choices.
>
> We must realize that they may become sexually active although we don't approve. But we should make sure that they are protected from getting or making someone pregnant. We must teach our children right and wrong before they need the information provided in classes for teen-age parents.
>
> We are the adult community; it is our responsibility.[4]

The institute staff kept a three-year record (1974–77) of "Letters to the Editor" printed in the two local newspapers. During this time there were thirty-four "anti-sex-education" letters (most attacking the general philosophy of the Institute for Family Research and Education) and fifteen pro-sex-education letters (most in support of the philosophy of the institute). Broken down by *individuals,* the number of anti-sex-education letter writers totaled twenty-three versus fourteen pro-sex-education letter writers. To some extent, both in terms of numbers of letters and numbers of letter writers, the anti-sex-education advocates have been given more coverage in the newspapers than have proponents.

[3]   *The Post-Standard* (Syracuse, N.Y.), March 31, 1977. Reprinted by permission.

A further analysis by affiliation of the anti-sex-education letters revealed that seventeen of the thirty-four anti-sex-education letters were written by members of Catholics United for the Faith, which is a radical right-wing group. (Several other letters made reference to religious scriptures, but the writers did not state their religious affiliation.)

A random telephone survey we conducted in the same community, however, revealed that the majority of the community favored sex education, including distribution to teenagers of birth control information (Institute for Family Research and Education, 1977). Yet, in this community and across the nation, the media have had a tendency to keep sex education more controversial than is actually the case.

We need to prepare young people to choose for themselves the sexual, family, and occupational styles they desire, and this means defending freedom of expression for those whose views we may not share as well as strongly advocating our own positions. Margaret Mead (1977) described the kind of society we need to support:

> At this time in the history of our earth there is no social need to press any individual into parenthood. We can free men and women alike to live as persons—to elect single blessedness, to choose companionship with a member of their own or the opposite sex, to decide to live a fully communal life, to bring up children of their own or to be actively solicitous of other people's children and the children of the future. In the process, those who elect marriage and parenthood as their own fullest expression of love and concern for human life also will be freed. For they will know that they have been free to choose, and have chosen each other and a way of life together (Mead, 1976, p. 249).

We need to spread some of our own rumors about the bankruptcy of sexist beliefs and the benefits of free circulation of ideas. We cannot allow public opinion to be molded by a vocal minority of reactionaries—after all, we are the "establishment." The great majority who favor sex education need to organize politically for equal rights, for freedom from persecution because of sexual style or gender, and for freedom from censorship, the most basic of our rights. We need to liberate ourselves from the defensive posture of merely coping with the opposition, and instead become activists whose concerns do not wait to be roused only in reaction to attempted suppression of rights. We need to defend knowledge and freedom of choice, not apologize for them. Those who cry that "sex education" will destroy the family and the country are, in fact, ignorant of the very forces that strengthen both (Cassell, 1978; Scales, 1978).

Perhaps we speak harshly of "vocal minorities" and "extremists" or "reactionaries." Our goal is not to criticize gratuitously or degrade any particular group, but rather to work openly toward solutions for our pressing social dilemmas.

Ultimately, any politics of humanistic sexuality must be tempered with a balance of individual and social rights and responsibilities; the individual is the child of society, which is, in turn, humanity's own creation. The struggle for power in the determination of public policies is as old as society itself; when those policies do not represent the opinions and better judgment of society, suffering and decay of family life as well as other institutions are inevitable.

The year 1979 marks the hundredth anniversary of the birth of Margaret

Margaret Sanger leaving Brooklyn Court of Special Sessions after arraignment, January 4, 1917.

Reprinted with permission from Planned Parenthood–World Population, New York.

Sanger, a remarkable woman of her time—creator of the term *birth control* and champion of the right of all women to make responsible choices in family planning. For her views, she was jailed nine times. It seems fitting to us to end this section with some relevant quotations from the person who founded the first birth control clinic in the United States in 1916.

> Millions of women are asserting their right to voluntary motherhood.
>
> No woman can call herself free until she can consciously choose whether or not she will be a mother.
>
> The development of womanhood must precede motherhood.
>
> The rights of women have found voices . . . intermingled with millions of voices demanding freedom.

References   Cassell, C. Who is the opposition? *IMPACT 1978.* Syracuse, N.Y.: Institute for Family Research and Education, 1978, 19–21.

Families drive out 2 singles. *New York Times,* 18 November 1976, 20.

General Mills Incorporated. *Raising children in a changing society.* Minneapolis: General Mills, Inc., 1977.

Goffman, E. Gender advertisements. *Studies in the anthropology of visual communication,* 1976, *3* (2) (entire issue).

Gould, L. Hers. *New York Times,* 30 June 1977, C2.

Institute for Family Research and Education. *Final report—A community family life education program for parents.* Syracuse, N.Y.: IFRE, 1977.

Judge blames rape on sexy clothes. *Chicago Tribune,* 28 May 1977, 6.

Lewis, A. Tyranny of a majority. *New York Times,* 13 June 1977, 29.

Mead, M. Bisexuality: What's it all about. In S. Gordon and R. W. Libby, (Eds.), *Sexuality today and tomorrow.* No. Scituate, Mass.: Duxbury, 1976, 245–249.

Scales, P. We are the majority—but who would know it? *IMPACT 1978.* Syracuse, N.Y.: Institute for Family Research and Education, 1978, 14–17.

Sex and today's teenager. *Circus,* 29 September 1977, 20–21.

Sex education booklets removed. *Kansas City Star,* 8 June 1975.

Sol Gordon thanks the opposition. *Fort Worth Press,* 19 September 1975, 3.

Will our humanity also be aborted? *New York Times,* 5 July 1977, 28.

Women vs. women. *Newsweek,* 25 July 1977, 34–38.

Twelve

Rights and Responsibilities in the Egalitarian Era

> The democratic family assumes that children may adapt better to their environment than did their parents, and that therefore their parents cannot take for granted the superiority of their own knowledge, perceptions, attitudes, and skills. Thus it not only causes but can only exist under conditions of chronic change. The democratic family is based on an expectation that tomorrow will be different from today, and that there is, hence, some ambiguity as to how to socialize the child. "Socialization for what" is its fundamental question.
>
> P. Slater, 1977

The task for today's parents, educators, and social planners is to prepare youth to exist under conditions of chronic change. More than in the previous generation, today's children are able—and required—to choose their own sexual styles, work styles, and family styles. We no longer assume that marriage and parenthood are for everyone, although the majority of today's children will marry and tend to have one or two children. In the face of these fundamental changes, one of the responsibilities of adults is to help youth make better choices about love, sex, and the family.

We need to redefine the values of the family. Despite the emergence of a "new breed" of parents whose personal lives may often come before spending time with their children, 68 percent of the "new breed" and 77 percent of the "traditional" parents in a General Mills study indicated that "strict, old-fashioned upbringing and discipline are still the best ways to raise children" (General Mills, 1977, p. 80). It is precisely in this strict, authoritarian family, however, that open communication is least likely to occur. We cannot return to the "traditional" family where the father alone was provider and the mother's lot was to bear many children before she died (often in childbirth). A return to this "traditional" family would mean reverting to a scene that "often preoccupied itself with a grim struggle for survival and opposed the egalitarian strivings of both women and children, as well as those of men . . . and where the father's dominance more often than not created a wall between him and the rest of the family" (Gordon, 1975, p. 18).

Despite the professional talk about the "death" or "demise" of the family, and despite statistics showing an increase in age at marriage and in divorce, Americans are the marrying kind (figure 12.1). Over 90 percent will marry at some point, and most will have two children (Population Institute, 1977). Four out of every five divorced adults remarry, half within four years (Everly, 1977). The structure of the family as a basic social unit is not dead, but some of the values that ordered the "traditional" family are dying. Gordon (1975) has described the emergence of this more egalitarian family:

> For the first time in history, we are beginning to see glimmerings of the excitement, the joy, and the power of family life, based fundamentally on the fact that the husband and wife marry, not for political or economic reasons, but because they love each other. Women and men respect each other and if they decide to have children it is because they want

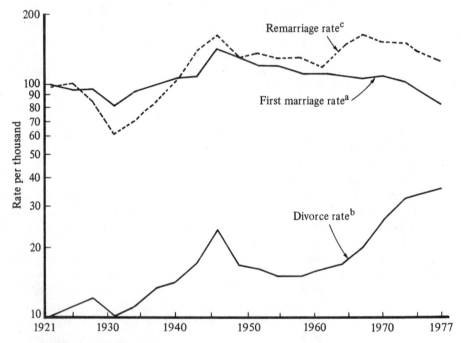

Figure 12.1 Rates of First Marriage, Divorce, and Remarriage for U.S. Women: 1921–1977.

[a] First marriages per 1,000 single women 14 to 44 years old.

[b] Divorces per 1,000 married women 14 to 44 years old.

[c] Remarriages per 1,000 widowed and divorced women 14 to 54 years old.

Adapted from Hugh Carter and Paul C. Glick, *Marriage and divorce: A social and economic study,* Rev. ed. (Cambridge, Mass.: Harvard University Press, 1976), p. 394; updated for 1975–1977 by the Population Reference Bureau in "Marrying, Divorcing, and Living Together in the U.S. Today," *Population Bulletin* 1977, vol. 32, no. 5, p. 5.

them. They can spend time having fun together, and many are beginning to discover that religion is neither a burden nor a farce, but a faith, a ritual, and an affirmation of the spirit that brings joy, comfort, and relaxation to a hectic, complex life.

Children are discussing their ideas with their parents, who no longer feel that the less their children know about sexuality and other "adult" pleasures, the safer they will be. Parents are communicating with their children, devoid of demands consisting entirely of "don't's" with no rationale.[1]

This hopeful description is not yet typical of communication between most parents and children. For most families, sex is the first communication block, the first evidence a child has that some things cannot be discussed or can only be talked about under certain conditions. In their preoccupation with avoiding it, many adults have rendered sex vastly more important than most young people consider it. Although 77 percent of Sorensen's (1973) teenagers agreed that "some people I know are so much involved with sex that it's the most important thing in their lives," this should be considered along with the additional finding that of twenty-one activities ranked in order of importance, sexual activities came near the bottom for both boys and girls. Most important for all adolescents were "having fun" and "learning about myself"; for thirteen-to-fifteen-year-olds, "getting along with parents" was very important; for sixteen-to-nineteen-year-olds, "becoming independent" and accomplishing "meaningful things" were primary goals.

Parents and Responsible Sexuality

Although Sorensen's study is marred by some methodological shortcomings, he did report provocative data. Nearly 40 percent of the 411 adolescents said they hadn't gotten to know their fathers, and one-fourth said they hadn't gotten to know their mothers. Is it any wonder that an estimated 577,500 youths between ten and seventeen ran away from home in 1975 (Opinion Research Corporation, 1976) or that children under fifteen are the only age group that has recently shown an increase in admission rates to mental hospitals (Ford Foundation, 1977). Sorensen (1973) found that many children only tell what they think parents want to hear, a finding supported by the General Mills (1977) study. Most young people *don't* talk with their parents about sex (Scales, 1976) or about such other "sensitive" issues as death, money, family problems, and personal feelings (General Mills, 1977). When there is communication, it is likely to be moralistic and to stress prohibitions and behavioral restraints. It is a sad irony that studies consistently show that females who feel most guilty about their sexual feelings and behavior are most likely to get

---

[1] Excerpted from "The egalitarian family is alive and well." This article first appeared in *The Humanist*, May/June 1975 and is reprinted by permission.

pregnant (Hacker, 1976; Moore & Caldwell, 1976; Mosher, 1973).

The background for parent-child communication rests with communication between the parents. How many children grow up believing that touching is only a prelude to sexual intercourse? That any demonstration of affection invariably leads to deep physical involvement? That their own parents rarely, if ever, are playfully affectionate with each other? How many children begin their own relationships thoroughly ignorant of how to communicate about sensitive issues because they've only caught furtive glimpses of how parents and other adults deal with important matters? How many have had their curiosity deflected with words like "when you're older"? (Mitchell, 1974). Parents themselves need to be educated about sex before they can become more effective sex educators of their own children.

Sex education from parents needs to be based on straight talk, devoid of commands to behave in a given way "because I said so" or because "you'll be sorry." Here are a few more of the "frequently heard phrases guaranteed to turn off adolescents" as compiled in the book *YOU* (Gordon, 1978):

> "Wipe that smile off your face . . ."
> "Just a minute . . ."
> "When I was your age . . ."
> "We trust you . . ."
> "Act your age . . ."
> "After all we've done for you . . ."
> "It's about time you . . ."
> "What will the neighbors say?"

Parents have often believed that a little guilt over sexual behavior is a deterrent, but just the opposite is true: Guilty people are no less likely to have sex, although they may wait a little longer for their first experience (Mosher, 1973; Hacker, 1976; Byrnne, 1977). In all the research we have reviewed, *an acceptance of sexuality has emerged as crucial to behaving responsibly.* Sex education per se cannot reduce unwanted pregnancy if our communication continues to be based on a denial of adolescent sexuality. Trying to make adolescents feel guilty about sex accomplishes two things: it raises the likelihood of that adolescent getting pregnant or getting someone pregnant; and it diminishes the likelihood that the adolescent will come to the parent for guidance on any important issue.

Although over 80 percent of sexually experienced teens appear to have had less than four partners (Scales & Gordon, 1977), the proportion who have had more than just one partner has increased 30 percent in the five years between 1971 and 1976 (Zelnik & Kantner, 1977). While a little less than half of all young people are not sexually active in their teens, the sexually experienced are having sex with more partners, although the overall frequency of adolescent intercourse appears to have remained low and occasional. This change, in concert with other manifest social changes, such as the jump between 1960 and 1976 in the proportion of single, twenty-to-twenty-four-year-old women from 28 percent to 43 percent (Glick & Norton, 1977), and the increasing mean age at marriage means that the likelihood of increased "illegitimacy" is great, the chance of spreading venereal disease is high, and the opportunities for meeting and getting to know different people, some of them sexually, are increasing. In order to prepare today's youth for tomorrow's family, parents and other adults need to provide youth with guidelines for deciding what is "normal" and "abnormal," what is "mature" love as opposed to "immature" love, and how one can tell if someone is being exploitative. They need to know if you can really trust someone who says, "Trust me." In an atmosphere in which young people are given information (not just "facts") that they can see is in their own best interests, it is possible for parents and other adults to talk about the responsibilities that go along with sexual rights (Gordon & Wollin, 1975).

Rights and Responsibilities

Our list of interpersonal rights and accompanying responsibilities asks this one thing—that people treat themselves, as well as others, with honesty and compassion. In so profound an area as human sexuality, the rights of the individual must be tempered with the rights and requirements of a healthy society. Human rights are constantly evolving, and the ones we set forth here are the most immediately compelling; there are, however, countless others, depending on the particular individual and situation.

In deciding specific policies, it is sometimes helpful to begin with the larger areas of freedoms and work backward toward social and legal reforms. Every community program, media presentation, scholastic curricula, and religious action that this book advocates must be mindful of these simple, but essential guidelines. Leaders in every field should occasionally refer to this list, or others like it, in order to maintain the highest standards of personal and professional integrity.

Freedom from Sexist and Sexual Stereotyping

At the heart of our difficulties in promoting responsible sexuality has been the inability to thoroughly undermine the traditional double standard. If men are consistently socialized to be "on the make" and women are consistently socialized to be "spontaneous" and "romantic," then sexual behavior will continue to be run by unspoken expectations and fantasies. In the absence of this kind of stereotyping, people are free to be themselves, and other people, equally free, can actually find out if they like the person! With the freedom to go beyond the "shoulds" of masculinity and femininity comes the ability to say Yes *or* No to experiences with a variety of people, based on nonneurotic desire and concern.

The community of educators and researchers has a responsibility in this area to prevent studies of sexual behavior from becoming standards of "performance" by which people can grade themselves. Young people are especially concerned with whether or not they are "normal."

Part of our message to youth needs to be that *all thoughts and fantasies are normal:* It is behavior that can be normal or abnormal. We need to provide young people with the guidance that *normal* behavior tends to be voluntary, pleasurable, and enhancing, while *abnormal* behavior tends to be involuntary, exploitative, and basically not pleasurable, although at times it may relieve tension.

Research can be extremely harmful to our long-range goals of helping people regulate their fertility and enjoy their sexuality. We have research that says the happiest marriages are those in which the man is stronger, has the last word, and is more intelligent (or thinks he is); marital happiness studies can thus convince impressionable people that they cannot have a happy marriage unless they conform to misleading statistics! But more compelling as a basis for action is the moral imperative supporting the women's liberation movement.

Years ago, women were not supposed to like sex. After all, novelists and commentators showed that a wife who was too pushy just might push her husband out of the house. Now, on the other hand, we have the "liberated" image that today's women like sex all the time. An even newer situation has developed in the marital and sexual counselor's office: For years, the main clients were women brought in by their husbands because they did not like sex enough (or acted as if they did not), and so were accused of being frigid. Now "research" shows that women are capable of multiple orgasms and that psychiatrists offices are filled with men who cannot stay hard enough or who cannot perform five times a night at the age of thirty. Other research establishes the peak years of "performance," and woe to the male: peaking at eighteen, well before the poor women catch up at twenty-nine. So therapists get young men of twenty coming in to the office saying, "I'm twenty! I'm past my prime, and I haven't even started yet!" What advantages are there to this kind of research? The researcher finds a couple at home and asks how many outlets they have. They think he is talking about electrical outlets, but once they know what he is *really* interested in, they lie. So the psychologist, who has had an excellent training in statistics, averages up all the lies into an average lie that makes everybody feel inferior!

We have to avoid research that creates artifacts people can use against themselves. Perhaps in the future, responsible researchers will include this warning on their study reports: "Caution: this research might be harmful to your mental health. It doesn't mean you're abnormal if you don't conform to our findings, but especially suggestible and vulnerable people shouldn't pay attention to them" (Gordon & Scales, 1977).

Freedom of Information
Knowledge leads to responsible sexuality. Our research suggests that those knowledgeable about sexuality tend to avoid unwanted pregnancy and venereal disease. Many obstacles, however, still operate against this principle.

Even mandating sex education is no guarantee that it is of high quality; on the contrary, experience has shown that schools are in a delicate position in a community and are frequently overresponsive to extremist elements who want to water down or even eliminate sex education courses. In any case, most sex education courses focus on the "plumbing" and ignore the more complex and sensitive issues of sexual attraction, sex roles, and sexual communication.

Freedom of information means more than exposure to the "facts" or even to discussions about those more sensitive issues. It means that teenagers need to know about their local resources. For instance, Urban and Rural Systems Associates (1976) found that 13 percent of the birth control clinics surveyed failed to inform attending teenagers that their records were, in fact, private. Since the main reason for not going to a clinic was "fear of parents finding out," this is a poignant reminder to publicize services more widely and in greater detail.

Freedom of information also means the ability to obtain birth control supplies and sexual counseling without legal restrictions on age or requirements for parental consent. While this is a controversial issue because the "rights" of the parents may be infringed, it is well to remember that no child asks his or her parents for their consent before having sex; it is a private affair which can be influenced but rarely dictated. If a child is already having sex, refusal of parental permission won't stop the sexual experiences, but it will dramatically raise the likelihood that the child will have, or be responsible for, an unwanted pregnancy. The parents and child may never talk openly again. In addition, how is a teenager expected to respond to the parental admonition: "If you get pregnant, I'll kill you" or "Don't come home." Obviously, it is a good idea to talk to parents—but ask the 600,000 young people who run away from home each year how they would feel about getting parental consent for medical services.

Freedom of information is an empty principle unless a young person can walk into a pharmacy and obtain birth control supplies. Although display and sale of condoms, even to minors, is now legal in all states, a nationwide study of pharmacies found that 40 percent refused to display condoms, mostly because they feared a negative "community" reaction. Of course, those who actually displayed condoms reported that fewer than 1 percent of their customers expressed negative reactions; most were indifferent to the displays (Kushner, 1976).

In a democratic society, freedom of information means freedom from censorship. We cannot expect young people to act responsibly, sexually or otherwise, if we allow a vocal minority to prevent young people's access to many kinds of information and points of view about "controversial" topics. We do the greatest disservice to all, young and old alike, when we allow a climate of fear to exist in many areas of our country. Censorship has become an ugly, totalitarian blight on the promise democracy still holds.

We live in a climate fearful of information, a curious statement in a society whose accomplishments are based on the high-speed manipulation of information. We have come to realize, to paraphrase Bob Dylan's words, that the times they have a-changed. The "cherished" beliefs of the 1950s about the roles and relations of the sexes, marriage and singlehood, abortion and child-lessness—the most basic assumptions about family and professional "careers"—were challenged in the 1960s, and many entered the 1970s in radically altered forms.

We need to teach the young not to fear communication, not to fear in-formation and the circulation of new ideas. We need to teach young people respect for others by respecting their ability to disregard ideas that they find to be ineffective or personally objectionable. Most of all, we need to encourage and stimulate their curiosity to discover. In New York City's Stuyvesant High, seventeen-year-old student newspaper editor Jeff Trachtman tried to survey his fellow students on premarital sex, sexual experiences, contraception, and so forth. The Board of Education "successfully" stopped him, saying that "professional educators" thought that the questionnaire "might have a poten-tially damaging effect on (students) or their right to privacy." We are protecting our children from the very information they need to live satisfying and nonexploitative lives.

We are in a situation now in which ignorance and myth are trend setters. People are not adversely affected by knowledge of other people's experiences, but they are adversely affected by assuming that they *know* about other peo-ple's experiences and by further assuming that they may not fit the sexual revolution that seems to be happening all about. People who are sensitive about their sexual behavior often feel, on the basis of assumptions, that everyone else is more sexually active than they are, so they must be "abnor-mal." We know that people can become paralyzed with guilt by homosexual thoughts, which they think no one else has, or by masturbation, which they think no other sexually adjusted person would "need" to do. It is precisely among this group that our zealous protection of the "right to privacy" has caused the most damage. The greatest threat to the families of tomorrow is the ignorance of young people today.

Freedom to Express Affection

It's no accident that people who reject friendships with members of the same sex or who go out of their way to be with members of the opposite sex exclu-sively (like women who say, "I can't relate to women; they bore me!" or the men who say "I love women! I need to be with women all the time!") are rarely able to establish a meaningful, mature, and lasting relationship with a member of the opposite sex.

Expressing affection covers a range of verbal and physical communica-tion. Often, parents leave the impression that physical touching is only a prelude to intercourse, and so the child concludes that one shouldn't touch another unless intercourse is wanted. As a result, quite a few friendships are blunted at the start. Most difficult in this regard is same-sex affection, including touching. Sometimes young people fear that wanting to touch another of the same sex, even in a nonsexual situation, such as providing comfort, implies that they are homosexuals. Fathers frequently refrain from hugging their sons after they get into school (except for sport situations) because of fear of promoting homosexuality. This is all nonsense. Affectionate fathers don't produce homosexual children any more than cold fathers do. As discussed earlier, all of our vaunted research techniques have not come up with a reliable explanation as to why some people prefer homosexuality and others do not.

The freedom to express affection necessarily entails the freedom to relate intimately with more than one person. This does not necessarily mean having sex or being "in love" with more than one person. What it means is that people have the right to a variety of relationships, some based on sex, some on talking late at night on the telephone, some on playing music together, or sharing a good meal at home. One of the problems with "love" is that love can be very narrowly defined as sexual love. Someone who defines love in this way may feel they are wasting time on "just friends." But romantic love is a recent, predominantly Western invention; great writers from the twentieth century back into the classical period have placed more importance on enduring friendship than on sexual expression.

It's too bad many people think that everything will be settled when they find "true" love. They think there must be no disagreements and that each partner will always want to be with the other. When a problem comes up, they are likely to end the relationship, thinking that love has died, and go off looking for someone else. The result may be that every relationship proves disappointing.

There *is* a difference between mature love and immature love. As we define it, immature love is when "caring" for oneself is much more important than your "caring" for the other person. Your love is a burden on the other person and the state of being in love is exhausting. You may neglect your studies, be jealous, irritable, and petty. Mature love, on the other hand, is when your "caring" about the other person is just a *little* more important than having the other person "care" for you. The relationship is mutually enhancing and energizing.

It is not true that being "really" in love is something that can happen only once in a lifetime. It is possible to be in love a number of times, with very different people. And these love relationships aren't always sexual. In our view, sex is only a small part of love.

Our society has overemphasized the importance of sex. In egalitarian relationships, the most important goal is not the pursuit of the ultimate orgasm. The real turn-on is getting to know and to care about another person.

The Responsibility to Avoid Exploitation

The freedoms discussed come with definite responsibilities. A man who freely expresses affection by telling women he loves them when he really doesn't is simply being promiscuous, not intimate. Exploitation derives too often from trying to live up to sex-role stereotypes of how one *should* feel or behave, and from feelings of inferiority. If someone's worth is based primarily on others' evaluations, then the opportunity to fall victim to someone who is thinking only of sex is great. Girls can exploit boys as well, by expecting them to live up to stereotypes that put women on a pedestal or by thinking that if they have sex with a boy then he will *have* to love them. The best way to avoid exploitation is to feel good about oneself. A judgment can then be made about whether the other person cares for you as a person, and not just as a sex object.

The Responsibility to Avoid Bringing an Unwanted Child into the World

The birthright of every child is to be loved and wanted. Unwanted births are significant causal factors in child abuse (Prescott, 1975), which is already increasing dramatically. The most conservative estimates are that at least one million children a year are physically abused by their parents and that about two thousand die as a result (National Committee for the Prevention of Child Abuse, 1977). In addition, the young, pregnant girl is more likely to have a premature baby, and then have to deal with the medical consequences (Alan Guttmacher Institute, 1976). The social consequences are just as severe, for a young mother is unlikely to finish school: her chances of getting a satisfying and well-paying job are drastically reduced. Even if a girl wants to become pregnant, these effects argue against teenage pregnancy. Sexually active people have a responsibility to use birth control. Current trends suggest that as many as 85 percent of all teenagers who give birth, including those who marry to "cover" the pregnancy, will start out, remain, or become single parents.

The Responsibility to Avoid Spreading Venereal Disease

If a person has more than one sexual partner, the chances become greater of contracting a venereal disease. The condom is still the best way to avoid this. Each partner should take responsibility for avoiding VD. If the woman thinks or knows that the man has several partners, then she should ask him to use a condom, regardless of whether she is taking the pill. She may need to be adamant about this, however, since many men may assume that the pill solves both problems. The man should be equally adamant if he knows the woman has multiple relationships.

Once contracted, VD is easier to detect in the man; many women show no symptoms of infection. People who think they have VD should go to a clinic or physician whose confidentiality they respect and get diagnosed and treated. In all states, teenagers (even minors) may obtain VD diagnosis and treatment without parental consent. Even if no symptoms occur, it is wise to have a checkup after having had sex with an unfamiliar partner.

Responsibility to Accept Individual Preferences

Every young adult has the right to decide sexual morality for themselves, free from patronizing or condescending attitudes on the part of adults and free from conformist pressures from friends. Although more young people than before are having sexual relations, many are not (approximately 45 percent in the 1977 Zelnik & Kantner study). The decision to remain a virgin, however, is becoming increasingly difficult in a society that allows so much importance to be placed on sexual rites of passage. Beyond deciding in general about virginity, respecting individual preferences means that every person should be free from harassment or psychological manipulations in the event they decide not to have sex with someone. If people have a high degree of self-acceptance and feel good about themselves, then they can accept other people's values without demanding that the other person live up to the image of what they think he or she *should* be.

We have made a special point of virginity because this book is about the sexual adolescent. Acceptance of individual preferences must be extended to all sexual preferences in the context of responsible behavior.

The Last Word[2]

The pseudosexual revolution of the 1970s has divorced love and intimacy from sex. The real sexual revolution, which we are promoting and hope to see in full flower in the 1980s, will reunite sexuality with love and caring. Increasingly, young people are fed up with sex as an avoidance of intimacy. They're viewing love and honest communication as the main *attraction*. Perhaps it is fitting to close with a message to the youth of America:

Self Acceptance

Joys can be shared
(Suffering is mainly personal)
Love energizing
Hate exhausting

Optimism is contagious
Pessimism debilitating

Envy, greed, jealousy, and
Prejudice are connected to
Self deprecation
while

---

[2] This brief section is written by Sol Gordon who feels free as the senior author to have the last word.

257

Admiration, Affirmation, and
Caring for others to
Self Acceptance

Why live in the past
if your future is the present?

No one can make you
Feel
Inferior without your
consent.

References   Alan Guttmacher Institute. *11 million teenagers.* New York: Planned Parenthood, 1976.

Brynne, D. A pregnant pause in the sexual revolution. *Psychology Today,* July 1977, 67–68.

Everly, K. New directions in divorce research. *Journal of Clinical Child Psychology,* 1977, *6* (2), 7–10.

Ford Foundation. Growing up forgotten. *Ford Foundation Letter,* 1977, *8* (1), 1.

General Mills Incorporated. *Raising children in a changing society.* Minneapolis: General Mills, Inc., 1977.

Glick, P. C., & Norton, A. J. Marrying, divorcing, and living together in the U.S. today. *Population Bulletin,* 1977, *32* (5).

Gordon, S. The egalitarian family is alive and well. *The Humanist,* 1975, *35* (3), 18–19.

Gordon, S. *You—a survival guide for youth.* New York: Times Books, 1978.

Gordon, S., & Scales, P. The myth of the normal outlet. *Journal of Pediatric Psychology,* 1977, 2 (3), 101–103.

Gordon, S., & Wollin, M. *Parenting—A guide for young people.* New York: Sadlier/Oxford, 1975.

Hacker, S. The effect of situational and interactional aspects of sexual encounters on premarital contraceptive behavior. Ann Arbor: University of Michigan, School of Public Health, Department of Population Planning, 1976.

Kushner, D. The condom comes out of hiding. *American Druggist,* 1976, *173,* 26.

Mitchell, J. *The circle game.* New York: Siquomb Publishing, 1974.

Moore, K., & Caldwell, S. *Out of wedlock pregnancy and childbearing.* Washington, D.C.: The Urban Institute, 1976.

Mosher, D. L. Sex differences, sex experience, sex guilt, and explicitly sexual films. *Journal of Social Issues,* 1973, *29* (3), 95–122.

National Committee for the Prevention of Child Abuse. *Prevent child abuse.* Chicago: NCPCA, 1977.

Opinion Research Corporation. Runaway incidence ascertained. *University Newsletter,* July 1976.

Population Institute. Focus: All in the family. *Population Issues,* March/April, 1977, 1.

Prescott, J. W. Abortion or the unwanted child: A choice for a humanistic society. *The Humanist,* March/April 1975, 11–15.

Scales, P. *A quasi-experimental evaluation of sex education programs for parents.* Doctoral dissertation, Syracuse University, 1976.

Scales, P., & Gordon, S. Contraceptive decision making among adolescent males. Syracuse, N.Y.: Institute for Family Research and Education, 1977 (unpublished paper).

Slater, P. *Footholds.* New York: Dutton, 1977.

Sorensen, R. C. *Adolescent sexuality in contemporary America.* New York: World, 1973.

Urban and Rural Systems Associates. *Improving family planning services for teenagers.* San Francisco: URSA, Pier 1½, 1976.

Zelnik, M., & Kantner, J. F. Sexual and contraceptive experience of young unmarried women in the United States, 1976 and 1971. *Family Planning Perspectives,* 1977, *9* (2), 55–73.

Appendix I

Stewart Bauman, M.D.

Contraception, Conception, Pregnancy, and Birth Facts for Everyone

People today do not expect their doctors to agree with their moral or sexual standards, but they do expect to participate in their own medical care, to be involved in health decisions, and to be able to talk about their moral struggles and changing roles. In other words, they want to be informed, consulted, and respected.

Physicians must face their social responsibilities, particularly in such badly neglected areas as contraception and abortion. Medical groups and hospitals generally obtain the most conservative legal counsel and surrender without protest to apparent legal restrictions. As a result, many physicians may require a husband's written consent before performing an abortion even though there is no such legal requirement. As a matter of fact, this action itself may be illegal.

In the following pages I shall attempt to correct many common myths that can lead to insecurity, guilt feelings, and, in some instances, unsound medical practices.

Once the decision to become sexually active has been reached, the very first consideration must be which method of birth control to use. Though some people complain, "There aren't any *really* good methods," there are actually several reasonably safe, effective contraceptives.

The pill, when used properly, is one of the most effective means of birth control available today. It consists of synthetic estrogen and progesterone, which suppress ovulation. Taking these hormones orally each day causes the

Dr. Bauman has been in both public and private practice of medicine for the past thirty years. He has had extensive experience with teenagers as a consultant for county family planning agencies and Planned Parenthood. He is currently Associate Clinical Professor in Obstetrics and Gynecology at the State University of New York in Syracuse.

The author wishes to acknowledge the leadership provided by Dr. Valerie Jorgensen, University of Pennsylvania, and Dr. Lise Fortier, past president of the Society of Obstetricians and Gynecologists of Canada. In their writings and lectures, both stress the basic problems in obstetrical and gynecological care.

body to simulate pregnancy. As in pregnancy, no eggs are released by the ovaries, and pregnancy cannot occur.

The pill provides both progesterone and estrogen every day for twenty-one days, followed by seven days of no pills, during which time the woman has her period. Use of this combination pill (favored by many doctors in the U.S.) is begun on the first Sunday after the period begins. If the period begins on a Sunday, then the pills should be started that night. As a result, there will be no periods on weekends. This may be considered most convenient by both men and women. Some doctors may advise starting the pill on the fifth day of the menstrual cycle, counting the first day as the first day of bleeding.

If a pill is forgotten, it should be taken as soon as remembered, even if it means taking two pills at once. Forgetting one pill rarely results in pregnancy, but an alternate method of birth control should be used for the rest of the month (e.g., condoms and foam).

The pill is at least 99 percent effective and has the added advantage that it does not require a great deal of preparation. Some women also find that their periods are shorter, with lighter flows and fewer menstrual cramps.

Some women experience side effects to the pill, though most are minor and require little or no medical care. The effects may include weight gain (usually caused by water retention), breast tenderness and enlargement, occasional nausea, and/or headaches. Women with a history of blood clotting, heart disease, or hepatitis may not be able to take the pill. Also, the pill makes women more susceptible to vaginitis, especially if they take an antibiotic at the same time.

For a very small percentage of women, the pill does cause serious complications. The greatest risk is in blood clotting, which has caused a few deaths. Recent research has shown that women over forty run much greater risks than younger women, particularly if they also smoke cigarettes. These facts highlight the necessity of ongoing consultation with one's physician, who can best advise which method(s) of birth control is indicated for each individual woman.

The intrauterine device (IUD) is a small piece of plastic inserted into the uterus. Most commonly used are the coil, loop, Copper 7, and Progestasert. The Copper 7 has a small, fine piece of copper wire wrapped around the plastic stem. This type must be removed and replaced every three years, for the copper is slowly absorbed into the uterine wall and becomes depleted. The Progestasert has a tiny membrane full of progesterone around its stem. This hormone is absorbed and the IUD must be removed and replaced every year. The coil and loop can be worn for many years without being replaced. Your doctor will advise you on the time for replacement.

A physician inserts the IUD into the uterus within seven days of the start of a woman's period. Although no one is absolutely certain why the IUD prevents pregnancy, it is from 97 to 98 percent effective. Women who have already given birth seem to adapt most easily to the IUD; never-pregnant women sometimes experience minor side effects such as increased menstrual bleeding and cramping, vaginal discharge and odor. Never-pregnant women also expel the IUD more frequently: For that reason, it is important for all women to check the string attached to the IUD frequently, to make sure it is still in place.

The diaphragm is the third common method of birth control prescribed by a doctor. It is a soft rubber dome with a flexible spring around the rim. It is coated with spermicidal jelly or cream and inserted into the vagina to block the cervical opening. The diaphragm is quite effective (95–97 percent) in blocking the sperm from getting into the uterus, and the spermicidal agent destroys any sperm that might have slipped by.

The diaphragm is effective in any coital position, provided it is properly inserted. It should not be put in more than one hour before intercourse, and an additional application of jelly or cream is necessary for each successive act of intercourse. The only side effect has been allergic reactions to certain spermicidals, but one nonallergic for the woman concerned can usually be found. The woman should be refitted after childbirth, miscarriage or abortion, surgery, or a weight loss or gain of more than ten pounds.

The condom (rubber) is a thin sheath made of latex or membrane from lamb's intestine ("skins") which fits over the erect penis and blocks the sperm from entering the vagina. The condom should be rolled onto the fully erect penis shortly before intercourse. A half-inch space should be left at the tip where the semen may collect. (Some condoms are made with a small "nipple," or reservoir, at the tip for this purpose.) After intercourse, the penis must be removed from the vagina before the erection subsides, and the condom should be held around the base of the penis while the penis is being withdrawn. This prevents spillage.

Some condoms are prelubricated, which helps prevent drying out and tearing, facilitates putting them on, and provides extra lubrication for coitus. Vaseline and other petroleum-based products should *never* be used, as they may destroy the latex. Water-based lubricants, such as KY Jelly, are better. Finally, condoms should not be kept in wallets or pockets, where heat, moisture, and pressure can damage them. Use each condom only once.

For added protection, it is a good idea to use vaginal foam along with the rubber. The woman injects foam into her vagina shortly before intercourse, using a special applicator. She can slip his condom on, and he can put in her foam, which helps make the act shared, loving, and fun.

Condoms and foam decrease the chances of contracting venereal disease and are the contraceptives most easily available to most young people. Condoms are best purchased at a pharmacy or obtained from one's doctor or clinic; vending machines in rest rooms and gas stations are not reliable.

Coitus interruptus is withdrawal of the penis from the vagina just before ejaculation. Since the first few drops of semen can contain sperm, this method is not reliable, though it is better than nothing. At any rate, this method re-

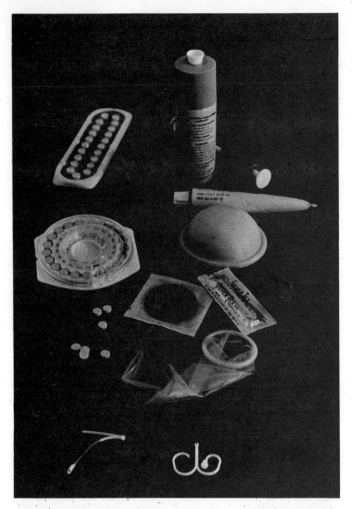

An array of modern contraceptive devices, from "the pill" and chemical foam (top) to intrauterine devices and condoms (bottom), is shown here.

Photo by Frank Siteman, © Stock Boston, Inc.

quires a great deal of self-control and can rob the experience of satisfaction.

The rhythm method of birth control (the only one sanctioned by the Catholic Church) is based on the determination of a woman's fertile period (time of ovulation). A woman generally ovulates about fourteen days *before* the start of her next period, though this varies tremendously from woman to woman. By charting her menstrual cycle *for one year*, and keeping track of her body's temperature, a woman can fairly accurately determine when she will ovulate (unless she is very irregular). Sexual intercourse is avoided for several days before and after a woman's predicted time of ovulation.

For women who object to contraception for religious reasons, or who want to use only "natural" methods, rhythm is the only real alternative. The schedule must be strictly adhered to, as only one slip-up can cause a pregnancy. Since recent research has also suggested that a particularly exciting or vigorous act of intercourse can trigger ovulation, the rate of failure with rhythm is understandable.

Sterilization for either men or women can be recommended only when the individual is certain he or she desires no children, or no more children. For men, the vasectomy, in which the two vas deferens are cut and tied off, must be considered irreversible; only about 20 percent of attempts at reversal succeed. In large medical centers where access to microsurgery is available, the success rate in reestablishing fertility is reaching 25 percent.

The most popular sterilization procedure for women is currently the laparoscopy. This involves a small incision in the woman's abdomen, through which a metal tube passes. The doctor locates the woman's Fallopian tubes, cuts them, and ties them off. (This is popularly called "band-aid" sterilization.)

Sterilization does not affect sexual functioning for either men or women, and may even improve responsiveness once the fear of pregnancy is removed. In a very few cases, the tubes of either men or women grow back and reconnect, resulting in restored fertility. But men or women who claim they lost their sex drive because of sterilization are most likely having psychological reactions. Some men fear that they are not "virile" if they cannot father a child, and some women feel that without the ability to bear children, they are not really women. In fact, all the operation does is prevent parenthood.

Infertility

Some couples find that conception does not occur after what they consider an unusually long time. In our male-dominated society, the usual sequence of events is for the husband to tell his wife to take *her* problem to the gynecologist. As a result, the wife feels guilty for failing to fulfill one part of the marriage contract. This situation is nonsensical and unnecessary and leads to unhappiness and frustration. Statistics show that about 50 percent of all failures to conceive are the result of male infertility.

Medical examination for infertility is necessary after an unsuccessful conception effort of nine months to one year in women under thirty, and six months in women over thirty years of age. It is best for a couple to go to a physician together. Moreover, no woman should undergo any infertility workup until her partner has been examined by a urologist or knowledgeable gynecologist in the field of male infertility and given a clean bill of health regarding his sperm count, motility, and cellular structure. This is simply because a man need only provide a sperm sample, whereas a woman's evaluation is expensive, time-consuming, and frequently unpleasant.

Unfortunately, many men refuse this rather simple examination for fear of being found deficient in sperm, an ego-shattering prospect for an insecure man. Education, explanation, and compassion can help a man in this situa-

tion. Many women have endured intensive examination, even abdominal surgery, when all the time their partners were shooting blanks.

Parenthood

One of the great decisions in a lifetime is whether to have children. Too often
this decision is less a product of informed choice than of fantasies, fears, and
social pressures. It is little wonder that the national divorce rate is rising and
that the problem of child abuse has grown to appalling proportions. Much unhappiness could be avoided if people were properly educated for responsible
parenthood and made aware of the impact children will have upon their lives.
Classes in parenting, especially at the high school level, are becoming more
common. Young people must be encouraged to learn about the effects of parenthood upon life-style, emotions, education, and finances.

Remember, the decision to have a family is between you and your partner. Choose wisely, with love, dedication, and joy. The decision not to have
children is legitimate, but it requires responsible action: choosing an effective
and acceptable method of birth control and using it as prescribed by a competent physician.

Pregnancy

When a woman thinks she is pregnant, she should see an obstetrician about
two to three weeks after missing a period. Her husband or lover should accompany her on the first visit and, if possible, on subsequent visits, especially
when complications or decision-making situations present themselves.

Choosing a doctor is often difficult. Unfortunately, you may have very
little background information about the doctor, the hospital, or hospital personnel. One of the most reliable indicators is the recommendation of satisfied
customers. Friends who have been happy with their doctors will be able to
give useful information. Remember, no doctor owns a patient. It is well within
your rights to change doctors if you feel dissatisfied or uncomfortable. However, it is common courtesy to notify the doctor's office of your decision.

Women should not rely on the urine pregnancy test as absolute proof
of pregnancy unless it is accompanied by a pelvic examination. The results of
the urine pregnancy test are occasionally wrong. As a result, valuable time is
lost, even to the point of jeopardizing a safe, early abortion. A pelvic examination is necessary to corroborate the laboratory urine test. Counseling services
offering pregnancy tests should urge their clients to have a pelvic examination.
An incorrectly positive pregnancy test can give false hopes or unnecessary
fears.

The Gynecological Examination

A woman's first visit to the obstetrician should not be cause for fear or embarrassment. Unfortunately, a cold, matter-of-fact, business-like physician
can add to a patient's fear and discomfort. Not surprisingly, most women

prefer to be fully clothed when they first meet the doctor; introductions are awkward when perched atop an examining table clad only in a dressing gown. A proper examination should, therefore, begin in the doctor's consulting office. Doctor and patient meet as equals and proceed to the first item of business: a complete medical history.

The pelvic examination should not be disagreeable if women understand the process and its purpose. The doctor will explain the procedure and answer any questions the patient has. For this examination the doctor uses a vaginal speculum (usually a metal instrument) to observe the vaginal walls and cervix. (It helps to warm the speculum first so it will not shock the woman.) The device gently spreads the vaginal lips apart, exposing the vaginal cavity and its contents. At this time the pap smear (check for cancer) is taken and material is obtained from cervical secretions for cultures for venereal disease, vaginitis, or other possible infections.

The pap smear is one of our truly great advances in gynecology. By this procedure, cervical cancer, one of the most common malignancies found in women, can be readily detected with a high degree of accuracy. Indeed, precancerous conditions (severe dysplasia) and localized early cancer (carcinoma in situ) can be diagnosed and properly treated before serious problems occur.

The pap smear is not a diagnostic tool but a screening procedure and tells us which patients need further investigation. The smear is obtained by taking a small wooden spatula and gently scraping the opening to the cervix. The material obtained is spread on a glass slide and sent to the laboratory for microscopic examination. The procedure is painless and there are no side effects. It should be performed on women of all ages at least once per year.

In addition to making a visual examination, the doctor draws blood samples to be tested for syphilis, sugar level, blood counts, blood type, Rh factor, and possibly other factors. Urine is collected for complete microscopic examination to discover any abnormal cells or such abnormal components as sugar and albumin.

The patient should not be afraid to ask the doctor about anything, including financial obligations and insurance coverage. A clear understanding of the entire process will contribute to a more relaxed relationship between physician and patient and go a long way to prevent unhappiness.

Most obstetrical centers sponsor educational classes for expectant parents. Dedicated members of the medical staff usually take an active part in conducting various sessions according to their specialties: anesthesiology, pediatrics, and obstetrics. Question and answer periods are encouraged. Classes are usually held on a weekly basis for men and women together.

These classes generally introduce the La Maze method of natural childbirth, a concept that has met with much opposition from the medical profession. However, in most centers it is now a viable option, and rightly so. Women interested in having natural childbirth should discuss this with their obstetrician as early as possible. If opposed to La Maze and similar methods, she or he may recommend colleagues who do encourage their patients to have natural childbirth. It is the patient's responsibility to make their expectations and preferences clear from the outset.

High-Risk Obstetrics

After the first few visits, the doctor will evaluate the patient's chances for a successful, normal childbirth. In other words, she or he will make a prenatal risk assessment. If the risk is severe, the patient may be referred to a high-risk obstetrical center for complete care.

The most important high-risk factors are:

1 diabetes requiring insulin
2 high blood pressure
3 chronic, serious kidney diseases
4 serious heart disease
5 prior birth to an infant requiring special or intensive care
6 prior low-birth-weight infants (less than 5.5 pounds)
7 Rh problems
8 drug addiction
9 history of miscarriages
10 prior infant born with malformations
11 prior pregnancy with death of fetus
12 other multiple factors considered moderate risk, but if three or four of the following are present together, the risk becomes high: anemia, venereal disease, excessive smoking (more than ten cigarettes daily), poor nutrition, prior infertility, recurrent urinary infections, chronic lung disease, thyroid or other glandular problems.

Genetic counseling is now coming into its own. If patients are considered high risk because of something in the family medical history or of a past experience with serious genetic implications, an expert in the field should be called in to outline the risks. The decision to abort must be voluntary and should only be made by the patient with support from her doctor and husband or partner.

Sex During Pregnancy

Like most aspects of sexuality, sexual behavior during pregnancy is rarely discussed. The notion that coitus during pregnancy can be harmful to the unborn child has no basis in fact and may cause unnecessary marital stress.

The fetus is completely immersed in a sterile "bag of water" (amniotic fluid). This fluid acts as a buffer. Any reasonable external force applied to the abdomen will be dispersed by this fluid and the fetus will suffer no ill effects.

For a majority of couples, sexual intercourse steadily decreases during pregnancy. This may be because of a fear of hurting mother or child, or the utterly false notion that pregnant women are sexually undesirable. In one study of pregnant women it was found that about 30 percent were instructed by their physicians to abstain from coitus from two to three months before their expected date of delivery. Abstinence rose to 55 percent in the ninth month. Yet no patients went into labor within twenty-four hours of coitus, and no effect on the prematurity rate was noted.

Orgasm is known to produce uterine contractions causing changes in fetal heart rate just as in labor. The contractions have not been linked to any fetal harm. In a normal pregnancy, sexual activity is a perfectly safe and desirable exercise. As long as the "bag of water" is intact, the only probable effect upon the fetus is that he or she thinks the waterbed is making waves.

There are, however, some circumstances when intercourse is inadvisable. Bleeding is one such danger signal; a second is the discharge of amniotic fluid. When the membranes rupture, the fetus is no longer protected by its antiseptic seal and is thus susceptible to infection. Occasionally, when the fetal head is low in the pelvis, vaginal intercourse may cause pain.

On the rare occasions when vaginal penetration is contraindicated, such techniques as oral, manual, or total body stimulation may be substituted. However, a word of caution. There have been rare reports of pregnant women having suddenly died following oral stimulation of the vagina (cunnilingus). This is due to air being forced into the vagina under pressure. As a result, large bubbles of air may enter the bloodstream and travel to the lung. This danger is present only during the last third of pregnancy. But even in nonpregnant women, air should never be blown into the vagina.

Traditional postures of intercourse may cause discomfort in the latter months of pregnancy. However, couples can experiment or find more comfortable positions such as side-to-side vaginal penetration or rear entry. Anal intercourse should not be practiced during pregnancy as severe vaginal infection could result.

Sex Determination

At present there is some evidence that a couple may be able to choose the sex of their child, a development with implications for equalizing the ratio of males to females. We now know that sperm carrying the male (Y) chromosome have greater speed and shorter life spans than sperm carrying the female (X) chromosome.

To conceive a male, a couple should abstain from intercourse for three days prior to the predicted time of ovulation to allow for the demise of the sperm from the last intercourse, resume coitus on the day of ovulation, and abstain again for two days afterward. Intercourse on the day of ovulation allows the faster moving male sperm to arrive first for fertilization.

To conceive a female, a couple should have intercourse during the seventy-two to thirty-six hours prior to ovulation. This increases the chances that the longer-lived X sperm will be present without the less viable male

271

sperm. There should be no coitus for forty-eight hours after ovulation if a female is desired.

Time of ovulation can be determined by using temperature charts, with or without pelvic exams, to establish the character of the mucus in the cervix, which changes when ovulation occurs.

To find the basal body temperature, take and record the oral temperature every morning before getting out of bed, before eating, smoking, or exercising. As the ovary prepares to release an egg cell (ovulate), the temperature usually falls below 98° Fahrenheit (36.7° Centigrade). When ovulation occurs, the temperature rises above 98°. This increase is presumptive evidence of ovulation. The temperature rise is usually 0.5° to 1° Fahrenheit (0.3° to 0.6° Centigrade). A basal body temperature thermometer is available at most drug stores. It is much easier to read than conventional thermometers, as it records only from 96° to 100°.

If a woman is not pregnant, her temperature returns to normal with the onset of menstruation. In early pregnancy, however, the temperature will remain elevated. Any factors that upset the normal course of events can cause increases in temperature not associated with ovulation. Such factors include illness, exercise, smoking, sexual intercourse, eating, or drinking.

Other tests for ovulation are more difficult and less reliable. These tests measure the acidity of secretions from the cervix and the change in character of the cervical mucus.

Recent studies indicate that preconception sex determination is successful in about 80 percent of the cases. But it is important to remember that the reliability of this method has not been definitely established. Even for couples whose planning has been meticulously careful, there can still be surprises in the delivery room.

Feminine Hygiene

Despite the gains of the feminist movement, women are still chained to some myths. In the area of feminine hygiene, this is very much in evidence. Women are still made to feel very self-conscious about their bodies. It is widely believed that the vagina is a source of offensive odors and slimy discharges, but the fact is that no offensive odors emanate from a healthy vagina. In my years as a practicing gynecologist, I have had my nose in close proximity to vaginas all day long and can personally verify this fact. If the vagina is malodorous, it is a sign that there is something wrong. Douching only substitutes one odor for another!

Television advertises a great many feminine hygiene sprays and douching solutions. Healthy women do not need such products. In some cases, douching may even be harmful. The vagina is probably the cleanest organ in the female body. It is much cleaner than the mouth. Indeed, it is much safer to be bitten by a vagina than by the human mouth. If a woman has a psychological need to douche, she should ask her doctor to recommend a safe solution. But by far the best solution to genital embarrassment is education. Women who understand the functions of their bodies and who practice hygiene do not need perfumed chemicals to feel confident and healthy.

A very sensitive organ, the vagina is highly susceptible to the various perfumes used in hygiene sprays and douches. Some chemicals can cause painful allergic reactions or alter the normal acid/alkaline balance and thus cause vaginitis. For the vast majority of women, it is absolutely unnecessary to take such risks. In those rare cases where douching is indicated, the physician should specify which preparation to use.

Amniocentesis

Amniocentesis is a test to detect Down's disease (mongolism) and other conditions in the developing fetus. In this procedure, a needle is inserted into the amniotic sac. A sample of amniotic fluid is then withdrawn and tested for abnormal constituents or lack of certain cells or chemicals.

Amniocentesis is done under local anesthesia, usually between the fifteenth and twentieth weeks of pregnancy when there is sufficient fluid for sampling. The procedure takes about fifteen minutes and there is no discomfort. The incidence of complications is very small, about 1 percent.

Amniocentesis is also useful later in pregnancy to determine the severity of Rh involvement of the fetus in a sensitized mother. In the case of Rh factor sensitization, a mother whose blood is Rh negative carries a fetus with Rh positive blood. The positive Rh blood causes the mother's blood to produce antibodies. These antibodies destroy the infant's blood. The level of antibodies rises with each pregnancy.

Amniocentesis can help assess the severity of fetal involvement, indicate the best time to remove the fetus from the uterus, and alert doctors to the best treatment for mother and child. Only 15 percent of the population is Rh negative. Of that percentage, only a small number become sensitized. If you have Rh negative blood, you should not be alarmed. Severe Rh problems are rare, and most respond to treatment.

In addition to its role in detecting Rh involvement, amniocentesis also gives a reliable estimate of the maturation of the fetal lungs. This indicates whether the fetus will have respiratory distress. When premature delivery is necessary, amniocentesis can help obstetricians decide when the fetal lungs are sufficiently mature to function outside the uterus.

It is also possible to determine the sex of a child from a sample of amniotic fluid.

Many fetal conditions, once obscure, are now being identified and classified. Fetoscopy, a method of introducing an instrument into the fetal sac, is now being perfected and used in some medical centers. This permits direct observation of the fetus, a useful tool for diagnosing preexisting deformities and diseases.

273

Neonatology

Within the last few years, the newborn death rate in this country has declined. One reason may be legalized abortion. Another is the progress of neonatology, the study of the fetal environment prior to conception, during intra-uterine life, and immediately after birth.

Another diagnostic procedure that has come into its own in recent years is ultrasound. In this procedure sound waves are transmitted toward the uterus and reflected back depending on the varying densities of tissues. In this way, the exact diameter of the infant's head can be measured with remarkable accuracy. Ultrasound also enables doctors to estimate the time of gestation. This helps determine whether the fetus is growing and developing normally. If it becomes necessary to deliver the baby prematurely, doctors can calculate just how premature the infant will be and make emergency preparations. Ultrasound is also useful in locating the afterbirth (placenta).

Ultrasound is not like X-rays. X-rays can be harmful to the fetus. According to our present knowledge, ultrasound has no such detrimental effects. Ultrasound is also used to diagnose multiple births and to detect abdominal and pelvic tumors. At this point, the technique is considered harmless.

Fetal Monitoring

In a discussion of recent advances in the care of mother and fetus, the technique of fetal monitoring during labor must be included. This procedure uses an electronic device to closely watch the changes in fetal heart rate as it relates to uterine contractions. There are normal effects upon the infant's heart rate as the uterus contracts in its attempts to propel the baby through the birth canal. These contractions can often be quite powerful and sustained. In some instances the fetus cannot stand the rigors of labor and dies as a result. This can often be prevented by fetal monitoring, which gives ample warning to do something before there is permanent damage.

Fetal monitoring presents no discomfort or danger to either fetus or woman. An electrode is placed on the fetus's scalp, and the trailing wire is attached to a recording machine. The fetal heartbeat is recorded as a tracing on a tape, much as an electrocardiogram tracing is recorded by a cardiologist. At the same time, a firm but comfortable strap is applied around the patient's abdomen. This belt has an electrode whose trailing wire is attached to the same machine. Thus, there are two simultaneous tracings, one of the fetal heart and one of the uterine contractions. The condition of the fetus can be watched very carefully by interpretation of the tracings.

Just a few years ago, Caesarean surgery was considered only as a last resort. The rate was about 4 percent of all births. Today, the Caesarean method is used much more frequently. The current rate is about 20–25 percent, and some predict it may reach 30 percent. This philosophy of handling the jeopardized fetus has contributed to a lower neonatal death rate. Also, it may lead to healthier babies being brought into this world. (Later we shall discuss the Caesarean operation in detail.)

A very useful procedure now being used more frequently is known as the "oxytocin challenge test." We are now able to predict with reasonable accuracy whether the fetus at high risk will be able to withstand the rigors of labor without harm. Just before the expected birth date, the prospective mother is admitted to the hospital. A drug (Pitocin) is given intravenously in calibrated amounts. This drug stimulates uterine contractions. In the meantime, a fetal monitor is attached to the patient's abdomen to record any changes in the fetus's heart. If the heart rate slows down just following each contraction (late deceleration) or other ominous patterns are noted, the fetus would probably be harmed by a full-scale labor. At this point, Caesarean surgery is considered. If the fetal heart patterns are normal, the test is usually repeated at seven-to-ten-day intervals. If the patterns remain normal, the patient is allowed to go into labor spontaneously, but is carefully watched throughout parturition.

A more recent addition to our diagnostic procedures is the "non" stress test. As in the preceding section, the patient is admitted to the hospital labor room or other appropriate space. However, instead of injecting Pitocin, the fetus is monitored for fetal movements and the effect of these movements on the fetal heart rate. This test is a screening device to determine which patients shall be investigated further with the challenge test. As a result, a large percentage of patients may be spared the intravenous injection of Pitocin, thus lessening the risk involved with any intravenous medication.

These innovative methods and philosophies have met with some opposition from practicing obstetricians. However, more and more physicians are beginning to see the light, and with pressures from patients and from nursing professionals, as well as enlightened physicians, we are steadily moving into an era of safer obstetrical care.

Nutrition and Vitamins

Faulty nutrition contributes to poor health. Experts have finally recognized the urgent need to educate the public about nutrition. For pregnant women, good nutrition and proper eating habits are absolutely vital.

In an age of fad diets and pill popping, there must still be a way to stay healthy and happy without compulsive attitudes or rigid schedules. Education, not advertising, holds the answer.

Vitamin popping is another American pastime. Many of the various components of the vitamin alphabet enjoy great popularity, only to fall out of fashion after a few years. These include vitamins E, C, A, B_6, and others. Vitamins A and D are fat soluble and are stored in the body. Thus, it is possible to suffer overdose from taking them in excessive amounts. The other vitamins require a daily intake, as there are no body stores. They are water soluble and excreted in the urine. These vitamins, if taken in excess, are simply eliminated as waste.

For pregnant women, doctors usually prescribe a multiple vitamin-mineral supplement, a capsule that contains adequate dosages of such antianemic factors as iron and folic acid. The iron content varies in each preparation as different combinations of iron are used. The dose is usually at the maintenance level, but if the patient is also anemic, a therapeutic dose of iron is separately prescribed. In addition to iron and folic acid, supplement capsules contain vitamins A, D, C, B_1, B_2, B_6, B_{12}, nicotinamide, and E, and such minerals as calcium, iodine, magnesium, copper, and zinc.

At times our culture seems preoccupied with eating. Some people have tried to make eating into a scientific exercise. Eating should be fun and healthful and satisfying. Whenever it becomes a compulsive (involuntary) behavior it is none of these things.

Medical science has still not solved the problem of obesity. Much energy and research are currently directed toward finding a rational solution to this problem. In the meantime, people should eat well-balanced diets and take supplements as needed. This means sufficient calories to maintain adequate weight and muscular frame, enough protein to maintain muscle, calcium and vitamins for a good bone structure, and sufficient carbohydrates and fat for enough energy to be active and live happily. Beware of the pseudoscientific approach to weight control and reduction. Until reliable data on this problem become available, stick to the known basics without resorting to fads or falling prey to clever advertising.

Weight Control

Just a few years back, doctors associated weight gain in excess of fifteen pounds during pregnancy with dire complications. Most feared was toxemia of pregnancy. This condition showed itself by rise in blood pressure, swelling (edema) of hands, feet, and face, albumin in the urine, and possible headaches and blurred vision. If unchecked, toxemia leads to kidney damage, convulsions, and possibly maternal and fetal death. Fortunately, this complication in its severest form is quite rare.

It has now been shown that dieting during pregnancy can be dangerous for both fetus and pregnant woman. Patients who restrict their diets may have low-birth-weight babies who, in turn, have more problems during the first year of life. The current standard is a maximum gain of about twenty to twenty-five pounds for the average woman. The cruel regimen of minimum weight gain is no longer acceptable in most obstetrical circles. So expectant mothers, stop feeling guilty about gaining weight and think instead about the joys of impending parenthood.

Systemic Infections During Pregnancy

1. *German measles.* Most virus infections can cross the placental barrier and injure the fetus. The best-known and most feared infection is the three-day German measles (rubella). It is now common knowledge that the rubella virus can cause the newborn to have heart trouble, cataracts in the eyes, deafness,

and many other afflictions. Many obstetricians draw blood at an early prenatal visit to test for immunity.

Schoolteachers and other women whose jobs involve coming into contact with many children should have a rubella blood test. If they are found to have no immunity, and they are *not* already pregnant, they should be inoculated.

If a woman contracts German measles during early pregnancy, the future for the fetus can be ominous. At this point, abortion might be considered. Abortion is a highly personal decision and should only be made by the woman and her partner with the support and guidance of the obstetrician. Some feel that abortion under these circumstances is not an acceptable alternative, but those who choose to continue pregnancy under such circumstances must understand that they take a grave risk and will require special care.

If during pregnancy a susceptible person comes into close contact with a known case of measles, an inoculation of gamma globulin can be given. This substance is a derivative of normal blood which carries immune bodies. If successful, it gives protection for about three weeks; subsequent exposure to rubella may require additional inoculations.

2. *Seven-day measles.* The other type of measles, the seven-day measles, is also a virus infection which can be transmitted to the fetus, causing miscarriage. Malformations of the fetus are not as devastating or as frequent as with German measles.

3. *Chicken pox.* Chicken pox is another type of virus infection that can be transmitted to the fetus. Actually, some newborns have come into the world with a full-blown case of chicken pox. The infant must be examined carefully for possible malformation.

Since an obstetrician/gynecologist is often the only physician a woman sees regularly, he has new responsibilities which were long considered outside his area.

He may give pregnant women some of the booster shots necessary to prevent infectious diseases. The two most important booster shots for adults are those for tetanus and polio. Most adults have not had a tetanus toxoid since they were infants. A booster shot is necessary when the last booster shot was ten or more years ago. In this age of automobile accidents and injuries it is good preventive medicine. It is safe during pregnancy. Influenza (flu) vaccine should be left to the discretion of the physician.

In recent years the herpes virus has become a serious threat to the health of many people, especially women. Infection of the vagina (vaginitis) has many causes. The herpes vaginitis is probably the most serious and most resistant to treatment. It is most commonly transmitted during sexual intercourse.

This condition is characterized by severe discharge, vaginal pain, and blisters around the vaginal orifice. These blisters can break, and terribly painful ulcers develop. At present there is no specific treatment. Antibiotics and painkillers are administered, and patients are urged to keep the affected area clean. For some women, the condition improves only to return at a later date. The situation is distressing, but for a majority of patients a cure usually results from supportive care. Painting with a dye followed by exposure to fluorescent light has been helpful in the past, but there is some evidence that this procedure causes malignant changes in the lesions.

Herpes vaginitis can be very serious in a pregnant woman. In the first three months it will usually cause a miscarriage, for the virus traverses the afterbirth (placenta) and kills the fetus. If the infection is contracted late in the pregnancy, the fetus will pick up the germ as it descends through the birth canal. It is usually so severe that death results shortly thereafter. If the diagnosis is made prior to delivery, delivery should be accomplished by Caesarean. This saves the newborn from coming into contact with the infected vagina.

Another type of vaginitis is not caused by a virus, but by the streptococcus germ, Group B hemolytic streptococcus. This type of vaginitis frequently has no symptoms, but it is very difficult to treat, and in pregnant women can be a problem. During the birth process the neonate can pick up the infection and become seriously ill or die. Much work is now being done to develop better diagnostic tools and new methods to eradicate this germ from the birth canal. At present, diagnosis requires special methods of culture and testing, methods usually not available except in large medical centers.

If not properly treated during pregnancy, the two most common venereal diseases, syphilis and gonorrhea, can cause severe damage to the fetus. An infant born through a birth canal infected with gonorrhea can pick up the infection, usually in the eye. If left untreated, it can result in serious injury to the eyeball and may result in blindness. In most states it is a law that medicated drops be put in the eyes of newborns to prevent such eye infection. However, there are still rare cases of severe gonococcal conjunctivitis. These usually respond rapidly to penicillin and do not cause permanent eye injury.

Syphilis is another dreaded disease in pregnancy. Laws require all pregnant women to have a blood test for syphilis early in pregnancy. Syphilis usually responds readily to penicillin. If the mother is not treated, the infant becomes infected and may die in the uterus or be born with signs of syphilitic infection almost anywhere in the body. Treatment of the mother in early pregnancy will most frequently insure the birth of a healthy child. Even in very large doses, penicillin administered to the mother does not have any harmful effects on the unborn child.

Vaginitis
The common causes of vaginitis are:

1 trichomonas
2 yeast
3 herpes virus

4 infections caused by various bacteria

5 gonorrhea

These conditions are characterized by vaginal discharge, itching, burning, pain and discomfort on urinating (the salty urine touches the bare tender areas). Treatment is quite successful, and in some instances both sex partners should be treated.

Parasites can also infest the genitals, causing itching and rash. The most common cause is the crab louse (crabs). This infestation is now easily treated by lotions or shampoos. Reinfection is common. Another common infestation is scabies (Sarceptes scabies). This is caused by tiny mites burrowing under the skin and causing terrible itching. This condition is also quite responsive to treatment.

It must be kept in mind that Flagyl, a drug commonly used to treat trichomonas vaginitis, is now listed by the Federal Drug Administration as a probable cause of fetal deformities if given early in pregnancy.

Drugs During Pregnancy

Drugs taken during pregnancy, especially in the first three months, can have deleterious effects upon the fetus. Some years back, after the tranquilizer Thalidomide was found to have caused infant deformities, research was undertaken in earnest to discover the potential effects of other drugs upon the growing fetus. The result was a long list of drugs dangerous for pregnant women. Among the drugs found harmful to the fetus are:

1. *Heroin and morphine.* The fetus can become addicted and, after birth, will show the classic signs of withdrawal.

2. *Sulfa drug.* If given to a woman near term, this drug causes severe jaundice of the newborn. Sulfa drug should be avoided in the latter weeks of pregnancy.

3. *Tetracycline.* This should be avoided from the third month of pregnancy. It can cause permanent yellow discoloration of the teeth.

4. *Tranquilizers.* Tranquilizers have long been suspected of causing fetal deformities. Recent studies indict such commonly used drugs as Valium, Librium, and Miltown. If a woman needs tranquilizers to function properly, she should use them in the smallest possible quantities during pregnancy. If she can give them up altogether, so much the better.

LSD has been the subject of much recent research with disturbing reports from many quarters. The latest research indicates that LSD damages the chromosomes in the newborn infant.

There is no question that pregnant women should avoid drugs. With strong emotional support from the important people in their lives, pregnant women should not *need* to take drugs.

5. *Hormones.* In the 1950s, it was common for obstetricians to prescribe Diethylstilbesterol (DES) during pregnancy, especially for women who had previously miscarried. It was thought that DES helped to maintain

pregnancy. It is now known that DES can cause cervical cancer in teenage girls whose mothers took DES during their pregnancy.

Any woman who has had miscarriages and was given pills by her obstetrician should contact the physician to ascertain if the drug was DES. If the fetus was exposed to DES, it is important *now* for that child to have a pelvic exam to show if there were negative effects. It should be noted that large numbers of pregnant women have been given DES, but the actual number of cancers in their offspring is small. Many infants were not affected.

Most of the research on DES effects has been done on females. However, a recently published study recommends close observation of teenage males whose mothers took this hormone during pregnancy. A preliminary report on humans indicates almost a 25 percent incidence of reproductive tract abnormalities in males exposed to DES while in the uterus.

The "morning after" pill used to prevent pregnancy is also DES. If abortion is not feasible, DES should definitely *not* be used because of its possible effects on the fetus. Instead, insertion of an intrauterine device (IUD) shortly after intercourse has been shown to be effective in preventing pregnancy. The IUD must be inserted within forty-eight hours of intercourse. The added advantage is continued contraception if the IUD is left in place.

Synthetic progesterone is another hormone commonly used during pregnancy. It is manufactured by the ovaries and it helps to maintain the pregnancy in the uterus. If a pregnant woman is deficient in the level of this hormone, she may miscarry. In the nonpregnant woman progesterone deficiency can interfere with the menstrual cycle.

Many physicians use progesterone as a pregnancy test. The woman takes progesterone for about five days. If she is not pregnant, she will begin to menstruate when the medication is withdrawn. If she is pregnant, menstrual bleeding will not follow withdrawal of medication. Progesterone used as a pregnancy test is now frowned upon by the vast majority of obstetricians because of the possible deleterious effect upon the fetus.

Progesterone is now known to affect a small percentage of infants while in the uterus. The effect is known as *virilization* in the female fetus. At birth, it may be most difficult to distinguish between the male and the female infant. The clitoris becomes very large and prominent, resembling a penis. The lips of the vagina become fused and may look like a scrotum. In the past, this problem has caused girls to be reared as boys, with psychological trauma for everyone concerned.

Positive gender identification can usually be accomplished by studying smears taken from inside the cheek. The presence of a uterus and ovaries can be surgically verified. Corrective surgery may be indicated to restore the opening to the vagina.

6. *Smoking.* It has now been definitely established that smoking has deleterious effects upon mother and fetus. Aside from the irritation of smoke itself, nicotine as a drug has undesirable side effects, especially during preg-

nancy. It causes constriction of blood vessels which nourish the baby, diminishing the oxygen and other nutrients necessary for proper fetal development. Another effect is the rise in the carbon monoxide content of the maternal blood, which diminishes its oxygen carrying capacity.

The heavy smoker stands a chance of having a low-birth-weight baby. A pack or more daily is heavy smoking. Ten cigarettes a day is moderate smoking. Pregnant women should limit themselves to no more than ten cigarettes a day.

Low-birth-weight children require more special care during the neonatal period. They are also more prone to problems during the first six months of life. Children who are under 5.5 pounds (2,500 grams) at birth are classed as low-birth-weight infants and account for 70 percent of all babies who die in the first three months of life. The mortality rate of these smaller babies during the first year of life is five times greater than that of larger infants. Anemia and malnutrition are common in small babies, and as a result, their resistance to prevalent infections is diminished. They frequently succumb when a larger child with adequate body defenses would survive.

Smoking marijuana is equally dangerous. It causes lung irritation and increased blood content of carbon monoxide, both of which may affect the fetus. Much research is being done to discover the exact effect of the active ingredient in marijuana. There is much controversy, however, so all smoking should be avoided during pregnancy.

7. *Amphetamines (speed, diet pills)*. Amphetamines are fast becoming one of the most abused items on the drug scene. They are readily available, fairly inexpensive, and are prescribed by some doctors to reduce the appetite of overweight people. Diet pills stimulate the central nervous system and may cause rapid pulse, elevated blood pressure, inability to sleep, tremor, extreme restlessness and dizziness. Tolerance to the drug usually develops in about two weeks. To maintain the false feeling of excitement, the dose may have to be increased to dangerous levels.

Amphetamines should have no place in the treatment of moderately overweight patients. They certainly should have no place in the medical management of pregnancy. Do not ask your doctor to prescribe speed.

As an aside, severe dieting, with or without pills, can upset the hormone balance in young people. A frequent result in women is the cessation of menstruation (amenorrhea). This, in turn, causes much distress and sometimes creates the fear of possible pregnancy. Avoid crash diets. Reduce gradually.

8. *Diuretics (water pills)*. Diuretics are often used with amphetamines to produce weight loss. Some pregnant women use them to combat water retention and elevated blood pressure. However, in the long run diuretics have no real benefit and may be harmful. In some patients with illnesses that require diuretic treatment, the doctor must make periodic laboratory checks on the chemical equilibrium of the body.

9. *Alcohol.* Alcohol must be classified as a potent drug whose large-

scale abuse is an alarming national problem. Its devastating effects upon health and family life are well documented. Alcoholism receives much publicity, but as yet no rational treatment has been found.

In large amounts, alcohol is definitely harmful to the fetus. Since poor nutrition and heavy smoking often go hand in hand with heavy drinking, pregnant alcoholics often have low-birth-weight infants. Alcoholic mothers cannot usually give their children proper care.

10. *X-rays.* Although technically not drugs, X-rays have the potential for great harm. Years ago, X-ray scientists frequently developed cancer from protracted exposure to radiation. It took years for scientists to make the connection. Today, X-rays are generally used only with extreme care. It should be emphasized that while excessive use of radiology is dangerous, overcaution deprives both doctors and patients of an important tool for diagnosis and treatment. Used judiciously, X-rays can help doctors provide the best medical care with a minimum of risk.

Pregnant women should avoid having X-rays, especially in the first three months, when the fetus is most vulnerable. If X-rays are indicated, the patient's abdomen should be shielded with a lead-lined apron.

One area of great controversy is the use of X-rays to detect breast cancer (mammography). This procedure has become a very useful tool for early diagnosis. The question is whether it should be used routinely in annual screening or only in high-risk cases. High-risk cases are those in which women have a family history of breast cancer or are over fifty years of age.

The list of drugs that are dangerous to the unborn child has grown rapidly, perhaps too rapidly. As a result, some perfectly safe therapeutic techniques may become suspect. The best policy is to avoid taking any drugs during the first three months of pregnancy, and to take only the smallest effective dose if drugs are necessary later on.

It is important to give your doctor a complete medical history, including all drugs you are currently taking, so that he can safely prescribe for your present needs. Lastly, we should remember that birth control pills contain synthetic hormones that could affect the fetus. Women who have stopped taking contraceptive pills should wait at least three months before becoming pregnant, because it takes the body approximately three months to eliminate all traces of synthetic hormones.

Exercise During Pregnancy

Most forms of physical activity are recommended during pregnancy. Not only does exercise help maintain muscle tone, it also has important psychological advantages.

The secret to a successful pregnancy is to keep life-style changes to a minimum. If you regularly bowl or swim or ride a bicycle, don't stop because you are pregnant. However, to start a new sport or exercise during pregnancy just promotes muscle strain. The graduated exercises included in most natural childbirth courses are an exception. These are extremely beneficial.

In other words, avoid exhaustion and extremes of physical stress. Be normally active and properly health conscious.

Preparing for Labor

As pregnancy progresses, the patient and her partner should be preparing for actual labor (parturition) and delivery. Expectant parents classes are usually available for a nominal fee in most communities. Your doctor can tell you when and where to enroll in such classes. Sign up! Classes are not only informative but also great fun.

Most courses consist of six sessions, each conducted by a specialist. These experts include anesthesiologists, pediatricians, obstetricians, and nurses. At the meetings you will learn about the concept of natural childbirth, a philosophy that stresses family involvement in the birth process. Labor can be very lonely; it is important to have company and support during parturition. If both the woman and her partner understand the anatomy and physiology of the birth process, there will be less tension, anxiety, and fear. Even couples who do not intend to use the La Maze method will profit from childbirth education.

After a long struggle and despite the opposition of many doctors, it is now commonplace to allow the man in the delivery room during childbirth, provided the couple completed a childbirth education program. Many couples find the experience exciting and gratifying.

The *New England Journal of Medicine* (May 27, 1976) reports that patients who are physically and mentally prepared for labor are more able to tolerate it and less likely to need analgesia and anesthesia. It should be noted that less medication does not necessarily mean shorter labor, fewer delivery problems, or fewer complications. Without medication, however, labor is less disagreeable, the family is drawn closer together, the atmosphere is more pleasant, and participation by the family leads to a more cooperative effort.

Remember, doctors do not deliver babies. It is more truthful to say that women give birth with the assistance and support of their doctors and their families. The birth of a baby is a family event. Everyone should be involved. The husband or male partner can be immensely helpful during labor and delivery. Children should be able to visit their mothers in the hospital and be allowed into the nursery to see their new sister or brother. Not only do such opportunities discourage fear and sibling jealousy; they also prevent the disruption of the warm and loving relationship between a mother and her older children.

In an attempt to achieve the ultimate in making childbirth a total family affair, many couples choose to experience the birth of their child in the comfort and intimacy of their own home. I certainly feel that a couple should have this option. However, the decision should be based upon facts, as far as possible. A recent communication by the American College of Obstetrics and

Gynecology pointed out that although the great majority of births proceed normally, 2 percent require services only available in a hospital to insure the safety of both mother and infant.

The pressure generated mainly by women's groups have interested some hospitals in providing an atmosphere that closely resembles a home delivery. This set-up, called the "Birthing Room," is furnished in the style of a warm, comfortable bedroom. There are curtained windows, walls painted relaxing colors, pictures on the walls, comfortable chairs and bed, possibly a stereo record player—in other words, all the comforts of home.

When the time for delivery arrives, it takes place in the Birthing Room, in the same bed occupied during labor. This eliminates the occasional frantic rush to the delivery room, an event many couples feel objectionable. Also avoided are the bright lights, sterile atmosphere, and numerous frightening gadgets of the delivery room.

In the tranquil atmosphere of the Birthing Room the rejoicing that accompanies the birth of a child can be spontaneous and not repressed. Meanwhile, the hospital facilities necessary to insure the safety and well-being of mother and child are immediately available.

Infant-maternal *bonding* is another concept gaining popularity. Basically, it is defined as giving the parents and newborn child an opportunity to get to know each other by touch, feel, and warmth immediately following birth and during the period of hospitalization. It starts with handing the infant to the parents shortly following the immediate care of the infant and then possibly putting the baby to breast. Recent studies tend to indicate that immediate and continued physical contact of child and parents has long-term beneficial effects in establishing a loving bond between members of the family.

Anesthesia During Labor

In the early part of labor, there is not much the doctor can do except give support by his presence and keep the prospective father and mother fully informed of the progress of labor. The knowledge that the fetus is doing well certainly helps the mother to relax.

Once the membranes have broken and the amniotic fluid is released, the internal fetal monitor is applied to the fetus's scalp. This gives a tracing on tape of the baby's heart and the exact timing and intensity of the uterine contractions. This method permits early detection of minor variations from the normal. With ample warning that something is amiss, corrective steps can be taken in time. If need be, the fetus can be delivered immediately either by Caesarean operation or other procedure.

Once the uterus is completely open (fully dilated) and the head descends to the opening of the vagina (crowning), the patient is taken to the delivery room. At this point, when the contracting uterus has done all it can by itself, the mother is asked to bear down with each contraction to assist in expelling the fetus.

When the fetus's head is fully crowned, some type of anesthesia may be offered. The most common types of anesthesia are: general, regional, and local. General anesthesia is rarely used. Ether and chloroform are relics of the past. However, gas (nitrous oxide) and oxygen skillfully administered give good results. As a general rule, since the baby can come at any time and frequently appears following a full meal, it is risky to put a woman in labor to sleep. Subsequent vomiting with inhalation of the vomitus can cause a very serious pneumonia. The fetus can also be adversely affected by the drug, which can traverse the afterbirth (placenta).

Regional anesthesia works on a selected portion of the body by blocking the nerves in the area. In obstetrics, various types of regional anesthesia are used. Saddle block is the most popular and best known. Untoward side effects are minimal and not usually serious. The most common is headache with spasm of the neck muscles, which is relieved by lying down without a pillow.

The pudendal block is becoming very popular, especially in conjunction with the La Maze method of prepared childbirth. It consists of an injection into both sides of the vagina and permits the obstetrician to make the opening to the vagina larger by incising the perineum (episiotomy). This procedure facilitates delivery and preserves the integrity of the muscles surrounding the rectum.

If the mother has not had general anesthesia, the infant is immediately given to her to hold and admire. Shortly after, in the recovery room, the baby will be put to the breast if the mother has elected to breast-feed.

Breast-Feeding

Breast-feeding is a personal decision. Most women will find it gratifying, but those who decide against it should not feel guilty.

Breast milk is a superior food for the baby. It is readily available, sterile, and the correct temperature. Its ingredients are perfect for the immature digestive system of the child. It satisfies the sucking needs of the infant and supplies antibodies for protection against many infectious diseases. The preliminary early milk is called *colostrum,* a clear liquid which may begin to leak out during pregnancy. Colostrum contains antibodies and also a mild laxative to clean out the baby's bowel. The curd formed by human milk is more easily digestible.

There are some circumstances under which nursing may be impossible. Working mothers may not be available at the necessary times. Some women may simply dislike the idea. But if you do decide to breast-feed, you should contact the La Leche League, a nonprofit organization, for support and advice. League members are available by phone in most communities. Your local hospital usually has the call list.

Caesarean Operation

The Caesarean operation is no longer considered as the last resort. The modern concept is that it is a method of delivery to be used before conditions become critical. There are times when unexpected hemorrhage or sudden deterioration of the condition of the fetus or the mother occurs. Such crises occur in only a small percentage of total births. With amniocentesis, fetal monitoring, and chemical tests of the pregnant woman's blood, there is ample time to detect and treat these conditions before they become critical.

A physician does not do a Caesarean without good reason. It is usual in a first pregnancy to permit the patient to have what is called a test of labor. Frequently a woman will be able to have a vaginal delivery after a doubtful beginning. The reasons for the test of labor are: It seems to be of some benefit to the child; labor thins out the lower part of the uterus and if surgery becomes necessary the wound in the uterus is technically easier to handle and heals more evenly; the cervix is a bit opened, thus facilitating drainage from the uterus; and it saves the patient from future surgery if vaginal delivery is accomplished. Most physicians feel that once a Caesarean operation is performed, all subsequent pregnancies should be delivered in this manner. The reason is that a scar in the uterus is a potential weak point and may rupture during strenuous labor.

How many Caesareans are permissible? A doctor should advise both parents about this. If a woman does not want any more children, it is a simple matter to tie the tubes at the last operation. This procedure does not add to the discomfort or lengthen the stay in the hospital. It is a reliable method of sterilization and usually has no effect on menstruation or sexual function.

Going Home

The patient usually leaves the hospital about the third day following a normal delivery. Going home is usually an occasion for excitement and fanfare. After about two weeks at home, however, the euphoria subsides and all becomes quiet. It is during this period that new parents need each other the most. Sometimes new parents experience feelings of inadequacy or despair. By far the best antidote for such feelings is loving cooperation.

Another good idea is to make plans far in advance of the expected birth date. Even choosing a name for the child can be difficult. Trying to make decisions in haste only makes matters worse. Embark upon this new phase in your life with confidence, understanding, and vigor.

Your doctor can recommend many helpful pamphlets that have information about types of baby furniture, nursery supplies, and baby clothing. Friends who have children can give you valuable advice.

Your obstetrician will give you time to decide upon a pediatrician for your baby. If you have no one in mind, he can suggest one. You must make this decision before the baby is born. In the event of unpredictable complications, the pediatrician might be called to the hospital on the spur of the moment.

Sexuality Post Partum

A common post partum restriction is the curtailment of sexual activity for six to eight weeks. This injunction, however, has no basis in science. Couples may have sexual intercourse whenever they choose. Some will experience sexual desires shortly after the return from the hospital. Most couples, however, will postpone intercourse for about three to four weeks after the birth of their baby.

There are many myths concerning fertility during the first eight weeks following parturition: It *is* possible to become pregnant during this period, even while nursing. Unless you want another pregnancy immediately, you must use a reliable method of birth control until you see your obstetrician for the six-weeks examination. At this time he will discuss the various methods of contraception, and you can choose the method best suited for your needs. Rubber condoms plus spermicidal foam are one reliable method of contraception during the first six weeks after delivery. The birth control pill is unacceptable for nursing mothers because it interferes with the milk-forming process (lactation). It suppresses the milk supply by the action of the hormones and interferes with proper nutrition of the infant.

The eight-week post partum period is one of transition. The female organs return to their nonpregnant state. Both parents undertake to meet new responsibilities and challenges from a changing perspective. No family group will operate exactly like any other, but it is important to remember that children learn by example. A child's pattern of behavior will strongly reflect those of parents and siblings. This means that parenthood, in addition to everything else, is a tremendously exciting opportunity to *teach*. Take advantage of it!

Appendix II

Melvin Zelnik & John F. Kantner

Contraceptive Patterns and Premarital Pregnancy among Women Aged Fifteen to Nineteen in 1976

We have, in two previous articles, presented comparative data on the premarital sexual and contraceptive (Zelnik & Kantner, 1977) and pregnancy-related (Zelnik & Kantner, 1978) behavior of two groups of fifteen- to nineteen-year-old American women—one surveyed in 1971 and the other in 1976. In summary, the data show:

> an increase in the prevalence of premarital sexual activity;
>
> an increase in the proportion of never-married sexually experienced teenagers who have always used contraception, and a smaller increase in the proportion who have never used contraception;
>
> among never-married contraceptors, an increase in the regularity of contraceptive use and in the use of more effective methods; but
>
> no change among sexually active whites, and only a small decline among blacks,[1] in the proportion who have ever been premaritally pregnant.

Reprinted with permission from *Family Planning Perspectives*, Vol. 10, No. 3, 1978.

Melvin Zelnik and John F. Kantner are Professors in the Department of Population Dynamics, School of Hygiene and Public Health, The Johns Hopkins University. The authors acknowledge the invaluable assistance of Judy Gehret, Nelva Hitt and Farida Shah. The 1976 study on which this article is based was supported by Grant No. HD05255 from the National Institute of Child Health and Human Development, DHEW. Generous assistance also was received from the Ford Foundation.

The data are derived from a national probability sample survey of ever-married and never-married women fifteen to nineteen years of age living in households in the continental United States. The sampling procedure involved stratification by race to ensure a substantial number of interviews with black respondents. The fieldwork was carried out under contract by the Research Triangle Institute and provided 2,193 completed interviews.

Thus, the data on contraceptive practices indicate that sexually active young women interviewed in 1976 were better protected against pregnancy than were comparable young women interviewed in 1971; but the data on premarital pregnancies do not show any change over the period in the proportions who had experienced a pregnancy up to the time of interview. This does not mean that improved contraception did not affect the incidence of pregnancy. But we cannot make the detailed comparisons of contraceptive use and pregnancy between the two surveys needed to explain the apparent contradiction.[2] However, the 1976 data alone, although far from perfect, do permit us to examine in far greater detail than we could from the 1971 survey the relationship of contraceptive use and premarital pregnancy.[3]

In this article, premaritally sexually active teenagers are classified by contraceptive-use status as "always-users," "never-users" or "sometimes-users" of contraception. This classification refers to contraceptive behavior up to the time of a premarital pregnancy, or if the teenager has never been pregnant premaritally, up to interview or marriage.[4]

We have noted previously that about 28 percent of teenagers (25 percent of whites and 40 percent of blacks) who have had premarital intercourse have ever experienced a premarital pregnancy (Zelnik & Kantner, 1978, table 2). Table 1 shows how these proportions vary widely according to contraceptive-use status (classified in the manner noted above). Roughly similar proportions—about three in ten—report that they are always-users and never-users, while about four in ten say they have used a method sometimes. Blacks are about one and one-half times more likely than whites to be never-users.

Most important, the data in table 1 show a strong negative correlation

Table 1   Percentage Distribution of Young Women with Premarital Sexual Experience,[a] by Contraceptive-Use Status, and Percent Ever Premaritally Pregnant for Each Status, According to Race

Contraceptive-Use and Pregnancy Status	Total		White		Black	
	Percent	N	Percent	N	Percent	N
Always-use	26.9	228	27.7	135	23.8	93
Ever pregnant	10.9		11.2		9.6	
Sometimes-use	42.1	343	44.6	215	33.3	128
Ever pregnant	23.9		22.6		30.0	
Never-use	31.0	312	27.7	147	42.9	165
Ever pregnant	58.0		52.2		71.2	
Total	100.0	883	100.0	497	100.0	386

[a]This and subsequent tables refer to women with premarital sexual experience who were aged 15–19 in 1976.

between contraceptive use and continuity of use, and pregnancy: 58 percent of never-users experienced a premarital pregnancy, compared to 24 percent of sometimes-users and only 11 percent of always-users. The difference in premarital pregnancy between regular use and nonuse of contraception is more striking for blacks than whites,[5] but the basic pattern is the same. For all teenagers, contraceptive use makes a substantial difference: Never-users are five times more likely to become pregnant than always-users, and two and one-half times more likely than sometimes-users.

We examine the association of pregnancy and contraceptive use in somewhat greater detail below. We continue to base contraceptive-use status on behavior up to pregnancy, marriage or the survey while at the same time subsuming the categories of always-, sometimes- and never-use under two more general categories. So that the reader may follow the presentation more easily, the scheme we use is outlined as follows:

I. Used contraception at first intercourse
   a. and always used it prior to pregnancy, marriage or survey
   b. but did not always use it prior to pregnancy, marriage or survey
II. Did not use contraception at first intercourse
   a. but used it prior to pregnancy, marriage or survey
   b. and never used it prior to pregnancy, marriage or survey

In terms of contraceptive-use status, Ia corresponds to always-use, IIb corresponds to never-use and Ib plus IIa corresponds to sometimes-use.

Used Contraception at First Intercourse

Almost 40 percent of all teenage women with premarital sexual experience used contraception the first time they had intercourse, with the proportion somewhat higher for whites than for blacks (table 2). There is a clear positive relationship between age at first intercourse and the likelihood of using contraception at that event: 55 percent of those who first had intercourse at ages

Table 2   Percentage of Young Women Who Used Contraception at First Intercourse, by Age at First Intercourse and Race

Age at 1st Intercourse	Total		White		Black	
	Percent	N	Percent	N	Percent	N
All	38.7	878	40.2	496	33.5	382
<15	24.5	237	23.8	97	25.8	140
15–17	40.9	564	42.0	338	36.2	226
18–19	54.8	77	54.1	61	**	16

Note: In this and subsequent tables, a double asterisk indicates N<20.

eighteen or nineteen used a contraceptive at that initial event—more than two times the proportion of those who first had intercourse before age fifteen.

Such a relationship may be related to changes in circumstances over time as well as to a direct effect of age at first intercourse and such concomitants as greater education and sophistication. That is because all young women who initiated intercourse at ages eighteen or nineteen began sex shortly before the survey, while those who started at younger ages had that experience at varying intervals preceding the survey. For example, the current fifteen-year-old whose first intercourse occurred at age fourteen began sex shortly before the interview, while the nineteen-year-old who initiated sex at fourteen began sex five years before the survey. It is probable that a fourteen-year-old in 1970 and in 1975 faced quite different situations regarding the availability and accessibility of contraception, for example.

If age at first intercourse were the sole factor accounting for the use of contraception at initial intercourse, we would expect that among those who began sex before age fifteen, the proportion using contraception at first intercourse would not vary with current age. On the other hand, if the calendar year in which intercourse first occurred is important—for example, because of the increased availability of contraceptives to teenagers in recent years—there should be variation by current age, with currently younger women having different rates of initial use than older women. The data in table 3 show that for

Table 3 Percentage of Young Women Who Used Contraception at First Intercourse, by Age at First Intercourse and Current Age, According to Race

Age at 1st Intercourse	Current Age			
	15–17		18–19	
	Percent	N	Percent	N
Total				
< 15	26.7	148	20.6	89
15–17	41.7	230	40.4	334
18–19	na	na	54.8	77
White				
<15	25.7	64	20.2	33
15–17	42.1	137	42.0	201
18–19	na	na	54.1	61
Black				
<15	28.7	84	21.3	56
15–17	39.8	93	33.7	133
18–19	na	na	**	16

Note: In this and subsequent tables, na=not applicable.

both races (reading down the columns), age at first intercourse remains positively associated with contraceptive use at that initial event. For blacks, and possibly for whites who began sex before age fifteen (though here, the Ns are small), there appears to be an increase in use over time (reading across the rows); while for whites who initiated intercourse between ages fifteen and seventeen, the year that sex began appears to make little difference. These data are consistent with reports indicating that in recent years contraceptives have become more available to younger teenagers (Paul, Pilpel & Wechsler, 1976), and that expansion of family planning services in organized clinic programs has increased availability proportionally more for blacks than for whites.[6]

What methods were adopted by those who used a contraceptive the first time they had intercourse? Table 4 shows that one-quarter of all those who

Table 4 Percentage of Young Women Practicing Contraception at First Intercourse Who Used a Medical Method of Contraception, by Age at First Intercourse and Race

Age at 1st Intercourse	Total		White		Black	
	Percent	N	Percent	N	Percent	N
All	25.1	326	20.1	198	46.6	128
<15	23.1	59	12.6	23	41.1	36
15–17	21.9	225	16.8	143	46.5	82
18–19	40.8	42	38.1	32	**	10

used contraception at first intercourse used a medical method (pill, IUD or diaphragm)—one-fifth of whites and nearly one-half of blacks. Again, there is a clear positive association between the age at which intercourse begins and the likelihood of adopting a medical method at initiation.[7]

Those who use contraception at the time of first intercourse can be subdivided into two groups: those who continue to use a method at every subsequent act of intercourse up to pregnancy, marriage or survey (always-users); and those who do not (sometimes-users). Having considered all of those who used a contraceptive at first intercourse, we now consider, briefly, each of the two subgroups.

Always-Users

Table 5 shows that about seven in ten of both whites and blacks who used a contraceptive at first intercourse reported that they always used a method. Although regularity of use does not vary with race, there are considerable differences depending on whether the first method used was medical or nonmedical: 87 percent of those who used a medical method of contraception at first intercourse continued to use contraception regularly, compared to 64 percent of

Table 5 Percentage of Young Women Practicing Contraception at First Intercourse Who Are Always-Users of Contraception, by Initial Method and Race

Initial Method	Total		White		Black	
	Percent	N	Percent	N	Percent	N
All	69.7	327	69.1	198	72.2	129
Medical	87.3	100	92.4	39	78.0	61
Nonmedical	63.8	227	63.2	159	67.1	68

those who started with a nonmedical method. Both blacks and whites who started with a medical method were more likely to continue use than those who started with a nonmedical method; but whites who started with a medical method were more likely to continue use than comparable blacks. However, black always-users were much more likely than whites to start with a medical method: 51 percent of black always-users began with a medical method, in contrast to 27 percent of the white always-users (table 6).

Table 6 Percentage Distribution of Always-Users of Contraception, by Initial Method and Race

Initial Method	Total (N=228)	White (N=135)	Black (N=93)
Medical	31.6	26.9	51.3
Nonmedical	68.4	73.1	48.7
All	100.0	100.0	100.0

Over time, one-quarter of the always-users changed the type of method employed between first and most recent contraceptive use.[8] One-third of those who started with a nonmedical method switched to a medical method; whereas only one in sixteen of those who began with a medical method shifted to nonmedical contraception (table 7). As a result, 53 percent of always-users were using a medical method at most recent use, compared to 32 percent at first use (table 6); and the racial difference that had prevailed at first use declined, so that 51 percent of the whites were using a medical method at last use, as compared to 63 percent of the blacks.

Table 1 showed that 10 percent of black always-users and 11 percent of white always-users had ever experienced a premarital pregnancy. However, there are substantial differences in the proportions of always-users who ever became pregnant, depending on whether they were using a medical or nonmedical method of contraception: Thus, 17 percent of always-users who employed a nonmedical method (at time of pregnancy or last intercourse pre-

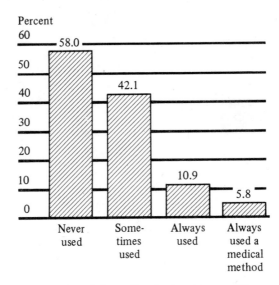

Figure 1 Percentage of Sexually Active Young Women Who Ever Had a Premarital Pregnancy, by Contraceptive-Use Status

Table 7 Percentage Distribution of Initial Method of Contraception Employed by Always-Users, According to Most Recent Method Used, by Race

Initial Method	Most Recent Method			
	Medical	Non-medical	All	N
Total				
Medical	94.0	6.0	100.0	84
Nonmedical	34.3	65.7	100.0	144
All	53.2	46.8	100.0	228
White				
Medical	93.2	6.8	100.0	36
Nonmedical	35.2	64.8	100.0	99
All	50.8	49.2	100.0	135
Black				
Medical	95.8	4.2	100.0	48
Nonmedical	28.6	71.4	100.0	45
All	63.1	36.9	100.0	93

ceding marriage or survey) experienced a pregnancy, three times the proportion of those who used a medical method (table 8).[9] Even more striking (as comparison of tables 8 and 1 shows), the proportion of never-users who became pregnant (58 percent) is ten times that of always-users who employed a medical method (6 percent). Among blacks, the proportion is fifteen times greater, and among whites, nine times greater.

Table 8 Percentage of Always-Users Who Became Premaritally Pregnant, by Method and Race

Method	Total		White		Black	
	Percent	N	Percent	N	Percent	N
All	10.9	228	11.2	135	9.6	93
Medical	5.8	128	6.1	69	4.9	59
Nonmedical	16.6	100	16.4	66	17.7	34

In summary:

1. Use of contraception at first intercourse, and especially use of a medical method, is associated with more consistent use of contraception.

2. One-third of always-users who start intercourse using a nonmedical method switch to a more effective medical method later, while almost all who begin with a medical method continue to use medical contraception.

3. Those who consistently use a medical method are one-third as likely to become pregnant as those who use a nonmedical method, and one-tenth as likely to get pregnant as those who use no method.

Used at Initiation, but Not Always

As indicated in table 5, 36 percent of those who used a nonmedical method at first intercourse subsequently failed to use contraception consistently, compared to just 13 percent of those initially using a medical method. Table 9 shows that among those who used contraception at first intercourse but not consistently thereafter,[10] one-third—half of the blacks and three in ten of the whites—became pregnant. Six out of ten of those who became pregnant reported that they did not intend to become pregnant, but the overwhelming majority of them—more than eight in ten—were not using contraception at the time pregnancy occurred.

No Contraception at First Intercourse

Just as we divided those who used contraception at first intercourse into two groups according to whether they continued to practice contraception consistently, we now divide teenagers who did not use contraception at first intercourse into those who did[11] and those who did not use any method subsequently (prior to a pregnancy, marriage or the survey).

Table 9 Percentage Distribution of Young Women Who Used Contraception at First Intercourse but Not Consistently Thereafter, by Whether Ever Premaritally Pregnant, by Whether Pregnancy Was Intended, and, If Not, by Whether Contraception Was Used at Time of Conception, According to Race

Pregnancy Status, Intent and Use of Contraception	Total (N=98)	White (N=63)	Black (N=35)
Never pregnant	66.8	70.8	47.8
Ever pregnant	33.2	29.2	52.2
Intended pregnancy	38.9	39.0	**
Did not intend	61.1	61.0	**
Used medical method	2.3	**	**
Used nonmedical method	13.2	**	**
Did not use	84.5	**	**
Total	100.0	100.0	100.0

Table 10 shows that almost half of the young women who did not use a method at first intercourse but adopted contraception later began with a medical method. This compares to just one-quarter adopting a medical method among those who began intercourse and contraception concurrently (table 4). The difference does not stem merely from the fact that those who delay contraception until some time after initiation are older than those who begin sex and contraception at the same time. Comparison of tables 4 and 10 shows that at each age of first intercourse, the proportion who start contraception with a medical method is greater among those who delay contraception than among

Table 10 Of Young Women Who Delayed Use of Contraception,[a] Percentage Who Began with a Medical Method, by Age at First Intercourse and Race

Age at 1st Intercourse	Total		White		Black	
	Percent	N	Percent	N	Percent	N
All	47.5	241	45.0	151	59.8	90
<15	46.0	67	39.4	36	67.8	31
15–17	48.4	158	47.1	102	55.1	56
18–19	**	16	**	13	**	3

[a] That is, did not use contraception at first intercourse but did use it prior to pregnancy, marriage or survey.

those who use it at sexual initiation. In fact, among both blacks and whites who had intercourse before age fifteen and who did not initially use contraception, the proportion starting with a medical method is as high as that among those who began intercourse and contraception at ages eighteen or nineteen. Thus, the higher level of initial use of medical contraception among those who start to contracept after they begin to have intercourse is not due to an older age at first use of contraception.

Of obvious importance is the length of the interval between first intercourse and first contraception. As may be seen in table 11, there was an average of 1.4 years between first intercourse and first contraception for those who initiated sex before age fifteen; whites tended to adopt a method somewhat sooner (1.2 years) than blacks (1.7 years). Those adopting a medical method waited an average of 1.8 years, while those adopting a nonmedical method waited only 0.9 years.

The young women who began intercourse between ages fifteen and seventeen waited just half a year to begin to contracept; there is no difference in this respect between blacks and whites or between those adopting a medical and nonmedical method. We have no information on the frequency of inter-

Table 11   Mean Number of Years Between First Intercourse and First Use of Contraception for Those Who Delayed Use of Contraception,[a] by Method and Race

	Method					
	All		Medical		Non-medical	
Age at 1st Intercourse	No. yrs.	N	No. yrs.	N	No. yrs.	N
Total						
<15	1.4	65	1.8	34	0.9	31
15–17	0.5	156	0.6	78	0.4	78
18–19	na	na	na	na	na	na
White						
<15	1.2	36	**	13	0.8	23
15–17	0.5	101	0.6	47	0.3	54
18–19	na	na	na	na	na	na
Black						
<15	1.7	29	1.7	21	**	8
15–17	0.6	55	0.7	31	0.5	24
18–19	na	na	na	na	na	na

[a]See table 10.

course during the interval between sexual initiation and the adoption of contraception.[12]

Twenty percent of those who delayed contraception became pregnant following the adoption of some method (22 percent of the blacks and 20 percent of the whites). Of those who became pregnant, nearly three-quarters did not intend the pregnancy (table 12). But of these, seven in ten were not using any method at the time they conceived.

Table 12   Percentage Distribution of Young Women Who Delayed Use of Contraception,[a] by Whether Ever Premaritally Pregnant, by Whether Pregnancy Was Intended, and, If Not, by Whether Contraception Was Used at Time of Conception, According to Race

Pregnancy Status, Intent, and Use of Contraception	Total (N=245)	White (N=152)	Black (N=93)
Never pregnant	79.7	79.9	78.5
Ever pregnant	20.3	20.1	21.5
Intended pregnancy	27.6	23.7	45.3
Did not intend	72.4	76.3	54.7
Used medical method	16.8	16.6	**
Used nonmedical method	13.9	14.6	**
Did not use	69.3	68.8	**
Total	100.0	100.0	100.0

[a]See table 10.

In summary, about one in five young women who started contraception at the time they initiated sex, but then failed to use contraception consistently, had an unwanted pregnancy, whereas about one in seven who delayed contraception until some time after initiating sex had an unwanted pregnancy (derived from tables 9 and 12). This difference appears to be due mainly to the fact that those who began use later were more likely to use a more effective medical method.

Never Used Contraception

As shown in table 1, 28 percent of whites and 43 percent of blacks with premarital sexual experience had never used contraception prior to pregnancy, marriage or the survey. Slightly more than one-half of the white never-users had experienced a premarital pregnancy, as had seven in ten of the black never-users. Of those never-users who had become pregnant, 66 percent of the whites and 72 percent of the blacks reported they did not intend to become pregnant (not shown in tables).

Following the outcome of the pregnancy, a very high proportion of eligible never-users[13] did in fact adopt contraception, and almost all of them adopted a medical method. Thus, seven in ten of the black never-users who became pregnant began to contracept subsequent to the pregnancy outcome, and virtually all of these adopted a medical method. Six in ten whites adopted contraception after the pregnancy outcome, and nine in ten adopted a medical method.[14] At the same time, one-fourth of the ever-pregnant never-users continued to be sexually active without using contraception (not shown).

The Premaritally Pregnant

So far, our discussion of the use of contraception in relation to premarital first pregnancy has focused on the proportion of sexually active young women who ever became pregnant. In table 13, we show for those who were premaritally pregnant whether contraception had ever been used prior to the time the pregnancy occurred.[15] The table shows that the bulk of premarital first pregnancies occur to that portion of the sexually active teenage population who do not use contraception before they become pregnant. Comparing table 1 with table 13, we see that 31 percent of sexually active teenagers are never-users, and that these comprise 58 percent of those who had a premarital pregnancy. Among blacks, 43 percent are never-users, comprising 71 percent of those who had a premarital pregnancy; among whites, the proportion of never-users is 28 percent, or 52 percent of those who had a premarital pregnancy.

Table 13 Percentage Distribution of Premaritally Pregnant Young Women, by Whether Contraception Had Ever Been Used Prior to Pregnancy, According to Race

Use of Contra- ception Before Pregnancy	Total (N=316)	White (N=151)	Black (N=165)
Ever used	41.9	47.6	28.7
Never used	58.1	52.4	71.3
Total	100.0	100.0	100.0

What proportion of *all* premarital pregnancies were reported as intended? Table 14 shows that seven in ten premarital pregnancies occurring to both whites and blacks were not intended.[16] However, only one in five of those who did not intend the pregnancy were using contraception when conception occurred; whites were somewhat more likely to have been using a method than blacks.

Overall, almost three in ten young women who became premaritally

Table 14 Percentage Distribution of Premaritally Pregnant Young Women, by Whether Pregnancy Was Intended and, If Not, by Whether Contraception Was Used at Time of Conception, According to Race

Pregnancy Intent and Use at Time of Conception	Total (N=316)	White (N=151)	Black (N=165)
Intended pregnancy	28.8	28.3	29.8
Did not intend	71.2	71.7	70.2
Used medical method	7.4	8.5	4.9
Used nonmedical method	13.7	17.0	6.0
Did not use	78.9	74.5	89.0
Total	100.0	100.0	100.0

pregnant married while pregnant. Those who intended the pregnancy were twice as likely to marry before the outcome as those who did not intend the pregnancy (table 15). Whether or not the pregnancy was intended, whites who conceived premaritally were four times more likely to marry while pregnant than were comparable blacks.

Table 15 Percentage of Premaritally Pregnant Young Women Who Married While Pregnant, by Whether or Not Pregnancy Was Intended, According to Race

Pregnancy Intent	Total		White		Black	
	Percent	N	Percent	N	Percent	N
All pregnancies	26.9	316	34.8	151	8.7	165
Intended	43.7	96	57.0	47	14.5	49
Did not intend	20.1	220	26.1	104	6.2	116

In table 16, we show the postpregnancy contraceptive behavior of *all* those who had a first pregnancy outcome while still unmarried. Seventy-two percent used contraception after the pregnancy outcome, and 83 percent of those contraceptors used a medical method. On the other hand, 16 percent continued to be sexually active but did not use any method after the outcome. Whites and blacks do not differ in the degree to which they use contraception, but blacks appear more likely to use a medical method. However, whites seem to be less likely to resume sex following the outcome of the pregnancy (at least over the short run) than blacks.[17]

Table 16 Percentage Distribution of Premaritally Pregnant Eligible[a] Young Women, by Use of Contraception Subsequent to Pregnancy Outcome, According to Race

Contraceptive Use After Pregnancy	Total (N=214)	White (N=75)	Black (N=139)
Used a method	71.8	70.8	73.3
Medical	83.0	79.6	88.3
Nonmedical	17.0	20.4	11.7
Did not use	16.2	12.5	22.1
Not sexually active	12.0	16.7	4.5
Total	100.0	100.0	100.0

[a]Refers to those who had a definite first pregnancy outcome while still unmarried.

Contraception and Abortion

One area the previous discussion has not touched upon is the association—if any—between abortion and prior contraceptive use. Are young women who become premaritally pregnant and obtain an abortion more or less likely to have used contraception at the time of conception than those who give birth or miscarry? In table 17, we provide two comparisons between women whose pregnancy ended in abortion and women with all other outcomes.[18] The first comparison involves all first premarital pregnancies; the second, all first premarital pregnancies that were reported as unintended.[19] When all first pregnancies are considered, those young women having an abortion are seen

Table 17 Percentage of Premaritally Pregnant White Young Women Who Were Using Contraception at Time of Conception, by Pregnancy Outcome, for All First Pregnancies and For All Unintended First Pregnancies

Pregnancy Intent	Pregnancy Outcome					
	All		Abortion		Other	
	Percent	N	Percent	N	Percent	N
All first pregnancies	18.2	151	27.1	38	14.5	113
All unintended first pregnancies	25.4	104	27.8	37	23.9	67

to be almost twice as likely to have been contracepting at the time pregnancy occurred (27 percent) as those with some other pregnancy outcome (14 percent). When we exclude from consideration those who were deliberately not contracepting because they intended to become pregnant, i.e., consider only unintended pregnancies, the difference narrows but still contradicts the assertion that those who obtain an abortion are less likely to have been contracepting at time of conception than those whose pregnancies have some other outcome.[20] Thus, although a substantial majority of young unmarried women who became pregnant and had an abortion were not contracepting at the time they became pregnant, they were no less likely, and were probably more likely, to be contracepting than young women who became pregnant unintentionally and did not have an abortion.

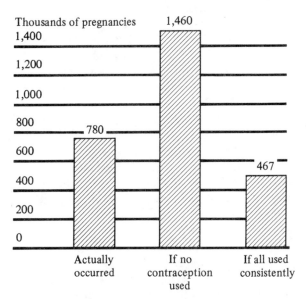

Figure 2   Number of Premarital Pregnancies Experienced by 15–19-year-olds in 1976, and Number That Would Have Occurred (a) If No Contraception Had Been Used and (b) If All Who Did Not Want a Baby Had Consistently Used Contraception

In summary, four in ten of those who became premaritally pregnant had practiced contraception at some time prior to their pregnancy. Although seven in ten did not want to get pregnant, only two in ten of this group were using any method at the time of conception. However, following the pregnancy, eight in ten of those who resumed sexual activity adopted a method, and eight in ten of these chose a medical method. Those who intended to get pregnant were more than twice as likely to marry in the course of pregnancy as those for whom the pregnancy was unintended. The data strongly suggest that teenagers are *not* using abortion as a substitute for contraception. More teenagers who obtained abortions than who gave birth or had other pregnancy outcomes were practicing contraception at the time they became pregnant.

Conclusion

When we recognize that eight in ten of those teenagers who have an unwanted pregnancy are not in fact using any method when the pregnancy occurs (Zelnik & Kantner, 1978, table 11), it becomes somewhat easier to understand why the level of premarital pregnancy continues to remain as high as it does in spite of increased and more regular use of contraception by teenagers.

It is clear that if a sexually active young woman uses a contraceptive regularly, she runs a relatively low risk of becoming pregnant (11 percent), and if she uses a medical method of contraception regularly, she runs an even lower risk (6 percent). It also is the case that a sexually active young woman who never uses a method is exceedingly likely (58 percent) to become pregnant.

Although four in ten sexually active young women initiate use of contraception prior to a pregnancy, one-third of these do not continue to use it consistently, even though most say they do not want to get pregnant. We cannot be certain what their reasons are for not continuing use. Misinformation about the real risk of unprotected intercourse when the partners are young and sex occurs seldom and episodically; the inappropriateness of long-term methods in the face of episodic sexual encounters, and embarrassment over obtaining coitus-dependent methods like condoms from unsympathetic druggists; differential availability of methods and services, especially to younger teenagers; or a need to dare the fates—all are among the many diagnoses and speculations that have been made. (We are currently analyzing the reasons proffered by the teenage respondents to our study, and will present the results in a future article.) It is a fairly safe assumption that sexual activity among adolescents is unlikely to decline. If unintended premarital pregnancies are to be reduced, it seems to us that it will be necessary to increase the proportion who use contraception and who use it consistently. This would require increased availability and accessibility of contraceptives through clinics, physicians and drugstores, as well, perhaps, as through nonthreatening neighborhood-based peer networks—especially for distribution of nonphysician methods like condoms and foam. Better information about pregnancy risk—in a form that teenagers can absorb and will believe—would also be needed if teenagers are to recognize the importance of consistent contraceptive use before they have the unfortunate experience of an unintended pregnancy. In addition, given the inexperience of teenage users, and a likelihood of contraceptive failure greater than that among married adults, accessible backup abortion services would undoubtedly still be needed for teenagers who continue to have unintended pregnancies but wish to avoid unintended births. Recent federal and state legislation restricting the availability of abortion under

Medicaid will especially handicap low-income teenagers who have unintended pregnancies.

Some of the data presented in this article may be disheartening to those alarmed over the magnitude of teenage pregnancy. Certainly, these findings leave no room for complacency. But they do show that many teenagers *are* using contraception, are using effective methods and are using them regularly (Zelnik & Kantner, 1977). And they show that use of contraception—even less than perfect use—makes a considerable difference in reducing the probability of an unintended pregnancy. Service providers should realize that the teenage pregnancy problem would be far greater than it now is if contraceptive services had been less available to sexually active teenagers than they were. The fact that considerable effort is still needed should not cause us to lose sight of the fact that many sexually active teenagers have availed themselves of services and, as a result, have not become pregnant.

In 1976, a little more than one million fifteen- to nineteen-year-olds experienced a pregnancy.[21] About 77 percent, or 780,000, of these pregnancies occurred premaritally. Based on the data from our study, it is probable that an additional 680,000 premarital pregnancies would have occurred (for a total of 1,460,000 premarital pregnancies) if no unmarried sexually active teenagers had used contraception.[22] These additional unwanted teenage pregnancies would have had to be resolved through more abortions, more out-of-wedlock births and more shotgun marriages. The social, psychological and economic consequences of unwanted pregnancies to teenagers, to their progeny and to society have been amply documented.

On the other hand, if all the teenagers who did not intend to give birth had been consistent users of contraception, there would have been about 467,000 premarital pregnancies (half of them intended)—313,000, or 40 percent, fewer than the 780,000 premarital pregnancies that actually occurred.[23] In other words, the difference between no use of contraception and always-use (by those who do not want to conceive) is about one million pregnancies.

These calculations, crude as they are, give an approximate idea of the number of premarital pregnancies that are now being averted through family planning efforts, and of the number that could be prevented if policy makers, educators and service providers were able to increase the number of teenagers who use contraception regularly and effectively to prevent unwanted conception.

Notes   [1]The decline for blacks may in fact be spurious (Zelnik & Kantner, 1978).

[2]The number of questions in the 1971 study on contraceptive use were far fewer and less detailed and specific than those asked in 1976. In addition, data on contraceptive use among the ever-married surveyed in 1976 refer specifically to the premarital state, whereas for 1971 the data cannot be split into premarital and postmarital segments.

[3]About 40 percent of the women fifteen to nineteen years of age in 1976 had experienced premarital intercourse; 80 percent of those who were married had had intercourse before marriage, compared to 36 percent of those still unmarried. This article applies only to premarital behavior. Thus, a respondent who was married at interview and who had had premarital intercourse, but had never used contraception while unmarried, is classified as a never-user whether or not she used contraception after marriage.

In discussing the contraceptive practices of premaritally sexually active women, we have removed from the analysis those women who have had premarital sexual intercourse only one time and thus cannot exhibit *patterns* of contraceptive use. In doing so we are undoubtedly excluding some who will continue to be sexually active; but we have no way of distinguishing between those who will continue such activity and those who will be sexually abstinent for some extended period of time. These "one-timers" represented 13.3 percent of all premaritally sexually active women, with remarkably little variation by race or current marital status.

[4]In our previous article, contraceptive-use status of never-married sexually active teenagers referred to contraceptive behavior up to the time of the survey. Over time, the sometimes-user group will increase as some never-users adopt contraception and as some always-users accidentally or intentionally fail to use it. The slippage into sometimes-use is a potential source of confusion if the proportions ever and never pregnant are computed for each contraceptive-use category, since pregnancy itself is likely to lead to a change from one category to another. Imagine, for example, that every non-user of contraception who becomes pregnant starts to use contraception after the pregnancy ends, and that every regular and consistent user of contraception who becomes pregnant stops using it after she becomes pregnant. In such a situation, the proportion ever pregnant among never-users and always-users would be zero since all who become pregnant would end up as sometimes-users. And the results would tell us little about contraceptive practices prior to pregnancy or about the relationship between use and pregnancy.

[5]Blacks who reported always-use were somewhat less likely than comparable whites to have been pregnant perhaps because a larger proportion used the more effective medical methods, while black never-users were more likely to have experienced pregnancy perhaps because of earlier initiation of intercourse and, therefore, greater exposure to risk (Zelnik & Kantner, 1977, tables 8 and 12).

306

[6]DHEW's National Reporting Service for Family Planning Services shows that between 1972 and 1976, the number of teenagers under age eighteen served in organized family planning clinics increased by 89 percent, compared to a 55 percent increase for those aged eighteen and nineteen. Services to black teenagers increased by 69 percent and to white teenagers by 65 percent.

[7]However, it must be remembered that those using a medical method at first intercourse represent only about one-tenth of all sexually active teenagers who have had premarital intercourse. It would be desirable to look at use of medical methods at initiation by current age to see the effect of changes over time. This is only one of a number of important questions concerning contraceptive and pregnancy behavior that we cannot attempt to answer because of the small number of sample cases that would be involved. Some of the differences we do tabulate involve Ns that are fairly small. The reader should view these with caution, especially where the differences are not great.

[8]Most recent use refers to time of pregnancy, or last intercourse preceding marriage or interview.

[9]Of those always-users who became pregnant, 29 percent were using a medical method at the time of pregnancy and 71 percent were using a nonmedical method.

[10]This group represents 28 percent of the sometimes-users shown in table 1.

[11]This group represents 72 percent of the sometimes-users shown in table 1.

[12]It should be pointed out that those who had intercourse in this interval and remained nonpregnant but subsequently began to use contraception are categorized as sometimes-users, while those who had unprotected intercourse and did become pregnant are classified as never-users.

[13]Eligible refers to those with a definite first pregnancy outcome while still unmarried. Thus, those who married while pregnant for the first time, and the never-married who at interview were currently pregnant for the first time, are excluded. We have not examined the postpregnancy behavior of the other contraceptive-use groups because of small Ns (table 16).

We have not computed the lag between the outcome of the pregnancy and the first use of contraception for never-users, since we have no way of knowing when sexual relations were resumed following the outcome of the pregnancy.

[14]If those who did not resume sexual activity following pregnancy outcome are removed from the base, there is no difference between blacks and whites in the proportion adopting contraception.

[15]This does *not* mean that those who had ever used a method prior to the pregnancy were in fact using one at time of conception.

307

[16]These tabulations include the always-users who became pregnant, none of whom intended the pregnancy.

[17]The qualifications are made here because of the small Ns involved.

[18]Included as an outcome is current pregnancy, since all of the pregnant women reported that they planned to have the baby.

[19]Because of a deficit, noted in a previous article, in the reporting by blacks of pregnancies terminated by abortion, data in table 17 refer to whites only (Zelnik & Kantner, 1978).

[20]The pregnancies referred to in table 17 all occurred premaritally, but the outcomes are premarital and postmarital. It is not surprising, but perhaps worth noting, that virtually all of the pregnancies that eventually ended in abortion were reported as unintended pregnancies.

[21]Based on the following: *For births:* National Center for Health Statistics, DHEW, "Final Natality Statistics, 1976," *Monthly Vital Statistics Report,* vol. 26, no. 12, Supplement, 1978. *For abortions:* totals from 1976 Alan Guttmacher Institute national survey, and percent to fifteen- to nineteen-year-olds, from Center for Disease Control, DHEW, *Abortion Surveillance: Annual Summary, 1976,* Atlanta, 1978. Involuntary fetal loss estimated to be 10 percent of total abortions plus births.

[22]Assuming that the 780,000 premarital pregnancies occurred to young women with the same contraceptive-status profile as that found in our study population, and that each contraceptive-status group had contributed to the total number of premarital pregnancies in the same proportion as found in our study.

[23]This is presuming that each contraceptive-status group had the same proportion of wanted pregnancies as in our study population, and that the level of contraceptive protection among those who did not want to get pregnant was the same as among the always-users in our study population.

References Paul, E. W., Pilpel, H. F., & Wechsler, N. F. Pregnancy, teenagers and the law, 1976. *Family Planning Perspectives,* 1976, *8,* 16.

Zelnik, M., & Kantner, J. F. Sexual and contraceptive experience of young unmarried women in the United States, 1976 and 1971. *Family Planning Perspectives,* 1977, *9,* 55.

Zelnik, M., & Kantner, J. F. First pregnancies to women aged 15–19: 1976 and 1971. *Family Planning Perspectives,* 1978, *10,* 11.

Appendix III

James W. Prescott

Abortion or the Unwanted Child: A Choice for a Humanistic Society

The antiabortion movement believes that the fetus, even in its embryonic stage of development, is human life and that any deliberate termination of embryonic or fetal life constitutes an "unjustified" termination of human life—that is, homicide. Conversely, proponents of abortion deny that the fetus is human life, particularly during its embryonic stage of development, and therefore believe that the termination of fetal life does not constitute homicide. Further, proponents of abortion justify the termination of fetal life by asserting that the woman has the ultimate right to control her own body; that no individual or group of individuals has any right to force a woman to carry a pregnancy that she does not want; that parents have the moral responsibility and constitutional obligation to bring into this world only children who are wanted, loved, and provided for, so that they can realize their human potential; and that children have certain basic human and constitutional rights, which include the right to have loving, caring parents, sound health, protection from harm, and a social and physical environment that permits healthy human development and the assurance of "life, liberty, and the pursuit of happiness."

These conflicts of "rights"—namely, the presumed rights of the fetus, the rights of the woman, the rights of the child, the presumed rights of adults to unlimited reproduction, and the rights of society—need careful consideration in evaluating the morality of abortion. How do we order the priorities of competing "rights"? Since rights confer obligations, does the failure to meet those obligations mitigate or abrogate the rights that gave rise to those obligations?

This article first appeared in *The Humanist* March/April 1975 and is reprinted by permission.

James W. Prescott is a member of the board of directors of the American Humanist Association, a member of the Washington Ethical Society, an editorial associate of *The Humanist,* president of the Institute of Humanistic Science, and a developmental neuropsychologist with the National Institute of Child Health and Human Development, HEW. The views expressed in this article are solely those of the author.

311

For example, when conception occurs in a uterine environment known to be adverse or a child is permitted to be born into an adverse environment, both of which threaten or deny the child's basic human and constitutional rights and opportunities for normal human development, should moral and constitutional questions be raised concerning the rights of such parentage? Is the right to parentage absolute? Do adults who are incapable of responsible behavior (for example, the severely mentally retarded) have the right to bring into this world children who will be neglected and abused and who will become infant and child mortality statistics? Is it not more moral and humane to prevent a life than to permit a life that may experience deprivation, suffering, and perhaps a brutal early death, which many of our child-abuse and infant and child mortality statistics reflect? Is mere physical existence our highest goal and greatest moral burden? Or is the quality of human life our highest goal and greatest moral burden? What are the social and moral criteria for justifying the sacrifice of human life? Perhaps the justifications for a "just war" should be considered in relation to certain arguments for and against abortion.

These questions of moral behavior, like that of abortion itself, are unlikely to be resolved by religious convictions or theological doctrine, since such convictions and doctrine vary considerably among free people and are, at best, arbitrary in their formulation and implementation. The extensive debates on abortion clearly indicate that no philosophical, religious, or scientific consensus exists concerning the question of whether fetal life is human life. A similar lack of consensus exists concerning the moral and ethical nature of the abortive act. Further, the US Constitution does not permit the legislation of religious beliefs or doctrine.

Consequently, it would appear constructive to examine the abortion question from a different perspective. Specifically, what are the effects of denied abortions—that is, of compulsory childbirth or of being an unwanted child—upon the development of the child; what are the consequences to society when parents are denied the right to have only wanted children; and what are the characteristics of societies that permit abortion in contrast to those that punish abortion. An examination of these questions from the perspective of the behavioral and social sciences, rather than from that of theology, should provide a basis to evaluate the merits of abortion on different grounds and to clarify the motivations and some of the social and psychological characteritics of the proabortion and antiabortion personality.

Consequences of Denied Abortion:
The Scandinavian Study

One of the most important studies that tried to evaluate the consequences of being an unwanted child upon the development of the child was conducted by H. Forssman and I. Thuwe of the Department of Psychiatry at Goteburg University in Sweden (1966). Therapeutic abortion was officially legalized in

Sweden in 1939 and liberalized in 1946 to include mental-health criteria. These Swedish investigators examined the development of children from birth to age twenty-one who were born during the years 1939 to 1941 to mothers who had applied for abortion but were denied. The sample included one hundred and twenty children, who were compared with a control group of children whose mothers had not applied for abortion. Of the unwanted children, 27 percent were born out of wedlock, whereas only 8 percent of the control children were born out of wedlock.

The statistically significant differences between the unwanted and the control children can be summarized as follows:

1. Sixty percent of the unwanted children had an insecure childhood, in contrast to only 28 percent of the control children. Criteria for an insecure childhood included official reports about unsatisfactory home conditions: The child was removed from the home by authorities; the child was placed in a foster or children's home; the parents were divorced or deceased before the child was fifteen; the child was born out of wedlock and never legitimized.

2. Twenty-eight percent of the unwanted children had received some form of psychiatric care, compared to 15 percent of the control children.

3. Eighteen percent of the unwanted children were registered with child-welfare boards for delinquency, compared to 8 percent of the control children.

4. Fourteen percent of the unwanted children had some form of higher education, compared to 33 percent of the control children.

5. Fourteen percent of the unwanted children received some form of welfare between the ages of sixteen and twenty-one, in contrast to 2.5 percent of the control children.

6. And finally, while 68 percent of the control children showed none of the social disabilities mentioned above, only 48 percent of the unwanted children were free of such characteristics.

It is worth noting that many of the differences listed were found in different social classes. In summary, unwanted children are more than twice as likely to suffer the social, emotional, and educational disadvantages as wanted children, on a variety of measures. Unwanted children appear to present certain costs to society: increased delinquency, a higher number of welfare recipients, a more poorly educated citizenry, and a greater number of psychiatric problems.

Child Abuse and Neglect:
Consequences of Being Unwanted

The killing of a child by its parents is an extreme outcome of being unwanted and is the final act of child abuse. Roman civil law recognized the right of the father to maim and kill his offspring (*patria potestas*), and a number of cultures have practiced the killing of female infants because they were valued less than male infants. Ceremonial sacrifices of infants and children have been documented in a number of cultures, and Abraham's willingness to kill his son for religious purposes is a biblical case in point. But the killing of one's own child in a modern civilization is uniformly met with revulsion and horror—even though child abuse, which is the precursor of filicide (the killing of one's own children) and neonaticide (the killing of the newborn), is widespread today. The central issue here is the role of abortion in preventing unwanted children and helping reduce the incidence of child abuse and infanticide. It should be recognized that being "wanted" and being "unwanted" are difficult psychological concepts, and E. Pohlman's " 'Wanted' and 'Unwanted': Toward Less Ambiguous Definition" should be consulted for a more extensive treatment of this subject (1965).

Phillip J. Resnick, in a study of one hundred thirty-one filicides (1969), found that 49 percent were associated with "altruistic" motives—for example, to relieve suffering; 21 percent were attributed to parental psychoses; 26 percent were attributed to the child's being "unwanted," which includes the child-abuse syndrome, and 4 percent were attributed to revenge on the spouse. Statistics, however, fail to convey the horror and tragedy of parents killing their own children, particularly when it could be prevented.

Several of the case histories are so grueling that they cannot help but raise the question of whether it is more humane to prevent human life than to compel it into an existence that possibly could result in a cruel and painful death. Dr. Resnick cites several means by which infants and children are killed. He states: "Head trauma, strangulation, and drowning were the most frequent methods of filicide. Fathers tended to use more active methods, such as striking, squeezing, or stabbing, whereas mothers more often drowned, suffocated, or gassed their victims."

It is unnecessary to catalogue the atrocities that are sometimes inflicted upon unwanted children. In Dr. Resnick's study of thirty-seven neonaticides (1970), he found that *83 percent of infant killings were attributed to being "unwanted" by the mother;* 11 percent to psychoses; 3 percent to "accidental" murder (child abuse); and 3 percent to "altruism." These infanticides must be seriously considered in any discussion of abortion, since for some people they may seem to be the only alternative to compulsory pregnancies.

The national fertility study reported by L. Bumpass and C. F. Westoff (1965) showed that, for the years 1960 through 1965, 22 percent of all births were unwanted by at least one spouse. This rose to 48 percent and 55 percent for families with five or six children. The greater proportion of unwanted births was reported from low-income and poorly educated families. Such family characteristics are serious impediments to providing quality care for children.

In addition to "unwanted births," "illegitimate births" also have been related to child abuse and neglect. In "Abortion on Request: The Psychiatric Implications," R. A. Schwartz (1972) cited statistics that indicate that illegitimate births rose from 3.5 to 9.7 percent during the period from 1940 to 1968 and that 90 percent of those illegitimate births were unwanted, while

R. C. Bensing and O. Schroeder (1960) reported, in *Homicide in the Urban Community,* that an extremely high illegitimate-birth rate is a good indicator of a high homicide rate.

In a recent study conducted by the Institute of Medicine of the National Academy of Sciences (Kessner, 1973) it was demonstrated that, for a New York City live-birth cohort, the neonatal death rate was two-and-a-half times as great for mothers who were judged to have received inadequate prenatal and postnatal care as for those who received adequate care. This suggests that our infant and child mortality rates may be used as an index of societal indifference and parental deprivation and neglect—that is, an index of dehumanization. The United States has one of the highest infant mortality rates among industrialized nations, ranking fifteenth with a rate of 18.5 per one thousand live births; and this can be attributed primarily to lack of adequate prenatal and postnatal care. There is little question that infants and children who survive depriving social and physical environments have (1) a high risk of arrested educational achievement, (2) low income potential, (3) a greater chance of poor health, and (4) a higher incidence of abnormal social and emotional behaviors, particularly asocial behaviors.

My own studies have shown very high and significant correlations between US infant mortality rates and homicide rates for the years 1940 to 1967, during which the entire country constituted the statistical sample (Prescott, 1971). In the years 1940 to 1955 from 15 to 25 percent of our homicide rates could be predicted from our infant mortality rates; in the years 1955 to 1967 from 25 to 75 percent of our homicide rates could be predicted from our infant mortality rates. The increase in the strength of these relationships indicates that those factors common to homicide and infant mortality are increasing in this country. In other words, it is becoming increasingly accurate to assert that those states that have high infant mortality rates also have high homicide rates and that those states with low infant mortality rates have low homicide rates.

The common factors associated with infant mortality, illegitimacy, and homicide assume greater significance in the context of the findings of J. Sklar and B. Berkov (1974), who demonstrated that legalized abortion reduces the number of illegitimate babies. They reported that for the year 1971 an estimated thirty-nine thousand more illegitimate babies and twenty-eight thousand more legitimate babies would have been born if legalized abortion had not been available. It was emphasized that the illegitimate births prevented represent almost one-tenth of all out-of-wedlock children born in the country in 1971. Two other effects of legalized abortion were reported: a reduction of the incidence of pregnancy-related marriages and subsequent marital disruption; and the prevention of illegal abortions, since it was estimated that between two-thirds and three-fourths of all legal abortions in the United States in 1971 were replacements for illegal abortions. These authors concluded that a return to restrictive and repressive abortion laws would result in an increase in

315

illegal abortions, pregnancy-related marriages, and illegitimacy.

Since illegitimacy has been linked to adult homicide and the killing of unwanted infants, it is clear that if abortion can reduce the number of illegitimate and unwanted children it can reduce the potential for future homicides and child abuse.

Given the alternative to abortion—that is, the birth of unwanted children, with all the adverse implications—it is clear that abortion is a beneficent and humanitarian act that values the *quality* of future human life more than the *quantity* of future human life. It is worth mentioning that the principle of the prevention of human life has its precedent in scripture—albeit in a different context—namely, Judas's betrayal of Jesus Christ: "It had been good for that man if he had not been born" (Matthew 26:24). Should this not be equally true for many children who are doomed to a life of misery and abuse, and for some who may meet an early violent death.

Cross-Cultural Studies

If abortion represents a disrespect for human life and constitutes an act of "murder," as is sometimes contended, then it would be expected that societies that permit and practice abortion should also be characterized by a disrespect for the quality of human life and by physical violence. This notion was tested by relating the coded scale "Punishment for Abortion" developed by B. C. Ayres to coded scales relating to child-rearing practices (1954), sexual behaviors, physical violence, and other characteristics of human relationships summarized by R. B. Textor (1967), from the Human Relations Area Files. Ayres identified eleven cultures that severely punish abortion and twelve cultures that have little or no punishment for abortion. The cultures that severely punish abortion are the Alorese, Ashanti, Azande, Balinese, Chir-Apache, Fon, Jivaro, Masai, Sanpoil, Fenda, and Wogeo. The cultures that have little or no punishment for abortion are the Ainu, Chagga, Dobuans, Dusun, Hano, Kurtatchi, Kwakiutl, Lesu, Marshallese, Papago, Pukapuka, and Tikopia.

The relationships between abortion and other practices of these cultures can be summarized as follows:

> 55 percent of cultures that punish abortion practice slavery.
> 92 percent of cultures that do not punish abortion do not practice slavery.
>
> 100 percent of cultures that punish abortion practice polygyny.
> 58 percent of cultures that do no punish abortion do not practice polygyny.
>
> 78 percent of cultures that punish abortion restrict adolescent sexual experience.

67 percent of cultures that do not punish abortion do not restrict adolescent sexual experience. (Virginity has a high or low value in these cultures.)

88 percent of cultures that punish abortion punish extramarital sex.
67 percent of cultures that do not punish abortion do not punish extramarital sex.

73 percent of cultures that punish abortion also kill, torture, and mutilate enemy captured in warfare.
80 percent of cultures that do not punish abortion do not kill, torture, and mutilate enemies captured in warfare.

100 percent of cultures that punish abortion are patrilineal rather than matrilineal.
71 percent of cultures that do not punish abortion are matrilineal rather than patrilineal.

70 percent of cultures that punish abortion place high pressure upon children to develop self-reliance.
78 percent of cultures that do not punish abortion do not place high pressure upon children to develop self-reliance.

Relationships defined in the first five groupings are all significant beyond the .05 level; relationships defined in the last two are significant at the .08 and .07 levels, respectively.

The data cited, particularly the variables of slavery, torture and murder, and punitive sexuality relating to punishment of abortion, do not support the antiabortionist point of view that abortion is tantamount to encouraging a more violent society. Rather, it provides support for the opposite point of view; specifically, societies that prevent and punish abortion also show disrespect for human life (the practice of slavery), are physically violent (killing, torturing, and mutilating the enemy), repress the expression of physical affection and pleasure (sexual repression), and place a high value on virginity.

These data, in turn, support the view of those who defend legalized abortion as a moral, humanitarian act that is characterized by a concern for the quality of human life, its integrity and dignity, and believe that these objectives are obtained by not permitting the birth of unwanted children. The most statistically significant findings are that 100 percent of cultures that punish abortion are patrilineal and that 71 percent of matrilineal cultures do not punish abortion. It is clear that the struggle of women for the right of self-determination and control over their own bodies involves the struggle to be free from male domination and authority. In this context it is perhaps not surprising to discover that cultures that enslave women to the bondage of compulsory pregnancy also practice other forms of human slavery.

317

Child Abuse and Abortion Punished: A Preliminary Study of Contemporary Social Attitudes

In an effort to determine whether the relationships between abortion, child nurturance, physical violence, and sexuality that were observed in preindustrial societies also exist for contemporary modern societies, a questionnaire was designed to assess these relationships. The Somatosensory Index of Human Affection was administered to ninety-six college students, whose mean age was nineteen years, and was factor analyzed. This statistical technique yields quantitative relationships among the variables or test questions. This questionnaire was administered and analyzed by Dr. Douglas Wallace of the Human Sexuality Program at the University of California School of Medicine at San Francisco.

Table 1 provides a factor structure—that is, a profile or description of a personality syndrome—that indicates the degree to which the attitudes and behaviors reflected in the questions belong together naturally. The numbers attached to each statement are called factor coefficients and indicate the weight that each statement has on the factor. A weight of 100 percent is represented by a coefficient of 1.0. Percent weights are determined by squaring the factor coefficient; for example, $.70^2$ is 49 percent. Thus a statement with .70 has twice the weight of a statement with .50 (49 percent versus 25 percent). In short, for nineteen-year-old college students these descriptive statements define a personality profile. Students who agree to one statement will also tend to agree with all the other statements. Students who disagree with one statement will tend to disagree with the other statements. It should be emphasized that this analysis defines the nature of the interrelationships among these variables and does not reflect the degree of agreement or disagreement with each statement. The nature of the relationship among these statements would remain the same by either agreeing with all the statements or disagreeing with all the statements. This student sample disagreed with the statements in the table. Consequently, the relationships described reflect associations along the dimension of relative disagreement, that is, little disagreement to strong disagreement.

An examination of the table fully supports a relationship among various attitudes to child abuse (hard physical punishment of children), punishment of abortion, repressive sexuality, a profile of physical violence (support of capital punishment and violence as necessary to solve our problems), alcohol (and drug) usage preferred to sex, an indifferent mother (deprivation of physical affection) and physically punitive father. Although these data on American college students are consistent with the data on preindustrial cultures, it should be recognized that a different subject sample could provide a different combination of statements from the total questionnaire.

These findings, when taken in the context of cross-cultural studies, clarify the psychosocial structure of the proabortion personality and the antiabortion personality. It would seem that the abortion issue carries with it deep per-

Table 1 Child Abuse and Abortion Punished: A Violent Society Characterized: Somatosensory Index of Human Affection—CS Factor I: 66.6%

hli-l.

.85	Hard physical punishment is good for children who disobey a lot.
.84	Prostitution should be punished by society.
.82	I tend to be conservative in my political points of view.
.81	Physical punishment and pain help build a strong moral character.
.80	Abortion should be punished by society.
.80	Responsible premarital sex is not agreeable to me.
.78	Nudity within the family has a harmful influence upon children.
.76	Capital punishment should be permitted by society.
.75	Violence is necessary to really solve our problems.
.74	Physical punishment should be allowed in the schools.
.73	Sexual pleasures help build a weak moral character.
.72	Society should interfere with private sexual behavior between adults.
.70	Alcohol is more satisfying than sex.
.69	Responsible extramural sex is not agreeable to me.
.61	Natural fresh body odors are often offensive.
.65	Drugs are more satisfying than sex.
.60	I get hostile and aggressive when I drink alcohol.
.54	I often feel like hitting someone.
.51	I often dream of either floating, flying, falling, or climbing.
.49	I would rather drink alcohol than smoke marijuana.
.47	I do not enjoy affectional pornography.
.45	My mother is often indifferent toward me.
.45	I drink alcohol more often than I experience orgasm.
.43	I can tolerate pain very well.
.42	I often get "uptight" about being touched.
.40	I remember when my father physically punished me a lot.

sonality characteristics and values that are largely influenced by experiences of physical pleasure and pain or their absence during the formative periods of development. The abortion issue cannot readily be resolved without an understanding of these complex emotional interrelationships that are determined by our social, cultural, and developmental family experiences. Further, the interpretation of the abortion issue as a "right to life" issue not only is an oversimplification of the problem but also is not consistent with these data. Those American college students who would punish abortion also support capital punishment, and, in primitive cultures, those who forbid abortion also practice slavery and kill, torture, and mutilate their enemies.

There is additional evidence with which to question the validity of the "right to life" principle advocated by antiabortionists. Jonathan Randall in a recent article in the *Washington Post* described the successful efforts of Simone Veil, health minister in Giscard d'Estaing's government, in obtaining a French Assembly vote (284 to 189) to legalize abortion. He described an incident during the German occupation of France in World War II, when a woman was executed for obtaining an abortion. The French law that prescribed the death penalty for having an abortion clearly makes a mockery of the "right to life" principle expressed by the antiabortionists. The relationship between support for capital punishment and prohibition of abortion is further strengthened by the voting patterns of members of the Federal Parliament of Canada during the years 1967 to 1969. The votes on Criminal Code Bill C–168 (27th Parliament, Second Session, 1967–1968), which proposed to abolish capital punishment, were statistically related to votes on Criminal Law Amendment Bill C–150 (28th Parliament, First Session, 1968–1969), which was an omnibus reform bill to permit abortion (previously a criminal offense under any circumstances) and to liberalize the adjudication of sexual offenders. Because of elections occurring between votes on these two bills, only ninety-eight voters on both bills were available for analysis. The results are summarized as follows: Fifty-eight (59 percent) voted for both reform bills; twenty-one (21 percent) voted against abortion reform; three voted for capital punishment and against abortion reform. These findings strongly support the relationship of advocacy of capital punishment with opposition to abortion and, conversely, opposition to capital punishment with advocacy of abortion. These relationships are supported by 80 percent of the voters. (This writer is indebted to Frank Borowics, professor of law, University of Windsor Law School, Windsor, Ontario, for obtaining the voting patterns for this analysis.)

With respect to religious beliefs and abortion, it is of more than passing interest that abortion practices in primitive cultures are not related to a belief in a supernatural deity or a spirit world. Similarly, religious preference and degree of religiosity were not related to abortion attitudes in the college sample. This, however, may change with a sample that is more conservative in religion. These data, when taken in the context of known contemporary religious differences on the abortion issue, are strongly supportive of the point of view that abortion attitudes are more related to developmental life experiences in human relationships and to the social-cultural mores of the society than they are to "religious" experiences and convictions. Recently a Jesuit priest, Reverend Joseph O'Rourke, of Boston, was expelled from the Society of Jesus for baptizing a three-month-old infant after Roman Catholic parish priests refused the baptism because the infant's Catholic mother refused to recant her public statements supporting individual freedom of choice concerning abortion.

These relationships were further illuminated by the recent annual meeting of the National Conference of Catholic Bishops, which debated and rejected on November 7, 1974, a fifteen-hundred-word statement that was opposed to capital punishment. On November 21, 1974, the bishops accepted a substitute motion on capital punishment: "The United States Catholic Conference goes on record in opposition to the death penalty" by a vote of 108 to 63. It should be noted that 37 percent of the Catholic bishops voting supported capital punishment. Clearly, the "right-to-life principle" is an inconsistent and arbitrary religious principle and provides no reasonable basis for resolving the abortion issue.

Conclusion

In summary, these data support the recommendations of the Presidential Commission on Population Growth and the American Future concerning abortion:

> With the admonition that abortion not be considered a primary means of fertility control, the Commission recommends that present state laws restricting abortion be liberalized along the lines of the New York statute, such abortion to be performed on request by duly licensed physician under conditions of medical safety. In carrying out this policy, the Commission recommends: That federal, state and local governments make funds available to support abortion services in states with liberalized statutes; That abortion be specifically included in comprehensive health insurance benefits, both public and private.

Moreover, these data strongly support the right of the woman to be pregnant by choice and to be a mother by choice as essential prerequisites for a humane and compassionate society.

References   Ayres, B. C. *A cross-cultural study of factors relating to pregnancy taboos.* Doctoral dissertation, Radcliffe College, 1954.

Bensing, R. C., & Schroeder O. *Homicide in the urban community.* Springfield, Ohio: Charles Thomas, 1960.

Bumpass, L., & Westoff, C. F. The "perfect" contraceptive population. *Science,* 1970, *169.*

Forssman, H., & Thuwe, I. One hundred and twenty children born after application for therapeutic abortion refused. *Acta Psychiatrica Scandinavica,* 1966, *42.*

Kessner, D. M. *Infant death: An analysis by maternal risk and health care.* Washington, D.C.: Institute of Medicine, National Academy of Sciences, 1973.

Pohlman, E. "Wanted" and "unwanted": Toward less ambiguous definition. *Eugenics Quarterly,* 1965, *12.*

Prescott, J. W. Early somatosensory deprivation as an ontogenetic process in the abnormal development of the brain and behavior. In I. E. Goldsmith & J. Moor-Jankowski (Eds.), *Medical Primatology, 1970.* Basel: S. Karger, 1971.

Resnick, P. J. Child murder by parents: A psychiatric review of filicide. *American Journal of Psychiatry,* 1969, *126.*

Resnick, P. J. Murder of the newborn: A psychiatric review of neonaticide. *American Journal of Psychiatry,* 1970, *126.*

Schwartz, R. A. Abortion on request: The psychiatric implications. *Case Western Law Review,* 1972, *23.*

Sklar, J., & Berkov, B. Abortion, illegitimacy, and the American birth rate. *Science,* 1974, *185.*

Textor, R. B. *A cross-cultural summary.* New Haven: Human Relations Area Files Press, 1967.

Appendix IV

James W. Prescott

Abortion and the "Right to Life": Facts, Fallacies and Fraud— Cross-Cultural Studies

The abortion issue has become volatile. Violence against abortion clinics to stop or interfere with abortions has been reported with some prominence in the press (Washington Star, 1976; MacNeil/Lehrer, 1978; Moyers, 1978; NARAL Newsletter, 1978; Abortion Under Attack, 1978). This violence has included fire-bombing, throwing gasoline and other flammable liquids on clinic staff—one staff member was temporarily blinded—vandalism, including slashing of phone lines and upholstery and destruction of operating equipment, forcible entry into operating theaters which interrupted medical procedures and threatened the medical safety of patients—antiabortionists chained themselves to the operating tables—bullets fired into clinics, and lesser forms of violence, including picket lines which harassed patients and prevented their entry into the abortion clinics.

These forms of violence were condoned and supported by the judicial actions of Judge Lewis Griffith of the General District Court in Fairfax, Virginia, who found the antiabortionists not guilty of trespassing and violence because they acted in the belief that they were saving lives (October 19, 1977) and by Judge Mason Grove of the same court, who declared the Virginia statute legalizing first trimester abortions unconstitutional. Fortunately, judicial restraint was obtained from Judge Albert Bryan, U.S. District Court, who issued a restraining order prohibiting the antiabortionists from going near or entering the abortion clinics (February 15, 1978). The National Abortion Rights Action League (NARAL) has noted that twenty to thirty violent attempts to stop abortion clinic procedures have been reported throughout the country.

This article first appeared in *The Humanist* July/August 1978 and is reprinted by permission.

Acknowledgment is gratefully extended to Mildred Beck; Washington Ethical Society, for her continued moral support in the preparation of this manuscript, and, particularly, to Bob McCoy for his critical reading of this manuscript and his many helpful suggestions for improvement, and to Executive Director Karen Mulhauser, NARAL, and staff for their assistance in providing some of the roll call votes used in this analysis and their observation that antiabortion senators voted against "pro-life" legislation.

In an update on violence against abortion clinics, NARAL (April 1978 newsletter) has reported that the restraining order in Fairfax, Virginia has resulted in no further incidents. Also, courts in Anchorage, Alaska; Silver Springs and Baltimore, Maryland; New London, Connecticut; and Omaha, Nebraska; have convicted trespassers for attempting to interfere with clinic operations.

Opposition to abortion has also been reported as a factor in early reports on the phasing out of the birth-defect detection program of the March of Dimes. Antiabortion leaders are reported to have said that parents have no right to decide whether a deformed child can be born, and they were displeased with the "phase out" plans of the March of Dimes prenatal screening program, which they asserted should be abruptly terminated (Washington Star, 1978). An official announcement of the National Foundation of the March of Dimes (March 28, 1978), apparently in response to public protest, reaffirmed its support of genetic services, including amniocentesis, as a means to prevent birth defects.

An escalation of the abortion conflict has resulted from recent United States Supreme Court decisions and congressional actions that have exempted the states from being required to pay for abortions with Medicaid funds. This has moved the conflict into each state where legislation is being vigorously debated on public funding of abortions.

Further polarization of this country by the abortion issue is seen on the religious front, where legal briefs are being prepared which assert that religious rights are being violated when the government uses an economic weapon to limit or deny the expression of religious convictions by a minority of poor citizens, for example, moral requirements of responsible parenthood, which includes the moral imperative to avoid bringing human life into an environment of abuse and neglect. The humanistic religious principles that provide moral justification for abortion are contained in the following resolution that was passed by vote of the membership of the American Humanist Association at its annual meeting on May 1, 1977, Los Angeles, California:

> **Resolution on Responsible Parenthood** The American Humanist Association reaffirms the ethical and moral responsibilities of all humanist parents to avoid bringing children into this world who are not wanted; to avoid bringing children into an environment of neglect and abuse; to assure that children are well-born; and to provide an affectionate, loving, and healthy environment for all children that they may enjoy an equal opportunity to realize the fullness and uniqueness of their own humanity.
>
> We affirm the moral right of women to become pregnant by choice and to become mothers by choice. We affirm the moral right of women to freely choose a termination of unwanted pregnancies. We oppose actions by individuals, organizations, and governmental bodies that attempt to

restrict and limit the woman's moral right and obligation of responsible parenthood.

We also affirm the right and moral responsibility of parents and future parents to be free from ignorance on matters of human sexuality and to have access to contraceptive methods in order to prevent unwanted pregnancies and abortions, and to avoid the spread of venereal disease.

We hold these moral rights of responsible parenthood as part of our humanistic religious heritage and consider infringements upon these moral rights as an infringement upon the free exercise of our humanistic religious principles as guaranteed by the First Amendment of the Constitution of the United States.

The diversity of religious moral beliefs on the abortion issue must be recognized. Additional moral dilemmas are raised when adults bring new human life into an environment that compromises or prevents the moral development of that new life. It would appear helpful to suggest that the consequences of such environments upon moral development should be reexamined within the biblical context: "It would be better for that man if he had never been born" (Matt. 26:24). This quotation from Matthew is attributed to Jesus Christ, who directed this comment at Judas for his betrayal. If the prevention of human life is considered morally desirable in this context, would the prevention of human life in other contexts not be equally morally desirable? The religious view on abortion is divided, and the Religious Coalition for Abortion Rights has summarized excerpts from statements about abortion rights as expressed by many national religious organizations. It is evident that the Catholic hierarchy has failed to exercise its ecclesiastical authority over the Catholic people (83 percent of all practicing Catholics use some form of birth control and only 6 percent are using the approved rhythm method) and that they are now turning to civil law to accomplish what they could not accomplish through ecclesiastical law. Archbishop Joseph Bernardin, in August 1977, who was then president of the Catholic Conference of Bishops, announced expanded antiabortion activities that would eliminate "the evil practice from our country" (The Abortion Rights Crisis, 1978). This attempt to impose a specific religious viewpoint on the American people through the use of civil and constitutional law is not limited to abortion. The Religious Coalition for Abortion Rights has also reported the following:

Father Paul Marx of the Human Life Center has written: "Prolifers who work toward the day when we shall no longer kill our unborn are only kidding themselves if they condone contraception—contraception is the chief cause of the present moral chaos. So-called contraception, in fact, often turns out to be silent (early) abortion induced by the Pill or the IUD (The Abortion Rights Crisis, 1978).

327

It is evident that these efforts involve a clear violation of and threat to the U.S. Constitution's First Amendment, which mandates the separation of church and state. Why should the fundamentalist religious minorities (Roman Catholicism is not alone in this antiabortion movement, although it is the principal financial and political supporter) seek to impose their religious viewpoint on abortion upon the rest of the country? And why should the antiabortion movement utilize violent methods to achieve their goal?

It is clear that differences of moral opinion concerning abortion are escalating confrontation in the religious and human rights domains. The antiabortionists claim that the fertilized ovum, the embryo, and the fetus have the full and equal status of human *personhood,* the termination of whose life is equivalent to killing a person. The proabortionists deny this assertion and hold that the termination of unwanted pregnancies is a moral, responsible act to avoid the immorality of bringing unwanted children into existence with all the risks of abuse, neglect, or an early violent death.

It is equally clear that these moral differences cannot be resolved or clarified from religious/philosophical arguments since these arguments begin with assumptions that are the very source of contention. Consequently, it was thought that an examination of social-behavioral characteristics for these two groups might shed some light on the morality of abortion behaviors themselves. With this objective in mind several research activities were initiated. These involved:

A. evaluation of the social-behavioral characteristics of preindustrial ("primitive") cultures that support and punish abortion;
B. relating abortion practices to infanticide practices in these preindustrial cultures;
C. evaluating voting patterns in the U.S. Senate, specifically, relating votes on abortion to votes on bills that support human violence and reject human nurturance; and
D. utilizing a psychometric instrument to evaluate attitudes on abortion to attitudes on other behaviors which carry clear social-moral values regarding respect and dignity for the quality of human life and its freedom of expression.

Some of these data have been briefly presented previously, but their summary and more extensive presentation here should assist the comprehensiveness of this report (Prescott, 1975a; 1975b).

Cross-Cultural Studies: Abortion and Violence

The data for this analysis was obtained from R. B. Textor (1967). This book provides statistical relationships among a number of coded scales of behaviors and societal characteristics for some four hundred preindustrial cultures that have been developed by a number of different cultural anthropologists. Consequently, these data become a universal resource to test hypotheses concerning how certain behaviors are interrelated. The coded scale on abortion was developed by Dr. Barbara Chartier Ayres, who provided information on twenty-three preindustrial cultures, where eleven cultures punished abortion severely and twelve cultures permitted abortion.

Table 1 summarizes the statistically significant social-behavioral characteristics associated with abortion practices. The value for the statistic "chi-

Table 1   Social-Behavioral Correlates of Abortion Practices

1. 55 Percent of Cultures Which Punish Abortion Practice Slavery
   92 Percent of Cultures Which Do Not Punish Abortion Do Not Practice Slavery
   $(\chi^2 = 3.81, P = .03, N = 23)$

2. 100 Percent of Cultures Which Punish Abortion Practice Polygyny
   58 Percent of Cultures Which Do Not Punish Abortion Rarely Practice Polygyny
   $(\chi^2 = 3.66, P = .04, N = 23)$

3. 78 Percent of Cultures Which Punish Abortion Restrict Youth Sexual Expression
   67 Percent of Cultures Which Do Not Punish Abortion Do Not Restrict Youth Sexual Expression. (Virginity Has a High or Low Value in These Cultures)
   $(\chi^2 = 2.49, P = .08, N = 21)$

4. 88 Percent of Cultures Which Punish Abortion Punish Extramarital Sex
   67 Percent of Cultures Which Do Not Punish Abortion Do Not Punish Extramarital Sex
   $(\chi^2 = 3, P = .05, N = 17)$

5. 73 Percent of Cultures Which Punish Abortion Also Kill, Torture, and Mutilate Enemies Captured in Warfare
   80 Percent of Cultures Which Do Not Punish Abortion Do Not Kill, Torture, and Mutilate Enemies Captured in Warfare
   $(\chi^2 = 3.92, P = .03, N = 21)$

6. 100 Percent of Cultures Which Punish Abortion Are Patrilineal Rather Than Matrilineal
   71 Percent of Cultures Which Do Not Punish Abortion Are Matrilineal Rather Than Patrilineal
   $(\chi^2 = 4.98, P = .02, N = 14)$

Source: R. B. Textor, *A Cross-Cultural Summary* HRAF Press, New Haven, 1967.

329

square" is given with the level of statistical significance for each of the social-behavioral correlates. The data in table 1 clearly links the punishment of abortion with the practice of slavery and polygyny; repressive sexuality; killing, torturing, and mutilation of enemies captured in warfare; and being patrilineal rather than matrilineal. The converse relationships are found for those cultures which permit abortion; that is, they do *not* practice slavery or polygyny; they are *not* sexually repressive; they do *not* engage in killing, torturing, and mutilation of enemies captured in warfare; they are matrilineal rather than patrilineal. These data provide no support for the antiabortionists' claim that their position reflects a respect for the dignity and quality of human life. In fact, these data provide support for the converse, namely, that antiabortion mentality is characterized by a lack of respect for the dignity, quality, and equality of human life. It is not surprising to find such values and social-behavioral patterns in patrilineal and not in matrilineal cultures.

Table 2 lists by name those twenty-three cultures which were punitive or supportive of abortion. In addition, those cultures which were rated as engaging or not engaging in killing, torturing, and mutilation of enemies captured in warfare are identified.

Table 2   Distribution of Cultures by Abortion Practices

Cultures Where Severe Punishment for Abortion Is High	Cultures Where Severe Punishment for Abortion Is Low or Absent
Alorese	*Ainu*
Ashanti	*Chagga*
Azande	Dobuans
Balinese	*Dusun*[a]
Chir-Apache	*Hano*
Fon	Kurtatchi
Jivaro	*Kwakiutl*
Masai	*Lesu*
Sanpoil	*Marshallese*[a]
Venda	*Papago*
Wogeo	*Pukapuka*
	Tikopia

Killing, Torturing, Mutilation of Enemy Is Low
Killing, Torturing, Mutilation of Enemy is High

Chagga and *Tikopia* Are Matrilineal Cultures Which Punish Abortion.
[a]Information Lacking in Textor Code 421

Table 3 lists by name those cultures which punish or permit abortion and which have also been identified as patrilineal or matrilineal. This information was available for fourteen of the twenty-three cultures, and two of the

Table 3 Abortion Practices in Patrilineal and Matrilineal Cultures

Abortion Punished Patrilineal Cultures (100 Percent)	Abortion Permitted Matrilineal Cultures (71 Percent)
Alorese	Dobuans
Ashanti	Hano
Azande	Kurtatchi
Fon	Lesu
Masai	Marshallese
Venda	
Wogeo	

Chi-Square = 4.98, P = 0.02, Phi = 0.60, N = 14

seven matrilineal cultures (29 percent) were found to punish abortion, whereas 100 percent of the patrilineal cultures were found to punish abortion.

Abortion and Infanticide

Table 4 lists by name those cultures which punish or permit abortion and whether infanticide is present or absent in these cultures. The ratings on infan-

Table 4 Abortion and Infanticide

Abortion Punished Infanticide Present (N=8; %=38)	Abortion Punished Infanticide Absent (N=2; %=10)
Azande	Ashanti
Chir-Apache	Balinese
Fon	
Jivaro	
Masai	
Sanpoil	
Venda	
Wogeo	

Abortion Permitted Infanticide Present (N=7; %=33)	Abortion Permitted Infanticide Absent (N=4; %=19)
Ainu	Hano
Chagga	Kurtatchi
Dobuans	Papago
Dusun	Pukapuka
Kwakiutl	
Marshallese	
Tikopia	

331

ticide were also provided by Dr. Ayres where twenty-one of twenty-three cultures were so rated. The statistical analysis by Textor showed no significant statistical relationship between abortion and infanticide practices in these preindustrial cultures (Textor, 1967). An inspection of table 4 will indicate that infanticide is practiced by as many cultures that punish abortion (eight cultures) as those that do not punish abortion (seven cultures). With respect to the absence of infanticide, it is of interest to note that there are twice as many cultures which permit abortion and *lack* infanticide than cultures which oppose abortion and *lack* infanticide. Only two of twenty-one (10 percent) of the cultures fit the expectations demanded by the antiabortion claim, that is, they are opposed to abortion and there is an absence of infanticide.

The claim of the antiabortionists that abortion is equivalent to killing a human person, that is, that feticide and infanticide are equivalent, is simply not supported by these data. Further, the social-behavioral characteristics that were related to the abortion variable did not relate to the infanticide variable. However, there was a tendency for patrilineal cultures to be linked with the practice of infanticide ($p = .08$); and significantly fewer infant/child support and nurturance measures were found in the infanticide cultures. It is emphasized, however, that the variables of slavery; polygyny; repressive sexuality; and killing, torturing, and mutilation of enemies captured in warfare, which are significantly linked to the abortion variable, are unrelated to the infanticide variable. Again, this analysis provides no support for the antiabortionists' claim that terminating an unwanted pregnancy is equivalent to killing a human person—a newborn (infanticide). If the antiabortionists' claim were correct, we would expect that antiabortion cultures would be peaceful and humane, respect the quality, dignity, and equality of human life, and not practice infanticide. None of these conditions characterize the antiabortion cultures.

In this context it should be noted that Nazi Germany was strongly opposed to abortion and provided the death penalty for both the woman who had the abortion and the abortionist. Hans Bleuel reported that the Reich Ministry of Justice sentenced women to hard labor for having an abortion and executed abortionists (Bleuel, 1974). Capital punishment was recommended for second offenders. Abortion was permissible solely on racial grounds. When one parent was of impure blood, abortion was permissible in the public interest. In this context, it was previously reported that a French woman was executed in German-occupied France for obtaining an abortion (Prescott, 1975a).

Voting Patterns in the United States Senate: Abortion, Violence and Nurturance

Since the cross-cultural data on preindustrial cultures characterized antiabortion cultures as violent and dehumanizing, it was considered desirable to attempt to cross-validate these relationships in modern complex cultures. One such attempt involved the analysis of voting patterns in the United States Senate, where votes on abortion were related to votes on capital punishment, continuing funding of the war in Vietnam, abolition of the "no-knock" laws (they permitted police to break into homes without court orders), and hand-gun control legislation. Some of these data have been previously published in a synoptic form (Prescott, 1975a; 1975b). This analysis will report in detail the voting characteristics of each senator, who will be identified by name. In addition, the voting characteristics of U.S. senators on human violence legislation will be compared with their voting characteristics on family nurturance legislation, as it is reflected in the ratings of the National Farmers Union (NFU) for each senator. The NFU voting reflects the degree to which senators support the farm family, poverty programs, food programs, and other welfare programs for children, the elderly, and other disadvantaged citizens. NFU ratings range from zero to one hundred, with low scores reflecting low family nurturance; and high scores reflecting high family nurturance (Barone, Vjifisch, & Mathews, 1977).

Table 5 summarizes the statistics that relate votes against abortion to votes on a variety of bills that support human violence and oppose civil liberties. These data show that there are highly significant statistical relationships between voting against abortion and voting to continue supporting the war in Vietnam; supporting the "no-knock" laws, and opposing hand-gun control legislation. These voting records are from 1974 and they provide clear and un-

Table 5 Senators Opposed to Abortion: Bartlett Amendment 1974

Descriptor	χ^2	P	N	PHI	%
Support Capital Punishment[1]	10.98	.0009	75	.38	71
Support Vietnam War[2]	14.05	.0002	65	.46	72
Support "No-Knock" Laws[3]	10.72	.001	71	.39	65
Oppose Hand-Gun Control[4]	11.68	.0006	74	.40	71

[1] S1401 Passed 54–33 March 13, 1974
[2] S2999 Passed 43–38 May 6, 1974 (Kennedy Amendment)
[3] S3355 Passed 64–31 July 11, 1974 (Ervin Amendment)
[4] S1401 Passed 58–31 January 13, 1974 (McClellan Amendment)

74%	Who Support Capital Punishment Do Not Support Abortion
64%	Who Do Not Support Capital Punishment Support Abortion
84%	Who Support Vietnam War Do Not Support Abortion
62%	Who Do Not Support Vietnam War Support Abortion
86%	Who Support "No-Knock" Laws Do Not Support Abortion
55%	Who Do Not Support "No-Knock" Laws Support Abortion
73%	Who Support Hand Guns Do Not Support Abortion
70%	Who Do Not Support Hand Guns Support Abortion

ambiguous documentation that antiabortion mentality in an advanced, "civilized" complex industrial society is no different from that observed in "primitive" preindustrial cultures where opposition to abortion is associated with authoritarian, fascist, violent, and dehumanizing non-nurturing behaviors.

The value of X^2 is a statistic reflecting the relationship between two variables. The P value is the probability that the relationship could occur by chance—the probability that the relationship between votes on abortion and capital punishment could occur by chance is six out of 10,000; the N value is the number of senators involved in the analysis; the *PHI* value is a correlation coefficient reflecting the strength of the relationship; the percent value indicates the magnitude of correct classification of senators in the voting relationship—the number of senators voting against abortion and for capital punishment, plus those voting for abortion and against capital punishment. The sum is expressed as a percent of all senators voting.

Table 6 lists two groups of senators. Senators in Group A voted against

Table 6   Senate Record on Family Nurturance, Abortion, and Capital Punishment: 1974 (Bartlett Amendment)

Group A High Family Nurturance Support Abortion No Capital Punishment		Group B Low Family Nurturance Against Abortion For Capital Punishment			
Senator	NFU	Senator	NFU	Senator	NFU
Abourezk	88	Allen	35	Hansen	12
Aiken	82	Bartlett	18	Helms	6
Brooke	88	Bellman	20	Hruska	24
Burdick	100	Bible	82	Huddleston	82
Case	100	Brock	24	Johnston	63
Clark	100	Buckley	0	Long	73
Cranston	100	Byrd, H. F.	29	McClellan	41
Hart	100	Byrd, R. C.	76	McClure	18
Hathaway	100	Cannon	76	McGee	81
Humphrey	100	Church	88	Montoya	76
Inouye	100	Curtis	24	Nunn	38
Kennedy	100	Dole	35	Randolph	82
Mathias	94	Domenici	56	Roth	35
Pearson	88	Ervin	35	Schweiker	88
Pell	94	Fannin	6	Stennis	29
Stevenson	94	Goldwater	12	Thurmond	18
Weicker	92	Griffin	44	Young	75
Williams	100	Gurney	33		
Mean NFU	96	Mean NFU	44	$\chi^2 = 11.90$	
Percent	24	Percent	47	P = .0006	
N	18	N	35	N = 75	

the 1974 Bartlett Amendment to the fiscal 1975 Labor–Health, Education, and Welfare Appropriations bill prohibiting Medicaid funds from being used to pay for, or encourage, abortion. A vote on a motion to table the amendment was defeated fifty to thirty-four on September 17, 1974. Group A senators also voted against the capital punishment bill S1401, which established new standards and procedures for the imposition of the death penalty. S1401 was passed fifty-four to thirty-three on March 13, 1974. The NFU ratings for 1974 are listed next to the name of each senator. Senators in Group B supported the Bartlett Amendment and voted for capital punishment. Each senator's 1974 NFU rating is also listed next to his name.

An inspection of table 6 indicates that eighteen of *seventy-five* senators voting on both bills (24 percent of the total) supported abortion, opposed capital punishment, and had a mean (average) NFU rating of ninety-six. Eighteen of *thirty* senators (60 percent) voting for abortion voted against capital punishment. Group A senators are nonviolent, have high family nurturance, and support abortion. Group B senators (thirty-five of *seventy-five*, or 47 percent of all senators voting on both bills) oppose abortion and support capital punishment. Thirty-five of *forty-five* senators (78 percent) voting against abortion voted for capital punishment. Their mean NFU rating is forty-four, which is less than half the family nurturance of those senators who support abortion. These relationships are statistically significant ($p = .0006$), which means that the probability of this relationship occurring by chance is six out of 10,000. These data confirm the relationships obtained in preindustrial cultures which link antiabortion to human violence and low nurturance (slavery and punitive sexuality). It should be observed that some senators in Group B who oppose abortion and support capital punishment receive high NFU family nurturance scores (17 percent: six of thirty-five). The exceptions are evaluated in table 7, where it should be noted that senators who receive NFU scores from zero to seventy-nine fall in the approximate lower half of the distribution of scores, and senators who receive scores from eighty to one hundred fall in the upper half of the distribution of scores.

Table 7 lists those senators in Group C and Group D. Group C senators represent ten of seventy-five (13 percent) of the senators voting on both bills where they vote against abortion and against capital punishment. This represents the true "right-to-life" position, and it is not surprising to find these senators with very high family nurturance ratings where their mean NFU rating is ninety-three. This 13 percent is remarkably similar to the 10 percent of primitive cultures that reflected the "right-to-life" position described in table 4—both represent clear minority positions. With respect to only those senators voting against abortion, this statistic becomes ten of *forty-five* (22 percent). Group D senators represent twelve of *seventy-five* (16 percent) of senators voting for both bills where these senators vote for abortion and for capital punishment. As a group they also have a mixed or highly variable NFU rating of family nurturance whose mean is seventy-eight, which falls be-

335

Table 7 Senate Record on Family Nurturance, Abortion, and Capital Punishment: 1974 (Bartlett Amendment)

Group C High Family Nurturance Against Abortion No Capital Punishment		Group D Mixed Family Nurturance Support Abortion For Capital Punishment	
Senator	NFU	Senator	NFU
Biden	94	Baker	64
Eagleton	88	Chiles	65
Hartke	92	Haskell	100
Hughes	100	Jackson	100
McGovern	94	Magnuson	100
McIntyre	88	Moss	100
Metcalf	88	Scott, H.	67
Muskie	100	Scott, Wm.	19
Pastore	94	Stafford	100
Proxmire	88	Stevens	82
		Symington	94
		Taft	47
Mean NFU	93	Mean NFU	78
Percent	13	Percent	16
N	10	N	12

National Farmers Union Rating (1974)
0–79 = Low Family Nurturance

National Farmers Union Rating (1974)
80–100 = High Family Nurturance

Capital Punishment Senate Bill S1401 (v73)
Passed 54–33 (3/13/74)

Abortion Bill: Bartlett Amendment to Fiscal 1975
DHEW Appropriations Defeated 50–34, 9/17/74

low the median. This group of senators is the most difficult to interpret; however, any attempted interpretation should give close attention to each senator's NFU rating of family nurturance, which can serve as an important anchor point. Group D senators are clearly not a uniform group and are dichotomous with respect to their family nurturance.

In order to validate the relationships obtained in the 1974 voting records of the U.S. Senate, this analytic study was repeated for votes on abortion in 1977 involving the Helms Amendment to the Labor–HEW Appropriation bill for 1978, which stated: "None of the funds contained in this Act shall be used to perform abortions except where the life of the mother would be endangered if the fetus were carried to term." This amendment failed in a vote of sixty-five to thirty-three on June 29, 1977 (Rollcall Vote No. 258 Legislature).

For this analysis a more striking test of the relationship between abortion and family nurturance was conducted by first identifying those senators who received the lowest 25 percent of NFU scores on family nurturance and those who received the highest 25 percent of NFU scores on family nurturance. NFU ratings from 1976 were used for this analysis, and NFU scores from zero to thirty-nine represented the lowest 25 percent of senators on family nurturance; and NFU scores ninety to one hundred represented the highest 25 percent of senators on family nurturance. These two groups of senators were then compared on the basis of how they voted on the Helms Amendment described above. This resulted in a sample size of forty-two senators who represent the extremes of the NFU ratings on family nurturance and who voted on the Helms Amendment.

Table 8 identifies these two groups of senators and their exceptions. Group A senators represent nineteen of *forty-two* (45 percent) of the sample, and they voted for abortion and were all characterized by very high family nurturance scores of ninety to one hundred. They also represent 76 percent (nineteen of *twenty-five*) of senators voting for abortion. Group B senators represent fifteen of *forty-two* (36 percent) of the total sample, and they voted against abortion and all had very low family nurturance scores (zero to thirty-nine). They also represent 88 percent (fifteen of *seventeen*) of the senators voting against abortion. Group C senators, the "right-to-life" senators, represent 5 percent (two of *forty-two*) of the total sample, and they voted against abortion and had very high family nurturance scores. They also represent 12 percent (two of *seventeen*) of the senators voting against abortion. Group D senators represent 14 percent (six of *forty-two*) of the total sample, and they voted for abortion but had very low family nurturance scores. They also represent 24 percent (six of *twenty-five*) of the senators voting for abortion.

The statistical significance of these relationships are extremely high; the probability of their occurring by chance is four out of 100,000. Again, these data strongly confirm that antiabortion mentality is primarily a non-nurturant mentality and provide no support for the antiabortionists' claim that their position reflects a respect for the quality, dignity, and equality of human life.

A converse analysis shows that 71 percent (fifteen of *twenty-one*) of this sample who have *very low* family nurturance scores oppose abortion, and 90 percent (nineteen of *twenty-one*) who have *very high* family nurturance scores support abortion.

In summary, the voting patterns of the U.S. Senate on abortion and on several bills of human violence and civil liberties, with ratings of their family nurturance by the NFU, clearly and unequivocally link opposition to abortion with the support of human violence legislation, opposition to civil liberties, and the absence of family nurturance. For the 1974 Bartlett Amendment the incidence of the true "right-to-life" position for the total voting Senate

Table 8 Senate Record on Family Nurturance and Abortion: Helms Amendment—June 29, 1977

Group A Very High Family Nurturance	Group B Very Low Family Nurturance No Abortion	Group C Very High Family Nurturance No Abortion	Group D Very Low Family Nurturance
19/42=45%	15/42=36%	2/42= 5%	7/42=14%
19/25=76%	15/17=88%	2/17=12%	6/25=24%
19/21=90%	15/21=71%	2/21=10%	6/21=29%
Abourezk	Allen	Ford	Baker
Bayh	Byrd, H. F.	Schweiker	Bellmon
Burdick	Curtis		Goldwater
Byrd, R. C.	Dole		Hansen
Clark	Domenici		Scott, Wm.
Cranston	Eastland		Tower
Culver	Garn		
Glenn	Griffin		
Gravel	Helms		
Haskell	Laxalt		
Humphrey	McClure		
Kennedy	Roth		
Leahy	Stennis		
Matsunaga	Thurmond		
McIntyre	Young		
McGovern			
Metcalf			
Nelson		$\chi^2 = 16.70$; P = .00004	
Riegle, Jr.		Phi = .63; N = 42	

National Farmers Union Rating (1976)
0–39 = Very Low Family Nurturance
90–100 = Very High Family Nurturance
Abortion Rating = Senate Rollcall Vote No. 258,
Helms Amendment June 29, 1977.

(against abortion and against capital punishment) is 13 percent, and is 22 percent (ten of forty-five) of those opposed to abortion.

For the Helms Amendment, the "right-to-life" statistic (no abortion and high family nurturance) is 12 percent (two of seventeen). These data indicate that only a minority within the antiabortion movement can be considered to respect the quality, dignity, and equality of human life (12 to 22 percent). The remainder (78 to 92 percent) can be characterized as authoritarian, dehumanizing, fascist, violent, and lacking in family nurturance. This conclusion is based upon the collective evidence summarized herein and individual exceptions to these categorizations would have to be demonstrated with additional data. Utilizing caution, these percentage values can be used as preliminary estimates of the *true* "right-to-life" position within the antiabortion movement in the United States.

It is worth noting that an analysis of the relation between abortion and capital punishment was previously reported for the Canadian Parliament, where votes on bill C–168 to abolish capital punishment (1967–1968) were related to votes on bill C–150 to permit abortion (1968–1969). A highly significant relationship was obtained, with 59 percent voting for both reform bills, and 21 percent voting against both reform bills. Thus 80 percent supported the basic inverse relationship between capital punishment and abortion (P = .00001 (Prescott, 1975a; 1975b). Only 16 percent voted against capital punishment and abortion. The assistance of Frank F. Borowicz, professor of law, University of Windsor, in providing these roll call votes for analysis is appreciated.

The results from these analyses of voting records in the United States Senate are highly consistent with the relationships obtained in "primitive" cultures. Opposition to abortion is highly correlated with various forms of human violence, namely, the subjugation of women, the practice of slavery, punitive and restrictive sexuality, capital punishment, arbitrary human seizure, human torture, and support of warfare. It is perhaps worth emphasizing that compulsory motherhood is a form of slavery; therefore, it is not surprising to observe that these phenomena are highly interrelated in both "primitive" and modern cultures. For these reasons, it is of interest to note the historical tolerance, if not acceptance, of slavery in this country by the Roman Catholic hierarchy and other fundamentalist religious institutions. The subjugation and control of the people through religious orthodoxy is a form of human slavery. Questions must be raised as to why these religious institutions did not oppose the establishment of slavery in this nation with the vigor that they are opposing abortion today. If they had, we would not only have a different history but a different nation as well. Similar questions must also be raised with respect to capital punishment. The patrilineal structure of religious orthodox institutions, of primitive cultures that punish abortion, and of the male-dominated legislatures of this country that deny full and equal rights to women is a communality worthy of emphasis.

The roots of oppression, slavery, and fascism will be explored in the second part of this article. This will involve a formal evaluation of the interrelationships of failure of nurturance; repressive and punitive sexuality; and religious orthodoxy. In the words of Wilhelm Reich: "Fascism is not a political party but a specific concept of life and attitude toward man, love, and work. . . . It is generally clear today that 'fascism' is not the act of a Hitler or a Mussolini, but that it is the *expression of the irrational structure of mass man*" (Reich, 1973, pp. xxii, xx).

It is this universal property of the human mind—the reciprocal relationship between nurturance and violent oppression of thought and liberty—that will be examined with respect to abortion in Part II of this article.

This will conclude the theme of this article that the antiabortion movement as a "right-to-life" movement, which purports to respect the dignity, quality, and equality of human life, is one of the greatest frauds ever perpetrated upon the American public.

References Abortion under attack. *Newsweek,* 5, June 1978.

Barone, M., Vjifisch, G., & Mathews, D. *The almanac of American politics.* New York: E. P. Dutton, 1977.

Bleuel, Hans Peter. *Sex and society in Nazi Germany* (trans). New York: Bantam Books, 1974.

MacNeil/Lehrer Report, 21 March 1978.

Moyers, W. Abortion politics. *CBS Reports,* 22 April 1978.

NARAL Newsletter, 1978, *10* (1).

Prescott, J. W. Abortion or the unwanted child: A choice for a humanistic society. *The Humanist,* March/April, 1975a.

Prescott, J. W. Abortion: The controversy continued. *APA Monitor,* September/October, 1975b.

Reich, Wilhelm. The mass psychology of fascism (1933). New York: Farrar, Straus, and Giroux (new trans., 1969), 1973.

Textor, R. B. *A cross-cultural summary.* New Haven: HRAF Press, 1967.

The abortion rights crisis. *Religious Coalition for Abortion Rights,* Washington, D.C., February, 1978.

Washington Star, 6 March 1976.

Washington Star, 9 March 1978.

Appendix V

James W. Prescott & Douglas Wallace

Abortion and the "Right to Life": Facts, Fallacies and Fraud— Psychometric Studies

In the first part of this article it was shown that punitive attitudes toward abortion are significantly associated with a personality structure of violence and low nurturance. In the studies on primitive cultures it was found that punitive attitudes toward abortion were significantly associated with punitive attitudes toward sexual expression, i.e., low sexual affection and nurturance. The studies to be reported herein will extend that observed relationship of punitive abortion and repressive sexuality in primitive cultures to modern contemporary cultures. It will be argued from this and other data that punitive and repressive attitudes toward sexual expression, particularly of women, is the primary motivating force in the antiabortion movement and that the "reproductive" aspect of sexuality is a pseudo-issue in the "right-to-life" movement. The emphases upon the "reproductive" aspect of sexuality by the antiabortion movement serves to obscure the central and real issue in the abortion controversy, namely, that the primary function of human sexuality is for the experiencing and mutual sharing of sexual pleasure. It is this primacy of physical pleasure in human sexual relationships that cannot be accepted by the antiabortionist mentality for reasons that will be enumerated after the empirical data are presented to validate the relationship of opposition to abortion with repressive/punitive sexuality.

This article first appeared in *The Humanist* September/October 1978 and is reprinted by permission.

Douglas Wallace is Director of Research and Program Evaluation, Human Sexuality Program, Department of Psychiatry, University of California School of Medicine San Francisco.

The authors are indebted to Babette Josephs, NARAL and Richard E. Chapman, ADA, Philadelphia, Pennsylvania; and Ellen Yacklin, Pennsylvania Legal Services Center, Harrisburg, Pennsylvania, for providing the various roll call votes of the Pennsylvania legislature for analysis in this report. Appreciation is extended to Karen Mulhauser, NARAL for bringing to the authors' attention the comments of Congressman John M. Zwach.

343

Legislative Studies

On April 3, 1973, Representative Mullen, Pennsylvania House of Representatives, introduced amendments that would reinsert fornication and adultery into the Crimes Code. These amendments were attached to HB 518, which was a bill to prevent malicious mischief to caves! The definition of fornication as a sexual offense was: "A person who has sexual intercourse with another person of the opposite sex who is not his or her spouse commits fornication, a summary offense"; and the definition of adultery, as an offense against the family, was: "Whoever being married, has sexual intercourse with another person of the opposite sex, not his or her lawful spouse, is guilty of adultery, a misdemeanor of the third degree" (*Legislative Journal—House*, pp. 599–600, April 3, 1973). Mr. Mullen, in defense of his amendments, had the following to say:

> All I want to do here is not to insert anything new into the law. As a matter of fact, this is the law today and this has been the law in Pennsylvania since the founding of the Commonwealth back in colonial times. It has always been the law that adultery and fornication were wrong, and it has been the law for two reasons. First of all, it is against the law of God. I think all of us believe in God. All of us believe in the Ten Commandments, and one of the Ten Commandments is, "Thou shalt not commit adultery." If you delete this thing from the law, what you are in fact doing is condoning this type of conduct all over Pennsylvania, and this is not going to be good because, first of all, most of the people in Pennsylvania are religious people and they believe in the Ten Commandments" (p. 600).

The amendment passed 118 to 69 with 14 not voting. Rep. Williams, in opposing the amendment, noted certain moral inconsistencies in the Pennsylvania House voting record where they violated one of the Ten Commandments, "Thou shalt not kill," by supporting capital punishment. Humanists are aware that this amendment violates the First Amendment of the U.S. Constitution, which guarantees separation of church and state, since humanist religious views on the morality of human sexuality differ substantially from the Orthodox-Judeo and Fundamentalist-Christian positions.

On June 24, 1977, Representative Mullen, Pennsylvania House of Representatives, introduced an abortion amendment, which reads: "None of the funds appropriated in this act shall be used to promote or pay for abortions except where the life of the mother were endangered if the fetus were carried to full term."

The amendment passed 155 to 26 with 19 not voting (*Legislative Journal—House*, pp. 1511–1522, June 24, 1977).

Although four years intervened between the passage of the antifornication and adultery amendments of 1973 and the antiabortion amendment of

1977, 90 representatives voted on both of these amendments. The voting relationship between these amendments was statistically evaluated and the results are summarized in tables 1 and 2. It was found that 86 percent who oppose abortion, also support criminalization of fornication and adultery; and 85 percent who support abortion opposed laws to criminalize fornication and adultery. The statistical results were extraordinary: $X^2 = 29.79$, $p = .00000005$, $n = 90$, which means that the probability of this relationship occurring by chance is five out of 10,000,000.

These data provide substantial support for linking antiabortion mentality to a sexually repressive mentality. These findings were cross-validated by evaluating the voting records in the Pennsylvania Senate against abortion (February 22, 1978) and on the Antihomosexual Bill SB 83 (April 19, 1977). SB 83 reads:

> Notwithstanding any law or executive order or directive to the contrary, no individual or AUTHORIZED REPRESEN-TATIVE of a governmental agency having the power to hire individuals to fill vacant positions shall hire any admitted homosexual, ADMITTED SEX OFFENDER or individual convicted of a sex crime to fill any of the following positions: (enumerated)

The Antihomosexual Bill SB 83 was passed thirty-two to twelve.

Table 1 Pennsylvania House Record on Abortion (6/24/77) and Fornication/Adultery (4/3/73): Mullen Amendments

Group A Support Abortion Rights Support Sexual Rights	Group C Against Abortion Rights Support Sexual Rights
Fryer	Butera
Itken	Foster, W.
Johnson	Mebus
Rappaport	Morris
Richardson	Noye
Ritter	Pievsky
Scirica	Spencer
Williams	Taddonio
Wise	Wagner
Yohn	Weidner
Zeafoss	Wilson
N = 11	N = 11
Percent = 85 (11/13)	Percent = 14 (11/76)

There were only two Group D voters (Anderson and Dorr): support abortion rights and against sexual rights.

Appendix Five

Table 2 Pennsylvania House Record on Abortion (6/24/77) and For-
nication/Adultery (4/3/73): Mullen Amendments

Group B
Against Abortion Rights
Against Sexual Rights

Arthurs	Gallen	Lehr	Salvatore
Bellomini	Geesey	Letterman	Scanlon
Bennett	Geisler	Lincoln	Schaeffer
Brandt	Gillette	Lynch, F.	Shuman
Brunner	Gleeson	Manderino	Shupnik
Burns	Goodman	McClatchy	Smith, E.
Caputo	Grieco	Miller, Jr.	Thomas
Cessar	Halverson	Mullen, M. P.	Wargo
Demedio	Hamilton	Novak	Wilt
De Verter	Hasay	O'Brien, B.	Yahner
Dininni	Hayes, D. S.	O'Connell	Zeller
Dombrowski	Hayes, S. E.	Pancoast	Zord
Doyle	Katz	Petrarca	
Englehart	Kelly, A. P.	Polite	
Fee	Klingaman	Prendergast	
Fischer	Koiter	Renwick	
Foster, A.	Kowalyshyn	Rieger	
Gallagher	Laughlin	Ruggiero	

N = 66
Percent = 86%

The antiabortion amendment to SB 1254, which withheld Medicaid reimbursement for abortion except where necessary to save the life of the mother, was passed thirty-four to twelve.

There were thirty-nine Pennsylvania senators voting on both bills, and the results are summarized in tables 3 and 4. It was found that 89 percent oppose abortion and punish homosexuality; and 73 percent support abortion and support homosexual rights. The statistical analysis was highly significant: $X^2 = 15.00$, $p = .0001$, $n = 39$. The probability of this voting relationship occurring by chance is one out of 10,000.

These results fully validate the relationships obtained in the Pennsylvania House of Representatives which involved a different antisexual expression bill. These results considered collectively clearly support interpretation that antiabortion mentality is authoritarian in nature and attempts to subjugate the rights of the individual to the power of the state. There is, however, a special relationship between antiabortion mentality and antisexuality, which is illustrated from the following studies.

346

Table 3 Pennsylvania Senate Record on Abortion (2/22/78) and Anti-homosexual Bill SB 83 (4/19/77)

Group A Support Abortion Rights Support Sexual Rights	Group C Against Abortion Rights Support Sexual Rights
Arlene	Coppersmith
Duffield	Noszka
Hankins	Romanelli
Howard	
Lewis	
McKinney	
Messinger	
Reibman	
N = 8	N = 3
Percent = 73 (8/11)	Percent = 11 (3/28)

Table 4 Pennsylvania Senate Record on Abortion (2/22/78) and Anti-homosexual Bill SB 83 (4/19/77)

Group B Against Abortion Rights Against Sexual Rights		Group D Support Abortion Rights Against Sexual Rights
Andrews	Murray	Gekas
Dougherty	Nolan	Juberirer
Dwyer	O'Pake	Tilghman
Early	Orlando	
Fleming	Ross	
Gurzenda	Scanlon	
Hess	Schaefer	
Holl	Smith	
Hopper	Snyder	
Kelley	Stapleton	
Kury	Stauffer	
Manbeck	Sweeney	
Mellow		
N = 25		N = 3
Percent = 89 (25/28)		Percent = 27 (3/11)

Questionnaire Studies

The senior author developed a questionnaire called a "Somatosensory Index of Human Affection," which has become known as "The Index of Human Affection." This questionnaire evaluates a variety of values, attitudes, and behaviors involving parent-child relationships; human sexuality; alcohol and drug usage; ethnic and racial prejudice; and the morality of pain and pleasure in human relationships. The initial questionnaire involved forty-three items and has grown to 103 items plus a number of biographical questions. There is a six-point scale to respond to each question as follows: 1 = agree strongly; 2 = agree moderately; 3 = agree somewhat; 4 = disagree somewhat; 5 = disagree moderately; 6 = disagree strongly.

The following study will report upon the statistical relationships of the first fifty-three test questions to the statement: *Abortion should be punished by society.*

The encoding of the data and its analysis has been centralized at the University of California School of Medicine and has been the primary responsibility of the second author. Strategies of data analysis are the joint responsibility of the two authors.

Study A

Over the past five years the Index of Human Affection has been given to a variety of different individuals and groups, for example, those who attended public lectures given by the authors; college students (East and West Coast); high school students; alcoholics in treatment; drug abusers in treatment; incest offenders in treatment; members of professional societies and "growth communities" in California; women who had completed an abortion; and a group of lesbian women.

It was decided to report upon the entire sample collected as of May 1976. The broader composition of the sample described above has greater generalization than just a college sample, however, and the limitations of this sample are recognized. In the above sample, it was found that only 8 percent of the 688 males and 5 percent of the 1178 females agreed to the statement "Abortion should be punished by society." Consequently, the following analysis compares fifty-five males (against abortion) to 633 males (for abortion); and fifty-nine females (against abortion) to 1119 females (for abortion). These *for* and *against* abortion groups were then compared to their being in *agreement* or *disagreement* with the first fifty-six items of the questionnaire. Males and females were analyzed separately. The average age of the males was twenty-nine, with a standard deviation of eleven years; the average age of the females was twenty-seven, with a standard deviation of ten years.

Table 5 presents the social-behavioral correlates of abortion attitudes for males which are all statistically significant. Statistical significance ranges from p < .04 to p < .0001. The social-behavioral correlates are rank-ordered from the most significant to the less significant. The first column is the

Table 5 Social-Behavioral Correlates of Abortion; Males N = 688

X²	Percent Agree		Percent Ratio No. for Abortion	Question
	Against Abortion	For Abortion		
58.12	36	6	6.0	Prostitution should be punished by society (39).
22.54	29	8	3.6	Unmarried persons having sex with their lovers before marriage is wrong (23).
20.74	23	5	4.6	Society should interfere with private sexual behavior between adults (30).
18.34	44	14	3.1	I do not enjoy oral-genital sex (49).
15.90	35	13	2.7	Nudity within the family has a harmful influence upon children (9).
14.73[c]	59	32	1.8	Capital punishment should be permitted by society (32).
14.13	24	8	3.0	Physical punishment and pain help build a good moral character (37).
13.52	22	7	3.1	Sexual pleasures help build a weak moral character (38).
12.58	55	30	1.8	The government should have more control of the people (42).
12.35[b]	56	78	-1.4	My father has not adequately discussed sex with me (29).
9.62	22	8	2.8	Violence is necessary to really solve our problems (33).
7.86	46	27	1.7	I use and experiment with drugs quite often (12).
7.82	53	72	-1.4	My father did not hug and kiss me a lot (3).
5.66	69	51	1.4	I would rather drink alcohol than smoke marijuana (16).
5.32	49	32	1.5	Married persons having sex affairs with their lovers is wrong (25).
4.67	44	61	-1.4	People in government and business do not care about me and my family (43).
4.36[a]	32	19	1.7	Physical punishment should be allowed in the schools (22).

a: P < .04; b: P < .001; c: P < .0001

traditional X^2 statistic, the second column is the *percentage* of those *against abortion* that *agree* with the question item; the third column is the *percentage* of those who are *for abortion* who *agree* with the question item; the fourth column is the *ratio* of the *percentage agreement* for the "against abortion" and "for abortion" groups. Thus, for the first question item there are six times as many antiabortionists who agree with the statement "Prostitution should be punished by society" than by those who support abortion.

Similarly, 3.6 times as many antiabortionists agree that premarital sex is wrong than those who support abortion; and 4.6 times as many antiabortionists agree that "Society should interfere with private sexual behavior between adults" than those who support abortion. The negative sign before the ratio indicates that the percent agreement is greater for the "proabortion" group than the "no-abortion" group. Some effort should be spent in studying this table. In brief, it provides strong support for the point of view that the antiabortion mentality is very punitive toward sexuality; believes that sexual pleasures help build a weak moral character and conversely that physical pain and punishment help build a strong moral character; does not enjoy oral-genital sex; feels family nudity is harmful to children; uses drugs more frequently; prefers alcohol to marijuana; believes in physical violence, e.g. capital punishment and physical punishment of children; and believes that society has the right to interfere with the private sexual behavior of adults. The presence of negative signs indicating that the proabortion groups agree more with those statements was not expected and needs further study. The finding that males (not females) that support abortion report less sex discussion and physical affection from the father may be interpreted as reflecting a greater identification with the female in providing a source of physical affection in human relationships. The source of this particular relationship could be coming from any or all of the many subgroups in this sample, and further study of this relationship is obviously required. The finding that males who support abortion also agree more with the statement "People in government and business do not care about me and my family" may be a further reflection of greater identification with matrilineal rather than patrilineal values of our society. The less physical affection from the father may be a contributing factor to this relationship.

In summarizing this table of results, it can be concluded that the antiabortion mentality is characterized by authoritarian control of individuals; a high value on physical pain, punishment, and violence; and the most significant correlates are those of punitive and repressive attitudes toward sexual expressiveness and pleasure. In short, it is the personality profile of the neofascist.

Table 6 presents the same data analysis for females. Most striking is the finding that three of the four most significant correlates with antiabortion mentality for females are identical to those found for males: punishment of prostitution; punishment of premarital sex; and societal interference with the

Table 6 Social-Behavioral Correlates of Abortion; Females N = 1178

X²	Percent Agree Against Abortion	Percent Agree For Abortion	Percent Ratio No. for Abortion	Question
103.62	45	7	6.4	Prostitution should be punished by society (39).
61.10	40	8	5.0	Unmarried persons having sex with their lovers before marriage is wrong (23).
39.64	21	2	10.5	Marijuana is more satisfying than sex (45).
39.16	24	4	6.0	Society should interfere with private sexual behavior between adults (30).
31.32	14	2	7.0	Alcohol is more satisfying than sex (17).
29.51	32	9	3.6	Nudity within the family has a harmful influence upon children (9).
26.17	22	5	4.4	Sexual pleasures help build a weak moral character (38).
25.83	59	28	2.1	I do not enjoy sex films where the sex partners give each other pleasure (27).
23.74	15	3	5.0	Physical punishment and pain help build a good moral character (37).
20.58	17	4	4.3	Violence is necessary to really solve our problems (33).
19.57	23	6	3.8	I get hostile and aggressive when I drink alcohol (15).
18.32	15	3	5.0	Hard physical punishment is good for children who disobey a lot (21).
16.29[c]	49	25	2.0	The government should have more control of the people (42).
15.66[c]	69	42	1.6	Married persons having sex affairs with their lovers is wrong (25).
14.29	25	9	2.8	Physical punishment should be allowed in the schools (22).
13.30	44	23	1.9	Capital punishment should be permitted by society (32).
10.21[b]	47	27	1.7	Natural fresh body odors are often offensive (10).
9.56	9	2	4.5	Drugs are more satisfying than sex (18).
7.31	17	7	2.4	I enjoy sex films where the sex partner is physically beaten or hurt (26).
5.96	40	25	1.6	I often get "uptight" about being touched (8).
5.81	38	24	1.6	I often feel like hitting someone (36).
5.11	37	24	1.5	My mother does not really care about me (4).
4.16	21	9	2.3	I usually do not get much pleasure from my sexual activity (46).
3.70[a]	37	25	1.5	I remember when my mother physically punished me a lot (35).

a: P < .05; b: P < .001; c: P < .0001

private sexual behavior of adults. It is evident from examining table 6 that the punitive and repressive attitude toward sexuality is the most salient characteristic of the antiabortion mentality. A most striking relationship found for female antiabortionists that was not found for male antiabortionists was the high preference for marijuana to sex (10.5 to 1); of alcohol to sex (7.0 to 1); and of drugs to sex (4.5 to 1). These constitute the highest ratios obtained in this analysis. An interpretation of their preference for marijuana, drugs, and alcohol to sex is that drugs and alcohol become compensatory responses to a sexually repressed and nonsatisfying sex life. Another salient difference between the male and female antiabortion mentality is that female antiabortionists report a significantly greater deprivation of maternal affection and maternal punishment that was not observed for male antiabortionists.

Apart from these two distinguishing characteristics of the male and female antiabortion mentality, there is a high communality of punitive/repressive sexuality; high moral values for physical pain, punishment, and violence; and authoritarian control of the individual by the state. In brief, the personality profile of the neofascist shows no significant sex difference.

Study B

Given the unusual heterogeneity of the sample in study A, it was considered desirable to cross-validate the above findings on a more homogeneous sample. Two college student samples, American and Canadian, completed the questionnaire, and their responses to the first forty-three questions are the subject of this report. A different statistical technique was employed in the analysis of these data, called factor analysis, which combines the variables (forty-three questions) in groupings or clusters according to their mathematically defined relationship to one another, i.e., how much do they have in common with one another. The specific form of factor analysis employed is known as principal components analysis with varimax rotation.

This procedure results in several factors or "profiles" which are defined by the clustering of test items that constitute the factor or "profile." Each test item or question has a "weighting" or coefficient that ranges from −1 to +1 and reflects the "weight" or degree of influence that a particular test question has upon the factor or "profile." This statistical technique identifies the "redundancy" among the various test questions, i.e., "How much do they measure the same thing," and permits a reduction of the total test battery (in this case forty-three items) to a much smaller number of factors (in this case sixteen factors). For the purposes of this report only two factors will be described, for they are the only factors that contain a significant "weight" on the abortion variable.

For the American sample, 9 percent of the males (fifty-four) and 3 percent of the females (ninety-four) agreed that society should punish abortion. For the Canadian sample, 10 percent of the males (sixty-three) and 4 percent of the females (one hundred fourteen) agreed that abortion should be punished by society. This means that the relationships described below reflect mostly variations in the strength of "disagreement" category with minor representation from the "agree" category.

Table 7 presents the test questions that have a weighting or coefficient of .35 or greater. Seven of the forty-three questions have such a coefficient value, where the abortion question "Abortion should be punished by society" has the highest coefficient. The precise weighting is obtained by squaring the coefficient, which is then interpreted as a percentage. On this factor the abortion variable has a coefficient of .64 or a weighting of 41 percent, i.e., 41 percent of this test question is represented on this factor or profile. Just as each test question has a certain percentage or weight on each factor, each factor accounts for a certain percentage of the total percentage of the test battery, which is 100 percent.

Table 7   American College Sample: Abortion and Punitive Sexuality; N = 148; 54 Males, 94 Females

Coefficient	Descriptor
.64	Abortion should be punished by society (31).
.52	Sexual pleasures help build a weak moral character (38).
.50	Nudity within the family has a harmful influence upon children (9).
.44	Physical punishment and pain help build a strong moral character (39).
.41	Prostitution should be punished by society (39).
.38	Physical punishment should be allowed in the schools (22).
.35	The government should have more control of the people (42).

Factor 2: 13 Percent Variance

Table 7 identifies factor 2 in this analysis and accounts for 13 percent of the total test variance of 100 percent. (Factor 1 accounted for 17 percent of the variance, and each succeeding factor accounts for less variance until 100 percent of the test battery variance is accounted for.) Factor 2 is labeled "Abortion and Punitive Sexuality" because of the particular test questions that identify the factor. An inspection of factor 2 indicates that punishment of abortion is highly associated with punishment of sexual behavior and a moral value system that considers that sexual pleasures help build weak moral characters and that pain/punishment help build strong moral characters. Associated with this social/moral value system is the advocacy of physical punishment of children and that the government should have more control of the people.

These are the same variables that were found to have the most significant relationship to antiabortion in the previous and more heterogeneous sample.

Table 8 presents a comparable analysis for the Canadian sample, where factor 7 (of fifteen factors extracted) contains the strongest representation of

Table 8   Canadian College Sample: Abortion and Punitive Sexuality; N = 177; 63 Males, 114 Females

Coefficient	Descriptor
.63	Unmarried persons having sex with their lovers is wrong (23).
.58	Abortion should be punished by society (31).
.49	Prostitution should be punished by society (39).
.40	Married persons having sex affairs with their lovers is wrong (25)

Factor 7: 5 Percent Variance

the abortion question than any of the other factors. Again we find that punitive and repressive sexuality are the most significant (and only) variables linked to the abortion question. There are important differences between the American and Canadian samples. For the American sample there are correlates of high moral values of pain and punishment; advocacy of physical violence; and government control of the people linked to antiabortion or marginal support of abortion which were not found for the Canadian sample. It is of interest to note that capital punishment was not found to be significantly linked to antiabortion or marginal support of abortion that has been found in previous studies. For these college samples, it was surprising to find that 69 percent of American males; 63 percent of Canadian males; 41 percent of American females; and 52 percent of Canadian females support capital punishment. These findings indicate that the relationship between abortion and capital punishment is quite different for the young college student than it is for the older generation. If these findings are replicated for additional American and Canadian college samples, the implications for the future of humanistic values is not encouraging.

Tables 9 and 10 present those *factors* that have the second highest weighting of the abortion question for the American and Canadian samples, respectively. For the American sample there is the usual punitive/repressive sexuality but with a new characterisic—maternal indifference—another measure of failure of nurturance. For the Canadian sample the most significant new correlates are failure of parental sex education and low interspouse

Table 9   American College Sample: Maternal Indifference, Punitive Sexuality, and Abortion Punished; N = 148; 54 Males, 94 Females

Coefficient	Descriptor
.54	Unmarried persons having sex with their lovers is wrong (23).
.48	My mother does not really care about me (4).
.38	Abortion should be punished by society (31).
.32	Society should interfere with private sexual behavior between adults (30).

Factor 15: 3 Percent Variance

Table 10 Canadian College Sample: Low Home Sex Education and Abortion Punished; N = 177; 63 Males, 114 Females

Coefficient	Descriptor
.89	My father has not adequately discussed sex with me (29).
.63	My mother has not adequately discussed sex with me (28).
.34	I have rarely seen my parents hug and kiss each other (1).
.27	Abortion should be punished by society (31).

Factor 2: 15 Percent Variance

physical affection. It is of interest that parental variables involving affection, indifference, and sex education are linked to the abortion issue, although they are clearly secondary factors.

In summarizing these psychometric data we can rank-order those social-behavioral characteristics that characterize the antiabortion mentality from most salient to less salient as follows:

1 punitive/repressive attitudes toward sexual expression, which includes both moral and political characteristics;
2 subjugation of the rights of the individual to the authority of the state and society;
3 a high moral value system for pain and physical punishment, which includes capital punishment;
4 drugs, alcohol, and marijuana are compensatory behaviors for sexually repressed behaviors; and
5 low parental affection, caring, and sex education.

The data presented in this two-part article have identified two basic motivational factors in the antiabortion personality, namely, a puritanical view of human sexuality and the authoritarian control by the state and society of an individual's right of self-determination. These authoritarian and punitive/repressive sexual attitudes are particularly well dramatized by the exchange between Senator Bayh and Congressman Zwach, Sixth Congressional District, Minnesota, on May 6, 1974, before Senator Bayh's Subcommittee on Constitutional Amendments.

Senator Bayh: I don't want to push, but will just make this reference. I don't think you relish this role, but as long as we are going to have this problem which arises from the question of when life begins, I think it is incumbent upon me to explore in infinite detail all the ramifications and the very strong feelings presented on both sides of this. If the proposition you make, that from the point of fertilization you have life, if that is accurate ——

Mr. Zwach: Yes.

Senator Bayh (continuing): Then it is taking life to use a substance or to have a device inserted, even prior to the act

355

of intercourse, that prohibits implantation. That is why I asked the question.

Mr. Zwach: No. I wouldn't interpret my position as saying that. My position is that after there is the creation of life, a coming together and a new life is formed, then taking that life would be destroying life and wrong.

I think America could very well consider a little bit of self-discipline in this area. *We seem to take for granted that we have to have people become pregnant. I think this in itself is a sickness of America, that you have to have intercourse: you have to.* We seem to get away from the matters of the spirit and deal almost totally with selfishness, personal selfishness, self-worship rather than in the areas of spiritual values. There is virtue in self-denial, there is virtue in self-discipline, there is virtue in self-control; virtues which, I think, have made our country great. It is a question, as we follow this easy way, whether it results in a great deal of destruction of the values that are fundamental in our way of life (pp. 148–149).

There is little question that the major hidden current in the antiabortion movement is the negative moral values associated with sexual pleasure and the accompanying authoritarian values to limit and suppress the expression of sexual pleasure. The "right-to-life" issue in the abortion controversy is a pseudo-issue which obscures the real issue of sexual pleasure, which is considered illicit and immoral. The fundamental confrontation in the abortion controversy is the primary function of human sexuality—reproduction or the mutual sharing of physical affection and sensual pleasure. Humanists hold the position that the primary function of human sexuality is for the expression and mutual sharing of physical affection and pleasure as indispensable for the development of personhood and social unity. Fundamentalist monotheism holds the converse, that the primary function of human sexuality is reproduction and that "uncontrolled" experiencing of sexual pleasure not only leads to loss of personal salvation but also to social disunity.

There is not sufficient time or space to elaborate and clarify these issues in this article. Suffice it to say that an understanding of the abortion controversy requires an understanding of Pythagorean philosophical dualism; its basic foundation for monotheistic religious values; and social-political systems of patrilineal cultures that maintain and support these philosophical dualistic-monotheistic religious institutions whose essential objective is the regulation, suppression, and ultimate denial of the equality of women in their expression of their own sexuality.

The relationship of deprivation of physical affection and pleasure and human relationships to violence, exploitation, and authoritarian control has been documented, elsewhere (Prescott, 1975a; 1975b; 1977). The linkage of these relationships to philosophical dualism and monotheistic religious values, however, has only been briefly summarized (Prescott, 1975b; 1976; 1977).

It would be remiss not to acknowledge the historic contribution of Wilhelm Reich (1969), who arrived at these same insights from a substantially different data base. Reich states:

> More than the economic dependency of the wife and children on the husband and father is needed to preserve the institution of the authoritarian family. For the suppressed classes, this dependency is endurable only on condition that the consciousness of being a sexual being is suspended as completely as possible in women and in children. *The wife must not figure as a sexual being, but solely as a child-bearer—Sexually awakened women, affirmed and recognized as such would mean the complete collapse of the authoritarian ideology* (p.105).

All of these issues are so completely interwoven that it is not possible to clarify the detailed structure of their interlocking nature in this paper. This will be the subject of a future essay.

Appendix Five

References   Prescott, J. W. Abortion and the unwanted child: A choice for a humanistic society. *The Humanist,* March/April 1975a, 11–15.

Prescott, J. W. Body pleasure and the origins of violence. *The Futurist,* April 1975b. (Reprinted: "Bulletin of the Atomic Scientists," November 1975b, 64–74.)

Prescott, J. W. Phylogenetic and ontogenetic aspects of human affectional development. In *Progress In Sexology, Proceedings of the 1976 International Congress Sexology* (R. Gemme and C. C. Wheeler, eds.). New York: Plenum Press, 1977, 431–457.

Prescott, J. W. Violence, pleasure and religion. *Bulletin of the Atomic Scientists*, March 1976, 62.

Reich, Wilhelm. *The mass psychology of fascism* (1933). New York: Farrar, Straus, and Giroux (new trans. 1969).

Appendix VI

Selected Resources

Basic Resources for the Professional

Begin by writing to the following organizations for bibliographies and subscription blanks, and request to be placed on mailing lists:

> The Alan Guttmacher Institute, 515 Madison Avenue, New York, N.Y. 10022.
>
> The American Association of Sex Educators, Counselors, and Therapists, 5010 Wisconsin Avenue, N.W., Suite 304, Washington, D.C. 20006.
>
> Creative Media Group, 123 Fourth Street, N.W., Charlottesville, Va. 22901.
>
> Ed-U Press, 123 Fourth Street, N.W., Charlottesville, Va. 22901.
>
> Guidance Associates, 757 Third Avenue, New York, N.Y. 10017.
>
> Institute for Family Research and Education, 760 Ostrom Avenue, Syracuse, N.Y. 13210.
>
> National Alliance for Optional Parenthood, 3 No. Liberty Street, Baltimore, Md. 21201.
>
> P. K. Houdek, *Sex News,* 7140 Oak, Kansas City, Mo. 64114.
>
> Perennial Education, Inc., 477 Roger Williams, P.O. Box 885, Ravinia, Highland Park, Ill. 60035.
>
> Population Institute, 110 Maryland Avenue, Washington, D.C. 20002.
>
> Population Reference Bureau, 1337 Connecticut Avenue, N.W., Washington, D.C. 20002.
>
> Sex Information and Education Council of the United States, 84 Fifth Avenue, New York, N.Y. 10001.
>
> Zero Population Growth, 1346 Connecticut Avenue, N.W., Washington, D.C. 20036.

For You to Read First Gagnon, J. H. *Human sexualities.* New York: Scott, Foresman and Co., 1977.

Gordon, S., & Libby, R. W. (eds.). *Sexuality today—and tomorrow.* North Scituate, Mass.: Duxbury Press, 1976.

361

Otto, H. A. (ed.). *The new sex education.* Chicago: Association Press/Follett Publishing Co., 1978.

Readings in human sexuality—78/79. Guilford, Conn.: Dushkin Publishing Co., 1978 (annual editions).

Sex is aweful. Journal of Current Social Issues, 1978, *15* (1). Available from 287 Park Avenue South, New York, N.Y. 10010.

For Giving to Teenagers to Read (paperbacks only)

Chiappa, J. A., & Forish, J. J. *The VD book.* New York: Holt, 1976.

Gordon, S. *You would if you loved me.* New York: Bantam Books, 1978.

Gordon, S. *You.* New York: Times Books, 1978.

Hamilton, E. *Sex, with love: A guide for young people.* Boston: Beacon, 1977.

Kelly, G. F. *Learning about sex.* New York: Barron's Educational Series, 1976.

Lieberman, E. J., & Peck, E. *Sex and birth control.* New York: Thomas Y. Crowell, 1973.

Ten heavy facts about sex (comic book). Available from Ed-U Press, 123 Fourth Street, N.W., Charlottesville, Va. 22901.

The Wardell Pomeroy books for the intellectually-minded and the Eric W. Johnson and Sol Gordon books for those who are not. (See "Important Books" on the following pages.)

For High School Teachers to Consider as Texts

Gordon, S. *Psychology for you.* New York: Sadlier/Oxford, 1978.

Gordon, S., & Wollin, M. McD. *Parenting—a guide for young people.* New York: Sadlier/Oxford, 1975.

For Parents

Gordon S., & Dickman, I. R. *Sex education: The parents' role,* Public Affairs Pamphlet #549. New York: Public Affairs Pamphlets, 1977.

For Those Concerned Especially with Teenagers

Alan Guttmacher Institute. *11 million teenagers.* New York: Planned Parenthood, November 1976.

Baldwin, W. *Adolescent pregnancy and childbearing—growing concerns for Americans. Population Bulletin,* 1976, *31* (2), (entire issue).

Canfield, L. Am I normal? *The Humanist,* March/April 1978, 10–12.

Zelnik, M., & Kantner, J. Contraceptive patterns and premarital pregnancy among women aged 15–19 in 1976. *Family Planning Perspectives,* 1978, *10* (3), 11–20.

List of Resources for the Professional

Two Highly Significant Documents

All our children, the American family under pressure. New York: Harcourt Brace Jovanovich, 1977.
The Carnegie Council on Children's extensive, five-year study that outlines a comprehensive policy of family health.

Population and the American future: Report of the Commission on Population Growth and the American Future. New York: New American Library, 1972.
The full report of the commission is available from the Superintendent of Documents, Government Printing Office, Washington, D.C. 20402.

Important Books

Altman, D. *Homosexual: Oppression and liberation.* New York: Avon, 1973.

Baker, R., & Elliston, F. *Philosophy and sex.* New York: Prometheus, 1975.

Barbach, L. G. *For yourself—the fulfillment of female sexuality.* New York: Signet, 1975.

Bell, A. P., & Weinberg, M. S. *Homosexualities: A study of diversity among men and women.* New York: Simon and Schuster, 1978.

Bell, R. R., & Gordon, M. (eds.). *The social dimension of human sexuality.* Boston: Little, Brown & Co., 1972.
Articles representing a cross-section of cultural and subcultural attitudes. Topics include premarital, marital, and extramarital sex; liberated women and female sexuality; homosexuality; commercialized sex.

Belotti, E. G. *What are little girls made of: The roots of feminine stereotypes.* New York: Schocken Books, 1976.

Bernstein, A. *The flight of the stork.* New York: Delacorte Press, 1978.

Blank, J. *The playbook for men—about sex.* Burlingame, Calif.: Down There Press, 1976.
A fun book that helps men explore their common sexual hang-ups.

Block, W. A. *What your child really wants to know about sex and why.* Englewood Cliffs, N.J.: Prentice-Hall, 1972.
Questions kids ask and approaches to answering.

Boston Women's Health Book Collective. *Our bodies, ourselves.* New York: Simon and Schuster, 1973; revised 1976.
An extremely candid statement by an important group of liberated women, although perhaps too polemical in parts. Some of the facts should be checked with Guttmacher's book, but, in general, the book is an extremely important statement of what women are thinking these days. English and Spanish versions are available from the Collective at Box 192, West Somerville, Mass. 02144.

Brain, R. *Friends and lovers.* New York: Basic Books, 1976.
An illuminating account of the patterns of friendship in a variety of cultures and their meaning for our own lives.

Brecher, E. M. *The sex researchers.* New York: Signet, 1971.
A historical account of Western man's efforts to understand his own sexuality within a scientific framework. In nontechnical language, it deals with the problem of evaluating sex research.

Broderick, C. G., & Bernard, J. (eds.). *The individual, sex and society.* Baltimore: The Johns Hopkins Press, 1969.
A text for training professionals for sex education programs. Puts sex education in the context of the viewpoints of the teacher and the individual school.

Brown, L. R. *The twenty-ninth day.* New York: W. W. Norton, 1978.

Brown, R. M. *Rubyfruit jungle.* New York: Bantam, 1977.
Fine novel of lesbian love and life-styles.

Bullough, V. L. *Sexual variance in society and history.* New York: John Wiley and Sons, 1976.

Bullough, V., & Bullough, B. *Sin, sickness and sanity.* Bergenfield, N.J.: New American Library, 1977.

Buscaglia, L. *Love.* Thorofare, N.J.: Charles B. Slack, 1972.
A beautifully written book geared to both adolescents and adults.

Byler, R., Lewis, G., & Totman, R. *Teach us what we want to know.* Connecticut Board of Education, Mental Health Materials Center, 1969.
An essential "report of a survey on health interests, concerns and problems of 5,000 students in selected schools from kindergarten through grade 12."

Calderone, M. S. (ed.). *Sexuality and human values.* Chicago: Association Press/Follett Publishing Co., 1975.

Carmichael, C. *Non-sexist childraising.* Boston: Beacon, 1977.

Chapman, E. D. *The sexual equation.* New York: Philosophical Library, 1977.

Cherniak, D., & Feingold, A. *VD handbook.* Available from PO Box 1000, Station G., Montreal, Canada.

Chiappa, J. A., & Forish, J. J. *The VD book.* New York: Holt, 1976.
The most complete, readable book on the subject; includes a self-quiz on VD.

Clark, D. *Loving someone gay.* New York: Celestial Arts, 1977.
A gay therapist offers sensitive, intelligent guidance to gays and those who care about them.

Colton, H. *The joy of touching.* New York: Peebles Press, 1979.

Commission on Obscenity and Pornography. *Report of the Commission.* New York: Bantam, 1970.
Synopsis of the research and recommendations of this presidential commission. Useful for helping to dispel myths about the effects of sex education.

David, H. P., Friedman, H. L., vanderTak, G., & Sevilla, M. J. *Abortion in psychosocial perspective: Trends in transnational research.* New York: Springer Publishing Co., 1978.

Delaney, J., Lupton, M. U., & Toth, E. *The curse.* Bergenfield, N.J.: New American Library, 1977.

DeLora, J. S., & Warren, C. A. B. *Understanding sexual interaction.* Boston: Houghton Mifflin, 1977.

Dinnerstein, D. *The mermaid and the minotaur—sexual arrangements and human arrangements.* New York: Harper & Row, 1976.

Dodson, B. *Liberating masturbation.* New York: Bodysex Designs, 1974.
"A meditation on self-love" for women; good for men to read also.

Dykeman, W. *Too many people, too little love.* New York: Holt, Rinehart & Winston, 1974.

Ellis, A. *The sensuous person: Critique and corrections.* Secaucus, N.J.: Lyle Stuart, 1972.
A devastating critique of the popular sex books, including David Reuben's. A sensational best-seller. It is one of Albert Ellis's most important books if you can handle his casual style and liberal use of obscenities.

Filene, P. G. *Him/her/self—sex roles in modern America.* New York: Mentor, 1974.

Francoeur, A. K., & Francoeur, R. T. *Hot & cool sex.* New York: Harcourt Brace Jovanovich, 1974.

Furstenberg, F. F. *Unplanned parenthood—the social consequences of teenage childbearing.* New York: Free Press, 1976.
Superb description of the problems related to early parenthood, based on a well-done study conducted over five years.

Gagnon, J. H. *Human sexualities.* New York: Scott, Foresman & Co., 1977.
Illustrated; explores the social and psychological factors that shape the many variations of human behavior.

Gagnon, J. H. (ed.). *Human sexuality in today's world.* Boston: Little, Brown & Co., 1977.
Collection of up-to-date articles from outstanding authorities, written in a popular style; VD, teenage sexuality, women's liberation, sex differences are included.

General Mills Inc. *Raising children in a changing society.* Minneapolis: General Mills, Inc., 1977.

Gochros, H. L., & Gochros, J. S. (eds.). *The sexually oppressed.* New York: Association Press, 1977.

Goldberg, H. *The hazards of being male.* New York: Signet, 1976.

Goldstein, M., Haeberle, E., & McBride, W. *The sex book: A modern pictorial encyclopedia.* New York: Herder & Herder, 1971.
Defines in plain language sex-related terms that are in current professional and popular usage. With explicit photographs.

Gordon, L. *Woman's body and woman's right.* New York: Penguin Books, 1977.

Gordon, S. *The new you.* New York: Bantam Books, 1979. New poems and slogans.

Gordon, S. *Girls are girls and boys are boys—so what's the difference?* Charlottesville, Va.: Ed-U Press, 1979.
Explores physical differences between boys and girls and focuses on breaking down traditional sexist orientations to life-style choices (ages 7–11).

Gordon, S. *Facts about sex for today's youth.* Charlottesville, Va.: Ed-U Press, 1978.

Gordon, S. *Facts about VD for today's youth.* Charlottesville, Va.: Ed-U Press, 1979.

Gordon, S. *YOU—a survival guide for youth.* New York: Times Books, 1978.

Gordon, S. *Psychology for you.* New York: Sadlier/Oxford Books, 1972; 1977.
A humanistic introductory text for high school or junior college.

Gordon, S. *You would if you loved me.* New York: Bantam, 1978.

Gordon, S., & Gordon, J. *Did the sun shine before you were born?* Charlottesville, Va.: Ed-U Press, 1977.
A sex education primer intended to be read aloud or to be given to beginning readers. Focuses on families, relationships, pregnancy and childbirth (ages 3–6).

Gordon, S., & Libby, R. W. (eds.). *Sexuality today—and tomorrow.* North Scituate, Mass.: Duxbury Press, 1976.
Thorough collection of articles on the politics of sex, changing sex roles, morals and social ethics.

Gordon, S., & Wollin, McD. *Parenting: A guide for young people.* New York: Sadlier/Oxford Book Co., 1975.
A planning for parenthood text for high school students; helpful for exploring how parents can broaden sex education into education for family life.

Gornick, V., & Moran, B. K. (eds.). *Women in sexist society—a study in power and powerlessness.* New York: Signet, 1972.
A collection of essays from a psychosocial perspective.

Green, R. *Sexual identity conflict in children and adults.* New York: Basic Books, 1974.
Well-written and extensively researched volume on the development of masculinity and femininity.

Greenberg, S. *Right from the start.* Boston: Houghton Mifflin Co., 1978.

Greer, G. *The female eunuch.* New York: McGraw-Hill, 1971.
Still one of the most important statements on the women's liberation movement.

Gross, B., & Gross, R. (eds.). *The children's rights movement.* Garden City, N.Y.: Anchor Press/Doubleday, 1977.

Subtitled *Overcoming the oppression of young people,* this book is a collection of important articles by Robert Coles, Margaret Mead, Benjamin Spock, and others.

Grummon, D. L., & Barclay, A. M. (eds.). *Sexuality: A search for perspective.* New York: Van Nostrand Reinhold Co., 1971.
One of the best of general compilations. Includes probing articles by Ira Reiss, Albert Ellis, Lester Kirkendall, and Alan Guttmacher.

Guttmacher, A. *Pregnancy, birth and family planning.* New York: Viking Press, 1973.
An excellent one-volume review of the important findings concerning birth control.

Haeberle, E. J. *The sex atlas—a new illustrated guide.* New York: Seabury Press, 1978.

Haight, A. L. *Banned books.* New York: R. R. Bowker, 1978.

Hamilton, E. *Sex, with love.* Boston: Beacon, 1977.
Deals with concerns of the twelve- to fifteen-year-old.

Hardin, G. *Stalking the wild taboo.* Los Altos, Calif.: William Kaufmann, 1973.
An important book dealing with the irrational manner in which society handles critical subjects, such as abortion and sex education.

Harrison, B. *Unlearning the lie—sexism in school.* New York: Liveright, 1973.
An informative book which deals with the stereotypes surrounding sex roles and ways of effecting change.

Hartley, S. *Illegitimacy.* Berkeley: University of California Press, 1975.
Statistically packed treatment explaining illegitimacy around the world.

Hatcher, R. A. et al. *Contraceptive technology, 1978–1979.* New York: Irvington Publishers, 1978.

Hilu, V. (ed.). *Sex education and the schools.* New York: Harper & Row, 1967.

Hite, S. *The Hite report.* New York: Macmillan Publishing Co., 1976.

Hobson, L. Z. *Consenting adult.* New York: Warner Books, 1976.

Hole, J., & Levine, E. *Rebirth of feminism.* New York: Quadrangle Books, 1971.
An objective, early analysis of the women's liberation movement.

Hottois, J., & Milner, N. A. *The sex education controversy.* Lexington, Mass.: Lexington Books, 1975.

Hunt, M. *Gay: What you should know about homosexuality.* New York: Farrar, 1977.

Hunt, M. *Sexual behavior in the 1970's.* Chicago: Playboy Press, 1974.
Though not as scientifically exact as it could have been, this is a large-scale survey of the sexual attitudes and behaviors of U.S.

adults. Very helpful for appreciating the variety of sexual life-styles in America.

Institute for Family Research and Education. *Community sex education programs for parents.* Charlottesville, Va.: Ed-U Press, 1977.
A guidebook based on three years of programs reaching over 1,400 parents.

Johnson, E. W. *Love and sex in plain language.* New York: Bantam, 1967.
An older book on how babies are born, what sexual intercourse is, the "different kinds of love." Written simply and concerned with fostering respect in relationships.

Jones, K. L., Shainberg, L. W., & Byer, C. O. *Sex and people.* New York: Harper & Row, 1977.

Kagan, B. *Human sexual expression.* New York: Harcourt Brace Jovanovich, 1973.
Thoughtful basic analysis covering anatomy, social psychology, and variations in sexuality.

Kappelman, M. *Sex and the American teenager.* New York: Reader's Digest Press, 1977.

Keith, L., & Brittain, J. *Sexually transmitted diseases.* Aspen, Colorado: Creative Infomatics, 1978.

Kelly, G. F. *Learning about sex—the contemporary guide for young adults.* New York: Barron's Educational Series, 1976.
Accurate but not overly technical, this nonmoralistic book treats sexuality as part of a whole person.

Kimmey, J. *Legal abortion: A speaker's notebook.* New York: Association for the Study of Abortion, Inc., 1975.
Responses to frequently raised arguments against legal abortion.

Kirkendall, L. A. (ed.) *A new bill of sexual rights and responsibilities.* Buffalo, N.Y.: Prometheus Books, 1977.

Konopka, G. *The adolescent girl in conflict.* Englewood Cliffs, N.J.: Prentice-Hall, 1966.

Lader, L. *Abortion II: Making the revolution.* Boston: Beacon Press, 1973.

Landers, A. *The Ann Landers encyclopedia: A to z.* Garden City, N.Y.: Doubleday, 1978.

Lash, T. W., & Sigal, H. *State of the child: New York City.* New York: Foundation for Child Development, 1976.
Fascinating report on the economic, educational, and social condition of children in our largest city.

Lehrman, N. *Masters and Johnson explained.* Chicago: Playboy Press, 1970.
A concise and readable explanation of their major findings about sexual response and feelings; gives a good background.

LeShan, E. *Sex and your teenager.* New York: Warner, 1973.

Libby, R. W., & Whitehurst, R. N. (eds.). *Marriage and alternatives,*

exploring intimate relationships. Glenview, Ill.: Scott, Foresman, 1977.
Collection of articles covering a wide range of alternate sexual styles.

Lieberman, E. J., & Peck, E. *Sex and birth control—a guide for the young.* New York: Thomas Y. Crowell Co., 1973.
A thorough treatment for the young adult or the adolescent who likes to read.

Life Cycle Library for young people. Chicago: Parent and Child Institute, 1969.

Lopez, R. I. (ed.). *Adolescent medicine, Topics,* vol. I. New York: Spectrum Publications, 1976.
Contains: The doctor, the teenager, and sex by S. Gordon; Infectious diseases in adolescence by P. J. Landrigan, C. D. Carter, J. F. Modlin, R. H. Henderson, and P. Q. Edwards; and Contraception and conception by L. L. Cedarquist.

Luker, K. *Taking chances: Abortion and the decision not to contracept.* Berkeley: University of California Press, 1976.

Maccoby, E. E., & Jacklin, C. N. *The psychology of sex differences.* Stanford: Stanford University Press, 1974.
Monumental volume, complete with annotated bibliography of pertinent research. Well written and thoroughly researched, it is a basic source.

Marine, G. *A male guide to women's liberation.* New York: Holt, Rinehart and Winston, 1973.
The first important book which declares that the women's liberation movement also involves the liberation of men.

Mazur, R. *The new intimacy—open ended marriage and alternate lifestyles.* Boston: Beacon Press, 1973.
Another good volume on sexual variety that is useful for helping parents appreciate the changing values about relationships their children are experiencing.

Mazur, R. *Commonsense sex.* Boston: Beacon Press, 1968.

McCarthy, B. *What you still don't know about male sexuality.* New York: Thomas Y. Crowell Co., 1977.
The best of the male books on sexuality by one of the authors of the pioneering *Sexual awareness.*

McCarthy, B. W., Ryan, M., & Johnson, F. A. *Sexual awareness: A practical approach.* San Francisco: Boy & Fraser, 1975.

McCary, J. L. *Human sexuality,* 3rd ed. New York: D. Van Nostrand Co., 1978.
Still one of the best books on sexuality for college students.

McCary, J. L. *Sexual myths and fallacies.* New York: Van Nostrand Reinhold, 1971.
The best collection of myths available, accompanied by detailed explanations.

McCuen, G. E., & Bender, D. L. *The sexual revolution.* Minneapolis: Greenhaven Press, 1972.

369

Miller, D. *Adolescence: Psychology, psychopathology, and psychotherapy.* New York: Jason Aronson, 1974.

Money, J., & Tucker, P. *Sexual signatures: On being a man or a woman.* Boston: Little, Brown & Co., 1972.

Money, J., & Ehrhardt, A. A. *Man/woman, boy/girl: Differentiation and dimorphism of gender identity from conception to maturity.* Baltimore: The Johns Hopkins University Press, 1972.
Very important review of the myths about sexual stereotyping and many of the so-called human nature and biological differences between men and women.

Money, J., & Musaph, H. (eds.). *Handbook of sexuality.* North Holland: Excerpta Medica/Elsevier, 1977.

Morrison, E., & Price, M. U. *Values in sexuality.* New York: Hart Publishing, 1974.
A variety of exercises and interpersonal situations to improve communication about sexuality.

Moustakas, C. E. *Loneliness and love.* Englewood Cliffs, N.J.: Prentice-Hall, 1972.

National Academy of Sciences. *Toward a national policy for children and families.* Washington, D.C.: National Academy of Sciences, 1976.

Newman, S. H., & Thompson, V. D. (eds.). *Population psychology: Research and educational issues.* Washington, D.C.: Superintendent of Documents, U.S. Government Printing Office, 1976.

Nichols, J. *Men's liberation: A new definition of masculinity.* New York: Penguin, 1975.
Excellent examination of how traditional sex roles can encourage troubled relationships.

Oakley, A. *Sex, gender and society.* New York: Harper & Row, 1972.
Emphasizes the important factor of culture in determination of sex roles.

Oaks, W., Melchiode, G. A., and Ficher, I. (eds.). *Sex and the life cycle.* New York: Grune & Stratton Academic Press, 1976.

Offit, A. K. *The sexual self.* Philadelphia: J. B. Lippincott, 1977.

O'Neill, N., & O'Neill, G. *Open marriage.* New York: Avon, 1973.
An extremely important book for stimulating discussion in high school home economics and college marriage courses, as well as in women's studies.

Osofsky, H. *The pregnant teenager.* Springfield, Ill.: Charles C. Thomas, 1972.
A careful review of literature with some important humanistic conclusions by a gynecologist/obstetrician who has had much experience working with teenage girls.

Otto, H. A. (ed.). *The new sexuality.* Palo Alto: Science and Behavior Books, 1971.
A collection of articles by leading authorities on sex, covering such topics as premarital sex, the affair, sex as fun, nudity, sexual lifestyles, group marriage, homosexuality.

370

Otto, H. A. (ed.). *The new sex education: The sex educator's resource book.* Chicago: Association Press/Follett Publishing Co., 1978.

Paulsen, K., & Kuhn, R. A. *The woman's almanac.* New York: J. B. Lippincott, 1975.
Compendium of facts and articles from health to finances.

Peck, E., & Senderowitz, J. (eds.). *Pronatalism: The myth of mom & apple pie.* New York: Thomas Y. Crowell, 1974.

Petras, J. W. *The social meaning of human sexuality.* Boston: Allyn and Bacon, 1978.

Pierce, R. I. *Single and pregnant.* Boston: Beacon Press, 1970.
An excellent handbook for single, pregnant girls and those who counsel them. It discusses available alternatives and includes a list of sources for counseling and medical aid.

Pleck, J., & Sawyer, J. (eds.). *Men and masculinity.* Englewood Cliffs, N.J.: Prentice-Hall, 1974.

Pomeroy, W. B. *Your child and sex: A guide for parents.* New York: Dell, 1974.
Discusses communication problems in sex and offers suggestions for helping parents to become more open talking about sex.

Pomeroy, W. *Boys and sex.* New York: Delacorte Press, 1968.

Pomeroy, W. *Girls and sex.* New York: Delacorte Press, 1969.

Project teen concern, (HSA) 78-5600. Rockville, Md.: U.S. Department of Health, Education and Welfare, Public Health Services, Health Services Administration, Bureau of Community Health Services, 1978.

Qualls, C. B., Wincze, J. P., & Barlow, D. H. (eds.). *The prevention of sexual disorders: Issues and approaches.* Providence, R.I.: Brown University, 1978.

Readings in human sexuality 78/79, annual editions. Guilford, Conn.: The Dushkin Publishing Co., 1978.

Roberts, J. I. *Beyond intellectual sexism—a new woman, a new reality.* New York: McKay, 1976.
Collection of feminist essays, including several cross-cultural articles on the continuing inequality of the sexes.

Rosenzweig, N., & Pearsall, F. P. (eds.). *Sex education for the health professional: A curriculum guide.* New York: Grune & Stratton Academic Press, 1978.

Rubin, I., & Calderwood, D. *A family guide to sex.* New York: Signet, 1973.
An examination of the issues surrounding sex education in the home as well as supportive agencies, such as the church and school. A good primer for parents.

Salk, L. *Preparing for parenthood.* New York: Bantam, 1975.

Salk, L. *What every child would like his parents to know.* New York: David McKay Co., 1972.
This commonsense book on promoting a child's emotional health in-

371

cludes chapters on sex education and sex experience that answer questions parents have about providing sex information and guidance.

Schiller, P. *Creative approach to sex education and counseling,* 2nd ed. Washington, D.C.: American Association of Sex Educators, Counselors, and Therapists, 1978.

Schlegel, A. (ed.). *Sexual stratification: A cross-cultural view.* New York: Columbia University Press, 1977.

Schlesinger, B. (ed.). *Sexual behavior in Canada: Patterns and problems.* Toronto: University of Toronto Press, 1977.

Schofield, M. *The sexual behaviour of young adults.* London: Allen Lane, 1973.
A seven-year follow-up study of eighteen-year-olds in England.

Sears, H. D. *The sex radicals.* Lawrence, Kan.: The Regents Press, 1977.

Semmens, J. P., & Krantz, K. E. *The adolescent experience.* New York: Collier-Macmillan, 1970.
Covers various aspects of the adolescent experience, including the problems counselors have in understanding adolescents.

Sherman, A. *The rape of the A.P.E.* Chicago: Playboy Press, 1975.

Silverstein, C. *A family matter: A parents' guide to homosexuality.* New York: McGraw-Hill, 1977.

Slater, P. *Footholds: Understanding the shifting family and sexual tensions in our culture.* Boston: Beacon Press, 1977.

Somerville, R. M. *Introduction to family life and sex education.* Englewood Cliffs, N.J.: Prentice-Hall, 1972.
A modern look at the family, its changing structure and roles. Somerville also discusses sex education in the context of the family and the larger society.

Sorensen, R. C. *Adolescent sexuality in contemporary America.* New York: World Publishing, 1973.
An important in-depth study of personal values and sexual behavior of a national sample of 411 adolescents aged thirteen to nineteen. Though flawed in some respects, it is a significant research effort in the study of sexual behavior among American teenagers.

Steen, E. B., & Price, J. H. *Human sex and sexuality.* New York: John Wiley & Sons, 1977.

Storaska, F. *How to say no to a rapist and survive.* New York: Warner Books, 1976.

Tripp, C. A. *The homosexual matrix.* New York: McGraw-Hill, 1975.
The best book on the subject, drawing on anthropology, biology, religion, and sociology.

Urban and Rural Systems Associates. *Improving family planning services for teenagers.* San Francisco: URSA, 1976.
Final report of a federally sponsored study covering forty clinics in eight major cities.

Veatch, R. M. (ed.). *Population policy and ethics: The American tradition.* New York: Irvington Publishers, 1977.

Westoff, C. F., & Westoff, L. A. *From now to zero: Fertility, contraception, and abortion in America.* Boston: Little, Brown & Co., 1971.
An important survey by the former head of the National Commission on Population Growth and the American Future.

Wolfe, J. L., & Brand, E. (eds.). *Twenty years of rational therapy.* New York: Institute for Rational Living, 1977.

Woods, N. F. *Human sexuality in health and illness.* Saint Louis: C. V. Mosby Co., 1975.

World Health Organization. *Education and treatment in human sexuality: The training of health professionals,* Technical Report No. 52. New York: WHO Publications, 1975.

Zilbergeld, B. *Male sexuality—a guide to sexual fulfillment.* Boston: Little, Brown & Co., 1978.

Articles Ard, B. Premarital sexual experience: A longitudinal study. *Journal of Sex Research,* 1974, *10* (1), 32–39.

Arnold, C. B. The sexual behavior of inner city adolescent condom users. *Journal of Sex Research,* 1972, *8* (4), 298–309.

Baldwin, W. H. Adolescent pregnancy and childbearing—growing concerns for Americans. *Population Bulletin,* 1976 *31* (2), (entire issue).

Bidgood, F. E. The effects of sex education: A summary of the literature. *SIECUS Newsletter,* 1973, *1* (4), 11.

Byrne, D. A pregnant pause in the sexual revolution. *Psychology Today,* July 1977, 67–68.

Canfield, L. Am I normal? *The Humanist,* March/April 1978, 10–12.

Caplan, H. Roundtable: Contraception for teenagers. *Medical Aspects of Human Sexuality,* 1972, *6* (10), 191, 193–195, 199, 203, 207, 209, 212–214.

Cassell, C. A., & Dearth, P. B. An assessment of public health nurses' personal attitudes relative to human sexuality. *Journal of Sex Education and Therapy,* 1977, *3* (2), 43–48.

Cutright, P. Illegitimacy: Myths, causes and cures. *Family Planning Perspectives,* 1971, *3* (1), 25–48.

Cutright, P. Historical and contemporary trends in illegitimacy. *Archives of Sexual Behavior,* 1972, *2* (2), 97–118.

Cvetkovich, G., Grote, B., Bjorseth, A., & Sarkissian, J. On the psychology of adolescents' use of contraception. *Journal of Sex Research,* 1975, *11* (3), 256–271.

Darrow, W. W. Rising rates of gonococcal infections as the use of condoms diminishes. Proceedings of the Fertility Control Conference sponsored by Emory University School of Medicine, Pine Isle, Ga., June 14, 1977.

Diamond, M. Mass sex education: Student and community reaction. *Journal of Sex Education and Therapy,* 1976, *2* (2), 1–11.

Donovan, P. Student newspapers and the first amendment: Their right to publish sex-related articles. *Family Planning/Population Reporter,* 1977, *6* (2), 16–17; 23.

Finkel, M. L., & Finkel, D. J. Sexual and contraceptive knowledge, attitudes, and behavior of male adolescents. *Family Planning Perspectives,* 1975, *7* (6), 256–260.

Fox, G. L. Sex role attitudes as predictors of contraceptive use. Paper presented at annual meeting of National Council on Family Relations, Salt Lake City, Utah, August 20–23, 1975.

Gagnon, J. H. Sex research and social change. *Archives of sexual behavior,* 1975, *4* (2), 111–141.

Gilbert, R., & Matthews, V. G. Young males' attitudes toward condom use. In M. A. Redford, G. W. Duncan, and D. J. Prager (eds.), *The Condom: Increasing utilization in the United States.* San Francisco: San Francisco Press, 1974, 164–172.

Gilligan, C., Kohlberg, L., Lerner, J., & Belenky, M. Moral reasoning about sexual dilemmas. In *Technical Report of the U.S. Commission on Obscenity and Pornography,* vol. I. Washington, D.C.: U.S. Government Printing Office, 1970, 141–174.

Goldsmith, S., Gabrielson, M., Mathews, V., & Potts, L. Teenagers, sex, and contraception. *Family Planning Perspectives,* 1972, *4* (1), 32–38.

Gordon, S. Counselors and changing sexual values. *Personnel and Guidance Journal,* March 1976, 362–364.
Reprint available from Ed-U Press, 123 Fourth Street, N.W., Charlottesville, Va., 22901.

Gordon, S. The egalitarian family is alive and well. *The Humanist,* 1975, *35* (3), 18–19.

Gordon, S. Why sex education belongs in the home. *PTA Magazine,* February 1974, 15–17.

Gordon, S. It's not okay to be anti-gay. *The Witness,* October 1977, 10–13; 16.

Gordon, S., & Scales, P. The myth of the normal outlet. *Journal of Pediatric Psychology,* 1977, *2* (3), 101–103.

Gordon, S., & Scales, P. Preparing today's youth for tomorrow's family. In G. Albee and J. Joffe (eds.), *The primary prevention of psychopathology, Vol. III: Adolescence.* Hanover, N.H.: University Press of New England (in press).

Gordon, S., & Snyder, C. Tomorrow's family. *Journal of Current Social Issues,* 1978, *15* (1), 31–34.

Green, C. P., & Potteiger, K. Teenage pregnancy: A major problem for minors. Four-page fact sheet available from Zero Population Growth, 1346 Connecticut Avenue, N.W., Washington, D.C. 20036.

Griffiths, J. Can the rapist be cured? *Sexual Medicine Today,* 1977, *1* (2), 15–20.

Hacker, S. *The effect of situational and interactional aspects of sexual encounters on premarital contraceptive behavior.* Ann Arbor: University of Michigan, School of Public Health, Department of Population Planning, 1976.

Hale, D., Shavers, D. J., Arnold, S. R., & Fryer, M. A. *An innovative approach for reaching youth: A professionally performed one act play.* Chicago: Planned Parenthood, 1977.

Hofmann, A. D. Adolescent, sex, and education. *New York University Education Quarterly,* 1977, 7–14.

Honig, A. What we need to know to help teenage parents. *The Family Coordinator,* 1978, *27* (2), 113–120.

House, E. A., & Goldsmith, S. Planned Parenthood services for the young teenager. *Family Planning Perspectives,* 1972, *4* (2), 27–31.

Juhasz, A. M. Changing patterns of premarital sexual behavior. *Intellect,* April 1976, 511–514.

Juhasz, A. M. A chain of sexual decision making. *Family Coordinator,* 1975, *24* (1), 43–51.

Jurich, A. D., & Jurich, J. A. The effects of cognitive moral development upon the selection of premarital sexual standards. *Journal of Marriage and the Family,* 1974, *36* (4), 736–741.

Kantner, J. F., & Zelnik, M. Contraception and pregnancy: Experience of young unmarried women in the United States. *Family Planning Perspectives,* 1973, *5* (1), 21–35.

Kantner, J. F., & Zelnik, M. Sexual experience of young, unmarried women in the United States. *Family Planning Perspectives,* 1972, *4* (1), 9–18.

Lane, M. E. Contraception for adolescents. *Family Planning Perspectives,* 1973, *5* (1), 19–20.

Lieberman, E. J. Leveling with young people about sex. *Journal of the American Medical Association,* 1969, 1, 210.

Luker, K. Contraceptive risktaking and abortion: Results and implications of a San Francisco Bay area study. *Studies in Family Planning,* 1977, *8* (8), 190–196.

McCoy, K. You and your sexuality: Your rights and responsibilities. *Teen,* August 1977, 24–25.

Miller, P. Y., & Simon, W. Adolescent sexual behavior: Context and change. *Social Problems,* 1974, *22* (1), 58–76.

Mosher, D. L. Sex differences, sex experience, sex guilt, and explicitly sexual films. *Journal of Social Issues,* 1973, *29* (3), 95–122.

Needle, R. H. Factors affecting contraceptive practices of high school and college-age students. *Journal of School Health,* 1977, *47* (6), 340–345.

Offer, D. Sexual behavior of a group of normal adolescents. *Medical Aspects of Human Sexuality,* 1971, *5* (9), 40–49.

Oskamp, S., Mindick, B., & Berger, D. Longitudinal study of success versus failure in contraceptive planning. Paper presented at annual meeting of the American Psychological Association, Chicago, September 1975.

Osmond, M. W., & Martin, P. Y. Sex and sexism: A comparison of male and female sex role attitudes. *Journal of Marriage and the Family,* 1975, *37* (4), 744–759.

Paul, E. W., Pilpel, H. F., & Wechsler, N. F. Pregnancy, teenagers, and the law, 1976. *Family Planning Perspectives,* 1976, *8* (1), 16–21.

Prescott, J. W. Abortion or the unwanted child: A choice for a humanistic society. *The Humanist,* March/April 1975, 11–15.

Presser, H. B. Early motherhood: Ignorance or bliss? *Family Planning Perspectives,* 1974, *6* (1), 8–15.

Reichelt, P. A. The desirability of involving adolescents in sex education planning. *Journal of School Health,* 1977, *47* (2), 99–104.

Reichelt, P. A., & Werley, H. H. Contraception, abortion, and venereal disease: Teenagers' knowledge and the effect of education. *Family Planning Perspectives,* 1975, *7* (2), 83–88.

Reiss, I. L., Banwart, A., & Foreman, H. Premarital contraceptive usage: A study and some theoretical explorations. *Journal of Marriage and the Family,* 1975, *37* (3), 619–630.

Rosenberg, P. P., & Rosenberg, L. M. Sex education for adolescents and their families. *Journal of Sex and Marital Therapy,* 1976, *2* (1), 53–57.

Ross, S. The youth values project. Washington, D.C.: Population Institute, 1978.

Rutherford, R. N. Contraceptive use: How to advise teenagers. *Osteopathic Physician,* 1972, *39* (5), 99–102.

Scales, P. Males and morals: Teenage contraceptive behavior amid the double standard. *Family Coordinator,* 1977, *26* (3), 210–222.

Scales, P. How we guarantee the ineffectiveness of sex education. *SIECUS Report,* 1978, *6* (4), 1–3.

Scales, P. Youth and the future of ignorance. Paper presented at annual meeting of American Association of Psychiatric Services for Children, Washington, D.C., November 18, 1977.

Scales, P., Etelis, R., & Levitz, N. Male involvement in contraceptive decision making: The role of birth control counselors. *Journal of Community Health,* 1977, *3* (3), 54–60.

Scales, P., & Everly, K. A community sex education program for parents. *Family Coordinator,* 1977, *26* (1), 37–45.

Scanzoni, J. Sex role change and influences on birth intentions. *Journal of Marriage and the Family,* 1976, *38* (1), 43–60.

Sex and today's teenager. *Circus,* 29 September, 1977, 20–21.

Shah, F., Zelnik, M., & Kantner, J. F. Unprotected intercourse among unwed teenagers. *Family Planning Perspectives,* 1975, *7* (1), 39–44.

Somerville, R. M. Family life and sex education in the turbulent sixties. *Journal of Marriage and the Family,* 1971, *33* (1), 11–35.

Students victorious in Fairfax suit. *Student Press Law Center Reports,* 1978, *6,* 3–4.

Stycos, J. M. Desexing birth control. *Family Planning Perspectives,* 1977, *9* (6), 286–292.

Syntex Laboratories. An in-depth look at the male role in family planning. *The Family Planner,* 1977, *8* (2–3), 4.

Teenage pregnancy: Whose problem, whose responsibility? New York: Planned Parenthood, 1978.

Teen-age sex: Letting the pendulum swing. *Time,* 21 August, 1972, 34–38; 40.

Teevan, J. J. Reference groups and premarital sexual behavior. *Journal of Marriage and the Family,* 1972, *34* (2), 283–291.

Vener, A. M., Stewart, C. S., & Hager, D. L. The sexual behavior of adolescents in Middle America: Generational and American-British comparisons. *Journal of Marriage and the Family,* 1972, *34* (4), 696–705.

Wills, G. Measuring the impact of erotica. *Psychology Today,* August 1977, 30–34; 74–76.

Yarber, W. L. New directions in venereal disease education. *The Family Coordinator,* 1978, *27* (2), 121–128.

Zelnik, M., & Kantner, J. F. Sexual and contraceptive experience of young, unmarried women in the United States, 1976 and 1971. *Family Planning Perspectives,* 1977, *9* (2), 55–71.

Zelnik, M., & Kantner, J. F. First pregnancies to women aged 15–19: 1976 and 1971. *Family Planning Perspectives,* 1978, *10* (1), 11–20.

Pamphlets
Abortion clinic directory. New York: American Civil Liberties Union, 1976.

Adolescence for adults. Report by Blue Cross and Blue Shield of Western New York.
A collection of essays to help adults understand the concerns of young people.

The Alan Guttmacher Institute. *11 million teenagers.* New York: Planned Parenthood, November 1976.
Comprehensive description of the problem of adolescent pregnancy in the United States. An essential resource.

American Social Health Association. *Body pollution.* Palo Alto, Calif.: ASHA. 1978.
Free pamphlet on venereal disease.

Fact Sheet. Available from Student Coalition for Relevant Sex Education, 300 Park Avenue South, Fourth Floor, New York, N.Y. 10010.

377

Ferrigo, M., & Southard, H. *Parents' privilege* (for parents of young children); *A story about you* (for grades four, five, and six); *Finding yourself* (for junior high school); *Preparation for marriage* (for ages sixteen to twenty); and *Facts aren't enough* (for adults who have responsibility for children). Chicago: American Medical Association and Washington, D.C.: National Education Association.

Gordon, S., & Dickman, I. R. *Sex education: The parents' role,* Pamphlet # 549. New York: Public Affairs Committee, 1977.
Answers questions, discusses how to become an askable parent, what to do if your child doesn't ask, and includes a list of resources for parents.

Hayes, M. V. *A boy today . . . a man tomorrow.* Available from Optimist International, 4494 Lindell Boulevard, St. Louis, Mo. 63108.

Landers, A. *Teenage sex and 10 ways to cool it!* Chicago: Field Enterprises, 1976.

Landers, A. *High school sex and how to deal with it—a guide for teens and their parents.*
Available from PO Box 11995, Chicago, Ill. 60611. Enclose $.50 and a large, self-addressed, stamped envelope.

Lyman, M. *Sex education at home—a guide for parents; Growing up—'specially for pre-teens and young teens; Teen questions about sex and answers.* Prepared by Planned Parenthood, Syracuse, N.Y.

Millar, H. *Approaches to adolescent health care in the 1970s,* Publication No. (HSA) 76–5014 Rockville, Md.: USDHEW, 1975.

Mothers too soon. New York: Draper World Population Fund, 1975.

National Parent-Teachers Association. *The fine art of parenting: A PTA priority.* Prepared by PTA, Chicago.
Free pamphlet describing the need and suggested curriculum for parenthood education.

Attention is needed, action is called for. Prepared by National YWCA Resource Center on Women, New York.
A study of teenagers' needs as expressed by over 1,000 teenagers across the country.

Planned births, the future of the family and the quality of American life: Towards a comprehensive national policy and program. New York: Alan Guttmacher Institute, 1977.

The positive policy handbook. New York: Planned Parenthood, 1975.
Collection of organization statements on sexual health and education services for youth.

The professional training and preparation of sex counselors. Washington, D. C.: American Association of Sex Educators, Counselors, and Therapists, 1974.

Public Affairs Committee. 381 Park Avenue South, New York, N.Y. 10016. This nonprofit group has some very useful pamphlets for parents:

Bienvenu, M. J., Sr. *Parent-teenager communication—bridging the generation gap,* Pamphlet No. 438 (a good little book);

Bienvenu, M. J., Sr. *Talking it over at home—problems in family communication,* Pamphlet No. 410 (an effectively written booklet on improving the process of intrafamilial communication);

Hymes, J. L., Jr. *How to tell your child about sex,* Pamphlet No. 149 (sensible, enlightened; aimed at parents of young children);

Irwin, T. *The rights of teenagers as patients,* Pamphlet No. 480 (a brief, but thorough all-around guide to the status of teenage legal rights);

Schwartz, J. V. *Health care for the adolescent,* Pamphlet No. 463.

Religious Coalition for Abortion Rights. *The abortion rights issue: How we stand.* Washington, D.C.: RCAR, February 1976.
Compendium of positions taken on abortion by over twenty religious groups.

Scales, P. (Ed) *Searching for alternatives to teenage pregnancy.* Baltimore: National Alliance for Optional Parenthood, 1978.

School-age parenthood: Consequences for babies, mothers, fathers, grandparents, and others, Bulletin #667. Pullman, Wash.: Cooperative Extension Service, Washington State University, April 1976.

Sex, love and intimacy—whose life style? New York: Human Sciences Press.

SIECUS study guide series, especially No. 1 (*Sex education*), No. 5 (*Premarital sexual standards*), No. 13 (*Concerns of parents about sex education*), and No. 14 (*Teenage pregnancy: Prevention and treatment*). New York: Human Sciences Press.

Suggestions for defense against extremist attack. Prepared by Commission on Professional Rights and Responsibilities, National Education Association, Washington, D.C.
Helpful for working with controversy and community opinion; based on sex education in the schools but insightful for parent group organizers as well.

Syracuse University Student Committee on Human Sexuality. *Sex in a plain brown wrapper.* Syracuse, N.Y.: Institute for Family Research and Education, 1973.

World Health Organization. Technical report series, especially No. 572 (*Education and treatment in human sexuality: The training of health professionals*) and No. 583 (*Pregnancy and abortion in adolescence*). Available from Q Corporation, 49 Sheridan Avenue, Albany, N.Y. 12210.

Youth and the Family. Center for Youth Development and Research, University of Minnesota, 48 McNeal Hall, St. Paul, Minn. 55108.
A 1976 pamphlet describing goals of parent education for sexuality and moral development, and possible community responses to youth conflicts.

You've changed the combination. Prepared by Rocky Mountain Planned Parenthood, Denver.
Great pamphlet on sex roles. Also, *So you don't want to be a sex object;* a pamphlet especially for women, but should be read by everyone.

Zeroing in on school-age pregnancy. Prepared by Child Welfare League of America, New York.

Zorabedian, R. *The view from our side: Sex and birth control for men.* Publications Department, Family Planning Program, Box 24069, Butler Street, S.E., Atlanta, Ga. 30303.

Canadian Pamphlets and Guides

Facts and fancy—about birth control, sex education and family planning. Ottawa: Family Planning Directorate, Tunney's Pasture, Ontario, 1976.
Great pamphlet on misconceptions about sexuality, with detailed factual answers.

Sex education—a teacher's guide. Ottawa: Ministry of National Health and Welfare, 1977.

Australia

The best source for Australian publications is Family Life Movement of Australia, 150 Concord Road, North Stratlefield, New South Wales, 2137.

Training Guide

Sex education for adolescents and youth. Prepared by American Association of Sex Educators, Counselors, and Therapists, Washington, D.C.
Emphasis on strategies and techniques for teaching adolescents about preventive health care.

Selected Journal Issues Devoted to Sex

American Journal of Public Health, 1971, *61* (4).
Includes five papers on adolescent sexuality.

Critic, March/April 1972. Available from 180 N. Wabash Avenue, Chicago, Ill. 60601.
This issue on sex of a contemporary Catholic magazine is worth the $1.00 cost ($1.25 by mail).

Family Coordinator, 1976, *25* (4).
Published by the National Council on Family Relations, Minneapolis, the entire issue is devoted to fatherhood.

Family Planner, 1970, *3* (4).
Published by Syntex Laboratories, Palo Alto, Calif. See also March/April 1977, *8* (2–3), The male role in family planning, and Spring 1978, *9* (2–3), Teenage sexuality and family planning.

Family Planning Perspectives, 1972, *4* (4) and 1976, *8* (4).
Published by Alan Guttmacher Institute, New York. See also 1978,

10 (4), Teenage mothers and fathers; Early childbearing and subsequent fertility, Contraceptive services for adolescents, Teenage childbirth and welfare dependency. An important issue.

How's your sex life? *Ms.* (New York), November 1976.

Humanist, 1978, *38* (2).
Articles on sex research, normality, sexual imagery, sex roles, sex and the law, adolescents and sex.

Journal of Clinical Child Psychology, 1974, *3* (3). Adolescent sexuality.

Journal of Current Social Issues, 1978, *15* (1). Sex Is aweful.
Articles on tomorrow's family, the media, teenage motherhood, religion. Contains an excellent bibliography.

Journal of Research and Development in Education, Fall 1976, *10* (entire issue).

Journal of School Health. School-age parents. Kent, O.: American School Health Association, 1975.
Devoted to issues of prevention, legislative changes, and comprehensive services.

Journal of Sex Research, 1969, *5* (3).
Issue devoted to sex and the young. See also, 1973, *9* (2). Devoted to adolescents in the 1970s.

Journal of Social Issues, 1973, *29* (3).
Published by Society for the Study of Social Issues, Ann Arbor, Mich., this issue is devoted to obscenity and pornography. See also 1976, *32* (3), on sex roles, and 1977, *33* (2), on social psychological issues of sexual behavior.

Personnel and Guidance Journal. The counselor and human sexuality. March 1976.
Issue on sexuality in teaching and in counseling.

Population Bulletin, 1976, *31* (2). Adolescent pregnancy and childbearing—growing concerns for Americans by W. H. Baldwin.

Society, 1977, *14* (5). The sexual bond. Available from Box A, Rutgers, The State University, New Brunswick, N.J. 08903.

Teen Special. Discover yourself.
Published by Petersen Publishing Co., this issue is packed with informative articles about living and growing—and fun, revealing quizzes that allow young people to participate in the process of self-discovery. Ninety-six pages.

Proceedings *Adolescent fertility.* D. J. Bogue (ed.). Proceedings of the First Inter-Hemispheric Conference on Adolescent Fertility, 1976. Airlie, Va.: Inter-American Center, 1977.

Adolescent sexuality and health care: A national concern. Report on the Wingspread Conference. Syracuse, N.Y.: Institute for Family Research and Education, 1974.

An exploration of the limits of contraception. Proceedings of the Ontario Science Centre Conference. Don Mills, Ontario, Canada: Department of Public Affairs, Ortho Pharmaceutical (Canada) Ltd., 1975.

The male role in family planning. Sacramento: Planned Parenthood Association, June 1975.

Problems of the adolescent as related to pregnancy and birth control. New York: Adolescent Clinic, Department of Pediatrics and Department of Obstetrics and Gynecology, The Jewish Hospital and Medical Center of Brooklyn, May 2, 1971.

Proceedings of the fertility control conference. Pine Isle, Ga.: Emory University School of Medicine, June 14, 1977.

Proceedings of the population workshop on who shall live and how? Control over birth and death and the quality of life. Charlotte: The University of North Carolina, Institute for Urban Studies and Community Service, April 21–23, 1971.

Teenagers and contraceptive services. New York: Maternity, Infant Care/Family Planning Projects, New York City Health Department, January 28–29, 1972.

Survey   *School health in America.* Prepared by American School Health Association, Kent, O 44240.
A survey of state school health programs, 1978.

Journals and Newsletters   *Abortion Research Notes.* Available from Transnational Family Research Institute, 8307 Whitman Drive, Bethesda, Md. 20034.
A worldwide review of programs, legislation, and resources.

Abortion Surveillance and *VD Fact Sheet.* Available from the Center for Disease Control, Atlanta, Ga. 30333.
Annual summaries of national and regional statistics.

Alternatives: Marriage, Family and Changing Life Styles. Available from Sage Publications, 275 So. Beverly Drive, Beverly Hills, Calif. 90212.

Alternatives in Marriage and the Family. Available from the Alternative Marriage and Relationship Council of the U.S. (AMRCUS), 909 69th Avenue, Philadelphia, Pa. 19126.

Archives of Sexual Behavior. Available from Plenum Publishing Corp., 227 W. 17th Street, New York, N.Y. 10011.

Behavior Today. Available from *Behavior Today,* 1156 15th Street, N.W., Washington, D.C. 20005.
Weekly newsletter covering psychological and social issues.

British Journal of Sexual Medicine. Available from 359 Strand, London WC2R OHP, England.

COFO Memo. Published by the Coalition of Family Organizations; available from American Association of Marriage and Family Counselors, 225 Yale Avenue, Claremont, Calif. 91711.

Quarterly describing how the federal government is likely to affect family life in the U.S.

Concerns. Monthly newsletter available from Midwest Family Planning Association, 3746 W. Irving Park Road, Chicago, Ill. 60618.

Current Population Reports. Occasional series available from U.S. Department of Commerce, Bureau of the Census, Washington, D.C. 20036.

Equilibrium. New publication available from Zero Population Growth, 4080 Fabian Way, Palo Alto, Calif. 94303.

The Family Coordinator. Journal available from National Council on Family Relations (NCFR), 1219 University Avenue, S.E., Minneapolis, Minn. 55414.
Contains descriptions of community programs, book and resource reviews, and research important for program organizers.

Family Planner. Available from Syntex Laboratories, 3491 Hillview Avenue, Palo Alto, Calif. 94304.

Family Planning Perspectives. Available from Alan Guttmacher Institute, 515 Madison Avenue, New York, N.Y. 10022.
Bimonthly publication of research, legislative, and scientific trend review.

Family Planning/Population Reporter. Bimonthly legislative report available from Planned Parenthood Federation of America, 1666 K Street, N.W., Washington, D.C. 20006.

Forum: The International Journal of Human Relations. Monthly publication available from Forum International Ltd., 909 Third Avenue, New York, N. Y. 10022.

Getting It Together. Newsletter available from Youth and Student Affairs, Planned Parenthood Federation of America, 810 7th Avenue, New York, N.Y. 10019.

Impact. Annual newsletter of National Family Sex Education Week available from Institute for Family Research and Education, 760 Ostrom Avenue, Syracuse, N.Y. 13210.

Intercom. Monthly international newsletter on population available from Population Reference Bureau, 1754 N Street, N.W., Washington, D.C. 20036.

Journal of Homosexuality. Available from Harvard Press, 149 Fifth Avenue., New York, N.Y. 10010.

Journal of School Health. Available from American School Health Association, Kent, O. 44240.

Journal of Marriage and the Family. Available from National Council on Family Relations, 1219 University Avenue, S.E., Minneapolis, Minn. 55414.

Journal of Sex Education and Therapy. Available from American Association of Sex Educators, Counselors, and Therapists, 5010 Wisconsin Avenue, N.W., Suite 304, Washington, D.C. 20016.
Some research, resource reviews, and articles about clinical and community work.

383

Journal of Sex Research. Available from Society for the Scientific Study of Sex, Inc., 208 Daffodil Road, Glen Burnie, Md. 21061.

Law and Population Monograph Series. Available from the Law and Population Programme, Fletcher School of Law and Diplomacy, Tufts University , Medford, Mass. 02155.
Includes The world's laws and practices on population and sexuality education and Pregnancy and abortion in adolescence: Legal aspects.

Medical Aspects of Human Sexuality. Available from Hospital Publications, Inc., 360 Lexington Avenue, New York, N.Y. 10017.

Ms. 370 Lexington Avenue, New York, N.Y. 10017.

National Abortion Rights Action League Newsletter. National Abortion Rights Action League, 706 Seventh Street, S.E., Washington, D.C. 20003.

The National Exchange. Periodic newsletter describing crisis and health-oriented resources available from 706 Seventh Street, S.E., Washington, D.C. 20003.

The National Reporter (monthly newsletter): The right to choose: Facts on abortion; 15 facts you should know about abortion; and Teenage pregnancy: A major problem for minors. All available from Zero Population Growth at 1346 Connecticut Avenue, N.W., Washington, D.C. 20036.
ZPG also staffs a hotline you can call for information on the latest about population problems and action: 202-785-0092.

People. Available from IPPF Distribution Dept., 18-20 Lower Revent Street, London SW1Y 4 PW, England.
A quarterly publication reporting world-wide efforts to balance resources and population to promote planned parenthood, and to improve the human condition.

Planned Parenthood News. High-quality newsletter available from Planned Parenthood, 810 Seventh Avenue, New York, N.Y. 10019.

Planned Parenthood-World Population Washington Memo. Available from Alan Guttmacher Institute, 515 Madison Avenue, New York, N.Y. 10022.

Population. Briefing papers on national and international population issues available from Population Crisis Committee, 1835 K Street, N.W., Washington, D.C. 20036.

Population Activist Newsletter. Resource publication available from Campus Action Program, Population Institute, 110 Maryland Avenue, N.E., Washington, D.C. 20002.
Also available is a list of resources prepared by the Resource Center of the Population Institute at the same address.

Population Bulletin. Available from Population Reference Bureau, 1337 Connecticut Avenue, Washington, D.C. 20036.

Population Issues. Excellent bimonthly publication available from Organization Liaison Division of the Population Institute, 110 Maryland Avenue, N.E., Washington, D.C. 20002.

Contains articles on population, the American family, women's rights, book reviews.

Population Reports. Available from the Population Information Program, Johns Hopkins University, 624 North Broadway, Baltimore, Md. 21205.

Pregnant Pause. Newsletter available from Population Institute Rock Project, 8961 Sunset Boulevard, Los Angeles, Calif. 90069.

Preterm. Newsletter available from Preterm University-Cedar Medical Building, 10900 Carnegie Avenue, Cleveland, O. 44106. The Fall 1976 issue (vol. 3, no. 1) is devoted to the issue of male involvement in sexual decision making and includes several bibliographies.

School Health Review. Available from American Association for Health, Physical Education and Recreation, 1201 16th Street, N.W., Washington, D.C. 20036.

Sex and Marital Therapy. Available from Human Sciences Press, 72 Fifth Avenue, New York, N.Y. 10011.

Sex News. Available from P. K. Houdek, 7140 Oak, Kansas City, Mo. 64114.
A monthly digest of resources.

Sex Roles, A Journal of Research. Available from Plenum Publishing, 227 W. 17th Street, New York, N.Y. 10011.

Sexual Health and Relationships. Available from PO Box 627, Northampton, Mass. 02060.

Sexual Law Reporter. Available from 1800 N. Highland Avenue, Suite 106, Los Angeles, Calif. 90028.
Includes reports of current developments in sexual law plus original articles on rape, transsexualism, abortion, prostitution, and homosexuality.

Sexual Medicine Today. Available from International Medical News Service, 600 New Hampshire Avenue, N.W., Washington, D.C. 20037.

Sexuality Today. Newsletter on current issues available from ATCOM, Inc., The ATCOM Building, 2315 Broadway, New York, N.Y. 10024.

Student Press Law Center Newsletter. Available from 1750 Pennsylvania Avenue, N.W., Room 1112, Washington, D.C. 20016. Information on the First Amendment as it affects student journalists and journalism teachers in high school and college.

Studies in Family Planning; Country Profiles; Reports on Population/Family Planning. All available from Population Council, 245 Park Avenue, New York, N.Y. 10017.

VD Spotlight. Available from Citizens Alliance for Awareness, 222 W. Adams, Suite 312, Chicago, Ill. 60606.

Vital and Health Statistics Series. Available from National Center for Health Statistics, Rockville, Md. 20782.

National, regional, and some local statistics on numerous health indices, including illegitimate pregnancy, birth rates, marriage, and divorce statistics. Send for the *Current listing and topic index to the vital and health statistics* for an overview of what is available. Also, for a registry of important federal and state statisticians, research directors, and health officers, ask for the annual *Directory of registration areas, United States and Canada.*

Worldwatch Paper Series. Available on yearly subscription basis from Worldwatch Institute, 1776 Massachusetts Avenue, N.W., Washington, D.C. 20036.
Covers global issues of population and ecology.

Religious Publications Concerned with Sexuality

Borowitz, E. B. *Choosing a sex ethic: A Jewish inquiry.* New York: Schocken Books, 1969.

Callahan, S. *Christian family planning and sex education.* Notre Dame, Ind.: Ave Maria Press, 1969.
An effort to develop a Christian approach to family planning, sex education, and premarital chastity.

Curran, C. E. *Contemporary problems in moral theology.* Notre Dame, Ind.: Fides Publishers, 1970.

Genné, W., compiler. *A synoptic of recent denominational statements on sexuality.* New York: National Council of Churches.

Goergen, D. *The sexual celibate.* Evanston, Ill.: Seabury Press, 1975.

Gordis, R. *Love and sex: A modern Jewish perspective.* New York: Farrar, Straus, and Giroux, 1978.
Drawing upon the thesis that there is no such thing as a Judeo-Christian heritage, Gordis examines how Judaism diverges from Christianity in love, sex, and marriage.

Greeley, A. *Love and play.* Chicago: Thomas More Press, 1975.

Hettlinger, R. S. *Growing up with sex.* New York: Seabury Press, 1971.
Written for preteens and young teens. Approaches values from the viewpoint of the individual and his own responsible decision making process.

Human sexuality: New directions in American Catholic thought. New York: Catholic Theological Society of the American Paulist Press, 1977.

Human sexuality: A preliminary study/the United Church of Christ. New York: The Pilgrim Press, 1978.

Human sexuality: The findings of the action research project in human sexuality. Minneapolis: The American Lutheran Church, 1978.

Keane, P. S. *Sexual morality: A Catholic perspective.* New York: Paulist Press, 1977.

Kennedy, E. *What a modern Catholic believes about sex and marriage.* Chicago: Thomas More Press, 1975.

386

Mace, D. *The Christian response to the sexual revolution.* New York: Abingdon Press, 1970.

McNeill, J. *The church and the homosexual.* Kansas City: Sheed, Andrews, and McMeel, 1976.

Nelson, J. B. *Embodiment: An approach to sexuality and Christian theology.* Minneapolis: Augsburg Publishing House, 1978.

Reuther, R. (ed.). *Religion and sexism.* New York: Simon and Schuster, 1974.

Taylor, M. (ed.). *Sex: Thoughts for contemporary Christians.* New York: Doubleday, 1972.

Wynn, J. C. (ed.). *Sex, family and society in theological focus.* Chicago: Association Press/Follett Publishing Co., 1970.

Sexuality and the Handicapped

Buscaglia, L. *The disabled and their parents: A counseling challenge.* Thorofare, N.J.: Charles B. Slack, 1975.

Dickman, I. R. *Sex education for disabled persons,* Public Affairs Pamphlet no. 531. New York: Public Affairs Council, 1975.

Exceptional Parent. Magazine devoted to the needs of children with disabilities available from Room 708, Statler Office Building, 20 Providence Street, Boston, Mass. 02116.

Gordon, S. *Living fully: A guide for young people with a handicap, their parents, their teachers, and professionals.* Charlottesville, Va.: Ed-U Press, 1975.

Greengross, W. *Entitled to love: The sexual and emotional needs of the handicapped.* London: Malaby Press Ltd., 1976.

Johnson, W. R. *Sex education and counseling of special groups: The mentally and physically handicapped and the elderly.* Springfield, Ill.: Charles C. Thomas, 1975.

Kempton, W. *Sex education for persons with disabilities that hinder learning: A teacher's guide.* N. Scituate, Mass.: Duxbury Press, 1976.

Kempton, W., Bass, M., & Gordon, S. *Love, sex, and birth control: A guide for the mentally retarded.* Syracuse, N.Y.: Institute for Family Research and Education, 1978. (Also in Spanish.)

Kempton, W., & Forman, R. *Guidelines for training in sexuality and the mentally handicapped.* Philadelphia: Planned Parenthood of Southeastern Pennsylvania, 1976.

Robinault, I. P. *Sex, society, and the disabled: A developmental inquiry into roles, reactions, and responsibilities.* New York: Harper & Row, 1978.

Sexuality and Disability. A new journal edited by Ami Sha'ked available from Human Science Press, New York.

SIECUS Report. The handicapped and sexual health. New York: Sex Information and Education Council of the United States, 1976.

Woods, N. F. *Human sexuality in health and illness.* St. Louis: C. V. Mosby Co., 1975.

Resource Centers

The Sex and Disability Unit, University of California, 814 Mission Street, 2nd Floor, San Francisco, Calif. 94103.

The Sex and Disability Project, George Washington University, 1828 L Street, N.W., Suite 704, Washington, D.C. 20036.

Films and Filmstrips for the Handicapped

Birth control methods: A simplified presentation for the mentally retarded. Available from Perennial Education, Inc., PO Box 855, Highland Park, Ill. 60035.

David Zelman's *Sex education curriculum for the mentally handicapped* combined with Winifred Kempton's slides, *Sexuality and the mentally handicapped.* Available from James Stanfield Film Associates, PO Box 851, Pasadena, Calif. 91102.

Don't tell the cripples about sex. Available from Multi-Media Center, 1523 Franklin, San Francisco, Calif. 94109.

The how and what of sex education for educables. Available from Hallmark Films, 1511 E. North Avenue, Baltimore, Md. 21213.

Like other people. Available from Perennial Education, Inc., PO Box 855, Highland Park, Ill. 60035.

On being sexual: For parents and professionals concerned with mentally retarded citizens. Available from James Stanfield Film Associates, PO Box 851, Pasadena, Calif. 91102.

Bibliographies

American Association of Sex Educators, Counselors, and Therapists, 5010 Wisconsin Avenue, Suite 304, Washington, D. C. 20016.

American Social Health Association, 260 Sheridan Avenue, Palo Alto, Calif. 94306.

Child Study Association of America, 853 Broadway, New York, N.Y. 10019.

D. C. Chapter of the World Population Society, 1650 No. 21st Road, No. 1, Arlington, Va. 22209. (April 1978 directory of the 84 population-related community organizations of the Washington, D. C. area.)

Human Sciences Press, 72 Fifth Avenue, New York, N.Y. 10011.

National Alliance for Optional Parenthood, 3 No. Liberty Street, Baltimore, Md. 21201.

National Council on Family Relations, 1219 University Avenue, S. E., Minneapolis, Minn. 55414.

Planned Parenthood-World Population, 810 Seventh Avenue, New York, N.Y. 10019.

Public Affairs Council, 381 Park Avenue, So., New York, N.Y. 10016.

U.S. Office of Education, Bureau of Elementary and Secondary Education, 400 Maryland Avenue, Washington, D.C. 20202.

Chelton, M. K. Adolescent sexuality: A self-training bibliography. *Emergency Librarian,* 1977, *5* (2).

Consortium on Early Childbearing and Childrearing. *Adolescent birth planning and sexuality: Abstracts of the literature.* Washington, D.C.: Child Welfare League of America, 1974.

Gordon, S. *Living fully: A guide for young people with a handicap, their parents, their teachers and professionals.* Charlottesville, Va.: Ed-U Press, 1975.

Interagency Task Force on Comprehensive Programs for School Age Parents. *A comprehensive approach to the problem of adolescent pregnancy: A general survey of the literature.* Washington, D.C.: U.S. Office of Education, January 1974.

Kinne, M., & Scully, P. *Annotated bibliography for teen projects.* New Orleans: Family Health Foundation.
A fine bibliography of many aspects of teenage sex education and birth control.

Multi-Media resource guide. San Francisco: Multi-Media Resource Center, 1976.

Office of Family Ministries, National Council of Churches of Christ in the U.S.A. *Resource guide for Christian education in sexuality.* New York: National Council of Churches, 1975.

Parenting Materials Information Center. *Parenting in 1976: A listing from PMIC.* Austin, Tex.: Southwest Educational Development Laboratory, May 1976.

Population education resources. Washington, D.C.: Zero Population Growth.
A very fine list of population and birth control sources and materials.

Population: International information on population problems and programs, demography, and development. New York: UNIPUB.

Resource Center on Sex Roles in Education. *A resource list for non-sexist education.* Washington, D.C.: National Education Association.

Scales, P. *Teenage pregnancy—a selected bibliography.* Baltimore: National Alliance for Optional Parenthood, 1978.

Sex is a touchy subject. Available from Richard Russo, 2343 San Juan Avenue, Walnut Creek, Calif. 94596.
A select bibliography of books, pamphlets, and films on sex and sexuality for young adults, prepared by Bay Area Young Adult Librarians, San Francisco, Calif.

SIECUS Report. New York: Sex Information and Education Council of the United States, 1976.
Special issue on the handicapped, contains selective bibliography on sex and the handicapped. See also vol. 5, no. 2 for a basic bibliography on human sexuality and vol. 5, no. 3 for a bibliography on religion and sexuality.

389

Singer, L. J., & Buskin, J. *Sex education on film, a guide to visual aids and programs.* New York: Teachers College Press, 1971.
A critical review of a variety of resources; supplies sample program on sex education for parents and teenagers.

Stewart, K. R. *Adolescent sexuality and teenage pregnancy: A selected, annotated bibliography with summary forewards.* Chapel Hill: Carolina Population Center, University of North Carolina, 1976.

Teen pregnancy bibliography. Washington, D.C.: National Alliance Concerned with School-Age Parents, 1977.

Magazines for Teens

Teen Times, 1977, vol. 32, no. 3. Available from Future Homemakers of America, 2010 Massachusetts Avenue, N.W., Washington, D.C.

True to Life. Sacramento: Reproductive Health Resources, 1977.
A popular, "confession" magazine format teaches about sexuality, relationships, and birth control.

What's Happening. Available from Emory University Memorial Hospital Family Planning Program, 80 Butler Street, S.E., Atlanta, Ga. 30303.
A magazine geared to answering teenagers' questions on sex and sexuality.

Films and Filmstrips for Teens

About sex. Available from Texture Films, 1600 Broadway, New York, N.Y.
Twenty-three-minute color film for junior high through adult ages, presenting sex information for young people in a light style.

Acquaintance rape prevention. Educational film series and curriculum by Oralee Wachter and Christina Crowley, available from O.D.N. Productions, Inc., 2051 Third Street, San Francisco, Calif. 94107.
Highly recommended for high school students.

Anything you want to be. A stunning film of the women's liberation movement available from New Days Films, PO Box 315, Franklin Lakes, N.J. 07417.
A good source of other films by and about women.

Gordon, S. *Getting it together is life itself.* Available from Educational Activities, Inc., PO Box 392, Freeport, N.Y. 11520.
The focus of this full-color sound filmstrip is that life is not a meaning—it is an opportunity.

Parenthood: A series. Available from Guidance Associates, 757 Third Avenue, New York, N.Y. 10017.
Includes Preparing for parenthood, Pregnancy, Preparing to give birth, and Birth.

Population and the American Future. Teacher's guides and film available on a loan basis from Population Affairs Films Collection, National Audio-Visual Center (G.S.A.), Washington, D.C. 20409.
The official film version of the *Report of the Commission on Population Growth and the American Future.*

The best source of films is Perennial Education, Inc., 477 Roger Williams, PO Box 885, Ravinia, Highland Park, Ill. 60035. For lists of other films, write to the following organizations:

E. C. Brown Center for Family Studies, Planned Parenthood, Guidance Associates, Box 300, White Plains, N.Y. 10602.

Child Study Association, Carolina Population Center, Center for Marital and Sexual Studies, 5199 East Pacific Coast Highway, Long Beach, Calif. 90804.

Focus International, Inc., 505 West End Avenue, New York, N.Y. 10024.

Multi-Media Resource Center, 1525 Franklin Street, San Francisco, Calif. 94109.

Parents' Magazine Films, Inc., 52 Vanderbilt Avenue, New York, N.Y. 10017.

Polymorph Films, 331 Newbury Street, Boston, Mass. 02115.

Public Television Library, 475 L'Enfant Plaza, S.W., Washington, D.C. 20024.

Viking Films, Ltd., 525 Denison Street, Markham, Ontario L3R 1BB, Canada.

National Organizations   The following organizations publish journals, newsletters, and reading lists of immediate interest to sex educators:

Alan Guttmacher Institute, 515 Madison Avenue, New York, N.Y. 10022.

American Association of Health, Physical Education and Recreation, National Education Association, 1201 16th Street, Washington, D.C. 20036.

American Association of Marriage and Family Therapy, 225 Yale Avenue, Claremont, Calif. 91711.

American Association of Psychiatric Services for Children, 1725 K Street, N.W., Suite 1112, Washington, D.C. 20006.

American Association of Sex Educators, Counselors, and Therapists, 5010 Wisconsin Avenue, N.W., Suite 304, Washington, D.C. 20016.

American Civil Liberties Union, 22 East 40th Street, New York, N.Y. 10016.

American Home Economics Association, 2010 Massachusetts Avenue, N.W., Washington, D.C. 20036.

American Library Association, Young Adult Services Division, 50 East Huron Street, Chicago, Ill. 60611.

American Medical Association, Department of Community Health and Health Education, 535 North Dearborn Street, Chicago, Ill. 60610.

American Orthopsychiatric Association, Inc., 1775 Broadway, New York, N.Y. 10019.

American Psychological Association, Population and Environmental Psychology Division, 1200 17th Street, N.W., Washington, D.C. 20036.

American Public Health Association, 1115 18th Street, N.W., Washington, D.C. 20036.

American School Health Association, 107 South Depeyster Street, Kent, Ohio 44240.

American Social Health Association, 260 Sheridan Avenue, Palo Alto, Calif. 94306.

American Venereal Disease Association, Box 385, University of Virginia School of Medicine, Charlottesville, Va. 22901.

Association for Creative Change, Box 2212, Syracuse, N.Y. 13220.

Association for Voluntary Sterilization, 708 Third Avenue, New York, N.Y. 10017.

Birth Control Institutes, Inc., 1242 W. Lincoln Avenue, Anaheim, Calif. 92805.

Carolina Population Center, University Square, University of North Carolina, Chapel Hill, N.C. 27514.

Center for Family Planning Program Development, 1666 K Street, N.W., Washington, D.C. 20006.

Center for Sex Education and Medicine, 4025 Chestnut Street, Philadelphia, Pa. 19104.

Child Welfare League of America, Inc., 67 Irving Place, New York, N.Y. 10003.

Citizens Alliance for VD Awareness, 222 W. Adams, Chicago, Ill. 60606.

Coalition for Children and Youth, 815 15th Street, N.W., Washington, D.C. 20005.

Communication Institute, 1777 East-West Road, Honolulu, Hawaii 96822.

Community Sex Information, Inc., PO Box 2858, Grand Central Station, New York, N.Y. 10017.

Consortium on Early Childbearing and Childrearing, Child Welfare League of America, 67 Irving Place, New York, N.Y. 10003.

Draper World Population Fund, 1120 19th Street, N.W., Suite 550, Washington, D.C. 20036.

E.C. Brown Center for Family Studies, 710 S.W. Second Avenue, Portland, Ore. 97204.

Education Foundation for Human Sexuality, Montclair State College, Upper Montclair, N.J. 07043.

Family Forum, 1539 North Courtney Avenue, Los Angeles, Calif. 90046.

Family Impact Seminar, Institute for Educational Leadership, George Washington University, 1001 Connecticut Avenue, Suite 732, Washington, D.C. 20036.

392

Family Life and Population Program, Church World Service, 475 Riverside Drive, New York, N.Y 10027.

Family Planning Program, Emory University School of Medicine, 80 Butler Street, Atlanta, Ga. 30303.

Institute for Family Research and Education, 760 Ostrom Avenue, Syracuse, N.Y. 13210.

Institute for Rational Living and Institute for Advanced Study in Rational Psychotherapy, 45 E. 65th Street, New York, N.Y. 10021.

Institute for Sex Research, Inc., Room 416, Morrison Hall, Indiana University, Bloomington, Ind. 47401.

International Planned Parenthood Federation, 18-20 Lower Regent Street, London, SW1Y 4PW, England.

International Projects Assistance Services, 123 West Franklin Street, Chapel Hill, N.C. 27514.

Maternity Center Association, 48 E. 92nd Street, New York, N.Y. 10028.

Midwest Population Center, 100 East Ohio, Chicago Ill. 60611.

National Abortion Rights Action League, 825 15th Street, N.W., Washington, D.C. 20005.

National Alliance Concerned with School-Age Parents, 7315 Wisconsin Avenue, Suite 211-W, Washington, D.C. 20014.

National Alliance for Optional Parenthood, 3 North Liberty Street, Baltimore, Md. 21201.

National Association of Social Workers, 1425 H Street, N.W., Suite 600, Washington, D.C. 20005.

National Center for Health Statistics, Center Building, 3700 East-West Highway, Hyattsville, Md. 20782.

National Coalition Against Censorship, 22 East 40th Street, New York, N.Y. 10016.

National Commission on Resources for Youth, 36 West 44th Street, New York, N.Y. 10036.

National Commission on Youth, PO Box 446, Melbourne, Fla. 32901.

National Congress of Parents and Teachers, 700 North Rush Street, Chicago, Ill. 60611.

National Council on Family Relations, 1219 University Avenue, S.W., Minneapolis, Minn. 55414.

National Education Association, 1201 16th Street, N.W., Washington D.C. 20036.

National Foundation, March of Dimes, Box 200, White Plains, N.Y. 10602.

National Gay Task Force, 80 Fifth Avenue, New York, N.Y. 10011.

National Operation Venus, 1213 Clover Street, Philadelphia, Pa. 19101 (National toll-free telephone: 800-523-1885; telephone in Pennsylvania (collect calls accepted): 215-567-6973; telephone in Philadelphia: 567-6969).

National Runaway Switchboard (Toll free, hassle free, referrals and information: 800-621-4000).

National Sex Forum, 1523 Franklin Street, San Francisco, Calif. 94109.

National Youth Alternatives Project, 1346 Connecticut Avenue, N.W., Washington, D.C. 20036.

The National Women's Health Network, Parklane Building, Suite 105, 2025 J Street, N.W., Washington, D.C. 20006.

Pathfinder Fund, 330 Boylston Street, Chestnut Hill, Mass. 02167.

Pharmacists Planning Service, Inc., 3000 Bridgeway Boulevard, Suite 202, Sausalito, Calif. 94965.

Planned Parenthood-World Population, 810 Seventh Avenue, New York, N.Y. 10019.

Population Action Council, 110 Maryland Avenue, N.E., Washington D.C. 20002.

Population Association of America, Box 14182 Benjamin Franklin Station, Washington, D.C. 20044.

Population Council, 1 Dag Hammarskjold Plaza, New York, N.Y. 10017.

Population Crisis Committee, 1120 19th Street, N.W., Suite 550, Washington, D.C. 20036.

Population Dynamics, 3828 Aurora Avenue, N., Seattle, Wash. 98102.

Population Information Program, Johns Hopkins University, 624 No. Broadway, Baltimore, Md. 21205.

Population Institute, 110 Maryland Avenue, Washington, D.C. 20002.

Population Reference Bureau, 1337 Connecticut Avenue, N.W., Washington, D.C. 20036.

Population Services International, 110 E. 59th Street, Suite 1019, New York, N.Y. 10022.

Pfizer Laboratories Divison, Pfizer, Inc., 235 E. 42nd Street, New York, N.Y. 10017.

Racism and Sexism Resource Center for Education, Council on Interracial Books, CIBC Resource Center, Room 300, 1841 Broadway, New York, N.Y. 10023.

Reproductive Biology Research Foundation (Masters and Johnson), 4910 Forest Park Boulevard, St. Louis, Mo. 63108.

Religious Coalition for Abortion Rights, 100 Maryland Ave, N.E., Washington, D.C. 20002.

Schmid Laboratories, Little Falls, N.J. 07424.

Sex and Disability Unit, University of California, 814 Mission Street, 2nd Floor, San Francisco, Calif. 94103.

Sex Education Coalition of Metropolitan Washington D.C., 2635 16th Street, N.W., Washington, D.C. 20009.

Sex Information and Education Council of the U.S. (SIECUS), 84 Fifth Avenue, New York, N.Y. 10001.

Society for the Scientific Study of Sex, Inc., 208 Daffodil Road, Glen Burnie, Md. 20601.

Student Press Law Center, 1750 Pennsylvania Avenue, N.W., Room 1112, Washington, D.C. 20016.

Transnational Family Research Institute, American Institutes for Research, 8307 Whitman Drive, Bethesda, Md. 20034.

World Population Society, 1337 Connecticut Avenue, N.W., Suite 200, Washington, D.C. 20036.

Worldwatch Institute, 1776 Massachusetts Avenue, N.W., Washington, D.C. 20036.

Youngs Drug Products Corporation, 865 Centennial Avenue, Piscataway, N.J. 08854.

Zero Population Growth, 1346 Connecticut Avenue, N.W., Washington, D.C. 20036.

Federal Programs

Adolescent Pregnancy Initiative, Office of Comprehensive Adolescent Program Services, Humphrey Building, Room 724H, 200 Independence Avenue, S.W., Washington, D.C. 20201.

Bureau of Elementary and Secondary Education, 400 Maryland Avenue, S.W., Room 2083, Washington, D.C. 20202.

Bureau of Health Education, Center for Disease Control, 1600 Clifton Road, N.E., Atlanta, Ga. 30303.

CDC–VD Control Division, Building I, Room 3051, 1600 Clifton Road, N.E., Atlanta, Ga. 30303.

Center for Population Research, National Institute of Child Health and Human Development, National Institutes of Health, Bethesda, Md. 20014.

National Clearinghouse for Family Planning Information, PO Box 2225, Rockville, Md. 20852.

Office of Education, 400 Maryland Avenue, S.W., Washington, D.C. 20202.

Office of Family Planning, 5600 Fishers Lane, Rockville, Md. 20857.

Office of Population Affairs, Humphrey Building, Room 719H, 200 Independence Avenue, S.W., Washington, D.C. 20201.

Office of Population, U.S. Agency for International Development, Washington, D.C. 20520.

Religious Organizations

The American Baptist Churches, Valley Forge, Pa. 19481.

The American Lutheran Church, 422 S. Fifth Street, Minneapolis, Minn. 55415.

The Christian Church (Disciples of Christ), PO Box 1986, Indianapolis, Ind. 56206.

The Lutheran Church in America, 231 Madison Avenue, New York, N.Y. 10016.

The Moravian Church in America, Northern Provincial Synod, 5 West Market Street, Bethlehem, Pa. 18018.

National Catholic Educational Association, 1 DuPont Circle, N.W., Suite 350, Washington, D.C. 20036.

National Council of Churches, Commission on Marriage and the Family, 475 Riverside Drive, New York, N.Y. 10027.

The Presbyterian Church, 341 Ponce de Leon Avenue, N.E., Atlanta, Ga. 30308.

Synagogue Council of America, 432 Park Avenue South, New York, N.Y. 10016.

The United Church of Christ, 296 Park Avenue South, New York, N.Y. 10010.

United Methodist Church, Board of Church and Society, Department of Population, 100 Maryland Avenue, N.E., Washington, D.C. 20002.

United States Catholic Conference, Family Life Bureau, 1312 Massachusetts Avenue, N.W., Washington, D.C. 20005.

Resources for Family Life Education Programs

The section on family life education programs was completed early in 1979. It includes references not found elsewhere.

Selected Curriculum Guides

Preparing professionals for family life and human sexuality education. Available from Michigan Department of Public Health, Bureau of Personal Health Services, Lansing, Mich. 48924.
An excellent 180-page mimeographed introduction prepared by Frances W. Hamermesh. Includes chapters on psychosexual development, values education, evaluation, and decision making.

Family life education: curriculum guideline. Available from Department of Education, Department of Health, Commonwealth of Virginia, Richmond, Va. 23216.
Includes an excellent goals statement.

Sex education guide for teachers. Available from Family Life Education Program, Flint Community Schools, Flint, Mich. 48502.
A brief and valuable statement from one of the early pioneers of family life education in the schools.

Sex education: a policy statement (and a sample course of study). Available from State Department of Public Instruction, Raleigh, N.C. 27611.
A very important, well thought out position paper.

Growth patterns and sex education: a suggested program. Kindergarten through grade twelve. Available from School Health Association, Kent, O. 44240.

This well developed program first published in 1967 is excellent except for the references which need updating.

Essential References for the Professional

Adolescent sexuality in a changing American society: social and psychological perspectives. Prepared by Catherine S. Chilman for the U.S. Department of Health, Washington D.C., 1978 (paper bound).
An impressive review of research up to 1976.

Understanding human sexuality. Hyde, J.S. New York: McGraw-Hill, 1979.
A fine, general book on human sexuality.

The sex education controversy. Hottois, J., & Milner, N. A. Lexington, Mass.: D.C. Heath, 1975.

The youth values project. Ross, S. Washington, D.C.: Population Institute, 1978.

Sex education for the health professional: a curriculum guide. Rosenszweig, N., & Pearsall, F. P. (eds.). New York: Grune & Stratton, 1979.
An important compendium with articles by the top experts in the field including Mary S. Calderone, Harold I. Lief, Theodore M. Cole, Paul H. Gebhard, Richard Green, and John Money.

Family life education curricula for the public schools. Charlottesville, Va.: Ed-U Press, in press.
A basic text for educators and community leaders who want to be sensitive about the needs of young people and their parents. Includes sections dealing with moral issues, teacher selection and training, model curricula, and research supporting sex education and the need for parent and community support.

Seminar for parents on adolescent sexuality: a leader's guide; Families and futures: helping self and others; and *Starting a healthy family: a teacher's guide.* Available from Education Development Center, Inc., School and Society Programs, 55 Chapel Street, Newton, Mass. 02160.

A teacher's round table on sex education. Available from National Association of Independent Schools, 4 Liberty Square, Boston, Mass. 02109.
Mimeographed report of a survey of current sex education programs by Mary Susan Miller and Patricia Schiller. Many good suggestions but most references are dated despite its 1977 publication date.

Taking sexism out of education (Stock number 017-080-01794-6). Available from Superintendent of Documents, U.S. Government Printing Office, Washington, D.C. 20402.
A 113-page paperback based on the findings and recommendations of the National Project on Women in Education.

A new attempt to teach morality. Important review (October 1978) available from Council for Basic Education, 725 15th Street, N.W., Washington, D.C. 20005.

The subtle points of controversy: A case study in implementing sex education. Hale, C., & Philliber, S. G. *Journal of School Health, 1978, 48* (10), 586–591.

Health education guide: a design for teaching K–12. Morris Barrett. Available from Lea and Febiger, 600 S. Washington Square, Philadelphia, Pa. 19106.
Eighteen teaching units including human sexuality and mental health. An excellent curriculum guide.

Parenting *Today's family in focus.* Available from The National PTA, 700 North Rush Street, Chicago, Ill. 60611.
A well-written, researched series of eight, four-page leaflets covering such topics as The family in today's educational world, Children's rights and how parents can protect them, and Children and values.

How to help children become better parents. A project developed jointly by the National PTA and the National Foundation March of Dimes; available from The National PTA, 700 North Rush Street, Chicago, Ill. 60611.
Nine well-documented leaflets dealing with a wide range of subject matter. Includes needs assessment survey, statistics on adolescent pregnancies, resolutions relating to parenting as adopted at PTA conventions, strategy and suggestions for interdisciplinary approaches.

Education for parenthood. Available from W. Stanley Kruger, Education for Parenthood Program, Office of Education, 400 Maryland Avenue, S.W., Washington, D.C. 20202.
A program to help teenagers prepare for effective parenthood through working with young children and learning about child development and the role of parents. Sponsored by the National Center for Child Advocacy, Children's Bureau, Office of Child Development, P.O. Box 1182, Washington, D.C. 20013.

Parenthood handbook project. Available from Social Studies Development Center, 513 North Park Avenue, Bloomington, Ind. 47401.
The handbook presents non-home economic teachers with a rationale for including parenthood education in their respective disciplines.

Teenage parenting. Available from Bank Street College of Education, 610 West 112th Street, New York, N.Y. 10025.
Materials designed to help pregnant teenage girls.

User's handbook. Prepared by Parenting Materials Information Center (federally supported and part of the ERIC system); available from Southwest Educational Development Laboratory, 211 East 7th Street, Austin, Tex. 78701.

Monographs *Project teen concern.* Available from Office for Family Planning, B.C.H.S., 5600 Fisher's Lane, Room 7-49, Rockville Md. 20852.

An implementation manual for an educational program to prevent premature parenthood and venereal disease developed by Planned Parenthood of Alameda-San Francisco for the Office for Family Planning (Bureau of Community Health Services of HEW). It includes sections on developing community support and teachers in-service training.

Classroom Resources

Family life education filmstrips and cassettes: *Getting it together is life itself, How can you tell if you are really in love,* and *Kids who have kids are kidding themselves.* Available from Educational Activities, Inc., P.O. Box 392, Freeport, N.Y. 11520.

A package of three consciousness-raising twelve-minute tapes professionally designed with original music by Laurie and Pete Gollobin and with text by Sol Gordon. Also availably singly.

Human growth-III and *A family talks about sex.* Available from Perennial Education, Inc., 477 Roger Williams, P.O. Box 855, Ravinia, Highland Park, Ill. 60035; in Canada, Viking Films, Ltd., 525 Denison Street, Markham, Ontario L3R 1B8.

The best films for classroom use including award winning films produced by the E. C. Brown Foundation.

Rape prevention education package. Available with instructional guides on free loan from National Center for the Prevention and Control of Rape, HEW, 5600 Fishers Lane, Rockville, Md. 20857.

A superb series of four films on "acquaintance" rape sponsored by HEW's National Center for the Prevention and Control of Rape.

Herpie—the new VD around town. Available from Ed-U Press, 123 4th Street, N.W., Charlottesville, Va. 22901.

An exceptionally fine twelve-minute filmstrip cassette (available with slides or as a videocassette) by Chic Thompson.

The facts about population ecology, The facts about human reproduction, and *The facts about birth control.* Available from Educational Materials Program, Carolina Population Center, 113 Mallette Street, Chapel Hill, N. C. 27514.

Three color-sound filmstrips/cassettes, teaching manuals, learners' manuals. Self-instructional audio visual packages for teenagers.

The stunted world of teen parents. Charlotte MacDonald. *Human Behavior,* January 1979, *8* (1), 53–55.

An excellent article for teenagers to read.

Preparing today's youth for tomorrow's family. *Youth Magazine,* July 1979 (Room 1203, 1505 Race Street, Philadelphia, Pa. 19102). Special issue of the United Church Press with excellent articles that could be the basis for discussions on self-concept and moral decision making.

Parenthood: a series (filmstrips and cassettes):
Preparing for parenthood;
Pregnancy;
Preparing to give birth;
Birth;

Adjusting to the new baby;
Mother and infant health care;
Skills for parents; and
Child development—pre-school years.
A first-rate series available from Guidance Associates, Box 300, White Plains, N. Y. 10602.

Going out—how do you feel about dating? Available from Guidance Associates.
A two-part series that teenagers will easily relate to.

Homosexuality: attitudes in transition. Available from Guidance Associates.
A two-part series dealt with in a highly sensitive and professionally sound way.

Classroom Texts

Sex, love or infatuation: How can I really know? Short, R.E. Minneapolis, Minn: Augsburg Publishing House, 1978.

Parenting—a guide for young people (paperback). Gordon, S., & Wollin, N. New York: Oxford Book Co., 1975.
Includes a chapter on whom not to marry, and, unlike most parenting programs, does not avoid the issue of sexuality.

Love and sex in plain language (paperback; 3rd rev. ed.). Johnson, E. W. New York: Bantam Books, 1978.
A perennial best seller with a well-deserved fine reputation.

You would if you loved me (paperback). Compiled by Sol Gordon. New York: Bantam Books, 1978.
A new approach to sex education combining humor and sound advice.

Facts about sex for today's youth (paperback). Gordon, S. Charlottesville, Va.: Ed-U Press, 1978.
Designed especially for young people who want information but don't like to read much. A conservative book that discourages teenagers from having sexual intercourse, but appreciates that we need to also meet the needs of those who are sexually active.

Discovering yourself I and *Discovering yourself II.* Available ($1.95 each) from *Teen* Magazine, Peterson Publishing Co., Magazine/Circulation, 6725 Sunset Boulevard, Los Angeles, Calif. 90028.
Two excellent anthologies of articles that have appeared in *Teen* magazine, 1978. They are first-rate self-concept articles written mainly by Kathy McCoy.

The heart of loving. Kennedy, E. Argus Press, 1973.
A beautifully sensitive book about the art of loving.

Love. Buscaglia, L. Greenwich, Conn.: Fawcett Books, 1972.
A wonderful, warm book.

For Classroom Population Programs

Population Institute, 110 Maryland Avenue, N.E., Washington, D.C. 20002.

Population Reference Bureau, 1337 Connecticut Avenue, N.W., Washington, D.C. 20036.

Worldwatch Institute, 1776 Massachusetts Avenue, N.W., Washington, D.C. 20036.

Centers and Sources for Information

American Red Cross, 17th & D Streets, N.W., Washington, D.C. 20006.

Family Life Publications, Inc., Resource Guide, Box 427, Saluda, N.C. 28773.

National Clearinghouse for Family Planning Information, P.O. Box 2225, Rockville, Md. 20852.

National Conference on Social Welfare, 919 18th Street, N.W., Suite 620, Washington, D.C. 20006 (request *Families and Public Policies in the United States*).

The National PTA, 700 North Rush Street, Chicago, Ill. 60611.

Public Affairs Pamphlets, 381 Park Avenue South, New York, N.Y. 10010.

SIECUS (Sex Information and Education Council of the U.S.) Publications Catalogue, Human Sciences Press, 72 Fifth Avenue, New York, N.Y. 10011.

Index

Abelson, H.: 173

Abortion: adoption as alternative, 71; American Civil Liberties Union, 96, 99; attitude shift, 172; controversy, 311–312; effects of liberalized abortion laws, 92–93, 102–104; Gallup Poll attitudinal survey, 90; Hyde Amendment, 95–97, 236; illegal, 100; political issue, 236; President Carter's position, 96; public opinion, 94–95; "Punishment for Abortion" scale, 316; related to contraceptive use, 302–304; research opportunities, 101–102; safety, 91, 92; services, 89

Abortion, adolescents and: access, 72; American Academy of Pediatrics Committee Statement on Youth, 103; "deterrent" theory, 101; effect of Hyde Amendments, 101; giving birth, 100–101; illegal abortion, 100; legality, 100; parental consent, 100; religious perspective, 93–94, 98, 133–137, 326–327; statistics, 60, 92, 93, 100–101, 103

Abortion, consequences of denied: child abuse, 313–316; cross-cultural studies, 316–317; related to support for capital punishment, 320–321; Scandinavian study, 312–313; Somatosensory Index of Human Affection, 318–319. See also Child abuse

Abortion, cross-cultural studies: infanticide, 331–332; social-behavioral correlates of abortion practices, 329; violence, 328–331

Abortion, opposition to: Committee for a Human Life Amendment, 138; compared with Holocaust, 97–98; compared with primitive cultures, 339; discrepant moral opinions, 328; as fraud, 340; mentality, 343–357; nonacceptance of pleasurable human sexual relationship, 348–357; phasing out March of Dimes prenatal screening program, 326; related to repressive/punitive sexuality, 343–347; right-to-life, 335, 336, 337, 338, 339; tactics, 97–99, 325, 326; voting

patterns of U.S. Senate on abortion, violence and nurturance, 332–339

"Abortion, Punishment for" scale: 316

Abortion, religious perspective. See Abortion

Abortion, Supreme Court decision: 89–91; 133, 326; basis, 91; Doe v. Bolton, 90; guidelines, 91; McRae v. Califano, 97; Roe v. Wade, 90; weakening, 96

Abortion under Attack: 325

Adams, W.J.: 168, 170

Adolescent intercourse. See Sexual intercourse among teenagers

Adolescent pregnancy: effect on unwed mother, 70–72; parental consent, 4–5; physical and mental health risks to mother and child, 72–75; Planned Parenthood of Missouri v. Danforth, 4; reasons for, 75–79; statistics, 3, 69. See Illegitimacy in teenagers; Pregnancy, premarital; Venereal disease in teenagers

Adolescent pregnancy, comprehensive family planning programs for dealing with: Consortium on Early Childbearing and Childrearing, 82–83; National Alliance Concerned with School-Age Parents, 82

Adoption, as alternative to abortion: 71

Affection, freedom to express: 254–255

Alan Guttmacher Institute: 11, 33, 69, 70, 71, 72, 89, 90, 164, 165, 177, 179, 182, 256

Alcohol, during pregnancy: 281–282

Alexander, M.N.: 125

"All in the Family:" 221

American Academy of Pediatrics Committee Statement on Youth: 103

American Association of Sex Educators, Counselors and Therapists: 80

American Baptist Convention. See Baptists, perspective on human sexuality

American Humanist Association: 326–327

American Social Health Association: 109